Page deliberately left blank

VOLUME 672

JULY 2017

THE ANNALS

of The American Academy of Political
and Social Science

The New Rural-Urban Interface

Special Editors:
DANIEL T. LICHTER
Cornell University
JAMES P. ZILIAK
University of Kentucky

⑤SAGE

Los Angeles | London | New Delhi
Singapore | Washington DC | Melbourne

Origin and Purpose. The Academy was organized December 14, 1889, to promote the progress of political and social science, especially through publications and meetings. The Academy does not take sides in controverted questions, but seeks to gather and present reliable information to assist the public in forming an intelligent and accurate judgment.

Meetings. The Academy occasionally holds a meeting in the spring extending over two days.

Publications. THE ANNALS of The American Academy of Political and Social Science is the bimonthly publication of the Academy. Each issue contains articles on some prominent social or political problem, written at the invitation of the editors. These volumes constitute important reference works on the topics with which they deal, and they are extensively cited by authorities throughout the United States and abroad.

Subscriptions. THE ANNALS of The American Academy of Political and Social Science (ISSN 0002-7162) (J295) is published bimonthly—in January, March, May, July, September, and November—by SAGE Publishing, 2455 Teller Road, Thousand Oaks, CA 91320. Periodicals postage paid at Thousand Oaks, California, and at additional mailing offices. POSTMASTER: Send address changes to The Annals of The American Academy of Political and Social Science, c/o SAGE Publishing, 2455 Teller Road, Thousand Oaks, CA 91320. Institutions may subscribe to THE ANNALS at the annual rate: $1070 (clothbound, $1209). Individuals may subscribe to the ANNALS at the annual rate: $122 (clothbound, $180). Single issues of THE ANNALS may be obtained by individuals for $38 each (clothbound, $52). Single issues of THE ANNALS have proven to be excellent supplementary texts for classroom use. Direct inquiries regarding adoptions to THE ANNALS c/o SAGE Publishing (address below).

All correspondence concerning membership in the Academy, dues renewals, inquiries about membership status, and/or purchase of single issues of THE ANNALS should be sent to THE ANNALS c/o SAGE Publishing, 2455 Teller Road, Thousand Oaks, CA 91320. Telephone: (800) 818-SAGE (7243) and (805) 499-0721; Fax/Order line: (805) 375-1700; e-mail: journals@sagepub.com. *Please note that orders under $30 must be prepaid.* For all customers outside the Americas, please visit http://www.sagepub.co.uk/customerCare.nav for information.

THE ANNALS

Editorial Office: 202 S. 36th Street, Philadelphia, PA 19104-3806
For information about individual and institutional subscriptions address:
SAGE Publishing
2455 Teller Road
Thousand Oaks, CA 91320

For SAGE Publishing: Peter Geraghty (Production) and Mimi Nguyen (Marketing)

From India and South Asia, write to:	From Europe, the Middle East, and Africa, write to:
SAGE PUBLICATIONS INDIA Pvt Ltd	SAGE PUBLICATIONS LTD
B-42 Panchsheel Enclave, P.O. Box 4109	1 Oliver's Yard, 55 City Road
New Delhi 110 017	London EC1Y 1SP
INDIA	UNITED KINGDOM

International Standard Serial Number ISSN 0002-7162
ISBN 978-1-5443-0236-2 (Vol. 672, 2017) paper
ISBN 978-1-5443-0235-5 (Vol. 672, 2017) cloth
First printing, July 2017

Information about membership rates, institutional subscriptions, and back issue prices may be found on the facing page.

Claims. Claims for undelivered copies must be made no later than six months following month of publication. The publisher will supply replacement issues when losses have been sustained in transit and when the reserve stock will permit.

Change of Address. Six weeks' advance notice must be given when notifying of change of address. Please send the old address label along with the new address to the SAGE office address above to ensure proper identification. Please specify the name of the journal.

⊞ANNALS

OF THE AMERICAN ACADEMY OF
POLITICAL AND SOCIAL SCIENCE

Volume 672   July 2017

IN THIS ISSUE:

The New Rural-Urban Interface

Special Editors: DANIEL T. LICHTER
and JAMES P. ZILIAK

FORTHCOMING

Inner City Schools: Inequality and Urban Education
Special Editors: LUKE ANDERSON and ELIJAH ANDERSON

The State of Unequal Educational Opportunity: The Coleman Report 50 Years Later
Special Editors: MARGOT JACKSON and SUSAN MOFFITT

The Rural-Urban Interface: New Patterns of Spatial Interdependence and Inequality in America

By
DANIEL T. LICHTER
and
JAMES P. ZILIAK

America's rural-urban divide seemingly has never been greater, a point reinforced by large geographic disparities in support for Donald Trump in the 2016 presidential election. But it is also the case that big cities and rural communities are more tightly integrated than ever and are increasingly interdependent, both economically and socially. This new rural-urban interface is highlighted in this collection of articles, which are organized and developed around the general concept of changing symbolic and social boundaries. Rural-urban boundaries—how rural and urban people and places are defined and evaluated—reflect and reinforce institutional forces that maintain spatial inequality and existing social, economic, and political hierarchies. This volume makes clear that rural-urban boundaries are highly fluid and that this should be better reflected in research programs, in the topics that we choose to study, and in the way that public policy is implemented.

Keywords: urbanization; economic restructuring; community; poverty; economic development; inequality; well-being

The United States is an increasingly urban—and urban-centric—society made up of densely settled big cities and rapidly expanding urban conglomerations. The hegemony of the nation's largest cities has been unmistakable (Lichter and Brown 2011). Cities are where culture is shaped and reshaped by politics, media, and money, where new jobs and technology are incubated, and where big ideas start and flourish. With the continuing urbanization of American society, big city issues and

Daniel T. Lichter is Ferris Family Professor in the Department of Policy Analysis and Management, professor of sociology, and director of the Institute for the Social Sciences, all at Cornell University.

James P. Ziliak is the Gatton Chair in Microeconomics, director of the Center for Poverty Research, and executive director of the Kentucky Federal Statistical Research Data Center, all at the University of Kentucky.

Correspondence: dtl28@cornell.edu

DOI: 10.1177/0002716217714180

interests have come to define America's most pressing social problems and to dominate key policy and political issues and programmatic solutions to them (Brown and Schafft 2012; Castle, Wu, and Weber 2011). Rural and small-town America is often left at the sidelines in policy discussions, far removed from the American cultural and economic mainstream. Yet as recently as 1940, the majority of the U.S. population lived in nonmetropolitan areas, many in small rural communities and on farms (Gibson 2012). Rural Americans—all 46 million of them—have seemingly been left behind, waiting to develop, prosper, and share in America's economic bounty. They are often invisible or, worse yet, are unfairly characterized as hicks, hayseeds, or hillbillies. But times are changing.

With the election of Donald Trump as America's forty-fifth president, rural America has struck back—with a vengeance (Scala and Johnson, this volume). The large majority share of rural voters in America's agricultural heartland; in small towns of the industrial "rust-belt" in Michigan, Wisconsin, and Pennsylvania; and in Appalachia responded positively to Trump's message of "America first" economic populism, nationalism (some say "white nationalism"), and fair trade. Exit polls in Pennsylvania show that Hillary Clinton lost to Trump decisively among rural and small-town voters, 71 to 26 percent (Evich 2016). In *Hillbilly Elegy* (2016), J. D. Vance vividly describes how declines in the coal industry have left small towns in Appalachia in ruins and the white working class in chronic poverty, dysfunction, and despair. The "carnage" is expressed in opioid and alcohol abuse, family breakdown, crime, and declining life expectancy. Arlie Russell Hochschild (2016), in *Strangers in Their Own Land*, gives voice to the anger and frustration of rural working-class whites—hardworking, self-sufficient, and god-fearing—who have patiently waited "in line" for financial success and the American dream, only to perceive "less deserving" immigrants and minorities as unfairly cutting in line. Identity politics and outside elites—establishment politicians and anonymous Washington government bureaucrats—presumably privilege less deserving others over "real Americans." White resentment has stoked outrage against the political status quo.

At the time of this writing, the rural-urban divide seemingly has never been greater. That rural Americans across the country voted in substantial numbers for Donald Trump makes this point; rural people tipped the national scale in Trump's favor and against urban and coastal elites, minorities, and immigrants. But, perhaps paradoxically, it may also be the case that urban and rural communities and people have also never been more tightly integrated and interdependent. It is often difficult to distinguish rural from urban people in America's increasingly

Note: The articles in this volume were first presented at a conference on "The New Rural-Urban Interface: A Research Agenda" held September 29–30, 2016, at the Annenberg Public Policy Center, University of Pennsylvania. The organizers gratefully acknowledge generous financial and institutional support from the American Academy of Political and Social Science, Cornell's Institute for the Social Sciences, University of Kentucky Center for Poverty Research, the Ferris Family Chair, and Scholars Strategy Network (Finger Lakes Branch), as well as administrative support from Jessica Erfer and Lori Sonken. The authors also benefited from helpful comments of Erin York Cornwell, David Brown, Domenico Parisi, Tim Parker, and Christopher Wildeman.

urban society. Visit any urban "hipster" neighborhood, and the cultural styles and emphasis on "local food" harkens back to a more pastoral agrarian past. As geographic concepts, however, rural and urban defy easy definitions. This is made even more difficult by the new rural-urban interface, which is our focus here and is expressed by the increasing back and forth flows of capital, labor, population, information and ideas, and material goods between rural and urban America. The new century is marked by a blurring of traditional rural-urban symbolic and social boundaries. Indeed, simple or unambiguous binary views of urban versus rural represent a conceptual and empirical roadblock to addressing underdevelopment and shared political and economic interests. Viewing "rural" and "urban" as competing rather than complementary sectors obscures fundamental spatial interrelationships that often drive economic development. In fact, the rural-urban interface is a zone of interdependence, not a clear border that neatly separates rural from urban people and places. It is America's growing spatial interdependence that has brought much of rural America into the economic and cultural mainstream but, perhaps paradoxically, also sowed the seeds of spatial inequality and divergent political views for rural people and places left behind. It also provides the motivation for this volume of *The ANNALS*.

Rural and urban are flip sides of the same coin; the things that divide rural and urban areas are real but arguably minor when compared to the things that unite most Americans. Rural America represents more than 70 percent of the land area. It is the nation's breadbasket. In 2017, as in the past, urban America has prospered and grown only because rural agricultural output and productivity has exceeded the most optimistic forecasts. In the mid-twentieth century the typical American family spent one-third of annual income on food; today it is about one eighth. Rural areas fuel the nation's economy—quite literally. They provide a reliable energy supply, from oil and gas, biofuels (from corn), and wind, solar, and hydroelectric power. Rural areas increasingly are places of consumption—to recreate and retire—for big city and suburban dwellers. They include places—mountains, lakes, and ocean coastlines—to visit, spend money, and enjoy. They are increasingly places to retire to in the golden years, when the fast pace and expense of urban life is traded for a simpler, quieter, and less expensive lifestyle. And this is attractive to city dwellers because rural areas often provide the same material comforts that they have grown used to in the city. The rural and urban boundaries that seemingly divide us today are neither immutable nor necessarily limiting. They are permeable and in a constant state of flux as rural communities and people become urbanized—and often wealthier (e.g., rural areas along the Atlanta-Charlotte corridor)—in an increasingly urban society, and as urban society—its people and its institutions—seemingly takes cultural and economic dominion over rural small towns and the countryside. The recent presidential election arguably has rebalanced spatial and social interactions—and our perceptions of them—that define the rural-urban interface. Rural America today is in the national spotlight.

It has also refocused the political spotlight on the rural-urban divide and spatial inequality. Rural America is too often ignored in the social sciences. Interestingly enough, the majority of all rural people (54 percent), as officially defined by the U.S. Census Bureau, now reside in America's metropolitan areas (Wunderlich 2015).[1] They live in the open countryside, on farms, and in unincorporated housing developments at the periphery of metropolitan cities and their suburbs. Metropolitan regions are expanding outward into the rural hinterland, gobbling up land along with rural people and communities (Garner, this volume). As such, rural and urban need to be treated as interdependent and mutually dependent. Such is our purpose here.

Our singular goal is to provide a definitive, authoritative, and up-to-date statement on the state of the rural-urban interface now—and on aspects of the rural-urban divide that will continue. It is past time to evaluate the scholarly profile of theory and research on emerging spatially interdependent social problems and issues. Rural-related theory and research arguably must be integrated with urban and global perspectives, and vice versa. The rural social sciences cannot be relegated to the intellectual backwaters of America's urban universities and public policy groups, devalued and ghettoized administratively. The reasons now seem obvious. Today's societal and global problems often have a large rural dimension (e.g., labor mobility, energy development, climate change, food production, waste disposal) that imposes new challenges that affect all Americans, regardless of where they happen to live. The social sciences require a new research synthesis that acknowledges the shared destinies of rural and urban people and places in a rapidly globalizing and interconnected world (Lichter and Brown 2015). The march of economic progress requires a new synthesis of policy research and action that acknowledges spatial interdependence (Brown and Shucksmith, this volume; Castle, Wu, and Weber 2011).

The articles included in this volume highlight four central themes that have animated recent theoretical and policy discussions on new or emerging patterns of spatial and social interaction at the rural-urban interface. They are (1) the urbanization of rural spaces—the spatial expansion of urban cultural hegemony; (2) changing rural-urban economic transactions and uneven economic development and growth; (3) institutional shifts—family, schools, politics—and their implications for rural and urban inequality; and (4) patterns of health and well-being at the rural-urban interface. To set the stage for our discussion, the next section presents a conceptual framework for thinking about the rural-urban interface, that is, the nature of changing and often permeable symbolic and social boundaries between rural and urban America. We conclude with a research agenda that explicitly makes "a place for space" in the larger social science literature (Logan 2012), emphasizing in particular the (growing) need to identify, define, and understand changing spatial relationships and to embrace a spatially inclusive approach to contemporary social problems and to political and economic solutions that address them.

Rural and Urban Boundaries

The idea of boundaries—as a conceptual tool—has gained new prominence in the social sciences. Lamont and Molnár (2002) define *symbolic boundaries* as agreed-upon ways to classify or categorize people (e.g., natives or immigrants), objects (e.g., sedans as opposed to SUVs), time (e.g., feudal society as opposed to postindustrial society), or, in our case, geographic space (i.e., rural or urban). For ease of communication, boundaries of all kinds are usually treated in practice as distinct and clearly demarcated rather than as the fuzzy or ambiguous concepts they almost always represent in reality. As we illustrate in this volume, conceptual and operational definitions of urban and rural are subject to great variation, and scholars and policy-makers not only adopt different classification schemes but also often view rural and urban as polar ends of a continuum in which America's people and communities are arrayed. Rural-urban is not a simple binary.

Officially, the U.S. Census Bureau defines urban as including people living in cities and communities of 2,500 population or more (or living in the "built-up" residential areas at the fringes of big cities and their suburbs) (U.S. Census Bureau 2017). Rural people live in small towns of fewer than 2,500 inhabitants, in the open countryside, or on farms. Few scholars, however, embrace this narrow definition based on population size, instead preferring to use the Census Bureau's official definition of nonmetropolitan interchangeably with rural. Nonmetropolitan is a residual category that represents 1,976 counties that do not satisfy the criteria required to be classified as metropolitan. Metropolitan areas are defined on the basis of county population size (i.e., exceeding 100,000 people) and the size of the principal city or cities located within the county (i.e., 50,000 people or more), as well as other physically adjacent counties that are closely integrated economically with the core metropolitan county. Even when rural and urban classification schemes are formalized by government, however, their use is not adopted uniformly among scholars, public policy-makers, or politicians. And, for better or worse, these official definitions of urban (or metropolitan) arguably have little if any common meaning or understanding among most everyday Americans, including political pundits. Urban or rural are experienced differently across America.

Clearly, the symbolic boundaries that separate rural from urban people and places are neither easily defined nor agreed upon (Johnson 2017; Wunderlich 2015). Moreover, unlike symbolic boundaries based on alternative classification schemes, *social boundaries* typically involve a value judgment or a qualitative assessment of the status or worth of people, objects, or space on either side of the boundary (Lichter and Brown 2011; Woods 2009). To illustrate, we can think about America's racial hierarchy and systematic patterns of prejudice or discrimination that value one group (i.e., the majority white population) over another (i.e., racial minority population). Similarly, poor people (based on the official poverty measure) are both stereotyped and stigmatized. The general point is straightforward: on many dimensions, the world is divided into "us" versus "them," and it is almost always better to be included in the in-group than the out-group. Boundary definitions—including definitions of rural and urban— similarly imply a clear social hierarchy that acknowledges that spatial distinctions matter, despite some ambiguity or lack of agreement on the essential characteristics that actually separate rural from urban people and communities. These boundary definitions provide a shorthand basis for making comparative value judgements or evaluative assessments that sometimes reinforce the existing status hierarchy and power arrangements.

The various themes of this volume of *The ANNALS* are organized and developed around the general concept of symbolic and social boundaries. Spatial boundaries are not immutable; rural and urban people and places should not be reified. Indeed, changing rural-urban boundaries reflect ongoing social processes of *shifting, crossing,* and *blurring* (Alba and Nee 2003). But it is also the case that boundaries both reflect and reinforce institutional forces that maintain the status quo or cement existing social, economic, and political hierarchies. Discrimination against an out-group often reinforces inequality and negative stereotypes. This is also true of the rural-urban dichotomy.

Boundary *shifting* refers to the redefinition of the boundary itself. For example, some rural areas, as a result of urbanization, metropolitan expansion, and municipal annexation, have become redefined as urban or metropolitan by the U.S. government. A simple example illustrates the broader point. Between 2010 and 2012, for the first time in U.S. demographic history, nonmetropolitan areas experienced absolute population decline—depopulation (see Figure 1). At first glance, this unprecedented population shift seemingly reflects well-known patterns of chronic out-migration of young people (of reproductive ages) and rapid population aging in America's remote rural areas. Less well appreciated is that rural depopulation, along with comparatively rapid urban growth, is also due to the fact that many growing nonmetropolitan counties were officially reclassified as metropolitan (or urban) on the basis of new population counts from the 2010 decennial census. Slow-growing or declining nonmetropolitan areas were left behind. Indeed, the Office of Management and Budget in March 2013 announced that 113 nonmetro counties (with 5.9 million people) switched to metro status, while 36 counties (with 1 million people) no longer qualified as metro, resulting in a net nonmetro population "loss" of 4.9 million from reclassification (Economic Research Service 2017). More than half of all nonmetro counties lost population (1,320) during 2010 to 2015, a historic high (Economic Research Service 2017).

Urban-rural boundaries clearly have shifted, but so also has the demographic and economic composition that has come to define the social boundaries that distinguish rural from urban people and communities. Changing symbolic definitions (based on official classification systems of rural and urban) sometimes upend the meaning of social definitions, which are necessarily being rewritten by rural residents who, without actually moving, now live and work in urban areas. They have been enveloped by urbanization—the centrifugal expansion of big city development into the hinterland in the form of urban sprawl. This creates ambiguity about whether reclassified rural people conform to conventional stereotypes or have been "left behind" materially. Indeed, the rural people living along California's Pacific Coast Highway; in Vail, Colorado; in the outlying housing developments in northern Virginia; or in the Florida Keys hardly conform to the usual rural or urban stereotypes. They cannot (by almost any definition) be considered backward, unsophisticated, or disadvantaged—which are included in the usual stereotypes of rural people. Rural America is heterogeneous and defies

FIGURE 1
Population Change by Metro/Nonmetro Status, 1976–2015

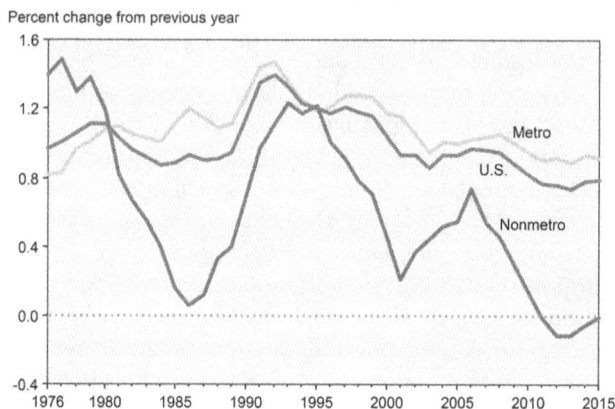

NOTE: Metro status changed for some counties in 1980, 1990, 2000, and 2010.
SOURCE: U.S. Department of Agriculture (USDA), Economic Research Service, using data from the U.S. Census Bureau.

facile generalizations. The same is true of urban America, but this has almost always been understood implicitly. Not surprisingly, social constructivist perspectives, where urban and rural people define themselves rather than others (including government bureaucrats and academics), are now on the ascendency (Fulkerson and Thomas 2013; Shucksmith and Brown 2016).

Boundary *crossing* refers to the back-and-forth movement of people, ideas, and money between rural and urban areas. For example, from a strictly demographic perspective, urban-to-rural migrants by definition cross the rural-urban divide to live and work. They bring "urban" to the countryside in terms of population (i.e., growth and density), culture, and economic development and growth. Migrants—in either direction—are cultural carriers that reshape communities in uncertain ways. As the aphorism goes, "you can take the boy (girl) out of the country, but you can't take the country out of the boy (girl)." Since the Great Recession, nonmetropolitan America has experienced net outmigration (see Figure 2). Between 2010 and 2013, 276,000 *more* people moved out of nonmetro areas than moved in; these rural-to-urban migrants—cultural carriers—might be viewed as promoting rural-urban spatial integration in much the same way that racial minority populations become more residentially integrated by moving into predominately white neighborhoods in the city. But it is not just people who cross spatial boundaries; so do ideas, money, and material things. Absentee owners from urban areas or big cities (e.g., food-processing companies, mining companies, or big-box retailers like Walmart) invest in rural communities, changing them forever. People living in rural "bedroom" communities may commute back and forth to their jobs in the city. Many rural and urban areas represent "places of consumption," where people living elsewhere do their shopping, seek

FIGURE 2
Nonmetro Population Change and Components of Change, 1976–2015

Percent change from previous year

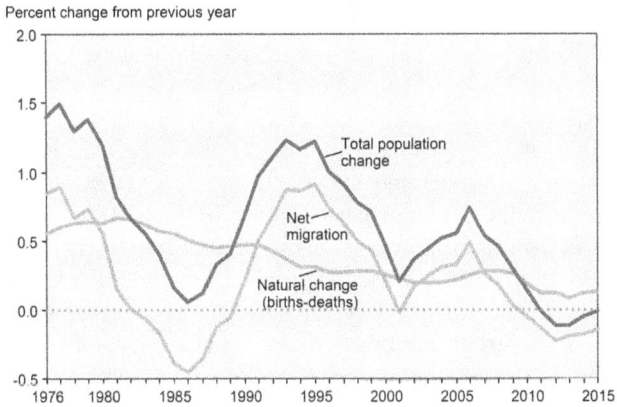

NOTE: Metro status changed for some counties in 1980, 1990, 2000, and 2010.
SOURCE: U.S. Department of Agriculture (USDA), Economic Research Service, using data from the U.S. Census Bureau.

entertainment, or recreate (even own second homes). Rural America also is sometimes thought of as a "dumping ground" for urban people (e.g., in the form of urban-generated toxic waste or prison populations), while also serving as a mode of rural economic development (Eason, Zucker, and Wildeman, the volume).

The point here is straightforward: Rural-urban boundaries are permeable—perhaps increasingly so in a technological age. More than ever before, so-called rural people are exposed to and interact with urban people and places, and vice versa. And it is this growing spatial interdependence—this back-and-forth of people, money, and culture—that has been greatly accelerated by innovations in transportation and information technology (i.e., satellite television, fiber optics and the Internet, and social media). In this sense, America is more spatially integrated than ever before. Vertical ties to mass society have eroded or even supplanted horizontal economic and social ties that traditionally were characterized by deeply felt community attachments, strong informal personal relationships (i.e., neighboring), and close family and kinship networks. Information and money travel quickly, eroding the "friction of space" and stitching together the fabric of rural and urban America as never before. They watch the same programs on TV and shop online for the same consumer goods. Some scholars even suggest that there is no "rural" left in America as urbanism has diffused throughout the countryside (Friedland 1982). People living in rural areas—even those far removed from big cities—have access to similar consumer items (food and clothing), telecommunication systems (satellite TV and cell phones), and modern transportation (modern highways and regional airports) that reduces isolation to urban amenities and material culture. Paradoxically, the historical isolation of rural areas has given way to a new exposure of rural people to material things (income and jobs) that also can elevate their own sense of economic or political marginality. This is hardly a one-way street. In any culturally diverse big city neighborhood (e.g., Williamsburg in Brooklyn or the Mission district in San Francisco), urban hipsters wear vintage clothing, sport long beards and shaggy haircuts, and reject trendy or chic fashions. The whole "local" movement of flea markets/farmers markets is drawn directly from rural America. Country music is enjoyed everywhere.

Finally, *blurring* refers to the fact that boundaries of all kinds can be "bright" or "dim," both spatially and socially. Culturally, rural people arguably have become increasingly like their urban counterparts, and this may be especially evident at the rural-urban interface—at the boundary that separates rural from urban people. As an illustrative case, Figure 3 shows the 2000 to 2010 growth of the urban population at the periphery of Atlanta (but within the larger metropolitan region); the rural-urban boundaries used to classify rural and urban people are highly ambiguous. Indeed, the boundaries of Atlanta's urban areas grew more rapidly than any other city in the nation between 2000 and 2010, increasing by more than 680 square miles over the decade (Berg 2012). The implication is clear: the symbolic and social boundaries that separate rural from urban are not a clear physical or cultural border or line at all but, rather, a zone of intense human interaction (which, in the case of Atlanta, may make up exurbia or the rural-urban fringe). Clearly, the boundaries that separate rural and urban people are sometimes difficult to observe; they are blurry. Rural and urban may instead be better represented as polar opposites; any blurring of boundaries is represented somewhere in the middle along the continuum.

Many articles in this volume of *The ANNALS* have embraced this view (i.e., using some variation of the U.S. Department of Agriculture (USDA) Economic Research Service's Rural-Urban Continuum Codes, which are sometimes referred to as the "Beale codes") (see Brown, Hines, and Zimmer 1975). For example, rural-urban boundaries at the periphery of major cities represent a zone of interdependence rather than separation, where residents live in a kind of interstitial zone, operating on either side of the rural-urban divide and presumably enjoying the best of both worlds. Their definition of themselves as rural or urban may be highly fluid and situational (Garner, this volume). It is in this interstitial zone where differences are often contested and where conflict occurs (Lichter and Brown 2011). These people and places have come to be defined as peri-urban, peri-rural, the urban-rural fringe, or exurban. The USDA's Economic Research Service has defined people as living in counties that are distinguished by metropolitan status, population size, and remoteness (i.e., proximity to metropolitan employment centers). They recognize that most Americans do not fall neatly or unambiguously on either side of a rural-urban divide. "Blurring the line" renders the conventional rural and urban binary classifications and stereotypes (i.e., social boundaries) less valid and sometimes meaningless.

Contrast this with the "bright" symbolic and social boundaries that separate the political or economic interests of declining rural central Appalachia from growing big cities in the region (e.g., Pittsburgh), or that separate predominately black rural communities in Georgia or Alabama from the Atlanta metropolitan

FIGURE 3
Atlanta Urbanized Area

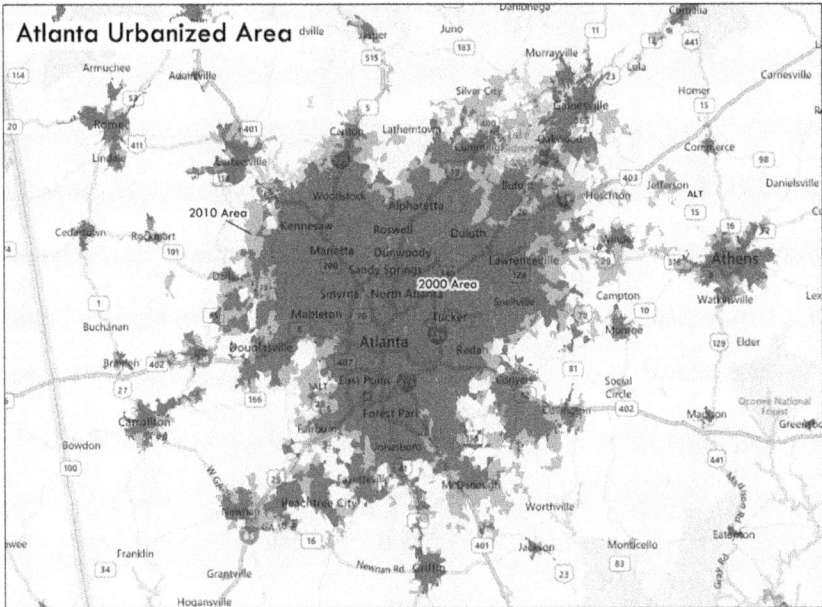

SOURCE: Nairn (2012) based on publicly available data from the 2000 and 2010 U.S. decennial Census at https://www2.census.gov/geo/maps/urbanarea/uaoutline/UA2000/ua03817/ua03817_00.pdf and https://www2.census.gov/geo/maps/dc10map/UAUC_RefMap/ua/ua03817_atlanta_ga/DC10UA03817.pdf.

NOTE: Dark purple = 2000 and 2010 urban areas; light purple = new urban for 2010.

area. In such cases, clearly demarcated and "bright" spatial boundaries may well reinforce well-documented social, economic, and political distinctions that may give rise to rural resentment—and to voting patterns that gave political energy to Donald Trump's presidential campaign (Monnat and Brown 2017; Scala and Johnson, this volume). Or they give rise to the usual stereotypes that animate the rural-urban divide in the public mind (i.e., rural hicks and hayseeds contrasted with urban elites or urban crime and welfare dependence). The U.S. Census Bureau and its data users (e.g., academics and government agencies, including the U.S. Department of Housing and Urban Development [HUD] and USDA) understand that these bright lines, usefully but crudely defined by conventional census geographic concepts (Wunderlich 2015), often hide substantial heterogeneity that exists *within* rather than *between* spatial categories. Rural-urban boundaries have become highly blurred. The implication is clear: our official classification systems can reveal spatial differences but are also at increasing risk of obfuscating them. And this is a central lesson from the various articles in this volume.

Intersecting Themes at the Rural-Urban Interface

This volume of *The ANNALS* is structured around four separate but interrelated themes that build on the idea of rural and urban symbolic and spatial boundaries.

The urbanization of rural spaces

From a cultural standpoint, rural America is often viewed as a cultural safe haven where "real Americans" live and where traditional values of family and kinship are stored and protected. Self-reliance and virtue abound, which are epitomized by the family farm and by the neighborliness of close-knit small towns. Urban areas instead are viewed as alienating, crime-ridden, and a threat to traditional American values and the rural idyll. The cultural contradiction, of course, is that rural places also are often seen as a cultural backwater, where only the unsophisticated and ill-bred live. Urbanites represent high-culture, sophistication, and excitement.

Any shifting, crossing, or blurring of symbolic and social boundaries has a decidedly demographic component. A century ago, the Chicago School in sociology emphasized that urbanization, population growth, and immigration contributed to growing heterogeneity, alienation, and a shift away from tightly knit and highly integrated communities, from a primary emphasis on personal relationships to secondary relationships. Indeed, this was a central tenet of Louis Wirth's ecological theory, as described in his classic 1938 paper on "Urbanism as a Way of Life." The shift from rural to urban society had pernicious effects on families and interpersonal relationships. Urban growth was associated with social disorganization in its myriad forms: crime, transience, interpersonal isolation, and family dislocation. Then, the U.S. settlement system was being upended by new immigration from southern and eastern Europe, new rural-to-urban migration, and massive outmigration from rural agricultural areas of the plantation South into northern industrial cities (i.e., the Great Migration). Now, theory and research has again centered on the implications of internal migration and population diversity, suburbanization, and exurbanization (i.e., the centrifugal drift of urban populations); the new geography and spatial diffusion of immigration (from the global South); the population boom and bust cycles of energy boom towns; and the explosive growth of outlying bedroom communities where daily commuting has separated work from everyday living. From a demographic perspective, what does it mean today to be rural (e.g., low density, small population size, underdevelopment) in an increasingly urban society?

In this volume of *The ANNALS*, it is clear that cultural and demographic changes are inextricably linked. A master demographic trend throughout most of the last century has been the concentration of population into urban or major metropolitan centers, along with the outward expansion from the urban core (i.e., suburbanization). In 1900, only 40 percent of the U.S. population lived in urban areas; today more than 85 percent officially live in metropolitan areas. At the same time, more than one-half of all U.S. residents now live in the suburban areas of metropolitan counties. To illustrate the issue, Garner (this volume) shows how outlying rural areas in the metropolitan Atlanta area have been enveloped—and changed—by the incursion of urban people spreading outward from the central city. Rural and urban have lost their traditional meaning, and this is revealed in how both old-timers and newcomers at the periphery of Atlanta now define themselves and describe their new attachments to their rapidly changing environment.

This history of urban concentration and dispersion also has been reshaped across the United States by growing racial and ethnic diversity (Hall, Tach, and Lee 2016), driven in large part by immigration and the large secondary effects of high fertility among immigrants (Johnson and Lichter 2016). Conventional stereotypes of rural and suburban America are now being revised by new minority population growth (Lichter 2013) that has become a demographic lifeline for some declining communities. Indeed, Lee and Sharp (this volume) document the extraordinary recent increases in racial and ethnic diversity across the urban size-of-place hierarchy, a change that has transformed many predominately white cities and suburbs, as well as rural areas, and raised new questions about racial disharmony and cultural and economic fragmentation (Legewie and Schaeffer 2016; Lichter 2013). The blurring of America's color line has accelerated with the emergence of new immigrant destinations—mostly of Hispanic and Asian origin. Garcia and Schmalzbauer (this volume) highlight the role of immigration in promoting new patterns of spatial interdependence of rural and urban America. They describe how the back-and-forth movement of new immigrants between different origins and destinations is stitching together communities and families as never before. More importantly, the cultural and economic implications for new immigrant-receiving communities are difficult to forecast; they depend heavily on whether the immigration originates from rural or urban areas. Minority economic incorporation and immigrant assimilation in American has taken on a new spatial form (Waters and Pineau 2016).

Rural-urban economic transactions

It is commonplace to highlight the economic hegemony of urban areas, which sometimes takes form in diverse literatures emphasizing internal colonization and urban exploitation of rural natural resources (e.g., in Appalachia coal country or oil fracking in Oklahoma and Texas), horizontal and vertical economic integration (e.g., in the food systems linked to big agriculture), recreational or tourist-related development (e.g., newcomers and old-timers in retirement villages), regional development policies (e.g., regional planning offices; consolidated school districts; and regional ambulances, hospitals, and police and fire departments), and branch offices and rural commercial activities (e.g., banking and insurance). We sometimes forget, however, that the economic influences between urban and rural areas are hardly asymmetrical. The biggest retailer in the world—Walmart—has its corporate headquarters in rural Arkansas.

In fact, the economies of rural and urban labor markets are highly integrated and interdependent in an increasingly global economy. A stark example of this is Google—a product of the urban core whose massive servers are housed and maintained in rural communities such as The Dalles, Oregon; and Moncks Corner, South Carolina. And the local benefits of self-employment and entrepreneurship often trickle down from America's largest metropolitan employment centers to other labor market areas, including rural ones (Tsvetkova, Partridge, and Betz, this volume). Money, information, and labor are portable across geographic space, providing especially useful illustrations of boundary crossing and diffusion across the entire rural-urban continuum. They also make the case for a regional perspective for local economic development (Brown and Shucksmith, this volume). The economic benefits, on balance, have been large historically. Using a new poverty measure—the Supplemental Poverty Measure—Nolan, Waldfogel, and Wimer (this volume) document rapid declines in poverty over the 1967 to 2014 period. Declines have been especially prominent in nonmetropolitan areas, owing in large part to the economic transformation and growth of many small and remote communities. Rural areas also benefit from a lower cost of living, perhaps as a cause or consequence of many rural areas seemingly becoming collecting grounds for economically disadvantaged populations. Indeed, lived experiences and economic well-being are often very different for poor people living in rural and urban communities and neighborhoods (see Alexander et al., this volume). Conventional statistical measurement approaches to poverty may mischaracterize day-to-day economic hardships and responses to them. This calls for new qualitative approaches—even a new nationally representative qualitative census of poverty—that identifies and monitors the different dimensions of poverty in both rural and urban areas (Alexander et al., this volume).

This is an important initiative. A distinguishing feature of American society is the intergenerational persistence of poverty and affluence (Torche 2015), which suggests a new crystallization of class boundaries and less openness in the American social stratification system (Beller and Hout 2006). Economic opportunity has a large spatial component that extends across the rural and urban continuum (Weber et al., this volume). In their groundbreaking work, Chetty and his colleagues (2014) use administrative records on the incomes of more than 40 million children and their parents to document the linear statistical association between the incomes of parents and children (i.e., a 10 percentile increase in parental income is associated with a 3.4 percentile increase in children's income). But perhaps more significantly, they show that intergenerational mobility varies enormously across the United States. They provide estimates of intergenerational mobility at the level of commuting zones, which are represented by aggregations of counties. They show that upward mobility is highest in the Great Plains, and also that rural areas exhibited more intergenerational mobility than their comparable urban counterparts. To illustrate the point, they present evidence of higher upward mobility among the children from low-income families from rural Illinois than those from the Chicago area. Of course, upward social mobility is linked to spatial mobility, which again makes our central point—that rural and urban boundaries are highly permeable. Other regions (e.g., Appalachia or rural areas of black population concentration) are less geographically mobile, which contributes both to intragenerational and intergenerational persistence of poverty. At other levels of geography—inner cities—poverty is often perpetuated by segregation from one generation to the next (i.e., a clear marker of the urban ghetto, where the American underclass is concentrated and perpetuated; see Rugh and Massey 2014; Sharkey 2014). Alternately, movement to middle-class suburbs is almost always viewed as a marker of achieving the American dream.

Building on this work, Weber et al. (this volume) show that patterns of intergenerational mobility in micropolitan areas (i.e., nonmetropolitan counties with large urban places, which might be characterized as incipient metropolitan areas) promote upward intergenerational mobility. They also illustrate the blurring of boundaries between metropolitan areas and remote rural areas. These analyses provide a potentially powerful tool for place-based policy interventions designed to promote upward mobility and loosen the putative ascriptive constraints of place.

Changing American institutions

With accelerating social and economic change, observers often claim that our most fundamental institutions—families, schools, and religion—are now under assault, and that public confidence or trust in them has eroded (Pew Research Center 2015). This may be especially true of government despite the overwhelming belief that the federal government plays an important role in ensuring national security, public health, and personal safety and well-being. Opinions are often highly partisan along party lines, with Republicans much less positive than Democrats about the role of government and its effectiveness (Pew Research Center 2015). And this was certainly reflected in the 2016 presidential election.

The headline of a 2012 article in *The Economist* ("Is Rural America Still Politically Relevant?") seemed to cast doubt on the political power of rural voters, who bring very different issues to the ballot box. America's red states are overwhelming rural (i.e., much of the South, Great Plains, and Mountain West), while the blue states are concentrated in the old "rust belt" and coasts, with their big cities and large populations of racial minorities and immigrants. (Purple states are swing states with blurred political constituencies.) As Scala and Johnson observe (this volume), the 2016 presidential election will be remembered as "the year the white rural voter roared." But rural and urban voters—and their attitudes about the role or effectiveness of government—are not a monolith. Scala and Johnson point out that the shifting, blurring, and crossing of urban-rural boundaries bring needed caution to big generalizations about a rural backlash. Voting patterns are expressed very differently along the rural-urban continuum, with partisan voting patterns the least apparent in suburban and exurban areas (especially in the largest cities). And it is these areas that have become the destinations of new arrivals—both from red rural areas and blue areas from the city.

The rural-urban interface—where interaction and interdependency is substantial—is also clearly revealed in the way that we govern (Brown and Shucksmith, this volume), the way that we educate young people in schools

(Burdick-Will and Logan, this volume), and where we punish and incarcerate criminal offenders (Eason, Zucker, and Wildeman, this volume). Brown and Shucksmith (this volume) highlight the problems of regional government that typically involve different and overlapping layers of government at the rural-urban interface. The quality of local schools, as measured by local funding and performance, provides a clear example of the real world consequences of government organizations (i.e., school districts and elected school boards) that span jurisdictional boundaries. The quality of schools is often a central consideration in family migration decision-making (e.g., moving from low-resourced schools districts to suburban schools). The consequences of selective rural out-migration of the "best and brightest" have been expressed historically in poor school performance, inadequate school funding (because of eroding property taxes), and school closings. Burdick-Will and Logan (this volume) uncover the issues at the rural-urban interface, and document the great disparities in school composition, achievement, and resources that may ultimately reinforce spatial inequality rather than reduce it.

New spatial interdependencies between rural and urban areas are also illustrated in an expanding literature on mass incarceration. Prison building and incarceration have provided an economic boom for some rural areas but also made them increasingly economically dependent on the importation of mostly urban offenders and the influence of state and federal sentencing mandates (Hooks et al. 2004). This is a symbiotic relationship between rural and urban America that has uncharted social, economic, and political consequences in the long term. Indeed, Eason, Zucker, and Wildeman (this volume) illustrate these economic and political spatial interdependencies, showing how mass incarceration plays out along the rural-urban continuum and how the penal and justice system often reinforce spatial inequality in crime and punishment.

Health and well-being at the rural-urban interface

Changing rural-urban boundaries are also revealed in the new "geography of despair" in America, which manifests itself in heightened rural mortality from violence, suicide, and alcohol and opiate abuse. In the past, these were characterized as urban maladies. Today, life expectancy in America is lowest in Central Appalachia, in the so-called Carolina-Georgia black belt, and in the Mississippi Delta region. More troubling is that, for the first time, the Centers for Disease Control and Prevention (CDC) now reports declines in life expectancy among less-educated rural whites, especially in impoverished and remote counties of Appalachia. The diffusion of urban maladies to the countryside is presumably responsible for deleterious health outcomes and to the behavioral patterns that contribute to them (Case and Deaton 2015). Among rural young people, deaths from opiates (especially from heroin, OxyContin, and Fentanyl) are at an all-time high, even exceeding deaths from automobile accidents. Inequality in mortality has increased in America, and observed health behaviors (e.g., nutritional intake, smoking, and drugs) and disparities have a large spatial dimension (Currie and Schwandt 2016).

This volume of *The ANNALS* highlights some emerging spatial patterns along the rural-urban continuum. In doing so, it provides a point of departure for new work on geographic disparities in health and well-being. For example, the article by Lawrence, Hummer, and Harris (this volume) describes the early onset of obesity in America, which threatens the health of young adults across the rural-urban continuum. They examine disparities in body weight, blood pressure, and other indicators of cardiac and vascular health, which seem to drive higher rates of mortality in rural areas. And these patterns are reinforced by economic disparities and by early exposure to unfavorable environmental conditions. Individuals who grew up in densely settled areas, but later moved elsewhere, had better cardiovascular health than otherwise similar immobile populations. Whether these spatial patterns reflect causal processes or are due to positive health selection of migrants has implications for the measurement and etiology of geographic disparities in health. Exposure to favorable and unfavorable living conditions (and the peer or neighborhood effect they imply) are highly fluid, perhaps especially at the rural-urban interface where conventional geographic classifications are most ambiguous.

Economic disparities in income and poverty are associated with disparities in economic and geographic access to health care and physical and emotional well-being. Hunger and food insecurity also has a spatial dimension. There is a vibrant literature on so-called food deserts, which denote neighborhoods, communities, and regions where residents lack access to nutritious food, such as affordable fresh fruits and vegetables (Walker, Keane, and Burke 2010). Indeed, Gundersen and colleagues (this volume) show that food insecurity is not evenly distributed across geographic space, nor are public responses to the problem (e.g., charitable food banks). They highlight the spatial interdependence and interpenetration of extralocal or national organizations into local rural communities in need. The result is that rural food insecurity is mitigated by urban interventions in the form of organizations like Feeding America and its many national corporate sponsors, such as the Buffett Foundation, and by federal programs like the Supplemental Nutrition Assistance Program (SNAP) that "make up" for the comparatively low levels of cash assistance for the poor in rural states.

Finally, the well-being of populations across the rural and urban divide (and continuum) can be measured by the uneven exposure to blighted communities and neighborhoods. HUD emphasizes, with its name, its programmatic priorities, which target government assistance on housing in the nation's cities. But not unlike the opiate epidemic, urban blight has diffused to rural communities and the countryside. Indeed, the economic decline in many rural communities—and increasingly in older close-in suburban communities—is observed in the form of abandoned, vandalized, and boarded up storefronts, which often instill fear of crime among residents. This point is clearly made by York Cornwell and Hall (this volume) by following a national sample of housing units over time. They show, for example, that abandoned and vandalized buildings are common in urban cities but have also increased rapidly in suburban, exurban, and rural areas. The social boundaries that have typically defined rural and urban areas—those based on housing blight and decay—are perhaps less clear-cut today than in the past. "Neighborhood problems are not just big city or urban problems" (York Cornwell and Hall, this volume).

Lessons Learned

Our fundamental goal—and the goal of this volume—is to highlight the new rural-urban interface in America. It is to better understand the rapidly changing spatial and social boundaries that animate our shared cultural, economic, and political interests and the spatially interdependent relationships that have become part and parcel of everyday life across America's cities, communities, and countryside. This is important, especially at a time when rural America is increasingly viewed as being left behind in public discourse, academic circles, and public policy (Lichter and Brown 2015). The result of the 2016 presidential election was a wake-up call. As we have argued here, it is time to elevate public awareness that the things that unite rural and urban America are arguably as important (if not more important) today than the things that divide us.

This central point—one of shared destinies—is reinforced by each of the articles in this volume of *The ANNALS*. We provide five key takeaway lessons that should inform future research and policy on spatial interdependence and inequality.

First, the symbolic and social boundaries that have traditionally defined rural and urban America are changing—and changing rapidly in a global economy. Rural and urban are ideal types that no longer exist in reality or in pure form. Spatial boundaries have *shifted* as rural communities and people are gobbled up by urbanization. With improvements in transportation and communication, virtually all Americans—rural and urban—have access to or are exposed to or influenced by people and places on either side of the rural-urban divide. Spatial boundaries are *crossed*, perhaps as never before, by people in our highly mobile society. And the spatial line or boundary that separates rural from urban arguably is not a line at all, but an interstitial space that has become less bright or clearly defined over time. Boundary *blurring* means that people and communities often experience both worlds—rural and urban—on a daily or regular basis.

Second, the new rural-urban interface means it is time to rethink how we divide up America in spatial terms. We need new approaches to social problems and policies that are spatially inclusive—that recognize that urban-centric approaches may by definition inadvertently miss or downplay the importance of topics that are inextricably linked to the health and well-being of rural America (Shucksmith et al. 2012). This includes natural resource development, food systems, climate change and the environment, and exclusionary settlement or segregation patterns (e.g., Indian reservations or new immigrant destinations). At the same time, rural-centric approaches must acknowledge growing cultural and economic ties to big cities, and the clear material benefits that have trickled down to the countryside over the past century. The economic interests of rural and urban people are shared and reinforced by new and growing spatial interdependencies.

Third, in an era of big data and high-speed computing, we need to rethink conventional classification schemes for measuring urban and rural people and communities. Most measures, developed in an earlier period, no longer neatly map onto the reality of U.S. settlement systems (Wunderlich 2015). Spatial classification systems are often wrongly institutionalized and difficult to change politically. They sometimes fail to acknowledge the new and growing spatial links that stich diverse populations together into an integrated system of interrelationships of all kinds. Our statistical system has not kept pace with the rapid pace of urbanization and globalism. This point is made clear by the fact that 54.4 percent of America's rural people, as officially defined by the U.S. government (and based on data from the 2015 American Community Survey), now live in metropolitan areas.[2]

Fourth, the current way that the nation is organized administratively may ultimately reinforce old or outdated symbolic and social boundaries of rural and urban in ways that make problem-solving more difficult. At the federal level, this is often reflected in the mission statements or funding priorities of various government agencies such as the USDA or HUD. The nation's university departments and research units (e.g., Department of Rural Sociology or Agricultural Economics) and academic specialty areas (e.g., urban economics) may reinforce a serious conceptual roadblock to understanding problems that are embedded in spatial interrelationships and interdependence. Dividing government agencies and university programs on the basis of old or outdated conceptual paradigms and measurement schemes requires some rethinking. For example, one recent development on the policy front that requires greater research attention is the replacement of federal-state matching grants with fixed block grants. The 1996 welfare reform, which eliminated the Aid to Families with Dependent Children and replaced it with the fixed block grant program called Temporary Assistance for Needy Families, is held up by some in conservative policy circles as the way to reorganize many other programs such as Medicaid and SNAP (aka "food stamps"). The devolution of responsibility to states may make programs more responsive to local needs across the rural-urban continuum, but may also expose the disadvantaged to large state-to-state inequities in welfare generosity.

Fifth, and perhaps most important, the singular lesson to be drawn from this volume is that spatial boundaries are highly fluid and this basic point should be better reflected in research programs, in the topics that we choose to study, and in the way that public policy problems are solved. An important lesson of the volume is that the reification of old, tired geographic definitions—and the norms and expectations associated with them—are often created on the basis of a demographic portrait of the country that no longer exists in America's increasingly diverse and urbanized population. The implications clearly extend to the political sphere, where effective policy prescriptions are only as good as accurate knowledge and appropriate norms allow. This calls for a new kind of dialogue between academics and those who swim in the waters of policy and politics, especially if civic improvement is a goal in both rural and urban places. Indeed, as we show here, most social and economic issues of the day have a large spatial component that, in one way or another, involves both rural and urban people and places. We need to forge a new—and modern—research agenda that acknowledges this fact and the shared interests that unify us rather than divide us into obsolete or narrowly defined categories that obfuscate rather than illuminate. This is especially important to ensure cost-effective public policy that makes a difference for all Americans (Brown and Shucksmith, this volume).

Notes

1. Timothy Parker, personal communication, April 17, 2017.
2. See https://storymaps.geo.census.gov/arcgis/apps/MapSeries/index.html?appid=9e459da9327b4c7e9a1248cb65ad942a.

References

Alba, Richard, and Victor Nee. 2003. *Remaking the American mainstream: Assimilation and contemporary immigration*. Cambridge, MA: Harvard University Press.

Beller, Emily, and Michael Hout. 2006. Intergenerational social mobility: The United States in comparative perspective. *The Future of Children* 16 (2): 19–36.

Berg, Nate. 28 March 2012. *America's growing urban footprint*. Citylab. Available from https://www.citylab.com.

Brown, David L., Fred K. Hines, and John M. Zimmer. 1975. *Social and economic characteristics of the population in metro and nonmetro counties: 1970*. Washington, DC: U.S. Department of Agriculture, Economic Research Service.

Brown, David L., and Kai A. Schafft. 2012. *Rural people and communities in the 21st century: Resilience and transformation*. Cambridge: Polity Publishers.

Case, Anne, and Angus Deaton. 2015. Rising morbidity and mortality in midlife among white non-Hispanic Americans in the 21st century. *Proceedings of the National Academy of Sciences* 112 (49): 15078–83.

Castle, Emery N., JunJie Wu, and Bruce A. Weber. 2011. Place orientation and rural-urban interdependence. *Applied Economic Perspectives and Policy* 33:179–204.

Chetty, Raj, Nathaniel Hendren, Patrick Kline, and Emmanuel Saez. 2014. Where is the land of opportunity? The geography of intergenerational mobility in the United States. *Quarterly Journal of Economics* 129 (4): 1553–1623.

Currie, J., and Hannes Schwandt. 2016. Inequality in mortality decreased among the young while increasing for older adults, 1990–2010. *Science* 352 (6286): 708–12.

Economic Research Service. 2017. *Recent population change*. Available from https://www.ers.usda.gov/topics/rural-economy-population/population-migration/recent-population-change/.

The Economist. 22 December 2012. Rural America's fight for relevance: The politics of rural America.

Evich, Helena Bottemiller. 13 November 2016. Revenge of the rural voter. *Politico*. Available from http://www.politico.com/story/2016/11/hillary-clinton-rural-voters-trump-231266.

Friedland, William H. 1982. The end of rural society and the future of rural sociology. *Rural Sociology* 47:598–608.

Fulkerson, Gregory M., and Alexander R. Thomas, eds. 2013. *Studies in urbanormativity: Rural communities in urban society*. Lanham, MD: Lexington Books.

Gibson, Campbell. 2012. *American demographic history chartbook: 1790 to 2010*. Available from http://www.demographicchartbook.com.

Hall, Matthew, Laura Tach, and Barrett A. Lee. 2016. Trajectories of ethnoracial diversity in American communities, 1980–2010. *Population and Development Review* 42:271–97.

Hochschild, Arlie Russell. 2016. *Strangers in their own land: Anger and mourning on the American Right*. New York, NY: New Press.

Hooks, Gregory, Clayton Mosher, Thomas Rotolo, and Linda Lobao. 2004. The prison industry: Carceral expansion and employment in U.S. counties, 1969–1994. *Social Science Quarterly* 85 (1): 35–57.

Johnson, Kenneth M. 20 February 2017. Where is "rural America," and what does it look like? *The Conversation*. Available from https://theconversation.com/where-is-rural-america- and-what-does-it-look-like-72045.

Johnson, Kenneth M., and Daniel T. Lichter. 2016. Diverging demography: Hispanic and non- Hispanic contributions to U.S. population redistribution and diversity. *Population Research and Policy Review* 35 (5): 705–25.

Lamont, Michèle, and Virág Molnár. 2002. The study of boundaries in the social sciences. *Annual Review of Sociology* 28 (1): 167–95.

Legewie, Joscha, and Merlin Schaeffer. 2016. Contested boundaries: Explaining where ethnoracial diversity provokes neighborhood conflict. *American Journal of Sociology* 122 (1): 125–61.

Lichter, Daniel T. 2013. Integration or fragmentation? Racial diversity and the American future. *Demography* 50 (2): 359–91.

Lichter, Daniel T., and David L. Brown. 2011. Rural America in an urban society: Changing spatial and social boundaries. *Annual Review of Sociology* 37 (1): 565–92.

Lichter, Daniel T., and David L. Brown. 2015. The new rural-urban interface: Lessons for higher education. *Choices* 29 (1): 1–6.

Logan, John R. 2012. Making a place for space: Spatial thinking in social science. *Annual Review of Sociology* 38 (1): 507–24.

Monnat, Shannon, and David L. Brown. 29 March 2017. More than a rural revolt: Landscapes of distress and the 2016 presidential election. *Speak for Sociology. A blog by the American Sociological Association*. Available from http://speak4sociology.org/2017/03/29/more-than-a-rural-revolt-landscapes-of-distress-and-the-2016-presidential-election/.

Nairn, Daniel. 26 March 2012. New census geographies tell an ambiguous urban story. *Discovering Urbanism*. Available from http://discoveringurbanism.blogspot.com/2012/03/new-census-maps-tell-ambigious- urban.html.

Pew Research Center. 2015. *Beyond distrust: How Americans view their government*. Washington, DC: Pew Research Center.

Rugh, Jacob S., and Douglas S. Massey. 2014. Segregation in post-civil rights America. *Du Bois Review* 11 (2): 205–32.

Sharkey, Patrick. 2014. *Stuck in place: Urban neighborhoods and the end of progress toward racial equality*. Chicago, IL: University of Chicago Press.

Shucksmith, Mark, and David L. Brown. 2016. Framing rural studies in the global north. In *Routledge international handbook of rural studies*, eds., Mark Sucksmith and David L. Brown, 1–26. London: Routledge.

Shucksmith, Mark, David L. Brown, Sally Shortall, Jo Vergunst, and Mildred E. Warner. 2012. *Rural transformations and rural policies in the US and UK*. London: Routledge.

Torche, Florencia. 2015. Analyses of intergenerational mobility: An interdisciplinary review. *The ANNALS of the American Academy of Political and Social Science* 26 (1): 37–62.

U.S. Census Bureau. 2017. 2010 Census urban and rural classification and urban area criteria. Available from https://www.census.gov/geo/reference/ua/urban-rural-2010.html.

Vance, J. D. 2016. *Hillbilly elegy: A memoir of a family and culture in crisis*. London: HarperCollins UK.

Walker, Renee E., Christopher R. Keane, and Jessica G. Burke. 2010. Disparities and access to healthy food in the United States: A review of food deserts literature. *Health & Place* 16 (5): 876–84.

Waters, Mary, and Marissa G. Pineau. 2016. *The integration of immigrants into American society*. Washington, DC: National Academies Press.

Wirth, Louis. 1938. Urbanism as a way of life. *American Journal of Sociology* 44:1–24.

Woods, Michael. 2009. Rural geography: Blurring boundaries and making connections. *Progress in Human Geography* 33 (6): 849–58.

Wunderlich, Gooloo S. 2015. *Rationalizing rural area classifications for the Economic Research Service: A workshop summary*. Washington, DC: National Academies Press.

Ethnoracial Diversity across the Rural-Urban Continuum

By
BARRETT A. LEE
and
GREGORY SHARP

Scholarship and popular opinion regard cities as more racially and ethnically diverse than rural communities. However, recent trends hint at the possibility of less distinctive diversity profiles on either side of the metro-nonmetro divide. To explore this, we compare the magnitude and structure of ethnoracial diversity in more than 27,000 census-defined places arrayed across ten different types of county contexts that spanned the rural-urban continuum in 2010. Even as average residents' exposure to diversity steadily declines as contexts become more rural and remote, place-based (unweighted) results show an uneven pattern of diversity across most of the continuum. Multivariate analysis supports the unevenness scenario: when place characteristics are taken into account, many of the associations between type of context and diversity weaken to the point of nonsignificance. Taken together, these findings suggest a blurring of rural-urban boundaries with respect to community ethnoracial composition.

Keywords: diversity; race-ethnicity; rural-urban continuum; census place; entropy index

Population diversity has long been considered a defining feature of the urban environment. As Chicago School sociologist Louis Wirth (1938) put the matter in his treatise on urbanism, cities are not only large and densely settled but heterogeneous in composition. Age, household type, socioeconomic status, and race-ethnicity rank among the major demographic dimensions of

Barrett A. Lee is a professor of sociology and demography at The Pennsylvania State University. He studies community diversity, racial segregation, neighborhood change, residential mobility, and urban homelessness. An interest in spatial manifestations of inequality runs throughout his work.

Gregory Sharp is an assistant professor of sociology at the University at Buffalo, SUNY. His current research examines ethnoracial stratification in housing in America, contextual effects on health, and community social organization in Los Angeles.

Correspondence: bal6@psu.edu

DOI: 10.1177/0002716217708560

diversity. The last dimension is arguably the most consequential, given its correlations with the others. During Wirth's career, the racial diversity of northern U.S. cities increased in response to the Great Migration of blacks from the rural South. Metropolitan ethnoracial diversity has risen even more impressively since the 1970s thanks to the arrival of Latinos and Asians, two immigrant groups with youthful age structures and high rates of natural increase (Frey 2015; Lee, Iceland, and Farrell 2014). Whatever the effects of the recent diversification trend—on the economy, politics, education, and social relations (see, e.g., Hopkins 2009; Lichter 2013; Portes and Vickstrom 2011)—these effects are assumed to be strongest in the nation's gateway cities. A large number of these cities now have majority-minority compositions.

The multiethnic character of large cities contrasts sharply with accepted wisdom about rural communities. These communities are often perceived as homogeneous in many respects, including their racial-ethnic mix (Lichter and Brown 2011). Certainly the "Lake Wobegon" image of places in the nonmetropolitan Midwest inhabited by descendants of Northern European immigrants has a factual historical basis (Lieberson and Waters 1988). Rural white homogeneity can also be traced to blatant forms of discrimination that kept people of color from settling in "sundown towns" (Loewen 2005) and, more recently, to the redrawing of municipal boundaries for exclusionary purposes (Lichter et al. 2007). Even when nonwhites are present, they may live in equally homogeneous settings—think African Americans in small "Black Belt" places, Mexicans throughout South Texas, or American Indian residents of reservation communities. Such examples, which reinforce popular stereotypes, stress the wide gulf between low-diversity nonmetro communities and their high-diversity metropolitan counterparts.

Our research proceeds from the premise that the destinations of international and domestic migration flows have changed sufficiently over the past half century to challenge this conventional view. Since the Immigration and Nationality Act of 1965, shifts in immigration-related policies at the federal, state, and local levels have increased foreign-born persons' freedom of movement within the United States while deflecting them from established gateways (Light 2006; Massey 2008; Tienda and Sanchez 2013). Many members of immigrant-rich groups are leaving behind saturated urban markets—where they traditionally have concentrated in ethnic enclaves—for the economic opportunities, affordable housing, and quality of life available in suburban and nonmetropolitan places. Their ruralward shift is especially striking, motivated in part by low-skill labor demand in agricultural processing, oil and natural gas production, and other sectors (Kandel and Parrado 2005). Similarly, rural retirement and amenity destinations are drawing immigrants to fill construction and service jobs (Johnson and Lichter 2013; Nelson, Lee, and Nelson 2009). Recruitment efforts and ethnic social networks

NOTE: Support for this research has been provided by a grant from the Eunice Kennedy Shriver National Institute for Child Health and Human Development (R01HD074605). Additional support comes from the Penn State Population Research Institute, which receives infrastructure funding from NICHHD (2P2CHD041025). The content of the article is solely the responsibility of the authors and does not reflect the official views of the National Institutes of Health.

continue to increase awareness of rural employment among Hispanics in particular, who show signs of further geographic dispersion outside the West and Southwest (Kandel and Cromartie 2004; Lichter and Johnson 2006).

As a result, nonmetro places have become more ethnoracially diverse, sometimes in dramatic fashion. A robust literature documents the nonmetro diversification trend and weighs its potential consequences for communities unaccustomed to incorporating minorities (Crowley and Ebert 2014; Lichter 2012; G. Sharp and Lee 2016). Consistent with the "blurring" theme of this volume, some of these communities qualify as "urban" in Census Bureau terms, exceeding a population threshold of 2,500 by themselves or as part of a cluster of adjacent places. Others are close to metro areas, a fact that increases their chances of being absorbed through centrifugal expansion or, at minimum, of being subject to metropolitan influences. This urbanization of rural America has been fueled by transportation advances, innovations in information technology, globalization, industrial restructuring, growing corporate dominance, and the pull—for recreation or extraction—of natural resources (Brown 2014; Lichter and Brown 2011). At the same time, many metro areas contain swaths of sparsely settled territory and nontrivial rural populations. The persistence of rurality in metropolitan settings is most evident in exurban or fringe zones, which tend to attract affluent white inhabitants (J. Sharp and Clark 2008). More generally, the share of racial residential segregation due to place-level sorting has increased over time, yielding homogeneous communities in the midst of metro-wide diversity (Lichter, Parisi, and Taquino 2015).

We evaluate a key implication of these intersecting trends: that the diversity profiles of rural and urban communities may no longer be as distinct as commonly thought. Our investigation addresses several limitations of existing research, including the inconsistent conceptualization and measurement of diversity and the rarity with which both rural and urban diversity are considered in the same study. Moreover, when rural-urban comparisons on any characteristic (not just diversity) are made, they tend to be crude, for example, between places inside and outside of metro areas or of different population sizes. Such approaches, which treat *rural* and *urban* in dichotomous or unidimensional fashion, may not adequately reflect the complexity of community types emerging at the new rural-urban interface. Neither do they recognize the potential for variation among communities within different kinds of metropolitan or nonmetropolitan settings. A preferable strategy, adopted here, emphasizes gradations along a rural-urban continuum, with a community's position on the continuum determined by aspects of the surrounding context in which it is embedded.

Our analysis compares 2010 patterns of ethnoracial diversity for more than 27,000 places found in the largest metro areas, the most remote rural counties, and a variety of contexts in between. The majority of the places are incorporated as cities, suburbs, towns, or villages, while others (termed census-designated places) lack municipal status; both types of places constitute meaningful social, symbolic, and institutional entities. We assign each place to one of ten rural-urban continuum categories based on the metropolitan status or proximity of its host county and, in nonmetro instances, the size of that county's urban population. Comparisons across categories allow us to address three central questions. First, how does the magnitude and racial-ethnic structure of diversity for places vary by position on the continuum? Second, are the average residents of places along the continuum exposed to similar or different diversity magnitudes and structures? And third, does county context capture features of places, such as housing and labor market characteristics, that are associated with ethnoracial diversity? Our answers to these questions shed new light on the ways in which contemporary forms of spatial interdependence can complicate traditional binary thinking about rural homogeneity and urban heterogeneity.

Background

Dimensions of diversity

The term *diversity* is regularly used in loose fashion to refer to the presence of African Americans, Latinos, or some other minority group in a community. Here we stick to a more precise demographic definition that emphasizes two aspects of the ethnoracial composition of the local population. The *magnitude* or level of diversity is determined by the number of racial-ethnic groups that make up the population and their relative sizes (White 1986). A place comprising many groups of equal size would be judged highly diverse. Obversely, homogeneity prevails when all residents belong to the same group, that is, when the population exhibits an absence of diversity. Several statistics are available with which to capture the magnitude dimension of diversity. We favor the entropy index (described in the methodology section) for both its conceptual congruence and its desirable statistical properties.

Diversity also varies in terms of *racial-ethnic structure*, or the specific groups constituting a population. The importance of the structural dimension lies in the fact that it may differ among places with identical diversity magnitudes. As an illustration, the entropy index values for a pair of "50-50" communities—one half white and half Asian, the other half black and half Hispanic—would be exactly the same despite the likelihood of divergent socioeconomic mixes and interethnic relations in the two communities. To understand ethnoracial diversity, we must know which groups are present, not just their number and sizes. Compositional bar graphs and a "majority rule" typology allow us to distinguish among places on the structural dimension.

Another valuable distinction can be made between *place-based* (or unweighted) and *person-based* (or weighted) diversity. In the former, all communities—from the principal cities of major metropolitan areas to the smallest rural villages—are considered conceptually equivalent and thus count the same from an analytic standpoint. However, more people in total may reside in the largest cities despite the greater number of villages. This uneven distribution of the population across types of communities suggests that larger places should count more (i.e., be weighted by size). It also means that the level or structure of place diversity experienced by the average American could differ from the average level or structure of place diversity if, as Wirth (1938) predicted, a positive relationship exists between community size and diversity. Given the validity of both approaches, our research compares person-based diversity exposure to place-based diversity across and within rural-urban continuum categories. Previous studies of which we are aware have chosen one or the other.

Urban versus rural?

A glaring lacuna in the diversity literature is the failure to examine communities over the full range of the rural-urban continuum in a single analysis. Due to minority overrepresentation in cities and the perceived homogeneity of rural settlements, diversity research focuses primarily on metropolitan areas, places, and neighborhoods (Frey 2015; Lee, Iceland, and Sharp 2012; Logan and Zhang 2010). Across metro units of varying spatial scale, rapid Hispanic and Asian growth has combined with absolute or relative white declines to erode the demographic primacy of whites, especially in the South and West. Most large cities now feature multigroup racial-ethnic structures, and fewer suburbs conform to the all-white image embedded in popular culture (Berube 2003; Hall and Lee 2010). Still, many metro places are dominated by one ethnoracial group, and some have even become more homogeneous over time (Lee and Hughes 2015).

A few recent studies do include both metropolitan and nonmetropolitan units. Parisi, Lichter, and Taquino (2015) document a substantial increase between 1990 and 2010 in the number of metro and nonmetro places with four-group racial-ethnic structures (white-black-Hispanic-Asian), although the metro-nonmetro gap in mean diversity magnitude widened during that period. A 1980 to 2010 comparison of diversity in metropolitan and micropolitan areas rather than places yields similar findings (Lee, Iceland, and Farrell 2014). Hall, Tach, and Lee (2016) show that the steepest upward-sloping trajectories of diversity change have disproportionately involved metro places instead of micropolitan or rural ones. Population size, an alternative to the metro-nonmetro dichotomy, exhibits a consistent positive correlation with ethnoracial diversity (Allen and Turner 1989; Hall and Lee 2010; Lee, Iceland, and Sharp 2012). However, it only taps a single dimension of the rural-urban continuum.

What is missing—and what we aim to provide—are finer-grained distinctions among the larger settings in which places are located. Metropolitan areas, for example, vary dramatically in population size, as the contrast between New York (18.9 million residents in 2010) and Carson City, Nevada (55,274) attest. Nonmetro counties vary as well, not only in size but in degree of urbanization and distance to the nearest metropolis. Intuitively, such features of areal contexts would appear to have implications for the diversity of their constituent places. Imagine three towns of a few thousand inhabitants each, one situated in a top-ten metro area, one in a nonmetro county adjacent to a medium-size metro area, and one far removed from any type of metropolitan environment. Because influences of the surrounding context are presumably strongest in the first town, the traditional urbanism paradigm espoused by Wirth (1938) would lead us to anticipate high diversity there as immigrants and minority groups—and the forces attracting them—disperse throughout the metropolis. These dynamics may operate to some degree in the second hypothetical town but be weakest in the third.

Fortunately, classification systems are available that capture basic differences across metropolitan and nonmetropolitan contexts. The U.S. Department of Agriculture's (USDA) nine-category rural-urban continuum (or RUC) scheme is particularly useful (USDA 2013). Its first three categories, which we expand to four, differentiate metropolitan counties by the total population size of the metro area to which they belong. The remaining six distinguish among nonmetropolitan counties based on the size of their urban population and proximity (adjacency) to a metro area. The RUC scheme facilitates a shift from dichotomous, urban versus rural thinking to a perspective that identifies gradations along a continuum of county contexts that are multidimensionally defined. The scheme's conceptual and operational advantages have made it popular in research on other topics. To date, though, it has not been used to study place ethnoracial diversity (but see Winkler and Johnson 2016).

Research questions

By sorting places into their appropriate RUC categories, we can shed empirical light on three descriptive research questions. The first question asks how the magnitude and racial-ethnic structure of place-based diversity varies over the rural-urban continuum. From a classic urbanism point of view, the most likely scenario would be a *linear decline* in diversity as one moves away from the largest metropolitan settings and toward the least urbanized, most isolated rural contexts. A *threshold* or stairstep pattern could occur if the metro-nonmetro distinction is meaningful, that is, if the drivers of ethnoracial diversity are present in all metropolises regardless of size but are absent from nonmetropolitan America. The blurring of rural and urban domains noted earlier, however, suggests more *unevenness* across continuum categories. For instance, places in highly urbanized nonmetro counties that are adjacent to large metropolitan areas might be as diverse as—if not more diverse than—their counterparts located in small metro contexts. Carried to an extreme, blurring logic yields the null hypothesis: that diversity levels and racial-ethnic structures for places do not vary by context, given the limited relevance of traditional urban-rural or metro-nonmetro distinctions in the contemporary United States.

Our second question reframes the first in person- rather than place-based terms. Namely, do the average residents of places at various points along the rural-urban continuum experience different or similar forms of ethnoracial diversity? The same hypothetical patterns just mentioned—linear decline, threshold, uneven, null—also apply to this question, yet the pattern receiving the most support need not be the same as for the first question. If people are disproportionately concentrated in larger places across and within the RUC categories, the exposure of individuals to diversity (which is what weighting places by population size tells us) will diverge from the place-based results (when places are weighted equally regardless of size).

The final research question inquires about correlates of the magnitude and structure of diversity among places. We are interested in whether the RUC categories independently predict place diversity or whether each category proxies more detailed characteristics of places found within a particular type of context. Three salient sets of characteristics have been identified in prior investigations (Allen and Turner 1989; Lee, Iceland, and Sharp 2012; Hall and Lee 2010; G. Sharp and Lee 2016). With respect to the *context of reception* provided by a place, location in the West or South (closer to Hispanic and Asian countries of origin) and a critical mass of foreign-born residents, which implies access to co-ethnic resources (social capital, employment niches, etc.), are related to higher diversity and more balanced racial-ethnic structures. A larger retirement-age population, however, tends to undermine ethnoracial diversity, perhaps because it signals a stagnant economy unattractive to immigrants and minorities or because its members are uncomfortable living near these groups. The dispropor-tionate whiteness of persons 65 and older probably contributes to the association between retirees and diversity as well (West et al. 2014).

A place's *housing and labor market characteristics*, reflective of economic opportunity, must also be considered. Access to housing—indexed by features such as affordability, an abundance of rental units, and new construction activ-ity—is a draw for most ethnoracial groups and hence should promote diversity. Higher incomes and lower unemployment rates have similarly widespread appeal. So does a local economy with types of jobs that suit a wide range of edu-cational and skill levels.

Last, places serving as *institutional hubs* for government, the military, and higher education are more likely to have diverse, multigroup compositions. Committed to affirmative action, these institutions provide avenues of upward mobility for people of color. The presence of correctional facilities, a less volun-tary kind of institution, is also positively associated with diversity in a community.

Methodology

Places as units

To address our three questions about variation in ethnoracial diversity across the rural-urban continuum, we extract data from the 2010 decennial census and the 2008–2012 American Community Survey (ACS) five-year summary file for 27,163 places with at least 100 residents. These places comprise cities, suburbs, towns, and villages that contain 74 percent of the total U.S. population, or 228.4 million people. Two-thirds of the places are incorporated, with legally vested powers and obligations, and the largest—principal cities of major metropolises—often approximate housing and labor markets. Among other duties, incorporated places are responsible for developing fiscal or policy responses to diversity-related issues that occur inside their boundaries. The remaining third of the sample consists of unincorporated or census-designated places. Residents recog-nize both incorporated and census-designated places by name and may feel some degree of attachment to them. More concretely, the ethnoracial diversity of a place influences the composition of local neighborhoods, schools, work settings, and voluntary organizations, not to mention the social relationships that form in these venues. On a number of criteria, then, places qualify as "real" communities in addition to being convenient statistical aggregations.

While most Americans live in our sample places, roughly one-fourth do not. The 80.4 million people excluded from the sample either reside in places with fewer than 100 inhabitants or are part of the nonplace population. They are also disproportionately white (80.2 percent versus 58 percent of those in places of 100 or more) and overrepresented in the six nonmetropolitan county contexts identified by the RUC classification scheme. These differences limit the applicability of our results to communities that exceed the minimal (100-person) size threshold imposed here.

Measuring diversity

We employ 2010 census tabulations to delineate six panethnic groups that form the building blocks for our diversity measures: Hispanics of any race, non-Hispanic whites, blacks, Asians (including Pacific Islanders), Native Americans (American Indians and Alaska Natives), and all other non-Hispanics (multirace and other-race individuals). Counts of these panethnic groups have been assembled for each place and, taken together, provide exhaustive, mutually exclusive coverage of the local population.

The panethnic counts are used to capture the two diversity dimensions of interest. The first dimension, magnitude, reflects how evenly residents of a place are divided among the six panethnic groups. We operationalize *diversity magnitude* with the entropy index, symbolized by E (White 1986). E takes a maximum value equal to the natural log of the total number of groups, or 1.792 in our six-group case. For ease of interpretation, we divide each diversity score by this theoretical maximum and multiply by 100, resulting in a 0 to 100 range of possible values. A diversity score of zero indicates complete homogeneity: that only one group inhabits a place. Of the 221 such places in our sample, 176 have all-white populations, 43 are entirely Hispanic, and 2 are entirely Native American. At the opposite extreme, a community that contains identical shares (16.7 percent) of each of the six groups would receive a score of 100. Although none of our places reach that level, the village of Hillburn, New York (near New York City), comes closest with an E score of 87.1.

Racial-ethnic structure, the second dimension of diversity, refers to the specific groups that live in a community. Our investigation captures this dimension in a couple of ways. At various points E scores are accompanied by bar charts that convey the group proportions underlying the magnitude of diversity. We also utilize a majority rule typology (see Farrell and Lee 2011) that classifies communities as group-majority (white-majority, Hispanic-majority, etc.) if one ethnoracial group constitutes more than 50 percent of the total population. White-majority places are further subdivided into white-dominant, in which whites are at least 90 percent of the local population, and white-shared, in which the white percentage is more than one-half but less than nine-tenths. We name white-shared subtypes based on any minority groups that constitute 10 percent or more of all residents (e.g., white-Hispanic, white-black-Hispanic). No-majority places are defined as those where none of the ethnoracial groups exceeds the 50-percent threshold. Applying this typology, we are able to gauge how places with particular kinds of racial-ethnic structures are distributed along the rural-urban continuum.

Rural-urban classification

The nine-category classification scheme developed by USDA's Economic Research Service allows us to assign places to different types of metropolitan and nonmetropolitan county contexts. We have revised the original scheme slightly, dividing the most urban category (RUC1) into counties in super metro and large metro areas (RUC1a and 1b, respectively). Operational definitions for the ten county contexts are as follows:

- *Super metro* (RUC1a)—county in metro area of 3+ million population; place N = 3,585;
- *Large metro* (RUC1b)—county in metro area of 1 million to 2,999,999 population; place N = 3,393;
- *Medium metro* (RUC2)—county in metro area of 250,000 to 999,999 population; place N = 4,639;
- *Small metro* (RUC3)—county in metro area of less than 250,000 population; place N = 3,372;
- *High-urban proximate* (RUC4)—nonmetro county with urban population of 20,000+, adjacent to metro area; place N = 2,472;
- *High-urban distant* (RUC5)—nonmetro county with urban population of 20,000+, not adjacent to metro area; place N = 808;
- *Low-urban proximate* (RUC6)—nonmetro county with urban population of 2,500 to 19,999, adjacent to metro area; place N = 4,008;
- *Low-urban distant* (RUC7)—nonmetro county with urban population of 2,500 to 19,999, not adjacent to metro area; place N = 2,474;
- *Rural proximate* (RUC8)—nonmetro county with urban population less than 2,500, adjacent to metro area; place N = 939; and
- *Rural distant* (RUC9)—nonmetro county with urban population less than 2,500, not adjacent to metro area; place N = 1,473.

Each continuum category contains a substantial number of places (from a low of 808 in RUC5 to a high of 4,639 in RUC2) and thus permits more nuanced comparisons of diversity magnitude and structure across a wider range of community contexts than usual.

Other variables

In the multivariate portion of the analysis, we use three sets of place characteristics to assess the robustness of any zero-order associations detected between diversity and position on the rural-urban continuum. The local context of reception is captured with indicators of region, immigrant presence, and the retirement-age population. Four conventional census-defined regions are recognized: Northeast, Midwest, South, and West. We operationalize immigrant presence as the percentage of foreign-born residents in a place. Despite potential collinearity concerns, this variable is only moderately correlated with the entropy index (r = .45), and some of the most immigrant-heavy communities prove to be among the least diverse (e.g., all-Hispanic towns in Texas and California). The percentage of residents 65 years of age or older constitutes our measure of the retirement-age population.

The second set of place variables covers aspects of the housing and labor market that may make a place more or less attractive to multiple ethnoracial groups. Housing characteristics include the stock of new homes (measured as the percentage of units built since 2000), the percentage of renter-occupied units, and rent burden (median rent as a percentage of household income). We represent labor market opportunities with median household income in the past 12 months, the percentage of civilians 16+ years old who report being unemployed, and an occupational diversity variable that reflects the range of job types available in a community. The diversity variable, constructed using the entropy index, quantifies how evenly workers are distributed across five general occupational categories extending from professional (management, business, science, and arts occupations) to blue collar (production, transportation, and material moving occupations).

Finally, we develop four measures of institutional hub status that denote whether a place specializes in government, military, higher education, or correctional functions. Places qualify as government hubs if the percentage of their employed residents holding federal, state, or local government jobs is at least double the percentage in the total (summed) place population nationally (coded 1 if yes, 0 otherwise). The same threshold has been incorporated into the remaining measures. For military specialization, the share of a place's labor force participants employed in the armed forces must be two times (or more) greater than the national percentage. In the case of educational and correctional specialization, we apply the doubling rule to the percentage of local residents who are enrolled in college or who are incarcerated in adult or juvenile facilities, respectively.

Results

Place-based diversity

Our initial research question concerns how ethnoracial diversity varies across places in different contexts along the rural-urban continuum. Average E scores, which tap diversity magnitude, are reported for the ten RUC categories at the right edge of Figure 1. At first glance, the diversity of places located in super metro counties stands out: their mean E (41.9) is twice that for the nonmetro

FIGURE 1
Mean Place Diversity by RUC Category

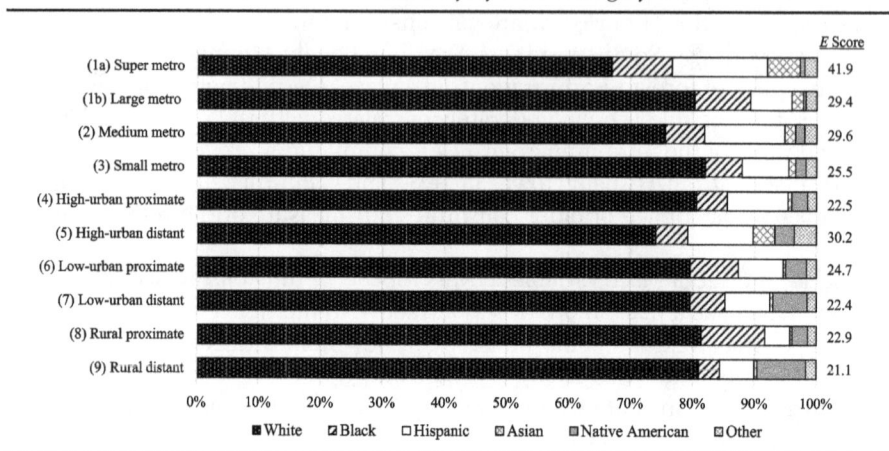

places located in rural distant counties. The largest principal cities (populations greater than 300,000) of the super metro counties epitomize the high diversity found in this context, with an average E of 67.7. But changes in diversity are hardly monotonic as one moves from the top to the bottom of the figure. Nonmetro places in the high-urban distant and low-urban proximate contexts, for example, reach the same diversity levels as their medium and small metro counterparts. In fact, the mean E for the high-urban distant places—which often contain one or two sizable minority groups—equals the mean for the large metro places. Taken together, these mean patterns best conform to the unevenness scenario.

The overlap in diversity across the rural-urban continuum becomes clear when we examine the boxplots of E scores in Figure 2. What initially catches the eye is the impressive amount of variation that exists in place diversity within each RUC context. A comparison of the boxplots also reveals the elevated diversity levels of super metro places. Observe, however, that the value of E at the 75th percentile for these places falls between the 25th and 75th percentiles of the distributions for the nine other continuum categories. Places at all points on the continuum have long top "whiskers" as well, with the most diverse places in five of the six nonmetro contexts exhibiting Es between 76 and 85. Thus, there seems to be little evidence of linear or threshold diversity declines with decreasing urban character, aside from the pronounced downward shift between the super metro and large metro contexts.

The racial-ethnic structures of communities in different continuum categories also appear broadly similar. Returning to Figure 1, the segments that make up each compositional bar reflect the representation of panethnic groups in the average place within that category. Whites constitute seven-tenths or more of place residents across the board, and Native Americans are overrepresented in nonmetro places, especially the low-urban distant and rural distant types. In the

FIGURE 2
Distribution of Place Diversity (*E*) by RUC Category

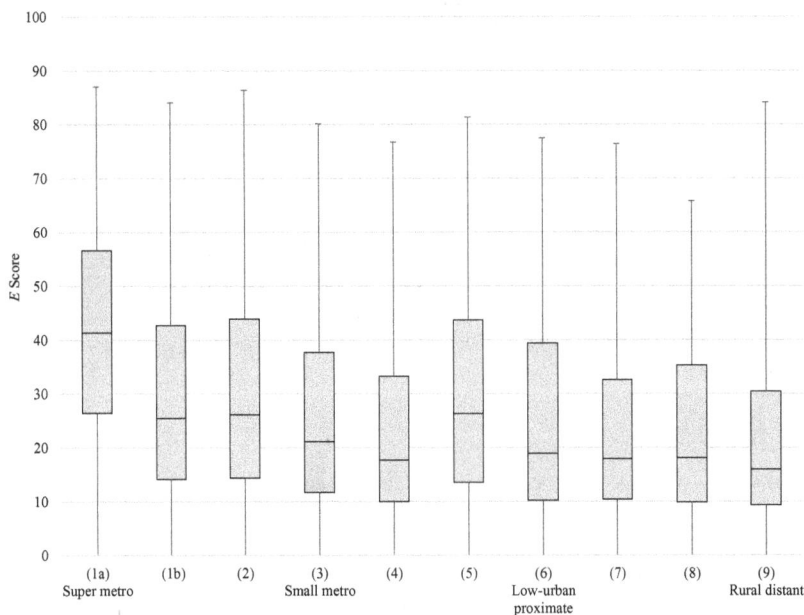

case of other groups, generalizations are less obvious. Blacks constitute a larger share of place populations in rural proximate settings than anywhere else. Hispanics reach double-digit percentages in super metro, medium metro, and high-urban distant places. Asian percentages, though relatively small, are highest in super metro and high-urban distant places, similar to the Hispanic pattern.

Our majority-rule typology helps to unpack the means summarized by the compositional bars. In online appendix Table A1, we show the distribution of places across types within each continuum category (see the online version of the article for the appendix). Once again, the distinctive ethnoracial structures of places in super metro counties can be seen. Almost three-fifths of these places are white-shared (whites in the numerical majority but less than 90 percent of the total population), with white-multigroup and white-Hispanic communities the most common subtypes. Super metro places are also the least likely to be white-dominant (whites making up 90 percent or more of all residents) and the most likely to qualify as no-majority. In contrast, the frequency of white dominance exceeds that of a white-shared composition in every continuum category other than the super metro context, sometimes by wide margins, and no-majority places are rare. With respect to majority-minority structures, rural proximate counties boast the greatest share of black-majority places, medium-size metro areas the greatest share of Hispanic-majority places and rural distant counties the greatest share of Native American–majority places.

Two lessons emerge from the place-focused portion of the analysis. First, places in super metro areas have higher diversity levels and more complex racial-ethnic structures than places elsewhere, on average. Oakland and Jersey City exemplify this point: their E scores fall in the mid-80s and they contain roughly equal percentages of white, black, Hispanic, and Asian residents. The second lesson is that sharp deviations in diversity patterns are not apparent over the rest of the rural-urban continuum; instead, a degree of unevenness prevails. Put another way, nonmetro places can be quite diverse, resembling their metro siblings. As an illustration, Unalaska, Alaska—in the rural distant category—displays a diversity magnitude (E = 84) that rivals those of Oakland and Jersey City and is driven by nontrivial proportions of Asians (34.1 percent), whites (33.7 percent), and Hispanics (15.2 percent). Other no-majority places in nonmetropolitan America include Winslow, Arizona (in the high-urban proximate category), Nanawale Estates, Hawaii (high-urban distant), Andarko, Oklahoma (low-urban proximate), and Crescent City, California (low-urban distant). All have entropy scores above 75 but varying combinations of panethnic groups.

Diversity exposure

Unlike the first question, which treats every place as equal, the second question guiding our research recognizes the varied distribution of populations among communities. Specifically, it asks how person-based (or weighted) estimates of ethnoracial diversity compare with place-based (unweighted) estimates not only for the total sample but across and within the ten contextual categories that make up the rural-urban continuum. For the sample as a whole, the weighted E reaches 50.5. This signifies the diversity level to which the average inhabitant of our 27,163 places was exposed in 2010. The racial-ethnic structure experienced by that hypothetical inhabitant remains primarily white (58 percent) but with nontrivial shares of Hispanic (19.5 percent), black (13.7 percent), and Asian (5.8 percent) dwellers. By contrast, unweighted or place-based means for the total sample indicate a much lower magnitude of diversity (E = 28.1), greater white representation (77.6 percent), and mean minority-group shares below 10 percent.

Such differences are consistent with the notion that exposure to diversity falls in a roughly linear manner as county contexts become less urban. The weighted E scores and compositional bars in Figure 3 support this inference. With the exception of the high-urban distant category, diversity magnitude declines rather steadily from the super metro to the rural distant end of the continuum. While the typical denizens of rural distant and rural proximate places encounter white-dominated homogeneity, ethnoracial heterogeneity is the norm for people living in super, large, and medium metro areas. These people experience high levels of diversity—Es ranging from the mid-40s to nearly 60—and racial-ethnic mixes in which 40 to 50 percent of their fellow residents are people of color. Hispanics constitute the largest minority in the super, large, and medium metro categories (roughly one-fifth of the population), followed by blacks (10–15 percent) and Asians (4–8 percent).

A category-by-category comparison of the Figure 3 results with those in Figure 2 shows person-based diversity levels to be higher than place-based ones across the board. That is, within each type of RUC context, more individuals live in bigger places that tend to be more diverse. We illustrate the principle in online appendix

FIGURE 3
Exposure to Place Diversity by RUC Category

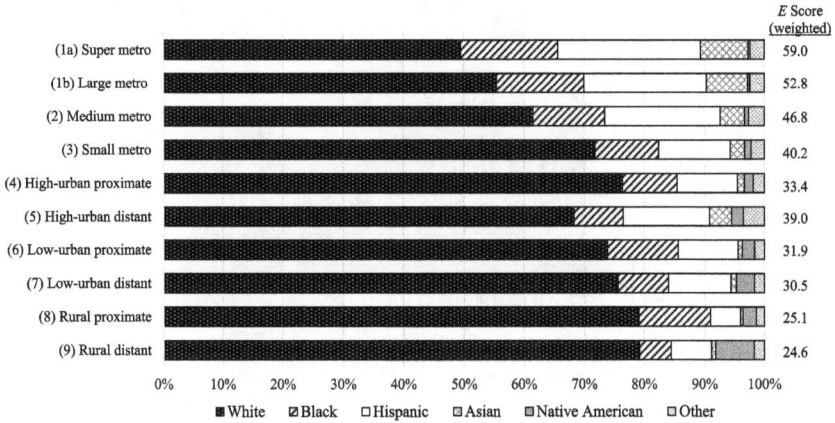

	E Score (weighted)
(1a) Super metro	59.0
(1b) Large metro	52.8
(2) Medium metro	46.8
(3) Small metro	40.2
(4) High-urban proximate	33.4
(5) High-urban distant	39.0
(6) Low-urban proximate	31.9
(7) Low-urban distant	30.5
(8) Rural proximate	25.1
(9) Rural distant	24.6

■ White   ⊠ Black   ▢ Hispanic   ⊟ Asian   ▣ Native American   ▢ Other

Table A2 (see the online version of the article for the appendix), using the ten largest places in the United States. Eight of the ten are located in super metro areas; the two that are not, San Antonio and San Jose, anchor large metro contexts. Diversity levels in most of the places substantially exceed that of the average super metro resident (E = 59.0), with New York leading the way (79.7). Aside from Hispanic-majority San Antonio, the cities are all no-majority in nature: the fact that three of them have white pluralities, two have black pluralities, and four have Hispanic pluralities attests to their varied multigroup racial-ethnic structures.

Accounting for diversity

As documented earlier, large cities do not enjoy a monopoly on diversity. Flows of migrants among RUC settings, immigrant moves to new destinations, and other redistribution processes have produced ethnoracially heterogeneous places in nonmetropolitan as well as metropolitan areas. Our final research question asks whether such variation in diversity across the rural-urban continuum reflects differences in the characteristics of places. To address this question, we first employ ordinary least square (OLS) estimation procedures to regress diversity magnitude (E) on nine dummy variables tapping the ten RUC categories (with the rural distant category, RUC9, the omitted reference). We then add the context of reception, housing and labor market, and institutional hub measures identified earlier. The same two-step approach is used to estimate logistic regression models in which dichotomous measures of the no-majority and white-shared types of racial-ethnic structure serve as dependent variables. Table 1 summarizes the results from the regression.

In the partial model for diversity magnitude, all RUC variables have significant positive associations with E relative to the rural distant category, and the largest effect is for location in a super metro setting. After the other place attributes are entered, however, the size of the super metro coefficient shrinks by roughly 50

TABLE 1

Regression Models of Diversity Magnitude and Majority-Type Structures on RUC Categories and Other Place Characteristics

Place Characteristic	OLS Regression of Diversity Magnitude				Logistic Regression of No Majority				Logistic Regression of White Shared			
	Partial Model		Full Model		Partial Model		Full Model		Partial Model		Full Model	
	b	(SE)	b	(SE)	b	(SE)	b	(SE)	b	(SE)	b	(SE)
RUC category (ref: rural distant [RUC9])												
Super metro (1a)	20.741	(.538)***	10.303	(.460)***	1.714	(.184)***	0.314	(.208)	1.325	(.069)***	0.351	(.083)***
Large metro (1b)	9.504	(.536)***	2.726	(.425)***	0.783	(.193)***	-0.158	(.209)	0.767	(.069)***	0.139	(.078)
Medium metro (2)	8.503	(.517)***	0.920	(.406)*	0.495	(.193)*	-0.568	(.206)**	0.702	(.067)***	0.043	(.075)
Small metro (3)	4.397	(.540)***	0.026	(.414)	0.202	(.205)	-0.416	(.217)	0.467	(.070)***	0.058	(.077)
High-urban proximate (4)	1.366	(.569)*	-1.104	(.435)*	0.132	(.218)	-0.337	(.229)	0.230	(.074)**	0.025	(.081)
High-urban distant (5)	9.038	(.757)***	1.869	(.572)**	1.253	(.221)***	0.422	(.236)	0.535	(.094)***	0.001	(.103)
Low-urban proximate (6)	3.535	(.527)***	0.886	(.398)*	0.556	(.194)**	0.186	(.205)	0.215	(.069)**	0.038	(.075)
Low-urban distant (7)	1.315	(.569)*	-1.263	(.428)**	-0.236	(.233)	-0.568	(.241)*	0.095	(.075)	-0.101	(.081)
Rural proximate (8)	1.734	(.722)*	-0.086	(.541)	-0.571	(.340)	-0.721	(.350)*	0.190	(.093)*	0.038	(.101)
Region (ref: Midwest)												
Northeast			-0.449	(.481)			0.815	(.161)***			0.193	(.048)***
South			13.680	(.481)***			1.775	(.136)***			1.331	(.038)***
West			11.252	(.481)***			1.385	(.145)***			1.098	(.044)***
% foreign-born (ln)			3.094	(.066)***			0.547	(.029)***			0.216	(.009)***
% 65+ years			-0.309	(.002)***			-0.051	(.007)***			-0.003	(.002)
% new housing (ln)			-0.015	(.021)			-0.032	(.025)			0.051	(.010)***
% rental housing			0.288	(.010)***			0.023	(.002)***			0.012	(.001)***
Rent burden (ln)			0.093	(.018)			0.025	(.036)			0.062	(.010)***
Median income (ln)			1.479	(.002)***			0.145	(.115)			0.596	(.045)***

(continued)

TABLE 1 (CONTINUED)

Place Characteristic	OLS Regression of Diversity Magnitude				Logistic Regression of No Majority				Logistic Regression of White Shared			
	Partial Model		Full Model		Partial Model		Full Model		Partial Model		Full Model	
	b	(SE)	b	(SE)	b	(SE)	b	(SE)	b	(SE)	b	(SE)
% unemployed			0.066	(.002)***			0.022	(.005)***			−0.011	(.002)***
Occupational diversity			0.023	(.002)***			0.029	(.004)***			−0.005	(.001)***
Government hub			2.173	(.002)***			0.172	(.093)			−0.021	(.041)
Military hub			3.718	(1.133)***			−0.070	(.133)			0.348	(.066)***
Education hub			0.825	(.486)			−0.638	(.216)**			0.728	(.090)***
Corrections hub			4.482	(.787)***			0.311	(.111)**			0.462	(.061)***
Intercept	21.123	(.450)***	−4.545	(2.924)	−3.776	(.176)***	−9.448	(1.431)***	−1.067	(.060)***	−7.920	(.531)***
Adjusted R^2	.111		.504									
−2 log likelihood					9,276		7,482		34,907		30,761	

NOTE: $N = 27{,}163$. See text for operationalization of place characteristics.
*$p < .05$. **$p < .01$. ***$p < .001$.

41

percent, and the remaining RUC coefficients are diminished as well, some becoming nonsignificant or negative. A similar pattern can be seen in the pair of logistic regression models for no-majority status. This similarity is not surprising since, by definition, E values will rise as community racial-ethnic structures incorporate more groups. Although positive and significant RUC coefficients are common in the partial model, most of them—including the super metro coefficient—fail to attain statistical significance in the full model or they reverse direction. And in the regressions for the white-shared type of structure, the super metro coefficient is the only positive and significant RUC indicator in the full model. These findings are robust to various model specifications (e.g., omission of percentage foreign born). More importantly, they demonstrate that position along the rural-urban continuum hardly seems decisive in predicting the diversity levels and structures of places.

On the other hand, a number of place characteristics, proxied in part by the RUC categories, do play a central role. As anticipated, the coefficients for the full models show high E values and diverse racial-ethnic structures to be more likely in places with receptive contexts (i.e., located in the South or West, having more immigrants, and having few older residents). Indeed, the context of reception measures make the largest contribution to overall model fit of any set of independent variables. Abundant rental housing, higher median income, and functional specialization as a military or corrections hub are also conducive to place diversity in at least two of the three models. Yet some discrepancies can be seen across models in how the predictors operate. The local unemployment rate, for example, exhibits the hypothesized negative association with diversity magnitude and no-majority status but is positively related to the white-shared type of structure, contradicting our reasoning about the appeal of economic opportunity. And occupational diversity, which reveals the expected positive relationship with our first two diversity measures (magnitude and no-majority status), also switches sign in the white-shared model.

Conclusion

This is the first study to examine racial and ethnic diversity across the rural-urban continuum for a full range of communities, encompassing small hamlets in the countryside as well as cities teeming with millions of inhabitants. The main substantive lesson from our study—consistent with the spatial interdependencies highlighted in this volume—is that diversity should no longer be considered an exclusive property of metropolitan America. When places are treated as equivalent (unweighted) units, diversity variation among RUC contexts is modest and conforms most closely to the unevenness scenario; places in super metro settings represent the lone outlier. At the same time, the person-based (weighted) approach offers some support for conventional wisdom about differences in diversity experienced by average metropolitan and nonmetropolitan residents. Thus, another lesson emerges from our first two research questions: the distinction between person- and place-based diversity matters.

Multivariate analysis pertinent to our third question provides additional evidence favoring the unevenness perspective. When we include relevant characteristics of places as predictors, many of the associations between the RUC categories and ethnoracial diversity become nonsignificant or take signs contrary to the linear decline hypothesis. Put another way, the RUC measures partially reflect whether places have contexts of reception, housing and labor market features, and institutional hubs that are more or less compatible with diversity.[1] Future research should explore how best to capture the larger settings that surround places. The USDA's RUC codes, for example, might be modified in fruitful ways (Winkler and Johnson 2016), or other classification schemes might be tried. Ideally, multilevel modeling strategies will move us beyond the dummy-variable representation of rural-urban context, illuminating how the detailed social and economic aspects of counties or areas shape the diversity of places nested within them.

Multilevel models could also prompt closer examination of aspects of place as well as context. One intriguing attribute is place population size, a simple unidimensional measure of rurality-urbanism that we criticized previously. A supplemental analysis (available upon request) reveals that the population of a place is strongly related to diversity, as Louis Wirth (1938) would have expected: the larger the place, the higher its diversity level and more complex its racial-ethnic structure. The positive and significant effect of size persists when separate multivariate models are estimated for places *within* each of the RUC contexts. This last finding suggests that something about the demographic scale of a place influences ethnoracial diversity irrespective of the context in which the place is embedded. Perhaps the "critical mass" principle proposed by Fischer (1976) operates well below typically urban thresholds. That is, even for smaller communities an incremental increase in population size may be sufficient to boost the likelihood that groups will coalesce around a shared attribute or interest such as race-ethnicity, form supportive networks and organizations, and ultimately attract additional members from elsewhere.

Its limitations notwithstanding, the current study upends long-held assumptions about urban heterogeneity and rural homogeneity. Our results suggest that if one measures urbanism by ethnoracial diversity, then a new urbanism has spread across rural and suburban spaces in a manner unforeseen by Wirth (1938). We regard the similar diversity patterns among places in most types of contexts as another manifestation of the blurring of traditional metro-nonmetro boundaries. Of course, similar diversity levels and structures may still have quite different consequences. Because of their extensive histories as destinations for immigrants and minorities, many metropolitan communities are accustomed to dealing with the educational, healthcare, housing, and other needs of a diverse population. Yet the recency and pace of ethnoracial diversification experienced by some nonmetro places poses challenges in virtually every institutional domain. To give but one illustration, the heavy rural vote for Donald Trump during the 2016 presidential election may have partly channeled a sense of anxiety among white inhabitants of small towns that was aroused by the growing presence of Latinos. Will these whites attempt to maintain political control at the local level, or will they move to a less threatening (i.e., less diverse) residential environment? In general terms, the issue is whether the potential benefits of diversity for rural places—especially the demographic, economic, and cultural revitalization that ethnic newcomers can bring—exceed the perceived costs to cohesion and quality of life. If not, increasing diversity could lead to greater intergroup avoidance and conflict rather than integration.

Note

1. These results hint at the possibility of spatial autocorrelation: that similarly diverse (or homogeneous) places tend to cluster together in space, violating the assumption of independent observations. If such autocorrelation is diagnosed, an appropriate next step would be to estimate spatial regression models that incorporate a lag term for diversity.

References

Allen, James P., and Eugene J. Turner. 1989. The most ethnically diverse places in the United States. *Urban Geography* 10 (6): 523–39.

Berube, Alan. 2003. Racial and ethnic change in the nation's largest cities. In *Redefining urban and suburban America: Evidence from Census 2000*, vol. 1, eds. Bruce Katz and Robert E. Lang, 137–53. Washington, DC: Brookings Institution Press.

Brown, David L. 2014. Rural population change in social context. In *Rural America in a globalizing world: Problems and prospects for the 2010s*, eds. Conner Bailey, Leif Jensen, and Elizabeth Ransom, 299–310. Morgantown, WV: West Virginia University Press.

Crowley, Martha, and Kim Ebert. 2014. New rural destinations: Research for the 2010s. In *Rural America in a globalizing world: Problems and prospects for the 2010s*, eds. Conner Bailey, Leif Jensen, and Elizabeth Ransom, 401–18. Morgantown, WV: West Virginia University Press.

Farrell, Chad R., and Barrett A. Lee. 2011. Racial diversity and change in metropolitan neighborhoods. *Social Science Research* 40 (4): 1108–23.

Fischer, Claude S. 1976. *The urban experience.* New York, NY: Harcourt Brace Jovanovich.

Frey, William H. 2015. *Diversity explosion: How new racial demographics are remaking America.* Washington, DC: Brookings Institution Press.

Hall, Matthew, and Barrett A. Lee. 2010. How diverse are US suburbs? *Urban Studies* 47 (1): 3–28.

Hall, Matthew, Laura Tach, and Barrett A. Lee. 2016. Trajectories of ethnoracial change in American communities, 1980–2010. *Population and Development Review* 42 (2): 271–97.

Hopkins, Daniel J. 2009. The diversity discount: When increasing ethnic and racial diversity prevents tax increases. *Journal of Politics* 71 (1): 160–77.

Johnson, Kenneth M., and Daniel T. Lichter. 2013. Rural retirement destinations: Natural decrease and the shared destinies of elderly and Hispanics. In *Rural aging in 21st century America*, eds. Nina Glasgow and E. Helen Berry, 275–94. New York, NY: Springer.

Kandel, William, and John Cromartie. 2004. *New patterns of Hispanic settlement in rural America.* Economic Research Service, Rural Development Research Report, No. 99. Washington, DC: U.S. Department of Agriculture. Available from http://www.latinamericanstudies.org/latinos/hispanic-settlement.pdf.

Kandel, William, and Emilio A. Parrado. 2005. Restructuring of the U.S. meat processing industry and new Hispanic migrant destinations. *Population and Development Review* 31 (3): 447–71.

Lee, Barrett A., and Lauren A. Hughes. 2015. Bucking the trend: Is ethnoracial diversity declining in American communities? *Population Research and Policy Review* 34 (1): 113–39.

Lee, Barrett A., John Iceland, and Chad R. Farrell. 2014. Is ethnoracial integration on the rise? Evidence from metropolitan and micropolitan America since 1980. In *Diversity and disparities: America enters a new century*, ed. John R. Logan, 415–56. New York, NY: Russell Sage Foundation. Available from https://www.russellsage.org/sites/all/files/logan/logan_diversity_ chapter13.pdf.

Lee, Barrett A., John Iceland, and Gregory Sharp. 2012. *Racial and ethnic diversity goes local: Charting change in American communities over three decades*. US2010 Project Report. New York, NY: Russell Sage Foundation. Available from http://www.russellsage.org/ research/reports/racial-ethnic-disparity.

Lichter, Daniel T. 2012. Immigration and the new diversity in rural America. *Rural Sociology* 77 (1): 3–35.

Lichter, Daniel T. 2013. Integration or fragmentation? Racial diversity and the American future. *Demography* 50 (2): 359–91.

Lichter, Daniel T., and David L. Brown. 2011. Rural America in an urban society: Changing social and spatial boundaries. *Annual Review of Sociology* 37 (1): 565–92.

Lichter, Daniel T., and Kenneth M. Johnson. 2006. Emerging rural settlement patterns and the geographic redistribution of America's new immigrants. *Rural Sociology* 71 (1): 109–31.

Lichter, Daniel T., Domenico Parisi, Steven M. Grice, and Michael C. Taquino. 2007. Municipal underbounding: Annexation and racial exclusion in small southern towns. *Rural Sociology* 72 (1): 47–68.

Lichter, Daniel T., Domenico Parisi, and Michael C. Taquino. 2015. Toward a new macro-segregation? Decomposing segregation within and between metropolitan cities and suburbs. *American Sociological Review* 80 (4): 843–73.

Lieberson, Stanley, and Mary C. Waters. 1988. *From many strands: Ethnic and racial groups in contemporary America*. New York, NY: Russell Sage Foundation.

Light, Ivan. 2006. *Deflecting immigration: Networks, markets, and regulations in Los Angeles*. New York, NY: Russell Sage Foundation.

Loewen, James W. 2005. *Sundown towns: A hidden dimension of American racism*. New York, NY: New Press.

Logan, John R., and Charles Zhang. 2010. Global neighborhoods: New pathways to diversity and separation. *American Journal of Sociology* 115 (4): 1069–1109.

Massey, Douglas S., ed. 2008. *New faces in new places: The changing geography of American immigration*. New York, NY: Russell Sage Foundation.

Nelson, Peter B., Ahn Wei Lee, and Lise Nelson. 2009. Linking baby boomer and Hispanic migration streams into rural America: A multi-scaled approach. *Population, Space and Place* 15 (3): 277–93.

Parisi, Domenico, Daniel T. Lichter, and Michael C. Taquino. 2015. The buffering hypothesis: Growing diversity and declining black-white segregation in America's cities, suburbs, and small towns? *Sociological Science* 2 (March): 125–57.

Portes, Alejandro, and Erik Vickstrom. 2011. Diversity, social capital, and cohesion. *Annual Review of Sociology* 37:461–79.

Sharp, Gregory, and Barrett A. Lee. 2016. New faces in rural places: Patterns and sources of nonmetropolitan ethnoracial diversity since 1990. *Rural Sociology* (online early view). Available from http://onlinelibrary.wiley.com/doi/10.1111/ruso.12141/epdf.

Sharp, Jeff S., and Jill K. Clark. 2008. Between the country and the concrete: Rediscovering the rural-urban fringe. *City & Community* 7 (1): 61–79.

Tienda, Marta, and Susana M. Sanchez. 2013. Latin American immigration to the United States. *Daedalus* 142 (3): 48–64.

U.S. Department of Agriculture. 2013. Rural-urban continuum codes. Economic Research Service, Documentation. Washington, DC: U.S. Department of Agriculture. Available from http://www.ers.usda.gov/data-products/rural-urban-continuum-codes/documentation.aspx.

West, Loraine A., Samantha Cole, Daniel Goodkind, and Wan He. 2014. *65+ in the United States: 2010*. Current Population Reports, No. P23-212. Washington, DC: U.S. Census Bureau. Available from http://www.census.gov/content/dam/Census/library/publications/2014/demo/p23-212.pdf.

White, Michael J. 1986. Segregation and diversity measures in population distribution. *Population Index* 52 (2): 198–221.

Winkler, Richelle L., and Kenneth M. Johnson. 2016. Moving toward integration? Effects of migration on ethnoracial segregation across the rural-urban continuum. *Demography* 53 (5): 1027–49.

Wirth, Louis. 1938. Urbanism as a way of life. *American Journal of Sociology* 40 (1): 1–24.

"Perfectly Positioned": The Blurring of Urban, Suburban, and Rural Boundaries in a Southern Community

By
BETSIE GARNER

In this article, I draw on ethnographic fieldwork and formal interviews from a community study in Rockdale County, Georgia, to illustrate the social construction of place-based identity within the rural-urban interface. Given decades of growth and expansion in metro Atlanta, Rockdale has become an object lesson of the boundary shifting and crossing typical of places located along the rural-urban fringe. A sustained pattern of demographic and ecological change in Rockdale has resulted in a lack of consensus about how to imagine the community's location on the rural-urban continuum. I show how symbolic and social boundaries between urbanity and rurality are blurred within the community as residents draw on local resources to construct alternatively urban, suburban, and rural identities. Additionally, I illustrate how local boosters take advantage of this blurriness to portray Rockdale County as a "perfectly positioned" community and how community members disregard the official rural-urban boundaries of governments or scholars and instead invest their own imagined boundaries with significant meaning.

Keywords: urban; suburban; rural; community; culture; identity; place

Seemingly clear-cut social theories often do not square with the complexity of empirically observed social phenomena. Certainly this has been the case for scholars of urbanity and

Betsie Garner is a PhD candidate in sociology at the University of Pennsylvania. She uses qualitative research methods to study family, culture, and place. Her work on gender and parenting recently appeared in Qualitative Sociology *and* Social Psychology Quarterly, *and her current project explores the discourse and practice of Southern hospitality in Rockdale County, Georgia.*

NOTE: This research was supported by a Dissertation Research Fellowship and multiple Gertrude and Otto Pollak Summer Research Fellowships from the sociology department at the University of Pennsylvania. The author is indebted to the journal issue's editors, two anonymous reviewers, and especially Sarah Zelner, each of whom provided helpful comments on earlier drafts of this article.

Correspondence: betsie@sas.upenn.edu

DOI: 10.1177/0002716217710490

rurality, who regularly make use of unambiguous definitions of "urban" and "rural" despite that in real life, differences between urban and rural places can be quite blurry. For example, Wirth (1938), who defined urban settlements as large, dense, and heterogeneous; and rural settlements, by implication, as small, sparse, and homogeneous, argued that "the city and the country may be regarded as two poles ... as ideal types of communities" (p. 3). He also pointed out, however, that the geographic mobility of people across the rural-urban divide blurs supposed distinctions between the two and that such differences are often overstated in the first place:

> The same man who is the farm laborer from April to September is also the city hobo from October to March. ... Is the Negro tenant or sharecropper in Mississippi any more closely associated with the farm owner than a similar employee of a steel company in Pittsburgh with the plant manager? (1964, 225)

Even though Wirth (1964) defined urbanity and rurality as a neat pair of polar opposites, he implored scholars not to accept his concepts as gospel and urged them instead to pursue the empirical study of local communities. "Rather than taking out conjectured rural-urban types for granted," he reasoned, "we might turn to what we actually find under specified conditions of life associated with what we call urban and rural communities" (p. 225).

Nonetheless, a vast sociological literature on rural-urban differences has too often relied on presupposed, dichotomous images of city and country life to establish the effects of urbanity and rurality on society. Ethnographers often proceed as if they believe iconic images of urban and rural life are accurate for the most part, just as quantitative researchers routinely include measures of rural or urban residence in their regression models without questioning whether these variables are appropriate proxies for whatever meaningful differences they are thought to capture.

If what Wirth argued half a century ago was true then, it is even truer now. Trends such as the deindustrialization of urban cores in the North (Wilson 1987); the rise of tourism, entertainment, and leisure in big cities (Grazian 2011; Zukin 1996); the sprawling expansion of metropolitan areas into nearby suburbs and exurbs (Bruegmann 2005); the decline of family farming in rural communities (Switzer 2012); the arrival of immigrants to new destinations (Marrow 2011; Winders 2013); the rapid suburbanization of formerly small country towns (Salamon 2003); and the mass relocation of people and jobs to cities in the South (Lloyd 2012) have all contributed to the growing notion that categorizing people or places as urban, suburban, or rural is increasingly difficult. As Lichter and Brown explain, "The bright boundaries that have defined urban and rural areas— and people—have dimmed over the recent past" (2011, 573). Despite these changes, however, the appeal of urban-rural difference persists, especially for local community members who imagine places and people as imbued with urban, suburban, or rural character (Bell 1994).

That urbanity and rurality continue to loom large in people's minds suggests that a social-constructionist approach to understanding urban and rural boundaries may be especially useful. Indeed, it is through social interaction in local communities that people construct evocative images of The City and The Country, and whether any given community is officially classified as urban or rural by a government authority or research team may have little to do with processes by which locals identify themselves as urban or rural people living in an urban or rural place. For example, even though 81 percent of Americans live in places that the U.S. Census Bureau considers urban, 53 percent of respondents in a recent survey of adults from across the country described their local communities as *sub*urban (Kolko 2015). Suburbia may feature prominently in popular understandings of the rural-urban continuum, but the Census Bureau offers no definition of "suburban" and instead relies on a dichotomous classification system in which 2,500 or more inhabitants constitutes the defining difference between urban and rural places (U.S. Census Bureau 1994). Accordingly, it is by turning to the local processes through which people construct cultural understandings of space, place, and identity that we may appreciate the importance of rurality and urbanity in people's day-to-day lives.

Drawing on two years of ethnographic fieldwork and sixty formal interviews, I use this approach to explore how a variety of people in Rockdale County, Georgia, imagine their community and themselves as alternatively urban, suburban, or rural. Rockdale is a community located between urban and rural extremes, with downtown Atlanta to its west and a relatively rural landscape to its east. It is widely regarded as a suburb—part of metropolitan Atlanta that lies outside of Atlanta's city limits—but it could also be described as an exurb situated along the rural-urban fringe or within an interstitial zone where boundaries are unclear and contested. During recent decades, the community has experienced significant demographic and ecological change, as metro Atlanta witnessed explosive population growth and expansive sprawl.

To illustrate these changes, I explain how local boundaries in Rockdale and metro Atlanta have shifted over time and how development projects have made boundary crossing more routine. I then explain the blurring of rural-urban boundaries in Rockdale by describing the ways in which residents selectively draw on various features of the local community to construct their own identities as alternatively urban, suburban, or rural people. My argument will be that the blurring of rurality and urbanity in Rockdale represents a symbolic resource for the social construction of many different place-based identities all within the same community. Furthermore, I show how some residents, including local government officials and business leaders, seek to capitalize on this blurriness by promoting Rockdale as a community that is—as the county slogan states— "perfectly positioned" to offer the best of both city and country living.

The Extremes of Urban and Rural Sociology

Sociologists have been interested in urbanity and rurality since the dawn of the discipline. What could be called our discipline's origin story unfolded in the

United States as University of Chicago scholars sought to understand how American society would be transformed by the dawn of modernity and the rapid increase of density and diversity in the country's largest cities. Informed by early conceptualizations of dichotomous urban-rural differences (Tönnies 1887/2002; Simmel 1903), they understood city living to be rational, impersonal, and perhaps even overstimulating due to the size, density, and heterogeneity of the urban environment; in contrast, the homogeneity and isolation associated with rural settlements were thought to make country living distinctly natural, emotional, traditional, and community oriented.

The enduring quality of this classic conceptualization is explained in part by urban ethnographers working in the Chicago School tradition who have portrayed big cities as diverse, chaotic, and even alienating by focusing on problems associated with racial and economic inequality in the inner-city neighborhoods of cities such as Chicago (Drake and Cayton 1945; Suttles 1968; Venkatash 2009), New York (Bourgois 2003; Duneier 1999; Newman 1999), Philadelphia (Anderson 2000; Edin and Kefalas 1997; Goffman 2014), and Boston (Whyte 1943; Harding 2010; Small 2004). At the same time, though, rural ethnographers have tended to emphasize closely knit and informal social relations in studies of small cities in Wisconsin (Macgregor 2010) and Indiana (Lynd and Lynd 1957), and isolated, rural communities in northern Iowa (Elder and Conger 2000) and upstate New York (Harper 1987).

Indeed, scholars have concentrated almost exclusively on places that epitomize either end of the rural-urban continuum, thereby focusing narrowly on the extremes of urban-rural difference while neglecting communities that defy easy classification as either urban or rural. This tendency is perhaps best illustrated by the institutional silos that organize sociologists into discrete disciplines according to their interest in *either* urbanity *or* rurality. A few noteworthy ethnographies of suburban communities notwithstanding (Gans 1967; Salamon 2003), this arrangement both implies that the study of suburbs is unimportant and suggests that to classify any given community as empirically urban or rural is a simple task. Yet in many metropolitan communities located somewhere between the city center and its hinterlands, decades of demographic and ecological change have resulted in blurred boundaries between The City and The Country.

This is especially true in the southern United States where the ecology of many metropolitan areas reflects a history of industrialization, urbanization, segregation, and immigration that is unique to the region. Urban sociologists in America have historically favored the ethnographic study of northern cities because, as Lloyd (2012) argues, "regional idiosyncrasy confounds the search for generalizable laws of social behavior … [and] Southern cities take shape in ways not well captured by the standard models of urban culture and morphology generated on the Northern prototype" (p. 484). Whereas densely built, pedestrian-friendly cities in the North have long histories of immigrant reception, ethnic diversity, industrialization, and more recently deindustrialization, southern cities, historically characterized by agrarian rather than industrial economies, are relatively sprawling and automobile-centric, and have only recently witnessed dramatic population growth along with the arrival of a large number of immigrants who complicate the region's black-white color line. (Examples include Birmingham, Nashville, and, of course, Atlanta.) Rushing (2009) explains that because of these differences, "few scholars recognize Southern cities as real 'American' cities" (p. 11), but I argue that communities in southern metropolitan areas, especially those where sprawling growth blurs the boundaries between urban and rural extremes, offer a unique opportunity to consider processes by which urban, suburban, and rural place-based identities are socially constructed instead of pre-ordained. Outside of the South, many other metropolitan areas that feature their own regionally specific histories of race relations, immigration, and demographic change nonetheless exhibit similar patterns of population growth and ecological sprawl. (Cities such as Phoenix and Tucson come to mind.) Indeed, even if urban ethnographers have harbored a regional bias that precludes the serious study of southern cities, opportunities to examine suburban communities across the entire United States abound.

Recently some scholars have called for a renewed effort to understand the blurring of rural-urban boundaries, and in a review of the literature, Lichter and Brown (2011) specify three types of processes that make rural-urban distinctions increasingly difficult to articulate: (1) boundary shifting happens when metropolitan areas expand outward in a sprawling fashion and bring urban and suburban influences into previously rural spaces; (2) boundary crossing is the movement of people back and forth along the rural-urban continuum, a practice aided by advancements in technology and infrastructure; and (3) the blurring of boundaries can be found in places along the rural-urban fringe, in the suburbs or exurbs, where communities fall under the influence of both nearby urban and rural forces.

According to Lichter and Brown (2011), communities such as Rockdale blur boundaries due to their close proximity to both The City and The Country:

> Conceptually, suburbs represent a rapidly growing associational bridge between big cities and nearby rural communities and the countryside. Suburban residents operate daily on either side of the rural-urban divide; as such, they blur conventional spatial and social boundaries. … The social, economic, and cultural connections that link the rural-urban fringe to both rural and urban areas are enormous. (p. 573)

This conceptualization emphasizes the interdependence between urban and rural communities and reminds us that places along the rural-urban continuum are connected. But it also perpetuates the idea that communities like Rockdale are indisputably suburban, that residents there imagine themselves to be living in a suburb that is linked to other distinctly urban or rural communities. Using this theoretical framework, the idea that urbanity and rurality may be contested *within* one particular local community, that residents of Rockdale may alternatively imagine themselves as living in an urban, suburban, or rural environment, is obscured from view. My findings, however, show not only that the City of Atlanta has become more connected to a variety of outlying communities than it once was, but also that whether Rockdale County itself should be understood as urban, suburban, or rural is increasingly up for debate.

Instead of conceptualizing suburban communities as linking adjacent urban and rural areas together, I frame Rockdale as a place that transcends urban-rural distinctions. My analysis of the community illustrates how places in which rural-urban boundaries have historically shifted, are easily crossed, and ultimately become blurred present residents with a variety of resources that make it possible for them to construct alternatively urban, suburban, or rural lifestyles and identities. I argue that rural-urban boundaries are blurred not just because suburbs serve as bridges connecting urban and rural spaces, but because community members who alternatively see themselves as leading urban, suburban, or rural lives simultaneously imagine themselves as belonging to the same local community, as living in the same place. I also show how this blurriness can be leveraged to construct an image of a community that offers "the best of both worlds" as a strategy for attracting new residents and businesses. In doing so, I hope to illustrate the value of the social-constructionist approach in revealing how, despite official definitions and expert opinions, urbanity and rurality are imagined and negotiated through the seemingly mundane interactions that make up daily life in local communities.

Studying Boundaries in Rockdale County

I began conducting ethnographic fieldwork in Rockdale County in summer 2014, and while I had never spent much time in the community before then, I was already familiar with the metro Atlanta area from having attended a local college and through several family connections in the region. After learning about trends in Rockdale, which reflected decentralized patterns of urbanization, industrialization, segregation, and immigration typical of many metropolitan areas in the South, I ascertained that it would be a good place to study themes related to regional culture and place-based identity within the changing southern United States.

Atlanta is quite decentralized and features three distinct high-rise districts—Downtown, Midtown, and Buckhead—surrounded by relatively low-density, automobile-dependent residential neighborhoods in which apartment complexes, townhomes, and single-family detached homes are heavily shaded by thick tree canopies. Given metro Atlanta's explosive growth and sprawling expansion in recent decades, residents have increasingly disregarded official boundaries between neighborhoods, cities, and counties and instead created their own mental maps of Atlanta by turning to the colloquial use of informal, socially constructed boundaries (Lynch 1960). For example, many people share the idiomatic understanding that Interstate 285, which forms a complete loop known as "the perimeter," constitutes the boundary between the City of Atlanta and its suburbs despite that it actually encompasses Atlanta along with several other incorporated cities such as Decatur, Brookhaven, and Chamblee. As one online resource, touted as Atlanta's "premier relocation guide," explains, the popular use of the acronyms ITP and OTP lend credibility to this imagined boundary:

> Whether you're inside or outside the perimeter can be the deciding factor in choosing your Atlanta neighborhood. For native Atlantans, these simple acronyms tell you a lot about the metro area. ITP, or "inside the perimeter," refers to the Atlanta city limits perfectly outlined by Interstate 285, which forms a loop around the city. OTP, or "outside the perimeter," contains the suburbs of Atlanta, all with their own characteristics and personalities outside I-285. For many Atlantans, being an ITP-er or an OTP-er is a way of life. (KnowAtlanta 2015)

That I-285 does not perfectly outline Atlanta's city limits in no way prevents people from imagining that it does, and this tendency to favor folk understandings of space over officially sanctioned boundaries makes the metro area an excellent place to study the social construction of rurality and urbanity.

To get to know people in Rockdale, I initially spent time socializing with neighbors, volunteering at nonprofits, visiting places of worship, frequenting shops and restaurants, and attending public events such as annual festivals and meet-and-greets with elected officials. In addition to participant observation and casual conversation, I conducted formal, semistructured and digitally recorded interviews with sixty individuals including parents and children, business owners, government officials, teachers and coaches, clergy, lifelong residents, and transplants and immigrants. In recruiting research participants, my goal was to capture as wide a range of experiences as possible and to include diverse points of view on topics such as place-based identity and change in the community. To that end, I sought out individuals particularly qualified to comment on specific types of experiences. For instance, I visited a Hispanic Baptist church to recruit Latino immigrants and attended events organized by the local government to recruit influential community leaders and business owners. I also relied on well-connected individuals to introduce me to respondents who were otherwise difficult to meet in public settings, including, for example, elderly, longtime residents of the county and families affiliated with minority religious groups not represented by local congregations.

Among these sixty formal interviewees were people from about thirty households, who also allowed me to spend additional time shadowing their daily lives. Some invited me into their homes for family meals and leisure activities while others asked me to accompany them to church, to work, or to a child's extracurricular activity. I offered interviewees who hosted me for extensive periods of participant observation their choice of a $50 Walmart or Target gift card. Many accepted the compensation, but some politely declined it. Some interviews took place in public settings such as coffee shops and restaurants, while others happened in private residences or workplace offices. During interviews with Spanish-speaking immigrants, I was assisted by a local bilingual translator. After conducting fieldwork and interviews, I typed up detailed notes and arranged for interview recordings to be professionally transcribed. I also amassed a collection of multimedia data on local community activity including newspaper articles, websites, photographs, and social-media exchanges. Finally, I used the software MAXQDA to qualitatively analyze all this material using a refined coding scheme.

Throughout my time in Rockdale, I have sensed that I am perceived alternatively as an insider or outsider depending on the context of an interaction. I undoubtedly benefit from the privileges enjoyed by white, middle-class, U.S.-born, heterosexual women in general, and most people seem to perceive me as trustworthy and nonthreatening. At the same time, my familiarity with metro Atlanta likely aided my ability to quickly build rapport with many community members. Though I assumed that my class and racial identity would affect my interactions with community members in various ways, I have found that residents from different backgrounds are equally willing to talk with me and invite me into their homes.

Boundary Shifting and Crossing in Rockdale

In 1870, the Georgia State legislature created Rockdale County by drawing a boundary around reappropriated portions of Henry and Newton counties, and by 1880 the county had grown to about 7,000 residents. Rockdale was predominantly rural then—its principal industry was agriculture, its largest employer a cotton mill—but a train depot located in Conyers, the county's only town, bustled with activity as farmers and cotton brokers transported their goods to market via the railroad. Along with its surrounding schools, churches, saloons, lawyers' and doctors' offices, retail shops, and government buildings, the depot functioned as the community's hub of business, transportation, and leisure (Farmer 1998).

If Rockdale owes its founding in large part to the railroad, then its subsequent growth can similarly be credited to the installation of Interstate 20 during the 1960s. Along with the rise of automobiles, the development of I-20 made boundary crossing along the rural-urban continuum far more efficient by connecting the county directly to downtown Atlanta and allowing it to better function as part of the larger metro area. Toilsome trips into Atlanta, which would have previously been reserved for special occasions, were suddenly transformed into easy drives of only half an hour or so, and as a result, the community attracted what one local historian described as a "growing population of commuters who wanted the serenity of a small town in which to live and still enjoy the ability to commute to their jobs in the city" (Farmer 1998, 26).

The I-20 project refocused commercial and residential development away from the historic downtown area near the train tracks and closer to state highways and other major roads connected to interstate exits. Georgia Highway 20/138 gradually became lined on both sides with big-box grocery stores, fast-food restaurants, and strip mall conglomerates as rural, arable land and heavily wooded lots were transformed into subdivisions featuring family-friendly floorplans. These suburban-style amenities, as well as high-quality public schools and low crime rates, attracted a steady flow of newcomers to the area throughout the following decades, and between 1970 and 1980 alone the county's population doubled in size from roughly 18,000 to approximately 36,000 (U.S. Census Bureau 1982, 1992).

Today, many of Rockdale's residents who relocated to the area in recent years explain that the community's large stock of affordable and spacious homes coupled with its close proximity to the interstate make it attractive. One woman explained that she and her husband decided to move to the Atlanta area from Florida when she landed a job at the state capitol downtown. The couple anticipated starting a family and wanted to buy a house, but they quickly concluded that Atlanta's gentrified neighborhoods were too pricey. "I'm so glad we came out here to Rockdale to look because we ended up getting a four-bedroom, three-bathroom, and my commute isn't that bad," she said, "I mean, I-20 is basically a straight-shot to my office." That many residents depend on the interstate for their daily commutes to work is evident each weekday when traffic backs up along I-20's entrance and exit ramps, but even for those who do not commute each day, easy access to Atlanta often has great appeal. "It's nice to be 15 minutes, 20 minutes to downtown," explained one retired woman, "I can go to the opera or the symphony or whatever you want to go to. And so we are, geographically, we're just so convenient."

The community's history of growing interdependence with Atlanta is not only reflected in these suburbanizing trends but also in the shifting of official boundaries in the surrounding metro area. The U.S. Census Bureau first defined the Atlanta Metropolitan Statistical Area for the 1950 reports as containing only three counties: Cobb, DeKalb, and Fulton. As surrounding areas such as Rockdale witnessed steady development and population growth, the definition grew to include more and more counties over time. Clayton and Gwinnett were added for the 1960 reports, and just a few years after the 1970 U.S. Census, ten more counties including Rockdale were added. This trend continued on, until the metro area was officially renamed the Atlanta-Sandy Springs-Roswell Metropolitan Statistical Area, which today contains a total of twenty-nine counties.

Longtime residents of Rockdale are uniquely able to reflect on the ecological changes that spurred increased boundary crossing and shifting in the area. On the Facebook group "You know you're from Rockdale County when," users share memories of the development projects that fundamentally altered their community's landscape. One woman wrote: "I'm so old that I remember when my grandfather Luther McDowell sold the right of way rights to the state of Georgia to change the route of 138 to run through the middle of his pasture! The Kmart [store] was where the farm house stood. His fish pond was where the Picadilly [restaurant] is now." Another woman simply stated that she remembered "when I-20 was not there." Even nonnative residents who had moved to the area more recently related a sense of astonishment at how the community's sparsely developed corners have been transformed into congested commercial and residential districts. One woman who had moved with her family from New Orleans to Rockdale in 2000 said that initially she would have described the area as quite country. "I had girlfriends and friends who used to come visit, and they would go back home saying, 'Girl, she live in the country ... all we see is cows and horses!'" But now she described seeing her community as a busy suburb, explaining "they've got some subdivisions where there's houses and houses and houses ... they put up *a lot* of stuff."

Rockdale's population has not only continued to grow but also to diversify. For decades, the county maintained a large white majority and featured a much smaller proportion of black residents, but the community's racial-ethnic makeup has been altered dramatically by the unprecedented arrival of numerous non-white newcomers. Black transplants include those who had simply relocated from nearby areas in metro Atlanta and others who had moved to the South from other regions of the country in a trend dubbed "The New Great Migration" (Frey 2004). Meanwhile, Hispanic and Latino newcomers have transformed Rockdale into one of the South's new immigrant destinations (Marrow 2011; Winders 2013). In 2000, non-Hispanic whites made up 73 percent of Rockdale's population, but by 2013 that figure had declined to only 38 percent (Krogstad 2015). Even though the county lost almost 15,000 white residents between 2000 and 2010 (U.S. Census Bureau 2000, 2010)—a pattern some locals interpret as "white flight"[1]—overall the total population has continued to increase. According to recent estimates, the county's population of nearly 89,000 residents is now a minority-majority community in which blacks constitute 52 percent of the population while non-Hispanic whites make up 35 percent, and 10 percent identify as Hispanic or Latino (U.S. Census Bureau 2015).

Changes in the racial composition of Rockdale's population have been mirrored by the rise of prominent black leaders in local government, business, and civic organizations, and many people describe the community as holding great promise for black families in particular. One black woman from a small, majority-white town in Alabama moved to Rockdale because she sensed that it offered unique opportunities for ambitious black people like herself. "I felt like I could go and get a piece of my pie," she explained. Indeed, many black families describe having achieved great success in the community and lead middle- and upper-middle-class lives. Yet white residents who associate blackness with racialized images of urban crime and poverty sometimes look at the success of their black neighbors with suspicion. One black woman, for example, who serves on her upscale subdivision's homeowners' association board reported that she once overheard a white woman say "all these blacks moving into these big houses must be selling drugs ... how else could they afford it?"

In the conversations that I participated in, white residents often made exceptions for "good" black neighbors and suggested that only certain types of black people are responsible for criminal behaviors associated with urban locales. "I wish we could just get the criminals off the streets ... I know some fantastic black families and I feel very sorry for them more than anybody," explained one white woman. "White people who are racist are going to lump all the black children together ... the kids who are not bad black kids are being lumped in with the ones who are." Others pointed out that both black and white residents of a certain type degrade the community's image, such as one white man who explained, "We've got black people moving in that—they're just Section 8, sucking up all the resources. But, it goes both ways. There's trashy white people moving in, too." He went on to say, "There are very affluent black people in this community. You don't see it because all you hear about in the news is the—I hate to say it—but the ghetto trash and the white trash." In casually associating "ghetto" with poor black newcomers, the man conjured up a familiar image of The City and suggested that at least some urban influences brought on by boundary shifting and crossing are unwelcome.

Blurred Boundaries in Rockdale

A significant portion of Rockdale's residents think of their community as a suburb of Atlanta and explained how a variety of distinctly suburban-style amenities are what make the community a convenient place to live. One retired couple who had previously lived in very rural areas explained that Rockdale offers them everything they want in a hometown including affordable houses in quiet subdivisions, a local hospital and associated medical specialists, community organizations such as churches and sports leagues, and an abundance of shopping and dining options. "We don't really go to Atlanta that often," explained the man. "Well we don't really have to leave Rockdale unless we want to," his wife added. "We have everything we need right here in our own town."

Indeed, much of Rockdale's ecology has a quintessentially suburban feel to it given the rapid development that took place in the 1970s, 1980s, and 1990s. Peering straight down Georgia Highway 20/138, a main thoroughfare right off the interstate, one's field of view is cluttered with brightly lit signs for numerous fast food chain restaurants. McDonalds, Dominoes, Starbucks, and many more advertise their latest promotions on large marquees and window banners, and dotted among these are sit-down, family-style restaurants, casual diners, and buffets, also of the chain variety, including Ruby Tuesday, Waffle House, Golden Coral, and Red Lobster. A smattering of immigrant-owned, casual-dining Mexican and Chinese restaurants offer the sort of Americanized dishes popular in suburban locales. Retail shopping in this district consists of well-known big-box stores such as Walmart, Target, and Home Depot; regional grocery store chains such as Publix and Kroger; popular department stores such as Kohls and T.J. Maxx; and smaller specialty stores with locations across the country such as Payless ShoeSource and Dressbarn. One large but vacant strip mall along the highway suggests that these developments have a somewhat temporary or transitory quality and could easily become neglected or abandoned. During the busy morning and evening rush hours, as well as in the late afternoon, the highway becomes congested with traffic as people line up to enter or exit the interstate or pop in at local stores and restaurants. With few locally owned establishments and little historic architecture, this zone looks much like any number of other suburbs in metro Atlanta, or in other cities.

Away from the busy commercial section along the highway, Rockdale is dotted with countless subdivision developments. Many feature neatly arranged homes of very similar design and formal, landscaped entrances where decorative signs proclaim the subdivision names: Laurel Woods, Honey Creek, Milstead Place, Druids Keep. Others have a slightly more spontaneous appearance with custom-built homes dotted among wooded lots and winding roads. Some subdivisions feature amenities such as pools, tennis courts, and clubhouses, and many post celebratory banners at their entrances each spring to announce the names of graduating high school seniors who live there. Clusters of these developments farther from town are typically anchored by their own nearby commercial areas, including basic amenities such as grocery stores, pharmacies, and gas stations.

Ecological features such as these provide residents with the symbolic resources to imagine themselves as living in a suburban community. One woman who moved to the area from New York City casually observed that Rockdale feels like a suburb to her because it lacks the sorts of immigrant-owned ethnic restaurants and food trucks that she had become accustomed to in Brooklyn. "We're used to authentic food [in New York]," she said, "like Spanish restaurants where the grandma is back there cooking." As for the food in Rockdale, "It's very commercial," she lamented. Even though she described missing the more urban food scene in Brooklyn, she nonetheless elaborated on the distinct appeal of Rockdale's other suburban features. In fact, she credits the community's affordable housing market with helping her to achieve the status of homeowner—something she thought would never be possible in New York. "I constantly tell people in New York, if they would just save enough money, you could live in Georgia like a queen." Likewise, the relatively low price of commercial rental space in Rockdale made it possible for her to establish a successful retail business. She compared her own rent to that of a friend who operates a similar shop in Midtown Atlanta's Atlantic Station development. "I could never run my business in a city like Atlanta," she said. "It's just way too expensive. I would be worried about money all the time. But here in the suburbs it's doable, you know?" In comparing her local food scene and real estate prices to those in more urban areas, the image of Rockdale as a suburban community is thrown into sharp relief.

Even though most of the county's recent growth has involved the development of suburban-style commercial and residential areas, some community members gravitate toward the historic downtown district that was originally built up around the railroad stop. Known today as Olde Town Conyers, this part of Rockdale is a quaint neighborhood that many people describe as having "character." Streets of adjoining, brick storefronts house various locally owned businesses including the Beasley Drug Company, which features an old-fashioned pharmacy and soda fountain, as well as a ballet school, ice cream parlor, coffee shop, and salon and spa. The popular restaurants Thai Palace and Las Flores are locally owned and operated and tend to impress guests in search of "authentic" rather than mass-produced or unduly Americanized dishes. Similarly, The Pointe Bar, Whistle Post Tavern, and Celtic Tavern promote themselves as local, neighborhood joints offering informal libations and entertainment late into the night. The area's relatively narrow streets lined with ample sidewalks and streetlamps make the neighborhood especially suitable for walking as opposed to driving.

Surrounding these shops and restaurants are various historic establishments including the stately county courthouse and related government offices; the restored train depot, which now functions as the Conyers Welcome Center; and the ornate First United Methodist Church and Conyers Presbyterian Church buildings, each more than 100 years old. The charming and well-maintained facades of historic bungalow homes in Olde Town feature deep porches filled with swings, rockers, and potted plants, and, in December, meticulously arranged strands of sparkling outdoor lights and evergreen wreaths pinched with bright red bows. Given the neighborhood's "authentic" ethnic restaurants, locally owned businesses, and restored historic homes, residents of Rockdale describe Olde Town as having a certain old-fashioned and charming feel to it, a sense that small-town customs and local history are being preserved.

Residents who are drawn to the idea of small-town living tend to orient their lives around this area. One woman explained how she enjoyed raising her son in what she called "a little centralized place," a walkable neighborhood with a variety of local amenities. "I want a community that looks like a little community, that's not strip mall here and strip mall there. I mean, if all of Conyers were like [Highway] 138, I wouldn't be here. Couldn't stand that. To me, Olde Town is the heart of Conyers, and it represents what it was and what it should be." She recalled how her son often spent time at the library or the pharmacy soda fountain and concluded, "I know these will be memories that he'll have when he's older." The family makes it a point to support locally owned businesses in Olde Town, including the same hair salon that I have frequented since moving to Rockdale. My stylist, a young woman who moved to Rockdale with her family as a child, similarly orients her life around Olde Town. Her father owns a successful business just a few doors down from the salon and recently purchased a beautiful historic house in the district. During one of my appointments, I asked about plans for her upcoming wedding, and she replied, "Oh did I tell you we're changing our venue? We decided to have it in my dad's backyard—the house right here in Olde Town! It's going to be really intimate and quaint, just perfect." She went on to tell me about her involvement with the committee planning Olde Town's annual Hometown Holiday Parade and her preference for coffee from the neighborhood's local shop over that from Starbucks. "It's so cozy here—I just love Olde Town," she said. By staying involved in the daily life of this historic neighborhood, families like these come to regard Conyers as more of a small town and think of Rockdale as a community that fosters a sense of local belonging.

Away from Olde Town and Interstate 20, subdivisions and shopping centers gradually give way to rural countryside. Homes have a less mass-produced appearance and are situated on larger plots of land than in Conyers. Some are large estates with hundreds of acres, featuring massive barns, grazing cattle, and horses all enclosed by well-maintained wooden fences, and others are more modest in size with vegetable gardens, chicken coops, and roaming house pets. Still others look quite old and shabby and suggest that once-thriving family farms have fallen on hard times, their rusting John Deere tractors and empty silos appearing to no longer be in use. Driving through these relatively sparsely populated areas, intersections occasionally feature a small gas station selling bait and tackle or a tiny church accompanied by a simple cemetery. Compared to neighborhoods within the city limits of Conyers, much of Rockdale's unincorporated territory has a distinctly country feel.

Similar to the small-town image of Conyers is that of rural landscape, which others invest with meaning as they construct identities as country people. By forgoing trips into Atlanta and avoiding the bustle of commercial activity along the highways, these residents' daily lives in Rockdale are understood to be distinctly rural. As one man explained, "I'm a redneck. I mean, you can look and see. I'm country." Together, with his wife, a woman who similarly described herself as "a country girl" who "grew up driving a tractor," the couple operate a small farm and sell fresh eggs and vegetables at local farmers' markets. Their picturesque farmhouse and well-kept chicken coops located on a large and secluded plot of land lends credibility to their country lifestyle. They described spending most of their free time entertaining friends and relatives at home and communicated a strong disinterest in venturing into Atlanta for any reason at all. "I think we've been to Atlanta twice since we've lived here," the woman explained. The couple lamented that they had recently been invited to a high-end wedding set to take place in Atlanta, and the woman half-jokingly asked for my opinion on the dress she had purchased for the event. "I tell people all the time I'm just a redneck country girl, and I'm proud of it," she said as she held up a formal black dress. "I'm not a fancy!" By distancing themselves from Atlanta and orienting themselves around Rockdale's more rural spaces and activities, people like this couple come to see their community as a part of "the country," a place far away from "the city."

Still others in Rockdale struggle to distinguish the community from Atlanta at all. For example, many who work in the city of Atlanta or otherwise spend a significant amount of time there describe feeling like they actually live in Atlanta, even though they simultaneously recognize that Rockdale is not officially part of the city. When asked how they typically respond to the question "Where are you from?" residents like these explain that they usually tell people they are "from Atlanta," and some even list Atlanta as their current residence on public-facing social media accounts.

In casual conversation, it often becomes clear that the label "Atlanta" is used with great imprecision, thereby blurring distinctions between the city and outlying communities such as Rockdale. For example, during an interview with a man who hails from a small town in south Georgia, I asked, "So when did you move here?" After he answered, our conversation continued, but moments later I realized he was describing a community that sounded very different from Rockdale. I interrupted and asked for clarification, "This was after you moved here? When you came to Rockdale?" He replied, "Oh no, this was in Atlanta. I didn't actually come to Rockdale until a few years later." Even though I had begun the interview by explaining that my research project is about Rockdale, he misinterpreted my use of "here" to mean the general metro Atlanta area, thereby revealing that distinctions between the urbanism associated with Atlanta and the suburbanism associated with places such as Rockdale are relatively insignificant in his mind.

Similarly, some residents point to features of Rockdale that they interpret as having a particularly urban feel as if to suggest that they imagine themselves as living in an urban community. One local restaurant, for example, has become known as a credible alternative to the many swanky restaurant options in Atlanta's trendy neighborhoods. Coaxum's Low-Country Cuisine's dressed-up southern dishes, glittering back-lit bar, and regular live music attract a steady stream of locals looking to enjoy a night out. When I mentioned to one of the managers that the restaurant seems popular, she replied, "Yeah, you don't have to go to Buckhead anymore for a nice meal or a nice bar. Why drive to some other part of Atlanta when we have the same thing right here?" In contrast to the many local chain restaurants in the area, places such as Coaxum's market to customers who would otherwise seek out similar experiences in Atlanta. And in doing so, they construct an image of Rockdale as featuring the same quality of attractions that can be found in more urban locales.

Rural-urban boundaries are blurred in Rockdale by the copresence of people who alternatively see themselves as living seemingly urban, suburban, or small-town and rural lives. At the same time, however, some people articulate this blurring of boundaries themselves when they describe their image of the community is one that features "the best of both worlds." One such man gave me a tour of his home, a large, stately house custom built in the 1980s and situated at the end of a long, wooded drive enveloped by several acres of grassy lawns and thick woods. Standing in his backyard one could easily feel miles away from civilization, but in reality his property is fewer than 10 minutes from a hospital, a school, an apartment complex, several subdivisions, and a collection of fast-food restaurants. He marveled at the beauty of his seemingly rural estate and the convenience of living in a suburb with easy access to downtown Atlanta. "This is a suburb—let me tell you about what's so beautiful about this county: from where I'm living right here, 30 minutes and you're down at Georgia Tech [in Atlanta] ... you're 30 minutes down there, but you come back here—you're out in the country. God, it's so nice to be here!" In one casual statement the man referenced both Rockdale's proximity to Atlanta and its credibility as either "a suburb" or "the country."

This same sentiment is echoed by the discursive strategy commonly used to attract new residents and businesses to the community. For example, Carrington Real Estate, a company serving metro Atlanta, describes Rockdale this way on their webpage:

Why Live Here: The Best of Both Worlds

The main reason why individuals make the move to Conyers is that they can have it all—a rural and scenic living space that has small town feel and is in close proximity to a major U.S. city. The low cost of living coupled with the town's vibrant community and wealth of activities make Conyers ideal for the modern family.

(Carrington Real Estate n.d.)

Likewise, Rockdale's slogan—"Perfectly Positioned"—was adopted by the county government in 2009 as a branding concept that would highlight the best-of-both-worlds concept. "We're perfectly positioned within the state. We're right on I-20, a few minutes from downtown Atlanta and only 20 minutes from an international airport, but we're still small," explained the public affairs deputy director. "We still have some country, so even though we're in a metropolitan area, we're in a perfect position to have the amenities of the big city without being in the big city."[2]

Discussion and Conclusion

Rockdale County is a community characterized by decades of dramatic ecological and demographic change. As Atlanta's growth spilled outward, rural-urban boundaries shifted, and Rockdale was eventually incorporated into the official Atlanta Metropolitan Statistical Area. At the same time, the installation of interstate highways made boundary crossing much easier than before, and the development of suburban-style commercial and residential outlets transformed the county's ecological environment. With these changes came dramatic population growth and diversification in Rockdale, further transforming the demography of the community. Together, these trends have culminated in a blurring of rural-urban boundaries. As the metro area encroached on the countryside and new infrastructure made travelling more efficient, the imagined distance between Atlanta and Rockdale seemingly diminished. The stark differences between The City and The Country softened, and Atlanta was no longer so very far away.

At the same time, however, rural-urban differences also became blurred *within* the community itself. Many residents today take advantage of the community's easy access to the interstate, affordable real estate prices, and numerous chain stores and restaurants to live what they understand to be a suburban lifestyle. Others turn to historic Olde Town Conyers or the rural countryside to imagine themselves as small-town or country people. Still others see Rockdale as a part of Atlanta and struggle to clearly distinguish between the two as they construct identities as urban dwellers. The wide variety of ways in which residents locate Rockdale along the imagined rural-urban continuum suggests that rural-urban differences have blurred not only between Rockdale and Atlanta but within Rockdale as well.

The blurring of boundaries in Rockdale reveals how communities located along the rural-urban fringe can provide residents with the symbolic and social resources to construct alternatively urban, suburban, or rural identities. Despite how government authorities and scholarly experts impose official rural-urban boundaries onto space, people living in local communities make sense of ecological and demographic change to construct their own images of urbanity and rurality. Put simply, people's place-based identities are socially constructed through interactions in their own communities, not inherited from demographers and statisticians. This process is especially well-illustrated by those residents of Rockdale who see their community as exhibiting the "best of both worlds." In particular, the development of the "Perfectly Positioned" slogan demonstrates how policy-makers capitalize on cultural understandings of space, not just legal definitions of place, to make local decisions that have real consequences.

One important implication of this argument is that policy-makers should look past officially imposed urban-rural designations and seek to understand how residents of local communities make sense of urbanity and rurality in their own lives. As the shifting, crossing, and blurring of rural-urban boundaries continues, we can expect to see the development of increasingly complex ecological forms in metropolitan areas across the country. By using ethnographic methods to understand how people invest symbols and spaces with meaning, we can look forward to creating nuanced concepts of urbanity and rurality in the future.

Notes

1. Rockdale Citizen. 2012. Rockdale Citizen Poll for Nov. 18, 2012. Available from http://rockdaleciti zen.com.

2. Rockdale Citizen. 2009. County seeks edge with new slogan. Available from http://rockdalecitizen .com.

References

Anderson, Elijah. 2000. *Code of the street: Decency, violence, and the moral life of the inner city*. New York, NY: W.W. Norton and Co.

Bell, Michael. 1994. *Childerley: Nature and morality in a country village*. Chicago, IL: University of Chicago Press.

Bourgois, Philippe. 2003. *In search of respect: Selling crack in el barrio*. Cambridge: Cambridge University Press.

Bruegmann, Robert. 2005. *Sprawl: A compact history*. Chicago, IL: University of Chicago Press.

Carrington Real Estate. n.d. Conyers, GA real estate. Available from http://atlanta.carringtonrealestate. com.

Drake, St. Clair, and Horace Cayton. 1945. *Black metropolis: A study of Negro life in a northern city*. New York, NY: Harper & Row.

Duneier, Mitchell. 1999. *Sidewalk*. New York, NY: Ferrar, Straus, and Giroux.

Edin, Kathryn, and Maria Kefalas. 1997. *Promises I can keep: Why poor women put motherhood before marriage*. Berkeley, CA: University of California Press.

Elder, Glen, and Rand Conger. 2000. *Children of the land: Adversity and success in rural America*. Chicago, IL: University of Chicago Press.

Farmer, Marion T. 1998. Conyers, a product of the transportation age. In *Rockdale County, Georgia heritage*, ed. Rockdale County Heritage Book Committee, 25–26. Waynesville, NC: Walsworth Publishing Co.

Frey, William. 2004. *The new great migration: Black Americans' return to the South, 1965–2000*. Washington, DC: The Brookings Institution.

Gans, Herbert. 1967. *Levittowners: Ways of life and politics in a new suburban community*. New York, NY: Columbia University Press.

Goffman, Alice. 2014. *On the run: Fugitive life in an American city*. Chicago, IL: University of Chicago Press.

Grazian, David. 2011. *On the make: The hustle of urban nightlife*. Chicago, IL: University of Chicago Press.

Harding, David J. 2010. *Living the drama: Community, conflict, and culture among inner-city boys*. Chicago, IL: University of Chicago Press.

Harper, Douglas. 1987. *Working knowledge: Skill and community in a small shop*. Chicago, IL: University of Chicago Press.

Kolko, Jed. 21 May 2015. How suburban are big American cities? *FiveThirtyEight*.

KnowAtlanta. 2015. Navigating Atlanta neighborhoods: ITP vs. OTP. Available from http://knowatlanta .com.

Krogstad, Jens. 2015. *Reflecting a racial shift, 78 counties turned majority-minority since 2000*. Washington, DC: Pew Research Center.

Lichter, Daniel, and David Brown. 2011. Rural America in an urban society: Changing spatial and social boundaries. *Annual Review of Sociology* 37 (1): 565–92.

Lloyd, Richard. 2012. Urbanization and the southern United States. *Annual Review of Sociology* 38:483–506.

Lynch, Kevin. 1960. *The image of the city*. Cambridge, MA: MIT Press.

Lynd, Robert S., and Helen Merrell Lynd. 1957. *Middletown: A study in modern American culture*. New York, NY: Harcourt Brace & Company.

Macgregor, Lyn C. 2010. *Habits of the heartland: Small-town life in modern America*. Ithaca, NY: Cornell University Press.

Marrow, Helen. 2011. *New destination dreaming: Immigration, race, and legal status in the rural American South*. Stanford, CA: Stanford University Press.

Newman, Katherine. 1999. *No shame in my game: The working poor in the inner city*. New York, NY: Russell Sage Foundation.

Rushing, Wanda. 2009. *Memphis and the paradox of place: Globalization in the American South*. Chapel Hill, NC: University of North Carolina Press.

Salamon, Sonya. 2003. *Newcomers to old towns: Suburbanization of the heartland*. Chicago, IL: University of Chicago Press.

Simmel, George. 1903. The metropolis and mental life. In *The Blackwell city reader*, eds. Gary Bridge and Sophie Watson, 103–10. Malden, MA: Wiley-Blackwell.

Small, Mario. 2004. *Villa Victoria*. Chicago, IL: University of Chicago Press.

Suttles, Gerald D. 1968. *The social order of the slum*. Chicago, IL: University of Chicago Press.

Switzer, Robert. 2012. *A family farm: Life on an Illinois dairy farm*. Chicago, IL: University of Chicago Press.

Tönnies, Ferdinand. 1887/2002. *Community and society*. New York, NY: Dover Publications.

U.S. Census Bureau. 1982. Preliminary estimates of the intercensal population of counties 1970-1979. Available from http://census.gov.

U.S. Census Bureau. 1992. Intercensal estimates of the resident population of states and counties 1988–1989. Available from http://census.gov.

U.S. Census Bureau. 1994. The urban and rural classifications, 12-1–12-24. Available from http://census.gov.

U.S. Census Bureau. 2000, 2010. Rockdale County, Georgia race and Hispanic or Latino origin tables for the 2000 and 2010 census. Available from http://factfinder.census.gov.

U.S. Census Bureau. 2015. QuickFacts: Rockdale County, Georgia. Available from http://census.gov.

Venkatesh, Sudhir. 2009. *Off the books: The underground economy of the urban poor*. Cambridge, MA: Harvard University Press.

Whyte, William Foote. 1943. *Street corner society*. Chicago, IL: University of Chicago Press.

Wilson, William Julius. 1987. *The truly disadvantaged: The inner city, the underclass, and public policy*. Chicago, IL: University of Chicago Press.

Winders, Jamie. 2013. *Nashville in the new millennium: Immigrant settlement, urban transformation, and social belonging*. New York, NY: Russell Sage Foundation.

Wirth, Louis. 1938. Urbanism as a way of life. *American Journal of Sociology* 44 (1): 1–24.

Wirth, Louis. 1964. Rural-urban differences. In *On cities and social life*. Chicago, IL: University of Chicago Press.

Zukin, Sharon. 1996. *The cultures of cities*. New York, NY: Blackwell Publishers.

Placing Assimilation Theory: Mexican Immigrants in Urban and Rural America

By
ANGELA S. GARCÍA
and
LEAH SCHMALZBAUER

Assimilation theory typically conceptualizes native whites in metropolitan areas as the mainstream reference group to which immigrants' adaptation is compared. Yet the majority of the U.S. population will soon be made up of ethnoracial minorities. The rise of new immigrant destinations has contributed to this demographic change in rural areas, in addition to already-diverse cities. In this article, we argue that assimilation is experienced in reference to the demographic populations within urban and rural destinations as well as the physical geography of these places. We analyze and compare the experiences of rural Mexicans who immigrated to urban Southern California and rural Montana, demonstrating the ways in which documentation status in the United States and the rurality of immigrants' communities of origin in Mexico shape assimilation in these two destinations.

Keywords: assimilation theory; undocumented immigrants; urban and rural immigrant destinations; Mexican migration

Ａmerica's diverse and mobile immigrant population is teaching us different ways to think about how ethnoracial minorities are assimilated into the broader society. Post-1965 immigration from Latin America and Asia has

Angela S. García is a professor in the School of Social Service Administration at the University of Chicago. She has published articles in the International Migration Review, Ethnic and Racial Studies, *and the* Journal of Ethnic Migration Studies.

Leah Schmalzbauer is an associate professor of sociology and American studies at Amherst College. She is most recently the author of Immigrant Families *(Polity 2016; with Cecilia Menjívar and Leisy Abrego), and* The Last Best Place? Gender, Family and Migration in the New West *(Stanford University Press 2014).*

NOTE: We thank Cecilia Menjívar, David FitzGerald, and two anonymous referees for their useful feedback.

Correspondence: agarcia@uchicago.edu

DOI: 10.1177/0002716217708565

considerably altered ethnoracial demographics in the United States, and minority populations have grown in urban as well as nonmetropolitan areas (Lichter 2012). According to census forecasts, more than half of all U.S. residents will belong to a minority group by 2044, and most children will be minorities by 2020 (Colby and Ortman 2015). Since the 1990s, shifts in immigrants' destinations have also brought sharp increases in foreign-born population to places in the South, Midwest, and the Mountain West, many of which are rural (Zúñiga and Hernández-León 2005; Massey 2008; Lichter and Johnson 2009; Singer 2004; Marrow 2011). Yet theories of assimilation typically position native whites in urban—and, increasingly, suburban—contexts as the American mainstream (Thomas and Znaniecki 1918; Park 1928; Warner and Srole 1945; Gordon 1964; Portes and Zhou 1993; Zhou 1997; Portes and Rumbaut 2001; Alba et al. 1999; Brown 2007).

We argue that engaging the complexities of the physical and demographic characteristics of place is critical to understanding contemporary assimilation. This means bringing assimilation theory and the scholarship on new immigrant destinations into a critical dialogue with the subjectivities of place, and fore-grounding the ways that immigrants experience assimilation across diverse rural and urban contexts (see Gibson 1988). Though the literature on new destinations highlights the different geographic regions that host immigrants, it largely over-looks the distinct landscapes, population densities, and built environments of these places. As immigrants adapt to the physical characteristics of their destina-tions, the process is fundamentally shaped by the terrain and environment of their communities of origin. Local demographics also matter. As the United States diversifies, segmented assimilation theory posits that coethnic communi-ties ease the challenges of assimilation (Portes and Zhou 1993; Zhou 1997; Portes and Rumbaut 2001). Yet this framework leaves unexplored the relationship between the absence or presence of coethnics and the rural or urban orientations of receiving locales. Moreover, assimilation theories do not seriously engage immigration status despite the large undocumented population in the United States and mounting evidence that legal status affects immigrants' experiences of integration (see National Academies of Sciences, Engineering, and Medicine 2015).

Given the deep demographic and physical variations across immigrant destina-tions, how can social scientists usefully employ the concept of assimilation? This article provides a reconceptualization of assimilation theory that centers on peo-ple, place, and the transnational rural-urban interface that connects them. In addition to economic, residential, and educational assimilation, immigrants incorporate into their destinations' demographic populations (including main-stream cultural patterns, values, and norms) and into the physical geography of destinations' built and natural environments. Moreover, immigrants' assimilation experiences are fundamentally shaped by their communities of origin, their expe-riences in prior receiving locales, and their documentation status.

This study aims to challenge and update contemporary understandings of assimilation. To do this, we draw on interview and observational data of Mexicans who immigrated to the United States from rural communities of origin, many of whom are undocumented. We center on their navigation of Southern California, a long-standing urban, ethnically diverse destination; and Montana, a new rural, ethnically homogeneous destination. Our data show the divergent assimilation paths that immigrants take, suggesting the utility of a place-based approach for assimilation theory. For example, we find that immigrants' legal status interacts differently with the physical and demographic environments of Southern California and Montana, producing different effects. Specifically, we show that coethnic communities in urban California ease the assimilation of Mexicans from rural origins despite the jar of urbanity, allowing them to mask their illegality by blending in. Though coethnics are largely absent in Montana, immigrants' connection to the landscape and rurality of the area eases their assimilation even as they are marked by skin color and language among a native white majority.

Assimilation Theory

Theories of assimilation center on how immigrants move into mainstream society by altering practices and behaviors to become like the native-born. Classic assimilation theory asserts that immigrants gradually become similar to the mainstream, commonly envisioned as Anglo and Protestant, over time (Thomas and Znaniecki 1918; Park 1928; Warner and Srole 1945; Gordon 1964). Critical of this "straight line" model, alternative theories argue that discrimination and exploitation contribute to the reproduction of disadvantage for ethnoracial minorities rather than their assimilation (Blauner 1969;. Acuña 1972). Alternatively, segmented assimilation theory holds that discrimination, coethnic immigrant communities, and inner-city residence influence immigrants' upward mobility into a white mainstream or downward trajectory toward an ethnic and racial underclass (Portes and Zhou 1993; Zhou 1997; Portes and Rumbaut 2001). While focusing on the process and pace of change, the ultimate test of assimilation across these theories consists of immigrants and their children reaching parity with native-born whites (Jiménez and FitzGerald 2007).

Assimilation theory is typically embedded in city-based studies of traditional immigrant gateways. The Chicago School's emphasis on the immigrant experience in that city guided future studies to center on urban places (Waters and Jiménez 2005, 106). Though some scholars have analyzed the assimilation of immigrants in rural areas, like Punjabis in rural California (Gibson 1988), contemporary works commonly focus on cities like New York (Kasinitz et al. 2010; Smith 2005), Miami and San Diego (Portes and Rumbaut 2001), Chicago (De Genova 2005), and Los Angeles (Bean, Brown, and Bachmeier 2015; Alarcón, Escala, and Odgers 2016). Responding to new immigrant destinations, scholars are increasingly analyzing immigrant assimilation outside of urban areas. Spatial assimilation approaches follow immigrants from initial settlement in inner cities to later settlement in suburban areas, for example (Alba et al. 1999; Brown 2007). Because this research translates residential movement to the suburbs into increasing proximity with whites, the progress of immigrant assimilation remains gauged on whites as the reference group (Wright, Ellis, and Parks 2005).

Marrow's work in rural North Carolina (2011) and Jiménez's study of rural destinations in Kansas and California (2010) follow a different path, using native whites, African Americans, and Latinos as mainstream benchmarks.

In their "new assimilation theory," Alba and Nee (2003) offer an another vision of the American mainstream, acknowledging that contemporary immigrant assimilation takes place within social contexts brimming with racial, ethnic, economic, cultural, and class-based differences. This diversity, they argue, implies there is no set mainstream to which immigrants uniformly orientate. Rather, the mainstream is subject to change: it is a composite of cultural practices and beliefs that forms a common national existence, and assimilation into it is achieved through shifts among both immigrants and natives. This conceptualization of the mainstream acknowledges America's deepening diversity and the two-way street of assimilation, but it is so broad that it becomes difficult to clearly define. A place-based view of the mainstream, on the other hand, serves to anchor the concept.

Placing Assimilation Theory

The burgeoning new destination literature demonstrates that the structural nuances of immigrants' destinations critically shape the processes and experiences of assimilation (Deeb-Sossa and Bickham Mendez 2008; Dreby and Schmalzbauer 2013; Marrow 2011). Immigrants are settling in cities, suburbs, and small towns in the South, Midwest, and Mountain West, as well as in new areas within traditional migrant receiving regions, like the Northeast (Singer 2004). It is thus tempting to use a lens of regional cultures, politics, and economies to better understand assimilation. While these regional aspects matter, geographic location alone does not explain vast differences in immigrants' experiences.

Hellen Marrow (2011) asserts that levels of urbanity or rurality and the ways in which they are spatially situated in relationship to each other are more important to assimilation than regional differences. Immigrants' assimilation is influenced by how they experience the subjectivities of places in addition to the relationships they form with natural landscapes or built environments (Schmalzbauer 2014; Hondagneu-Sotelo 2014). The process of assimilation is shaped, for example, by receiving locales that are racially and linguistically diverse or homogeneous, with dense or sprawling housing, robust or nonexistent public transportation systems, and polluted air or clear skies (Marrow 2011; L. Nelson and Hiemstra 2008). These aspects map more neatly onto levels of urbanity or rurality than they do onto specific regional geographies. From rural North Carolina to rural Montana, Mexican immigrants from rural sending-communities emphasize the appeal of small town life, suggesting it reminds them of "home" (see Marrow 2011; and Schmalzbauer 2014).

Rather than arriving to the United States as blank slates, immigrants—especially adults—are profoundly influenced by their sending-communities. In addition to maintaining transnational social connections, immigrants bring with them experiences and sensory memories of smells, sounds, sights, and feelings that structured and flavored daily life in their places of origin (see Levitt and Waters 2006; Levitt and Glick Schiller 2004). These, in turn, shape their actions, outlooks, and assimilation into their new social and natural environments. Taking inspiration from Bourdieu (1977), Schmalzbauer suggests that we consider immigrants' "geographic habitus," or the "dispositions they have developed through their relationships with the natural landscapes and built environments that have contextualized their lives," when thinking about experiences of assimilation (2014, 26). Hondagneu-Sotelo (2014) echoes this approach in her research with Latino migrant gardeners in urban Southern California, finding that migrants encounter peace and refuge in public gardens because the setting reminds them of their communities of origin.

Drawing from work that includes sending locales in studies of assimilation (Jiménez and FitzGerald 2007; Eckstein and Najam 2013; Levitt and Waters 2006; Levitt and Glick Schiller 2004), we expand the concept into a place-based realm that accounts for migrants' connection to the social and physical landscapes of their places of settlement. We suggest that when the landscape of a place resonates with immigrants' geographic habitus, they may experience a sense of connection even if they simultaneously feel socially marginalized. Likewise, when there is discord between the environment of immigrants' immediate destinations and their geographic habitus, they may feel detached from the place even as they develop social connections.

Place, Illegality, and Assimilation

Social and physical landscapes alone do not shape connection to place. Legal status and the critical way it undergirds the assimilation experience are of increasing importance. Indeed, analyses of place have taken on more importance as immigration enforcement has expanded from the border into the U.S. interior. Local police departments and Immigration and Customs Enforcement (ICE) increasingly collaborate, focusing on worksite deportations, minor criminal infractions, and traffic stops (Golash-Boza 2015). At the same time, cities and states are forming their own laws to reduce the rights and benefits available to undocumented immigrants with an eye toward "attrition through enforcement," or pushing them out (García 2013).

As a result, physical deportations have increased sharply alongside a swell of denigrating social constructions of migrant illegality that are particularly associated with Mexican ethnicity (Golash-Boza 2015; Chavez 2013). The association between immigration and criminality has fueled the convergence of immigration and dangerous deviance in the public imagination (De Genova 2005), resulting in an increase in anti-immigrant sentiment (Kil, Menjívar, and Doty 2009) and immigrants' experiences of "legal violence" (Menjívar and Abrego 2012). Consequently, undocumented immigrants live with the constant "threat of deportability," which produces fear and anxiety among the undocumented and those who live in close proximity to them (De Genova and Peuz 2010; Dreby 2015). We acknowledge that legal status is a burden born by immigrants throughout the United States, yet the ways in which this burden is experienced varies by place.

Licona and Maldonado (2014), for example, analyze the place-specific productions and experiences of illegality within a framework of (in)visibility. Visibility can be experienced either positively or negatively depending on the intersection of one's social position and location on the rural-urban interface. For example, in urban Latino enclaves, like those studied in Southern California, immigrant visibility may be benign or beneficial. Yet in new rural destinations, visibility may prompt increased surveillance, with invisibility emerging as a strategy of protection. In areas like Montana, with little to no long-standing multigenerational Latino populations, Mexican immigrants are conspicuously marked by their brown skin and are thus more vulnerable to being read as "illegal."

Data and Methods: Research within the Rural-Urban Interface

The data for this article were collected through two independent studies that centered on Mexican immigrants' experiences in urban and rural destinations. Contrasting an urban receiving locale (Southern California) with a rural one (Montana) provides us with important analytical leverage. We use the matched pair comparison to build a place-based model of assimilation that accounts for legal status in the United States and the rurality of Mexican sending locales while staying attuned to the complexities of the assimilation process on the ground. Although paired case comparison is limited in terms of generalizability, the case study approach is well suited to the theory-generating goals of this study.

Interviews (115) and observational data were gathered from working-class, adult Mexican residents of Southern California in two waves: during 2006–2007 in Inglewood and Anaheim, cities in Los Angeles County and Orange County,[1] and during 2012–2014 in Santa Ana and Escondido, cities in Orange County and San Diego County. Most participants were undocumented and came from rural communities in Mexico that contrasted greatly with their destinations in Southern California (see Table 1). The state is solidly majority-minority, and 95 percent of residents live in metro areas (U.S. Census Bureau 2012; see Table 2).

From 2006 to 2012, and for six months in 2014, interviews (76), observations, and focus groups were conducted in southwest Montana, also with working-class, adult Mexicans. All but one moved to Montana from another state, with California and Colorado the most common previous destinations. As with the California sample, most participants in Montana were undocumented and emigrated from rural communities of origin (see Table 1). Montana is the third largest state by geographic size in the continental United States, yet it boasts fewer than one million people, translating into a density of only six residents per square mile. Southwest Montana is mountainous and the distances between towns are expansive. The state is predominantly white and English speaking, with some of the lowest numbers of Latinos in the United States (see Table 2).

Despite the seemingly vast differences between urban California and rural Montana, they are connected by economic restructuring and migration. Migrants in both study sites hail from places in rural Mexico whose economies have been

TABLE 1
Characteristics of Immigrant Samples

	California	Montana
Total sample size (*N*)	115	76
% undocumented	89	42
% male	47	53
% rural origin	84	95
% employed outside home	88	61
% experience in other U.S. states	17	96

disrupted by trade and economic development and, thus, whose opportunity structures have withered (Fernández-Kelly and Massey 2007). The vast majority were initially drawn to the United States by urban employment opportunities. Yet economic restructuring drew some away from saturated urban labor markets like many in California (see Light 2006) to rural states, such as Montana, in search of wages and opportunities.

Montana's economy, as is the case in other Mountain West states, is shifting away from agricultural production and resource extraction toward consumption (Hines 2010; McCarthy 2008; Woods 2007). A growing number of wealthy white urbanites are migrating to the area for lifestyle reasons (see Schmalzbauer 2014), consuming natural and urban-transplanted amenities, such as cafes, shops, and galleries, while telecommuting to jobs in urban hubs or retiring into the remoteness of the countryside (Krannich, Luloff, and Field 2011; P. Nelson, Oberh, and Nelson 2010; Cloke 2006). The surge of urban lifestyle migrants into Montana has spurred the influx of rural-origin Mexican labor migrants to service their lifestyles: a form of linked migration (P. Nelson, Oberh, and Nelson 2010).

Across both sites, immigrant interviews were semistructured. Though some took place in public spaces, participants often preferred to be interviewed in their homes, allowing for further insight into their lives. During analysis, an inductive approach was used to look for recurrent themes across interviews. We coded interviews at least three times as interpretations of results were refined. A similar process was followed with ethnographic and focus group field notes, which were analyzed in relationship to the interview data. In each section of the article's analysis, we present quotes that represent the views expressed by most respondents in each site. All respondents' names in this article are pseudonyms.

Findings

Visibility and vulnerability

The demographics of receiving locales critically shape Mexican immigrants' experiences of visibility and their perceptions of the mainstream. Established

TABLE 2
Characteristics of Receiving States

	California		Montana	
	2000	2010	2000	2010
Total population	33,871,468	37,254,503	902,195	973,739
% non-Hispanic white	46.7	40.1	89.5	89.8
% Hispanic	32.4	37.6	2	2.9
% Asian	10.9	13	0.5	0.6
% black	6.7	6.2	0.3	0.4
% American Indian	1	1	6.2	6.3
% rural population	5.6	5	45.9	44.1
% metro population	94.4	95	54.1	55.9
% foreign born	26.2	27.2	1.8	2
% non-U.S. citizen	15.9	14.7	0.8	0.9
% Spanish in home	25.8	28.5	1.5	1.4

SOURCE: U.S. Census 2000, 2010.

urban enclaves and new, small, and dispersed immigrant communities differentially affect the ways that immigrants' skin color, language, and presentation of self are interpreted and thus how they experience the daily embodiment of their immigrant status. In Southern California and Montana, Mexican immigrants—and particularly the undocumented—share the fear of being targeted by police and immigration enforcement and respond with efforts to go unnoticed. Yet because Montana is predominately white, immigrants there experience greater visibility and vulnerability than in Southern California, and thus more difficulty blending into the local population.

In Southern California, immigrants in the study mostly settled in Mexican-majority urban neighborhoods where, as Yolanda, a 40-year-old stay-at-home mother from a town in Zacatecas put it, "The only Americans I see around here [in her Santa Ana neighborhood] are some police officers and school teachers." In this context, "Americans" refers to native-born whites, serving as a racial rather than simply a nationality marker. In addition to the array of accessible commodities and services in these areas—from Spanish-language radio and religious services to dance halls and nonprofit organizations, legal services, and medical clinics—the presence of coethnics brought a level of social comfort. The neighborhoods dotting the Southern Californian towns where fieldwork was conducted were so deeply Mexican that Enrique, a 28-year-old landscaper, said, "The people and things in this neighborhood are familiar to me. I thought living in California would be different, that I would be surrounded by big houses, fast cars, all that. ... Around here, it's all Mexicans like me. So in that sense, it's comfortable." Enrique's comment reflects both a sense of familiarity with his immediate destination and the segregated geography of most American cities, where residents sort into neighborhoods based on race, ethnicity, and class.

Whereas migrants to California found themselves surrounded by people with similar backgrounds, in Montana migrants were shocked upon arrival to find there were so few Mexicans. Olga, who migrated to Montana from Texas, explained that when she arrived in the late 1990s, "I was the only Hispanic in town. There were hardly any Hispanics anywhere around. I wasn't even able to buy corn tortillas." Similarly, Victoria, who moved to Montana from Colorado in 2006, reflected, "In Colorado, no matter what the day … there were a ton of Mexican gatherings and dances. Here there is nothing. Nothing, nothing, nothing." The small community meant there were few cultural amenities such as food staples and leisure options that catered to Mexicans, which in turn made them feel like outsiders.

Living in diverse Southern California cities brings with it the ability to go about daily life without ethnicity serving as a constant marker of otherness. Being able to blend in to broader social surroundings is particularly important for Mexican immigrants whose skin color, facial features, and language can identify them as both a distinct ethnoracial group and, in popular consciousness, as undocumented (Goldsmith and Romero 2008). With a sharp uptick in immigrant policing, detention, and deportation, undocumented Mexicans took steps toward legal passing, or taking on characteristics associated with the mainstream by masking their undocumented legal status (see García 2014). In Southern California, undocumented Mexicans were able to remain under the radar during everyday life because their native born coethnics offered cover.

This point is illustrated by Luis, a 37-year-old father of three who has lived in Santa Ana for about six years. Interviewed in the living room of his tidy, one-story rental home, Luis expressed apprehension about his undocumented status and the desire to keep his head down. Yet "as one of many," the city's large Latino population allows him to go about his daily life without feeling conspicuous. "We are all Mexicans around here," he commented. "I don't stick out. I'm not the only one speaking Spanish or listening to *El Show del Mandril* on the radio, right?" Luis leaned back in his sofa and laughed at this last thought, finding it difficult to imagine living in an area of the United States without a sizable Mexican population. "I feel protected here, I would say," he continued. "If you stay out of trouble with the police it's easy enough to go about your life without calling attention to yourself."

In Montana it is impossible for Mexicans *not* to call attention to themselves. In one of the whitest, most English-dominant states in the country, most feel marked by skin color and language, and they experience particular challenges connected to this impossibility of anonymity. Antonio shook his head with despair as he discussed the hardships that Mexican immigrants face in Montana. "Here we are more vulnerable. We are more visible. I mean, the less we are, the more visible we are, the more likely we are … well, we are easily identified. We are in danger. So when there's more people it's easier to be anonymous. Here you stand out from white quite a bit." The impossibility of anonymity is also exacerbated by common instances of public harassment. As Jose explained, "So you arrive here and it's strange. Difficult. And it is more difficult because sometimes you are buying something in Walmart or whatever store and then you realize that there is someone looking at you and they say 'In America speak English.' Or on the street, 'In America speak English!' So, for example, in Los Angeles … no one is going to say something to you if you're speaking Spanish.

The way space is organized and where migrants live within it also shape experiences of visibility, vulnerability, and perception. The urban density of the neighborhoods studied in Southern California allowed immigrant residents to connect with others in the community. Guadalupe, who arrived to Escondido from a village in Puebla, found that her immigrant neighbors served as a source of support and information, particularly when the city passed a 2006 ordinance to ban renting property to undocumented immigrants. "I didn't know many people in Escondido, but I needed to find out more to understand what was happening," she recalled. "My neighbor, Doña Sofía, has been in Escondido forever and she watches the news constantly … I knew she would have information on what was happening and what this law would mean for all of us." Guadalupe's conversation with Sofía led her to an immigrant right's meeting at a nearby church, where she developed connections to both immigrants and native locales. While immigrant residents of these Mexican neighborhoods experienced geographic isolation from more prosperous areas of town, the density of their neighborhoods served, at times, to foster social inclusion.

Mexicans in Montana, in contrast, tended to live far from town in individual trailers or homes, with few nearby neighbors. Because public transportation does not exist outside of Bozeman, driving is mandatory to accomplish basic tasks. Women were especially unlikely to have a driver's license or know how to drive. Thus Montana's geographic isolation led to social isolation, which furthered marginalization. Maira, who lives on a dairy farm, said, "Women here don't leave home. If you don't know how to drive and you try to go to the store they can stop and detain you for whatever error. So I know women who don't leave home, because they are afraid that on the road they'll get stopped by the police." Respondents frequently discussed reports of police asking for papers, further intensifying their fear. Rosalia became emotional as she recalled the first time that she was stopped by the police in Montana. A legal permanent resident, her status did not erase her vulnerability to profiling. "Well, I was stopped at a light waiting and there was a police behind me … he said, 'Are you here legally?' And I said, 'yes.' And he said, 'Then show me your work visa or green card. …' I am sure they only stopped me because I look Mexican." To be sure, immigrants in Montana and Southern California alike feared local law enforcement and immigration officials. Yet across both sites, *how* immigrants coped with this vulnerability differed. In Montana, they isolated themselves as much as possible, whereas in California, they engaged in legal passing to navigate daily life.

Perceptions and performances of urban and rural

Immigrants in Southern California looked to Latinos—both native and foreign born—as their targets of emulation. In this setting, the reference point for cultural assimilation, or the adaptation to the dominant cultural patterns, values, and

norms, was not exclusively the white majority as envisioned in much of assimilation theory. In Montana, the reference point for assimilation was the white mainstream. Yet fear prohibits many immigrants from attempting to penetrate the
identity barriers of skin color and language that encase it. Instead, in Montana,
most immigrants isolated themselves as much as possible.

In Southern California, interviewees associated rurality with undocumented
status, and avoided appearances associated with it. Originally from a town in
Zacatecas, Marta and Leo settled their family in Anaheim, on the western edge
of the city just a few miles from Disneyland's gates. Marta explained that her
sister, who migrated to Anaheim several years prior, coached her on how to outfit
her family in the city. "'No ironed jeans!' That's one thing she told me," Marta
remembered. "I used to always starch and iron Leo's jeans. I thought it made
them look nice. But my sister said that makes you look like you've just come from
the *rancho*." Instead, Marta and others sought to embody a more urban image on
par with that of native-born Latinos and whites. Leo, for example, worked as a
busser at a mid-range chain restaurant. The company uniform (kakis and a logoed
polo) helped to take the stress out of clothing selection before work, but Leo,
following the lead of the other employees, always changed at the end of his shift.
"I try to dress like the other guys when I leave work," he said. "There's a mix of
us on the floor. The servers are white, both men and women. All of the bussers
are Mexican like me, and in the kitchen are Mexicans, a guy from Guatemala,
some white guys on the line. … After work it's usually jeans or shorts and a t-shirt.
But everything clean, and not too baggy. New looking shoes, like sports shoes too,
that's what everyone wears," he explained. The attire, though quite common, was
still an adjustment from Leo's freshly starched jeans, but it made him feel "like
just another guy on the street," he said.

Unlike the performance prescription followed by immigrants in California, in
rural Montana, creased jeans, cowboy boots and hats, and large belt buckles—
attire from the *rancho*—fit seamlessly. While Bozeman's center is gentrifying, it
is surrounded by working ranch and farm land. Indeed, agriculture remains the
most important economic sector in the state.[2] Therefore, immigrants' pick-up
trucks and *vaquero*/cowboy attire serve as an assimilation asset. This is evident
during rodeo season when ranchers and their families come together to cele-
brate. On a hot, bright evening in 2010, the prefestivities for one of the largest
rodeos in southwest Montana were underway. Though the rodeo itself was to be
the main draw, the streets of the rundown town were filled with revelers. While
native-born white ranching families and the Mexican ranch hands did not overtly
mix, both groups seemed at ease in the space. Differentiated by language and
skin color, Mexicans and native-born whites were united by their cowboy attire,
the honoring of the rural, and the spirit of the rodeo, an event with Mexican and
Spanish origins.

In California, cultivating the right urban look was important, especially for
Latino males. While they used personal style as a form of legal passing, in interviews men also discussed how to use their dress to signal a lack of gang affiliation.
In cities like Escondido, which has embraced anti-immigrant policies (García
2014), avoiding the *pandillero* or gangster look was critical. Jorge, a 20-year-old

immigrant from a small town in Guerrero, lived with his older brother in Escondido when he was interviewed in 2013. He spent a portion of his first U.S. paycheck from his construction job on a pair of baggy jeans. "I took them home and tried them on, and my brother was so mad," he recalled. "I didn't really understand why! He said that the police would stop me, and the real *pandilleros* would come after me." After speaking with his brother, Jorge became convinced of the need to tread the line of urban appearance carefully. Explaining how he now dresses, Jorge said he tries not to look "like someone who just crossed the border, and not like a delinquent."

Similarly in Montana, migrants associated urbanity with criminality and gang activity in particular, while mapping morality onto "rural" (see also FitzGerald 2009, 125–52). Presenting themselves as rural protected them from the negative and dangerous associations produced by illegality. Martín, who sports a cleanly trimmed moustache, and ironed jeans and shirts, migrated to Montana in the early 1990s. He has since established his own construction business, and is well known among the small Mexican community. He expressed concern that the behaviors and presentations of urban Mexicans taint the way all Mexicans are perceived: "What I don't like is when they come, let's say, from California or from Chicago, and their fashion is where their pants are really baggy, like *cholos*. Then those who have bad values begin to rob or something like open a car and take a stereo. … And then they cause prejudice against all of us." Lucy, a Spanish teacher, offered a similar explanation for the stereotype burden confronting Mexican youth, particularly boys, in Montana schools. "The Mexican boys at the school all hang out together and speak Spanish. … The stereotypes keep coming from the students and from the administrators. They say, well they always hang out at their lockers together and … they have the baggy pants, they look the look." Gaby, whose son dropped out of high school when he was 16, said, "Well, everyone thought Ernesto was a *cholo*, so he finally started acting like one. That is why he dropped out."

Efforts to blend in across Southern California cities extended beyond clothing and demeanor to social and cultural norms. Eric, who came to Inglewood in 2004 at 24 from a rural village in Yucatán, offered an example. His first job in Inglewood was with a janitorial company that serviced hotels. Prior to migration he had worked in the hotel industry in Cancún, and his experiences there, in addition to his time in his home community, informed his way of understanding his U.S. work life. Eric was especially taken by the way male and female employees of the janitorial company, a mix of U.S.-born Latinos and recent immigrants from Mexico, associated during breaks and lunch. "In Cancún, the men and women stayed separate at work," he explained. "It was the same in my *pueblo*. In my job here, it's not like that. It's more around if the group is speaking Spanish or English at break, but not men on this side and women on that side," he explained. "I like that. … Acting in the old way makes you look like you're not from here."

While Eric appeared to accept this shift in gender relations and use it to advance his efforts to assimilate, other immigrants in California struggled with differences between rural and urban norms. On the issue of gender, Graciano complained that native-born Latinas and Mexican immigrant women apply pressure to their recently arrived counterparts to conform to less traditional gender roles: "They tell her, 'You're silly. Get dressed. Let's go to the club! Let's dance!' That's where the problem starts. There are a lot of men who bring their wives here and they get separated, due to the freedom there is in California." Although Graciano also strove to blend in with his attire and way of moving about Anaheim, where he migrated in 2004, he struggled with the mismatch between his rural orientation and values of a diverse, urban destination.

In Montana, immigrants associated conservative social values with the rural mainstream. Many asserted that the values that they brought with them from rural Mexico "fit in Montana." Thus incorporating into this destination did not require a shift in cultural norms like in other urban places they had lived. In their narratives, women held up the rural as morally superior to the urban, characterizing the latter as violent, drug-infested, and devoid of values. In several interviews, women celebrated that their husbands spent more time at home in Montana than in other destinations. Olivia, for example, said, "I wanted to come to Montana because my husband was an alcoholic … he was always out drinking with his cousins and friends. I wanted this to stop, and it did when we came to Montana. … Here it is more peaceful. Men go to work and they come home … to be with their family." And Victoria, who moved to Montana from Denver said, "Montana is good for our family. It is more like home. Here we know our kids are safe, we go to church, we have picnics, and we can stay together." While it was difficult for Mexican migrants to perform the whiteness of the social mainstream, they embraced what they understood as Montana's rural values.

Geographic habitus and assimilation

We argue in favor of placing assimilation theory on not just a social group, determined by demographic variables, but also a destination, defined by geographic space and physical landscapes. Assimilation into this kind of nuanced mainstream includes the textured feelings of belonging to, or exclusion from, the physicality of the destination itself—the landscape, air, smells, noises, and seasonal rhythms. Immigrants' sense of connection to such environmental aspects of their destinations is critically shaped by their experiences in their communities of origin and previous U.S. destinations. Despite the impossibility of anonymity in Montana, Mexican immigrants expressed a transnationally inspired sense of belonging that was tied to the area's geography. In Southern California, on the other hand, the ease of blending into a familiar presence of Latino communities was counterbalanced by the huge shift from rural to urban space, from noise and traffic to the social problems that they perceive in the American city.

The experiences of migrants in Montana are shaped by the other physical, social, and natural environments that have contextualized their lives. A striking theme throughout these data was the resonance that Montana's rurality had for rural Mexicans—a resonance that they described as being heightened because of their "escape" from "chaotic" and "dangerous" urban areas. Martín's words exemplify the connection many described: "I think I am accustomed to life here because where we are from in Mexico is also a small town, and it is very peaceful." Angel also emphasized the peace many associated with rurality. "It's better here [than in California]. Here it is more or less like Mexico. It is peaceful and beautiful. I am from a small, peaceful town. And I feel like here it is more or less the same," he said. For those who work in agriculture in Montana, the connection to the natural landscape was even stronger. Jesus, for example, describes working in the campo/countryside as the essence of his identity. "Well I am accustomed to it here, in the campo, to the lifestyle of the campo. I really like it here in Montana ... I prefer living in the peace of the campo ... the campo is part of who I am."

Unlike their counterparts in Montana, immigrants from rural communities in Mexico interviewed in Southern California found urban life jarring and harried. Even though he had lived in Santa Ana for five years, Edwin, an immigrant from rural Michoacán, expressed bewilderment at life in his busy corner of the city. "Look," Edwin said, pointing to a window of his small apartment in a densely populated Santa Ana neighborhood. The screen was grimy, casting a grey haze over the early evening view—a busy intersection; a congested stretch of road; and the glimmering neon-lit signs of fast food restaurants, a dollar store, and a laundry mat. "All day it is like this—car, car, truck, car, truck. ... It doesn't stop. There is no calm. Only traffic, horns, and lights," he said, shaking his head. "I miss the quiet of my pueblo, where only the roosters woke me up." Like Edwin, most of the immigrants interviewed in Southern California from rural sending-communities struggled with the urban landscape of their destinations.

Though the urban Californian bustle proved trying, options for respite were constrained. Between fear of police and immigration enforcement, apprehension about driving without licenses, and busy work and family schedules, it was common for immigrants to go for long periods without seeking escape from the city in the area's many beaches, nature preserves, or mountain areas. It only took Sandra, who lived in Escondido, about 30 minutes to drive from her apartment to the beach without traffic. "When I can, which is not so often, I like to go to the beach," the single mother of three said. "We bring food and a little canopy, and there we spend the day relaxing. The children in the water and sand, and me watching them and the waves. Those days, they are so nice with all of us together and this beach I'm telling you about is so beautiful." These trips were important to Sandra, offering her a chance to "relax and enjoy a moment of peace," but the infrequency meant that the hustle of urban life was a far more common experience. This point was developed by Marina and Jorge, a married couple who live in Anaheim with their young son. "We are both from a *rancho*," Jorge explained. "But here we must be city people. ... That means there is not much nature in our lives," he continued. "We spend our free time inside, mostly."

For Mexicans in Montana, the city represented confinement and stress, whereas the Montana countryside signified freedom and connection to home. Elena was born in Los Angeles. When she was still a baby, her parents returned with her to rural Mexico where she stayed until she was midway through primary school. They then returned to California for a couple of years before moving to Montana where they have lived for almost a decade. Elena was sad and homesick for Mexico while she was in California. Her sadness followed her to Montana where she was the only Mexican in her rural school and at first found it difficult to make friends. Yet despite the social marginalization she initially experienced, Elena felt a connection to the mountains, the river, and the feel of her new small town. She compared Montana to California, saying, "It was very boring in California. I had to stay in the apartment all day watching TV. In Mexico I was outside running everywhere. In California I missed the campo a lot. ... Montana reminds me of home. It's like I'm back in the mountains of Jalisco."

The connections that Mexicans in Montana feel to the rural countryside were strengthened through their work, most of which takes place outside. Although many immigrants bemoaned the snow and ice that can begin falling in October and stay through May, they celebrated working in the open air away from the frenzied rhythms of the city. Pablo, for example, who worked on a ranch building fencing, laying irrigation, and wrangling calves, said, "Do you know what I like? What I like is agriculture. I am a person of the campo. Here I feel free. I feel like I am in Mexico. For me, my work in the campo is liberty. ... I have worked in cities, but I do not like the city. I am not accustomed to live like they do. I am happy here. There is nothing so beautiful as to live in the company of animals and nature." In this manner, the rural geographic habitus Pablo brought with him across the border aided his assimilation into rural Montana.

Our data indicate that immigrants in both samples experience belonging not only through their connection with the local population but also through the physicality of a place. Immigrants who settled in Southern California expressed a mismatch between their geographic habitus and the built environment of their destinations, yet the large Latino population provided a sense of familiarity and, for the undocumented, cover. Those who settled in Montana, in contrast, expressed a sense of intimate connection with the area's physical environment and their perception of rural values, yet alienation from the mainly white population into which it was impossible to blend. Undergirding experiences in both locales were documentation status and experiences in communities of origin. These perceptions from immigrants, coupled with increased ethnoracial diversity in traditional urban and new rural destinations, indicate the utility of "placing" assimilation theory.

Discussion and Conclusion

As the United States experiences increasing levels of ethnoracial, religious, and linguistic change and as immigrants settle in rural areas, we argue for a more nuanced assimilation theory. This new understanding includes two dimensions of belonging: to the human population in immigrants' immediate destinations and to the physical environment, both natural and built, that surrounds them. Further, we argue that both of these dimensions are shaped by the level of rurality or urbanity of immigrants' communities of origin and prior destinations, as well as documentation status in the United States.

Conceptualizing assimilation theory in terms of people and place brings with it significant strengths. Like Alba and Nee (2003), we understand the social core into which immigrants assimilate as subject to continual shifts and changes. Our call to anchor assimilation theory within immigrants' receiving locales, however, offers flexibility and specificity. Understanding assimilation as locally based adaptation to people and place allows for a de-centering of the United States, whiteness, and cities, opening opportunity for assimilation analyses firmly based within a range of destinations. Though born in Chicago, assimilation theory should have broader applicability, particularly given that the majority of contemporary international migration occurs between developing countries in the global south (Ratha et al. 2011) and that within the United States, migration to rural areas is growing rapidly (Lichter 2012). Reconceptualizing assimilation theory in this manner also acknowledges the influence of communities of origin on immigrants' trajectories within their destinations (see Levitt and Waters 2006; Hondagneu-Sotelo 2014), allowing us to see the ways in which migration bridges the rural-urban interface across borders and within countries of destination.

A place-based notion of assimilation theory has concrete implications for policy as well, and we encourage future research to focus here. This article demonstrates that how Mexican immigrants—and particularly the undocumented—experience public visibility and audibility shapes their assimilation trajectories. Of particular salience is the level of access and comfort that they experience in connecting with public entities and non-Latino residents. Place-specific ethnoracial demographics also determine who works in the public and social services that migrants must maneuver to manage daily life. Helen Marrow (2009) suggests that these gatekeepers serve as "street level bureaucrats," with the power to determine access to critical resources, programs, and services. In rural new destinations where few street-level bureaucrats speak Spanish or understand eligibility requirements for immigrant populations, immigrants may intentionally seek invisibility, staying away from even those services to which they are entitled (Schmalzbauer 2014). Avoiding social services also impacts family members, especially U.S.-citizen children of undocumented parents, who may not receive needed care or resources (Yoshikawa 2011). The data we present support the conclusion that the less stigmatized and policed immigrants feel within their destinations, the more likely they will be to engage broadly with society.

This article is intended to spark a different course of thinking about assimilation theory. While we argue that centering on local contexts is imperative, assimilation processes themselves are multifaceted. The increase in the undocumented population in the United States and the sharp uptick in immigrant enforcement add layers of complexity, as immigrants without legal status push toward assimilation with special urgency. The acceptance that some immigrants find within urban Latino neighborhoods or the peace that others feel in rural mountain areas, then, may also be a means of coping with their marginalized legal and ethnoracial status. In this sense, part of assimilating into a place may be learning to cope. Indeed, this article argues that assimilation involves not only precisely measurable outcomes, such as immigrants' earnings or educational attainment as compared to those of a reference group, but also racialization and identity negotiation (see Ribas 2015). Finally, while we focus on the process of immigrant assimilation into immediate destinations, the process is not unidirectional. As immigrants enter communities—and especially new destination communities—they are agents in reshaping the social, cultural, economic, and physical landscapes of the places that they inhabit, often blurring boundaries between urban and rural identities and scholars' conceptual categories in the process.

Notes

1. The first author gathered these interviews with the assistance of other researchers in collaboration with the Mexican Migration Field Research Program (MMFRP), an initiative of the Center for Comparative Immigration Studies at the University of California, San Diego.

2. See Mt.gov.

References

Acuña, Rodolfo. 1972. *Occupied America: The Chicano's struggle toward liberation*. New York, NY: HarperCollins.

Alarcón, Rafael, Luis Escala, and Olga Odgers. 2016. *Making Los Angeles home: The integration of Mexican immigrants in the United States*. Oakland, CA: University of California Press.

Alba, Richard, John R. Logan, Brian J. Stults, Gilbert Marzan, and Wenquan Zhang. 1999. Immigrant groups in the suburbs: A reexamination of suburbanization and spatial assimilation. *American Sociological Review* 64 (3): 446–60.

Alba, Richard, and Victor Nee. 2003. *Remaking the American mainstream: Assimilation and contemporary immigration*. Cambridge, MA: Harvard University Press.

Bean, Frank, Susan Brown, and James Bachmeier. 2015. *Parents without papers: The progress and pitfalls of Mexican American integration*. New York, NY: Russell Sage Foundation.

Blauner, Robert. 1969. *Still the big news: Racial oppression in America*. Philadelphia, PA: Temple University Press.

Bourdieu, Pierre. 1977. *Outline of a theory of practice*. Cambridge: Cambridge University Press.

Brown, Susan. 2007. Delayed spatial assimilation: Multigenerational incorporation of the Mexican-origin population in Los Angeles. *City & Community* 6:193–209.

Chavez, Leo. 2013. *The Latino threat: Constructing immigrants, citizens, and the nation*. 2nd ed. Stanford, CA: Stanford University Press.

Cloke, Paul. 2006. Conceptualizing rurality. In *Handbook of rural studies*, eds. Paul Cloke, Terry Marsden, and Patrick Mooney, 18–28. London: Sage Publications.

Colby, Sandra, and Jennifer Ortman. 2015. *Projections of the size and composition of the U.S. population: 2014 to 2060 population estimates and projections*. Current Population Reports. Washington, DC: U.S. Census Bureau. Available from https://www.census.gov.

De Genova, Nicholas. 2005. *Working the boundaries: Race, space, and "illegality" in Mexican Chicago*. Durham, NC: Duke University Press.

De Genova, Nicholas, and Nathalie Peuz. 2010. *The deportation regime: Sovereignty, space, and the freedom of movement*. Durham, NC: Duke University Press.

Deeb-Sossa, Natalia, and Jennifer Bickham Mendez. 2008. Enforcing borders in the nuevo South: Gender and migration in Williamsburg, Virginia, and the Research Triangle, North Carolina. *Gender and Society* 22 (5): 613–38.

Dreby, Joanna. 2015. *Everyday illegal: When policies undermine immigrant families*. Berkeley, CA: University of California Press.

Dreby, Joanna, and Leah Schmalzbauer. 2013. The relational contexts of migration: Mexican women in new destination sites. *Social Forum* 28:1–26.

Eckstein, Susan, and Adil Najam. 2013. *How immigrants impact their homelands*. Durham, NC: Duke University Press.

Fernández-Kelly, Patricia, and Douglass Massey. 2007. Borders for whom? The role of NAFTA in Mexico-U.S. migration. *The ANNALS of the American Academy of Political and Social Science* 610:98–118.

FitzGerald, David S. 2009. *A nation of emigrants: How Mexico manages its migration*. Berkeley, CA: University of California Press.

García, Angela S. 2013. Return to sender? A comparative analysis of immigrant communities in "attrition through enforcement" destinations. *Ethnic and Racial Studies* 36 (11): 1849–70.

García, Angela S. 2014. Hidden in plain sight: How unauthorised migrants strategically assimilate in restrictive localities in California. *Journal of Ethnic and Migration Studies* 40 (12): 1895–1914.

Gibson, Margaret. 1988. Punjabi orchard farmers: An immigrant enclave in rural California. *International Migration Review* 22 (1): 28–50.

Golash-Boza, Tanya. 2015. *Deported: Immigrant policing, disposable labor and global capitalism*. New York, NY: New York University Press.

Goldsmith, Pat Rubio, and Mary Romero. 2008. "Aliens," "illegals," and other types of "Mexicanness": Examination of racial profiling in border policing. In *Globalization and America: Race, human rights, and inequality*, eds. Angela Hattery, David Embrick, and Earl Smith, 127–42. Plymouth, UK: Rowman and Littlefield Publishers.

Gordon, Milton Myron. 1964. *Assimilation in American life: The role of race, religion, and national origins*. New York, NY: Oxford University Press.

Hines, J. Dwight. 2010. Rural gentrification as permanent tourism: The creation of the "new" west archipelago as postindustrial cultural space. *Environment and Planning D: Society and Space* 28 (3): 509–25.

Hondagneu-Sotelo, Pierrette. 2014. *Paradise transplanted: Migration and the making of California gardens*. Berkeley, CA: University of California Press.

Jiménez, Tomás. 2010. *Replenished ethnicity: Mexican Americans, immigration, and identity*. Berkeley, CA: University of California Press.

Jiménez, Tomás, and David FitzGerald. 2007. Mexican assimilation: A temporal and spatial reorientation. *Du Bois Review: Social Science Research on Race* 4 (2): 337–54.

Kasinitz, Philip, Mary Waters, John Mollenkopf, and Jennifer Holdaway. 2010. *Inheriting the city: The children of immigrants come of age*. New York, NY: Russell Sage Foundation.

Kil, Sang, Cecilia Menjívar, and Roxanne Doty. 2009. Securing borders: Patriotism, vigilantism and the brutalization of the U.S. American public. *Sociology of Crime, Law, and Deviance* 16 (13): 297–312.

Krannich, Richard S., A. E. Luloff, and Donald R. Field. 2011. *People, places and landscapes: Social change in high amenity rural areas*. Dordrecht, the Netherlands: Springer.

Levitt, Peggy, and Nina Glick Schiller. 2004. Conceptualizing simultaneity: A transnational social field perspective on society. *International Migration Review* 38:1002–1039.

Levitt, Peggy, and Mary Waters, eds. 2006. *The changing face of home: The transitional lives of the second generation*. New York, NY: Russell Sage Foundation.

Lichter, Daniel. 2012. Immigration and the new racial diversity in rural America. *Rural Sociology* 77:3–25.

Lichter, Daniel, and Kenneth Johnson. 2009. Immigrant gateways and Hispanic migration to new destinations. *International Migration Review* 43:496–518.

Licona, Adela, and Marta Maldonado. 2014. The social production of Latin@ visibilities and invisibilities: Geographies of power in small town America. *Antipode* 46:517–36.

Light, Ivan. 2006. *Deflecting migration: Networks, markets and regulation in Los Angeles*. New York, NY: Russell Sage Foundation.

Marrow, Helen. 2009. Immigrant bureaucratic incorporation: The dual roles of professional mission and governmental policies. *American Sociological Review* 74:756–76.

Marrow, Helen. 2011. *New destination dreaming: Immigration, race, and legal status in the rural American South*. Stanford, CA: Stanford University Press.

McCarthy, James. 2008. Rural geography: Globalizing the countryside. *Progress in Human Geography* 32:129–37.

Massey, Douglas. 2008. *New faces in new places: The changing geography of American immigration*. New York, NY: Russell Sage Foundation.

Menjívar, Cecilia, and Leisy J. Abrego. 2012. Legal violence: Immigration law and the lives of Central American immigrants. *American Journal of Sociology* 117 (5): 1380–1421.

National Academies of Sciences, Engineering, and Medicine. 2015. *The integration of immigrants into American society*. Washington, DC: National Academies Press.

Nelson, Lise, and Nancy Hiemstra. 2008. Latino immigrants and the renegotiation of place and belonging in small town America. *Social and Cultural Geography* 9 (3): 319–42.

Nelson, Peter, Alexander Oberh, and Lise Nelson. 2010. Rural gentrification and linked migration in the United States. *Journal of Rural Studies* 26:343–52.

Park, Robert E. 1928. Human migration and the marginal man. *American Journal of Sociology* 33 (6): 881–93.

Portes, Alejandro, and Rubén G. Rumbaut. 2001. *Legacies: The story of the immigrant second generation*. Berkeley, CA: University of California Press.

Portes, Alejandro, and Min Zhou. 1993. The new second generation: Segmented assimilation and its variants. *The ANNALS of the American Academy of Political and Social Science* 530 (1): 74–96.

Ratha, Dilip, Sanket Mohapatra, Calgar Özden, Sonia Plaza, William Shaw, and Abebe Shimeles. 2011. *Leveraging migration for Africa: Remittances skills and investments*. Washington, DC: World Bank.

Ribas, Vanessa. 2015. *On the line: Slaughterhouse lives and the making of the New South*. Berkeley, CA: University of California Press.

Schmalzbauer, Leah. 2014. *The last best place? Gender, family, and migration in the new West*. Stanford, CA: Stanford University Press.

Singer, Audrey. 2004. *The rise of new immigrant gateways*. Washington, DC: Brookings Institution.

Smith, Robert C. 2005. *Mexican New York: Transnational lives of new immigrants*. Berkeley, CA: University of California Press.

Thomas, William Isaac, and Florian Znaniecki. 1918. *The Polish peasant in Europe and America*. Boston, MA: Gorham Press.

U.S. Census Bureau. 2012. *Growth in urban population outpaces rest of nation*. Washington, DC: U.S. Census Bureau. Available from http://www.census.gov.

Warner, Lloyd, and Leo Srole. 1945. *The social systems of American ethnic groups*. New Haven, CT: Yale University Press.

Waters, Mary C., and Tomás R. Jiménez. 2005. Assessing immigrant assimilation: New empirical and theoretical challenges. *Annual Review of Sociology* 31 (1): 105–25.

Woods, Michael. 2007. Engaging the global countryside: Globalization, hybridity and the reconstitution of rural place. *Progress in Human Geography* 31:485–507.

Wright, Richard, Mark Ellis, and Virginia Parks. 2005. Re-placing whiteness in spatial assimilation research. *City & Community* 4:111–35.

Yoshikawa, Hirokazu. 2011. *Immigrants raising citizens: Undocumented parents and their young children*. New York, NY: Russell Sage Foundation.

Zhou, Min. 1997. Segmented assimilation: Issues, controversies, and recent research on the new second generation. *International Migration Review* 31 (4): 825–58.

Zúñiga, Victor, and Rubén Hernández-León, eds. 2005. *New destinations: Mexican immigration in the United States*. New York, NY: Russell Sage Foundation.

Entrepreneurial and Employment Responses to Economic Conditions across the Rural-Urban Continuum

By
ALEXANDRA TSVETKOVA,
MARK PARTRIDGE,
and
MICHAEL BETZ

In this article, we explore how local employment growth in the urban-rural continuum is affected by economic trends in industries that comprise local economies and by growth in nearby metropolitan areas. Our county-level analyses reveal heterogeneous responses. Favorable economic changes due to a fast-growing local industry mix have the largest positive impact on self-employment growth in small metropolitan areas and the smallest positive impact in rural counties. Self-employment in rural counties is fostered by growth in nearby small metropolitan statistical areas (MSAs) and is hampered by growth in nearby large MSAs. In micropolitan counties that are close to small and medium growing MSAs, local self-employment tends to grow faster, while growth in nearby large MSAs has no effect. In urban counties, growth in a nearby large MSA is not related to local self-employment growth in the lower tiers of the urban hierarchy.

Keywords: urban-rural hierarchy; self-employment; wage and salary employment; urban-rural interdependence

The United States has undergone substantial urbanization in recent decades, with fewer than 50 million of its more than 320 million people living in rural areas (Lichter and Brown

Alexandra Tsvetkova is a postdoctoral researcher at The Ohio State University, Department of AED Economics. Her research on regional economic performance determinants has appeared in Energy Economics, Small Business Economics, Regional Science and Urban Economics, Economic Development Quarterly, *and other journals.*

Mark Partridge is the C. William Swank Chair of Rural-Urban Policy at The Ohio State University and a professor in the Department of AED Economics. He is also an adjunct professor at Jinan University, Guangzhou, China, and at Gran Sasso Science Institute, L'Aquila, Italy. He has published in journals such as the American Economic Review, Journal of Economic Geography, Journal of International Economics, Journal of Urban Economics, Journal of Business and Economic Statistics, *and* Review of Economics and Statistics.

Correspondence: tsvetkova.1@osu.edu

DOI: 10.1177/0002716217711884

2011). This has occurred through both rural-to-urban migration and the expansion of urban areas annexing surrounding nonurban counties. "Bleeding" of urban ways of life and industrial structures into nonurban regions, accompanied by the shrinking of agriculture and mining, traditional dominant sectors in rural areas, has blurred the borders between what we usually perceive as rural and urban in terms of social, economic, and political settings. Instead of a sharp divide and separate analyses for urban and rural contexts, social scientists are increasingly examining processes at the fringe. Gradually, arguments are made for more nuanced analyses to understand social, political, and economic phenomena occurring across the urban-rural hierarchy, as interdependencies replace urban dominance (Lichter and Brown 2011).

Much of the empirical economics research is based on the premise that metro centers dominate in their economic relationships with surrounding areas. Following a long-standing research tradition, such analyses often conclude that the economic fortunes of the nearby hinterlands are closely linked to the economic success of proximate urban areas, as urban growth "spreads" to the hinterlands via the so-called spread effects (Boarnet 1994). It is not surprising that U.S. research and policymaking has mostly focused on explaining and stimulating urban growth. Rural issues have received much less attention, and rural policy often aims to stimulate the natural resource sector rather than linking up with urban-led growth, despite a long-term decline in primary-sector employment.

An earlier strand of literature has discussed offsetting spread and backwash effects (Myrdar 1963). Spread effects occur when urban growth spills over to nearby rural areas, for example, through commuting, access to markets, and knowledge spillovers. Yet spread effects may be dampened or eliminated when proximity to large urban areas drains resources from rural communities. Such forces (termed "backwash effects") are observable when financial resources and human capital move to metropolitan areas (Domina 2006; Lichter, McLaughlin, and Cornwell 1995) or when rural businesses cannot compete against larger firms that predominate in urban areas (Gereffi, Humphrey, and Kaplinsky 2001).

Although considerable scholarly attention has been paid to the urban-rural continuum and its definitions in many social sciences (Lichter and Brown 2011; Isserman 2005; Schaeffer, Kahsai, and Jackson 2013), economists have mostly focused on urban phenomena and have been slow to consider variations across the broader urban-rural hierarchy. This article helps to fill this gap by studying how national economic changes or shocks in various industries produce different local self-employment and wage and salary employment responses and how job

Michael Betz is an assistant professor in the Department of Human Sciences at The Ohio State University. His research explores factors that drive local labor markets and demographic change in the United States, with a particular focus on differences between rural and urban areas. He has published in the American Journal of Agricultural Economics, Energy Economics, Papers in Regional Science, Rural Sociology, *and* International Regional Science Review.

NOTE: We appreciate the partial support of USDA AFRI grant #11400612, "Maximizing the Gains of Old and New Energy Development for America's Rural Communities."

growth in various-sized metropolitan statistical areas (MSAs) affects growth across the urban hierarchy.

One particularly interesting aspect of rural/urban economic interdependency is the relationship between urban economic growth and rural entrepreneurship. The importance of entrepreneurship for job creation and regional economic performance is well established (Audretsch and Keilbach 2004a, 2004b; Glaeser, Kerr, and Kerr 2015; Malecki 1994; Carree et al. 2015; van Praag and Versloot 2007). Self-employment is often used to approximate entrepreneurship in empirical studies, and it is increasingly recognized as a key component to economic growth (Goetz, Fleming, and Rupasingha 2012; Rupasingha and Goetz 2013) that uniquely contributes to economic well-being in remote and disadvantaged regions (Stephens and Partridge 2011; Stephens, Partridge, and Faggian 2013). Given the special role that self-employment is able to play in defining local economic well-being, we focus our analysis on the factors that influence self-employment growth. We further expand our analysis to separately analyze the determinants of paid employment growth to assess differences in the dynamics behind these two important economic outcomes, which, we hope, will contribute to informed policy debate, as our work expands the understanding of "cross-border economic processes" and variations in job creation drivers across heterogeneous groups of counties.

We expect the effects of the dissimilar industry structures and of nearby MSA growth on rural entrepreneurship to differ depending on MSA size and proximity. Proximity to larger, more diverse cities should allow local entrepreneurs to access workforce skills that they themselves lack (Helsley and Strange 2011). Denser cities also have more access to services or partnerships that can help to bridge skill gaps. In smaller cities that tend to have less industry diversity (Henderson 1997), the dynamics are likely different, as entrepreneurs often strive to fulfill local demand and are less likely to be dependent on skills and services available in larger metro areas. However, more pressing competition in and around larger cities may reduce business start-ups and self-employment growth. Recent research has shown that small and medium cities have outperformed the largest cities in terms of job and population growth (Dijkstra, Garcilazo, and McCann 2013, 2015; Partridge 2010), supporting the hypothesis that economic performance may differ depending on MSA size. Additionally, Partridge et al. (2008, 2009) find positive spread effects of urban population and job growth to nearby nonmetro areas, but only when the urban centers have fewer than 500,000 people.

Our results suggest that self-employment in nonmetro counties modestly increases in response to favorable economic changes, with the size of the effects in rural counties being less than half of the average effect size in micropolitan[1] counties. In contrast, the influence of growth in a nearby small MSA is on average two times larger than the corresponding effect felt in micropolitan counties. Unlike rural counties, in addition to growth spread effects from a small nearby MSA, micropolitan counties enjoy increased self-employment growth if a nearby medium MSA grows. Growth in a large nearby MSA, on the other hand, suppresses rural self-employment growth, in line with the backwash hypothesis. In the metropolitan subsample, self-employment positively responds to exogenous economic changes due to differential growth of its industries, with the effects being more pronounced in counties within small MSAs, whereas job growth in a nearby large MSA has no statistical impact on self-employment growth.

Proximity and a Distribution of Growth

Building on the urban-hierarchy lattice of the central place theory (CPT), the new economic geography (NEG) (Krugman 1991) explains the formation of agglomerations with the performance of firms and, by extension, regions. Together, NEG and CPT explain the advantages of location close to agglomerated economies, but the associated fierce competition can suppress growth in nearby hinterlands due to a "growth shadow" from the larger urban center (Dobkins and Ioannides 2001). Yet NEG and CPT frameworks alone cannot explain the spatial distribution of economic activity and the interdependence between cities and their nearby hinterlands (Partridge 2010). An alternative approach within traditional rural development literature has focused on spread and backwash effects from urban areas into rural areas (Henry, Barkley, and Bao 1997; Myrdar 1963; Partridge et al. 2007). It is possible that urban growth spreads into the countryside by creating job opportunities for commuters, market opportunities for rural businesses, and access to higher-level urban services for firms and households. In this framework, commuting helps rural businesses, as commuting households purchase services locally. On the other hand, it is also possible that growth shadows result because urban growth pulls resources from rural areas by dominating markets, attracting human resources (e.g., braindrain), and drawing rural financial capital.

The U.S. research that examines interdependences between rural and urban economic areas generally supports the spread effects hypothesis (Boarnet 1994; Henry et al. 1999; Henry, Schmitt, and Piguet 2001; Lichter and Brown 2011; Schmitt and Henry 2000). A main conclusion is that growth in cities has net positive effects on population, employment, and several other measures of economic performance in surrounding rural regions—that is, spread effects outweigh the backwash effects. However, U.S. policy-makers seem to be reluctant to rely on urban-led growth in certain rural settings.

As income inequality rises, not only among professional occupations, but perhaps more importantly in the largest U.S. MSAs where considerable pockets of severe poverty can be found,[2] the ability of cities to lift living standards in their own and surrounding counties may be questioned. Indeed, past U.S. research has not fully examined whether net spread and backwash effects vary by metropolitan size. For example, the largest cities may be associated with relatively stronger backwash effects because their congestion limits the geographic range of rural commuting. Likewise, recent research on developing countries suggests that those who migrate to secondary cities, as opposed to mega-cities, find higher standards of living, ensuring more inclusive economic growth (Christiaensen,

Weerdt, and Todo 2013). Others have found that small and medium cities in developing countries may play an important role in growth and poverty reduction (Berdegué et al. 2015), although such evidence is country-specific (Berdegué et al. 2015; Ferré, Ferreira, and Lanjouw 2012).

After a surge of interest in the 1960s and 1970s, U.S. research has been slow in appraising the economic role of places other than central cities (Irwin et al. 2010). Partridge (2010) compares growth in four MSA population groups, finding that small and medium cities outperformed larger ones in both employment and population growth rates. With regard to the effects of proximity to urban centers of various sizes, Partridge et al. (2009) report positive population spillovers from MSAs of up to 500,000 people into smaller urban areas and nonmetro counties, with no additional spillovers from the largest metro areas.

Empirical Model, Data, and Variables

Our expectation of the important role played by distance to nearby MSAs and by sizes of these MSAs is motivated by a CPT framework, where firms and households desire various services that are offered by different-size urban areas. Actors access goods and services available in the nearest city, but move on to progressively higher-level cities when the nearest city does not offer the products that they demand.[3] Each urban tier offers progressively higher levels of functions and services, implying that economic actors need to travel to successively higher-ordered urban areas, which imposes additional costs to acquire more advanced services.

We posit that our outcome variables (self-employment and wage and salary employment growth) are a function of a number of factors identified as employment growth determinants in the literature. They include (1) the industry mix term (described in greater detail below and in the appendix), which captures differences in local industry composition that lead to differing local growth rates; (2) employment growth rate in the nearest MSA; (3) distance to this MSA; (4) an interaction term between MSA growth and distance to the MSA to account for indirect effects; and (5) a set of control variables that previous research has identified as important for local employment growth: the 1990 share of employment in agriculture, 1990 share of adults with high-school diploma only, 1990 share of adults with graduate or professional degree, and 1990 own county's population and 1990 population in nearby (or own for metropolitan counties) MSA. Equation (1) presents our empirical specification.

$$\Delta Y_{ict} = \beta_0 + \beta_1 \Delta INDMIX_{ct} + \beta_2 \Delta MSAGR_{mt} + \beta_3 DIST_c,$$
$$+ \beta_4 INTERACTIONS_{ct} + X_{c1990}\beta + \theta_t + \varepsilon_{ct} \tag{1}$$

where subscript i denotes employment type (SE or WS employment), c refers to a county, m to a nearby MSA, and t indicates time period. We estimate equation (1) using ordinary least squares (OLS). Since our specification cannot capture all (fixed) county-specific growth factors that might influence self-employment and wage and salary employment[4] growth, we use three-year differences of the dependent and main explanatory (industry mix and MSA growth) variables.[5] For example, if a county's self-employment growth rate calculated with total county employment as the base was 0.5 percent between years 2004 and 2007 and the same measure was 0.1 percent between years 2001 and 2004, the value of the dependent variable in year 2007 is 0.4 percent. There are three observations for each county calculated in the same fashion and denoted by years 2007, 2010, and 2013. Our first-differencing removes unobserved county characteristics that might relate to its employment growth and may potentially bias estimation results. First-differencing between three years should also remove some of the potential measurement error that is more problematic in annual data. When estimating equation 1, we cluster errors at the Bureau of Economic Analysis (BEA) economic area level (defined by the patterns of economic interdependence) because of the possibility that the error terms within the economic areas could be correlated and adjusting for this correlation improves the efficiency of our estimates. There are more than 170 BEA areas. We use 3,067 continental U.S. counties as our observation units, separated into metropolitan (1,059),[6] micropolitan (679), and rural (1,329) subsamples using the 2003 Office of Management and Budget (OMB) definition.

Our main data source is a proprietary dataset of county employment from Economic Modeling Specialists, Int. (EMSI).[7] The data are detailed by four-digit North American Industry Classification System (NAICS) codes and broken down by class of worker,[8] which allows us to separate total county employment into self-employment and wage and salary employment. EMSI relies on a number of public data sources (the *Quarterly Census of Employment and Wages* [QCEW] from the Bureau of Labor Statistics, BEA's *Regional Economic Accounts*, and *County Business Patterns* from the U.S. Census Bureau) to help fill in values suppressed due to public confidentiality requirements.[9] In deriving our variables, we exclude the agricultural sector to avoid difficult issues of measuring farm proprietors and employment; thus, our dependent and explanatory variables (industry mix term, growth in self-employment, paid employment, as well as job growth in nearby MSAs) reflect nonfarm employment only.

The EMSI self-employment totals are derived from the American Community Survey (ACS). The ACS only reports those individuals who consider self-employment as their primary employment. This is an important advantage over measures of self-employment provided by the BEA that count someone as self-employed if she or he engages in almost any self-employment activity, even if it is not the primary source of income. Thus, unlike numerous existing studies of self-employment, our analysis is based on estimates that avoid "double-counting" self-employed by placing those who have casual self-employment earnings in addition to primary income from a paid position into the wage and salary employment group. The differences between the two main sources of self-employment data (BEA and EMSI) are best illustrated by examining year-to-year averages. The BEA reports consistent yearly increases in mean proprietors between 2001 and 2013. According to the EMSI data based on the ACS, however, mean proprietors grew until 2006 and declined afterward.[10] These divergent patterns seem plausible, as full-time self-employed firms were more likely to close after the onset of the Great Recession, whereas worsening income conditions (Farber 2011) pushed paid employees to look for additional income through casual self-employment.

Our first explanatory variable in equation (1) is industry mix. The industry mix term is a longtime workhorse in regional economics whose mathematical derivation is described in the online appendix. The industry mix term reflects how differing initial local industry compositions can lead to economic changes (or shocks) to local job growth due to various national factors differentially affecting national industry growth. Simply, the industry mix variable reflects the county's expected employment growth rate if all its industries grew at their corresponding national growth rates. Because the industry growth rates are based on national data, the local industry mix term is by construction exogenous to local growth; that is, growth in industries of one county does not affect growth rates of these industries nationally. This eliminates the possibility of reverse causation or endogeneity that can bias the regression coefficients. Since the industry mix term greatly mitigates endogeneity concerns, it is widely used in regional and urban economics as an independent variable or as an exogenous instrument in studies that rely on instrumental variable estimation techniques (Bartik 1991; Betz et al. 2015; Blanchard et al. 1992; Tsvetkova and Partridge 2016).

The next group of explanatory variables is employment growth rates in nearby MSAs of various sizes over the same three-year periods. We employ slightly different empirical specifications for the counties in the nonmetropolitan sample (rural and micropolitan subsamples) and in the metropolitan sample (counties within small and medium MSAs). For the nonmetropolitan sample, we interact nearby MSA growth rates with one of three dummy variables that indicate that MSA's size (population under 250,000, between 250,000 and 1 million, and above 1 million people in 1990). This allows us to specifically assess whether the impact of urban economic conditions has different spread and backwash effects depending on the size of the nearest urban area. A priori, it is unclear which city size has spread effects into rural areas. Close access to larger cities provides bigger markets and more services, but smaller urban areas may have less congestion creating more opportunities for commuters that support rural services. All models in the nonmetro sample include interactions of MSA employment growth/size dummy variables with distance to corresponding MSAs. For counties in the metropolitan sample, we include job growth in the nearest large MSA (more than 1.5 million residents in 1990) together with an interaction between job growth and distance.

Finally, all models include a set of distance variables that reflects remoteness or, alternatively in metro models, centrality of a county in the urban-rural hierarchy. This approach stems from the CPT, which delineates tiers in the urban system that have successively higher-ordered functions or services for households or businesses. In this vein, the four distance variables are distance to the nearest MSA and then incremental distances to MSAs with 1990 population of at least 250,000, 500,000, and 1.5 million people following Partridge et al. (2008) and Partridge et al. (2009).

FIGURE 1
Example of Distance Calculation

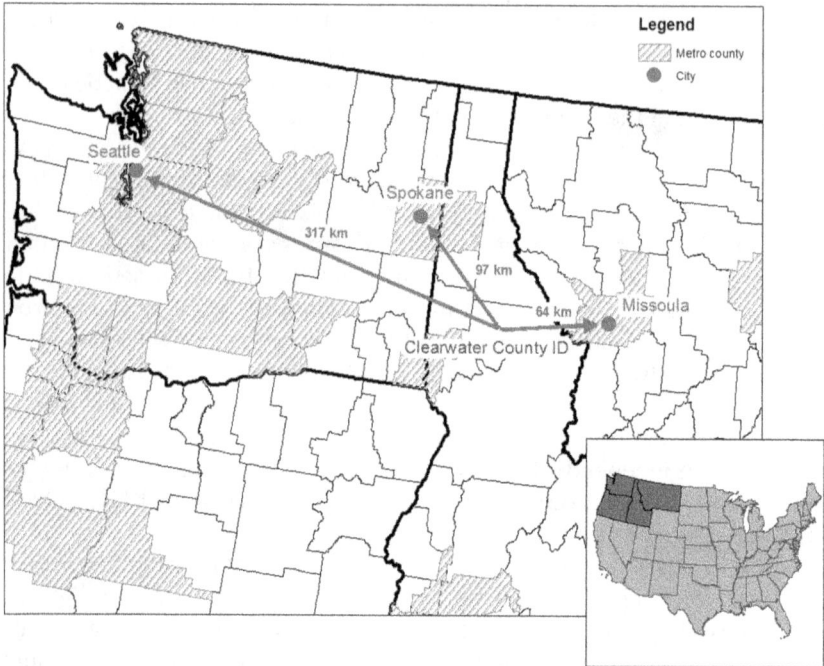

Figure 1 shows an example of the distance calculation. Clearwater County is a rural county in Idaho. The nearest metropolitan area, Missoula, Montana, had a population of about 90,000 people in 1990 and lies 64 kilometers away; that is, the distance to the nearest MSA for this county observation is 64. The nearest MSA in the next tier of the urban hierarchy with more than 250,000 residents is Spokane, Washington, with a population slightly exceeding 360,000 residents in 1990. This MSA is 97 kilometers away from Clearwater County, which means the incremental distance to an MSA with a population of at least 250,000 is 33 kilometers (97 minus 64). The third closest MSA in the next tier of the urban-rural hierarchy is the Seattle-Tacoma-Bellevue MSA, in Washington, which is 317 kilometers away and happens to fall in the highest tier (MSAs larger than 1.5 million residents in 1990). The incremental distance to an MSA of at least 500,000 residents is then 220 kilometers (317 minus 97) and zero to an MSA of at least 1.5 million people, because no further travel is required to get to a highest-tier MSA.

For the metropolitan sample, incremental distances are measured similarly, except that the distance to the nearest urban area is measured from the population-weighted centroid of the county to the population-weighted centroid of its own MSA, accounting for the notion that more distant counties in an MSA are often growing faster with more land availability. All distances are measured as straight-line distances because spillovers that are important for economic activity are likely to occur via numerous channels, such as travel time, job networks, and public service delivery, which are highly correlated with distance. An alternative intuitive measure, travel time, is not likely to offer sizable improvement over our operationalization as road travel time can be affected by time of day with rush hour, for example, which would introduce a measurement error that would be more systematically severe in large metropolitan areas and potentially may bias our results. If our choice of an approximation introduces some measurement error, the only tangible effect would be that distance coefficients are biased to zero and the standard errors would be measured less precisely (see Partridge et al. 2008),[11] so our results represent conservative estimates. Because the first-difference approach removes all time-invariant county-specific fixed-effects, including proximity or remoteness from urban centers, the estimated distance coefficients show how the effects of urban hierarchy accessibility are changing over time—for example, a significant positive coefficient would suggest that the role of distance in helping more remote areas to grow (for example, by "insulating" from urban competition) is increasing over time.

In addition to the explanatory variables described above, the vector $\mathbf{X}$ of other control variables includes a number of controls that are based on previous research into the employment growth determinants. Economic advantages from larger populations are captured by the 1990 values of logged county population and logged nearest MSA population (or own in the metropolitan sample). The share of adult population with a high school diploma (no bachelor's degree) and the share of the adult population with a graduate or a professional degree are proxies for the level of human capital. The data source for these variables is the U.S. Census Bureau. Finally, the models include the 1990 agriculture employment share using the EMSI data. Following the well-established economic literature, we use 1990 to lag the explanatory variables to mitigate any endogeneity including reverse causality concerns. As with the distance variables, with the county fixed-effects differenced out, the coefficients on the control variables reflect change in their importance over time. All models include time period dummies that account for business cycle effects such as the Great Recession. Table 1 shows summary statistics.

Estimation Results and Discussion

This section presents estimation results for both self-employment and wage and salary employment discussed below separately for the metro and nonmetro sub-samples. Since the dependent variables, industry mix term, and employment growth in nearby MSAs are calculated relative to total county employment, estimation coefficients on the main explanatory variables in each model are directly comparable. One should keep in mind that the industry mix variable is calculated using total employment that includes both self-employment and wage and salary

TABLE 1
Summary Statistics for the Variable by Sample

	Nonmetro Counties				Metro Counties			
Variable	Mean	Std. Dev.	Min.	Max.	Mean	Std. Dev.	Min.	Max.
ΔSE Total emp growth	−0.44	2.01	−26.81	29.67	−0.58	1.55	−30.86	12.89
ΔWS Total emp growth	0.62	13.51	−236.13	180.39	0.35	11.18	−151.64	128.03
ΔIndustry Mix variable	0.13	2.02	−9.33	10.73	0.12	2.01	−7.95	5.04
ΔNear MSA growth	−0.03	4.93	−28.04	25.27	0.25	4.72	−28.04	25.27
ΔNear MSA growth°dist	−34.4	830.4	−7,109.1	4,641.3	−45.66	882.1	−6,541.0	9,375.4
ΔNear 1.5m MSA growth	1.50	3.61	−14.45	10.51	1.23	3.85	−14.45	16.06
ΔNear 1.5m MSA growth°dist	25.4	203.0	−2,111.8	2,013.9	−16.0	104.4	−1,001.9	901.3
Distance to nearest MSA	97.63	59.10	17.01	408.19	24.43	19.98	0.00	96.87
Incr distance to 250k MSA	68.66	109.47	0.00	621.43	36.81	74.11	0.00	621.56
Incr distance to 500k MSA	42.84	65.69	0.00	426.36	36.62	68.04	0.00	490.54
Incr distance to 1.5m MSA	88.76	110.97	0.00	557.70	91.15	131.05	0.00	599.21
Agriculture share, 1990	14.59	9.35	0.08	63.53	7.27	7.31	0.01	40.90
Share of adults w HS, 1990	35.00	5.94	13.54	52.56	33.21	6.21	14.77	50.24
Share of adults w grad or prof degree, 1990	11.76	4.74	3.69	53.42	16.51	7.90	4.45	52.30
Population (ln), 1990	9.58	0.99	4.65	12.07	11.21	1.36	7.39	16.00
Nearby MSA population (ln), 1990	12.12	0.78	10.61	15.23	13.19	1.33	10.61	16.64
Observations	6,024				3,177			

NOTE: The table reports means that are not weighted by population.

employment, whereas the dependent variables separate these two employment groups. To meaningfully interpret the industry mix coefficients in Tables 3 and 4, we need to adjust for the share of self-employed (reported in Table 2) in the four subsamples that we analyze.

TABLE 2
Shares of Nonagricultural Self-Employment in Four Groups of Counties

County Type	County Subsample	Number of Counties	Share of Self-Employed
Nonmetropolitan	Rural	1,329	9.31
	Micropolitan	679	7.12
Metropolitan	Small MSA	365	6.16
	Large MSA	338	6.07

SOURCE: Authors' calculations based on the EMSI data.

Nonmetropolitan sample results

In this subsection, we discuss results for the nonmetro subsample broken down into rural and micropolitan groups.[12] Table 3 reveals clear differences in the effects of self-employment and wage and salary employment growth determinants. For self-employment, the industry mix term has a modest but positive impact on self-employment growth; however, the effect in micropolitan counties is twice as large. The gap is even larger if we account for the average nonfarm share of proprietors in the rural and micropolitan subsamples. Using Table 2, we can interpret the coefficient of 0.12 for rural counties as 0.03 percent spillovers. That is, a 1 percent increase in exogenous employment from having a favorable industry composition increases rural self-employment by 0.12 percent. Because rural self-employment averages 9.3 percent of total employment, this 1 percent of expected increase in total employment on average should consist of 0.09 percent of new self-employed jobs and 0.91 percent of new paid jobs, suggesting that self-employment grows by an additional 0.03 percent above what would be expected if the economic shocks created jobs in the same proportion as the share of self-employment. Likewise, the coefficient of 0.25 in the micropolitan subsample can be interpreted as 0.18 percent spillovers because micropolitan self-employment averages 7 percent of total employment. The spillover is six times larger than the one in the rural subsample, indicating that micropolitan counties on average create more self-employed jobs after a positive economic change.

Rural self-employment benefits from growth in the nearest small MSA. Every 100 new jobs in such metro areas on average are associated with 4.5 new self-employed jobs in rural surrounding counties, but only 2.7 new jobs in micropolitan surrounding counties, after three years. In addition to enjoying positive spread effects from small MSAs, micropolitan self-employment also benefits from growth in nearby medium-size metros. Micropolitan self-employment is not affected by economic conditions in nearby large MSAs, whereas self-employment growth in rural areas is suppressed if the closest MSA grows and happens to be large. The magnitude of the corresponding coefficients shows that rural backwash effects from nearby large MSAs are almost three times larger than positive spread effects from small MSAs. Insignificant coefficients on the distance-MSA-size-growth interaction terms suggest that distance to a nearby MSA does not affect the magnitude of the estimated MSA growth effects.

TABLE 3
OLS Estimation Results for Nonmetro Counties

Explanatory Variable	Total Self-Employment		Total Wage and Salary Employment	
	Rural	Micro	Rural	Micro
Industry mix	0.12°°	0.25°°	1.8°°°	1.1
	(0.06)	(0.12)	(0.49)	(0.88)
Nearest MSA growth (small)	0.045°°°	0.027°°°	0.19°°	0.34°°°
	(0.01)	(0.01)	(0.08)	(0.07)
Nearest MSA growth (medium)	0.018	0.032°°	0.16	0.52°°°
	(0.02)	(0.01)	(0.13)	(0.12)
Nearest MSA growth (large)	−0.12°°	5.5e–03	−0.32	0.037
	(0.05)	(0.04)	(0.22)	(0.23)
Distance to nearest MSA	1.4e–03°°°	1.5e–03°°°	4.7e–03	6.2e–03
	(0.00)	(0.00)	(0.00)	(0.00)
Nearest MSA growth x distance (small)	2.0e–05	5.6e–05	4.3e–04	2.9e–04
	(0.00)	(0.00)	(0.00)	(0.00)
Nearest MSA growth x distance (medium)	−1.6e–04	−6.9e–05	1.8e–03°°	6.1e–04
	(0.00)	(0.00)	(0.00)	(0.00)
Nearest MSA growth x distance (large)	−4.0e–04	1.2e–06	−5.3e–03°°°	−2.2e–03
	(0.00)	(0.00)	(0.00)	(0.00)
Incremental distance to MSA of 250k	1.1e–03°°°	1.0e–03°°°	4.5e–03	7.7e–03°
	(0.00)	(0.00)	(0.00)	(0.00)
Incremental distance to MSA of 500k	2.1e–04	2.5e–04	−7.3e–03°°°	−8.4e–04
	(0.00)	(0.00)	(0.00)	(0.00)
Incremental distance to MSA of 1500k	7.9e–05	−1.0e–04	−1.8e–03	1.7e–03
	(0.00)	(0.00)	(0.00)	(0.00)
Agriculture share, 1990	−1.2e–03	−.012°°	−.074	−.017
	(0.00)	(0.01)	(0.05)	(0.04)
Share of adults with HS only, 1990	7.6e–03°°	0.011°°°	0.015	0.041
	(0.00)	(0.00)	(0.04)	(0.03)
Share of adults with grad or prof degree, 1990	1.7e–03	0.013°°°	−0.046	−0.047
	(0.01)	(0.00)	(0.04)	(0.03)
Population (ln), 1990	−0.079°	−4.3e–03	−0.71°	0.059
	(0.04)	(0.04)	(0.36)	(0.45)
Nearest/own MSA population (ln), 1990	−0.021	−0.029	−0.073	−0.21
	(0.03)	(0.02)	(0.17)	(0.20)
Constant	0.028	−0.57	11°°	3.5
	(0.67)	(0.50)	(5.24)	(6.38)
R^2	.142	.233	.143	.302
Observations	3,987	2,037	3,987	2,037
Time period fixed effects	Yes	Yes	Yes	Yes

NOTE: Standard errors clustered at 177 BEA economic areas in parentheses.
°$p < .1$. °°$p < .05$. °°°$p < .01$.

TABLE 4
OLS Estimation Results for Metro Counties

Explanatory variable	Total Self-Employment		Total Wage and Salary Employment	
	Small	Medium	Small	Medium
Industry mix	0.34°°°	0.2°°°	0.82°	2.5°°
	(0.11)	(0.07)	(0.43)	(0.99)
Nearest MSA of 1.5m growth	0.012	–1.8e–03	0.26°°	0.43°°°
	(0.02)	(0.01)	(0.10)	(0.13)
Nearest MSA of 1.5m growth x distance	–6.1e–04	–1.7e–03°	–1.1e–03	5.2e–03
	(0.00)	(0.00)	(0.00)	(0.01)
Distance to nearest MSA	2.1e–03	4.1e–03	–0.035	3.2e–03
	(0.01)	(0.00)	(0.03)	(0.02)
Incremental distance to MSA of 250k	5.0e–04°	–0.018	–1.4e–03	–0.041
	(0.00)	(0.01)	(0.00)	(0.04)
Incremental distance to MSA of 500k	4.1e–04	1.8e–04	–6.0e–03°°°	–5.6e–03°
	(0.00)	(0.00)	(0.00)	(0.00)
Incremental distance to MSA of 1500k	–3.5e–04	–1.8e–04	–2.8e–03°	–2.3e–03
	(0.00)	(0.00)	(0.00)	(0.00)
Agriculture share, 1990	–9.8e–03	–0.021°°	–0.081°°	–0.056°
	(0.01)	(0.01)	(0.03)	(0.03)
Share of adults with HS only, 1990	0.013°°	0.016°°	–8.7e–03	0.016
	(0.01)	(0.01)	(0.03)	(0.04)
Share of adults with grad or prof degree, 1990	0.014°°°	0.019°°°	–0.027	–0.014
	(0.00)	(0.01)	(0.02)	(0.03)
Population (ln), 1990	0.072	0.13°°	–0.75	0.024
	(0.12)	(0.06)	(0.54)	(0.38)
Nearest/own MSA population (ln), 1990	–0.13	–0.12	0.66	–0.37
	(0.14)	(0.10)	(0.68)	(0.61)
Constant	–0.35	–1.3	4.6	9.5
	(0.89)	(1.37)	(6.22)	(8.27)
R^2	.288	.345	.412	.432
Observations	1,095	1,014	1,095	1,014
Time period fixed effects	Yes	Yes	Yes	Yes

NOTE: Standard errors clustered at 164 BEA economic areas in parentheses.
°$p < .1.$ °°$p < .05.$ °°°$p < .01.$

Turning directly to the main distance variables, which reflect changes in the effects of proximity over time, the positive and significant distance to the nearest MSA coefficient suggests that greater distance provides proprietor businesses increasing protection from urban competitors. Yet as noted above, some of the adverse urban competition effects are mitigated for growing small and medium MSAs, which is consistent with Partridge et al.'s (2008) findings that medium and small MSAs have larger spillovers. Incremental distance to the nearest metro area of fewer than 250,000 people also offers additional protection, but incremental distances to higher-tier cities are statistically insignificant. This might suggest that backwash is becoming more pronounced in the twenty-first century, which differs from the findings reported by Partridge et al. (2010).

Coefficients on the 1990 control variables tell several stories. First, the magnitude of the coefficients is very small, so that while some are statistically significant, we do not want to overstate their economic consequences. Next, the legacy of agricultural specialization in micropolitan counties appears to be associated with some growing reductions in self-employment. Relatively low levels of educational attainment have (modest) ever-increasing effects in promoting self-employment in both rural and micropolitan counties, whereas greater shares of adults with a graduate or professional degree have a growing impact on self-employment only in the micropolitan subsample. This may point to an increasing prevalence of necessity entrepreneurship in rural areas. In micropolitan counties the results seem to suggest increasing roles for both necessity and opportunity self-employment as follows from the positive and significant coefficients on both educational attainment measures. Larger rural counties, as measured by population in 1990, tend to have decreasing rates of self-employment growth, which is a little surprising unless incorporated businesses are crowding out self-employment, which mostly consists of partnerships and not limited liability corporations.

We now briefly describe the wage and salary results shown in the right panel of Table 3. They suggest that the dynamics behind nonmetro paid employment is different from that behind self-employment. In particular, a 1 percent exogenous change in employment due to local industry composition is associated with 1.8 percent more rural wage and salary employment (significant at the 5 percent level) but leads to a statistically insignificant 1.1 percent increase in micropolitan paid employment. One implication is that in sparsely populated rural counties, favorable economic changes have, on average, larger impacts.

The spread effects from the nearby small and medium MSAs are consistent with the self-employment results. The only difference is that growth-spread effects from small MSAs are stronger in micropolitan counties. No backwash effects are detected for wage and salary employment. Likewise, distance to nearest MSA of any size is statistically unrelated to wage and salary employment growth. In rural counties, two distance-growth interaction terms are significant. Although the lack of statistical significance of the main effects complicates interpretation, one may conclude that the protective effect of distance from growing medium MSAs is greater if they grow faster, whereas protective effects of distance from large MSAs is decreasing when these large metro areas experience faster growth. Incremental distance to the nearest medium MSA has a growing negative effect on rural paid employment growth, indicating greater job creation closer to such urban centers. This may be due to greater access to markets and suppliers, which promotes wage and salary employment. In the micropolitan subsample, to the contrary, incremental distance to urban centers of 250,000–499,999 residents in 1990 offers additional protection from urban backwash effects. Overall, the results for variables that measure distances seem to point to the changing presence of both spread and backwash effects of varying intensity, making it hard to draw firm conclusions.

Metro sample results

Table 4 presents the results for counties in small and medium MSAs. The table shows a wide variation in the effects of the main explanatory variables depending on employment type and the county's position in the urban hierarchy. With approximately equal 6 percent self-employment shares in small and medium metropolitan counties (from Table 2), economic growth driven by a favorable industry composition has stronger stimulating effects on self-employment in small MSAs—that is, after subtracting 0.06 from the respective industry mix coefficients, there are 0.28 percent spillovers in small as opposed to 0.14 in medium MSAs, showing considerably greater self-employment growth than the expected growth based on its average 6 percent (0.06) share. Job growth in nearby large metro areas and distance to these areas do not affect self-employment in lower-tier MSAs, although there is evidence that possible distance protection is weaker if nearby large MSA growth is greater. Both education variables are positive and statistically significant, again in line with the necessity and opportunity entrepreneurship perspectives.

In the wage and salary employment models, the industry mix term has differing effects in small and medium metro areas. In small MSAs, industry composition effects suggest that an exogenous 1 percent increase in total employment leads to only an 0.82 percent increase in wage and salary employment, which means that the growth displaces other paid employment. In medium MSAs, the corresponding 1 percent change is associated with 2.5 percent more wage and salary jobs, suggesting high positive multiplier or spillover effects. Growth in MSAs of at least 1.5 million people appears to have strong positive effects on both small and medium MSA paid employment growth, which is more pronounced in medium MSAs.

The direct effect of distance from the own-MSA core (distance to the nearest MSA) is statistically insignificant. For smaller MSAs, the negative and significant incremental distance to MSAs greater than 500,000 and greater than 1.5 million people suggests that the effects of remoteness are declining in smaller cities. In other words, being closer to larger MSAs has increasing importance. The results are similar for medium MSAs, though the incremental distance to MSAs of at least 1.5 million people is insignificant. Both results are consistent with growing spread effects from bigger cities to smaller cities because being closer to larger MSAs is positively related to paid employment growth.

Before we summarize our main findings in the next section, it is important to note that this study documents the differences in the effects of national economic conditions and of employment growth in nearby MSAs on local self-employment and paid employment as a function of a locality's position in the rural-urban hierarchy and of the size of a nearby MSA. Our research design ensures that we detect a statistically strong relationship since the main explanatory variables in the models are predominantly significant even after differencing and a use of instrument-like measures. Our research design, however, does not allow us to draw detailed conclusions on the specific mechanisms that lead to the documented differences. We, thus, rely on previous literature in our attempt to explain the phenomena that we present and welcome future research that would formally test potential explanations.

Conclusion

Since Birch's (1979) work on the importance of small businesses, economists and policy-makers have championed them as key economic drivers. At the same time, scholars are increasingly aware that entrepreneurship is not fostered inside a vacuum and that key environmental factors influence the probability of initial success and maturation of start-ups. Our study contributes to this discussion by investigating the relative local job growth effects from exogenous economic changes on self-employment and paid employment. We also investigate how these relationships change according to the locality's position within the urban-rural hierarchy.

Our analysis arrives at three important conclusions. First, we demonstrate that the response of local self-employment to exogenous economic shocks varies by the local county's position in the urban-rural hierarchy. Overall, self-employment in rural counties is the least responsive to such exogenous changes. In rural counties with higher shares of workers who have only a high school diploma, rising rates of self-employment may indicate the prevalence of "necessity entrepreneurship." Whether the emergence of necessity entrepreneurship is a drag on local growth is debatable—the answer likely varies across the urban hierarchy; however, the distinction between necessity and opportunity entrepreneurship often used in the literature (Low, Henderson, and Weiler 2005) may be a misnomer, especially in lagging and remote regions (Stephens and Partridge 2011).

Second, we document the presence of both spread and backwash effects. Most likely, these effects work simultaneously via various channels whose intensities depend on a number of factors. This article explores the role of two such factors—a position within the urban-rural hierarchy and a nearby MSA size—that indeed appear to play a role in what effect dominates. Overall, backwash effects are evident in the influence of large metro employment growth on self-employment growth in surrounding rural counties. In all other cases, either spread effects are predominant or no effects are detectable, most likely because of their offsetting impacts.

Finally, depending on the relative positions of counties within the urban-rural hierarchy and the type of employment considered, distance to nearby MSAs plays both protective (allowing faster self-employment growth in more remote nonmetro counties) and stimulating (promoting growth in counties closer to urban centers, in line with the view that access to markets and resources are important) roles, although the empirical evidence on the presence of the latter is weaker. While distance is not something that can be directly affected by policy levers, local decision-makers should exploit any advantages and realize limitations that their jurisdictions may face that stem from the jurisdiction's position on the urban-rural continuum. Future research may examine how exogenous changes in economic growth affect other outcomes such as income, poverty, and inequality to help to better tailor policy design within the urban-rural hierarchy.

Appendix

Industry mix variable is calculated as described in equation (A1). To keep our specification consistent, we difference the industry mix term over three years.

$$\Delta INDMIX_{ct} = INDMIX_{c\tau} - INDMIX_{c\tau-3} \text{ and,}$$
$$INDMIX_{c\tau} = \left(\sum_i IndShare_{ci\tau-3} NatGr_{i\tau-3,\tau}\right) \tag{A1}$$

where subscripts c, t, and τ indicate county, time period, and a year within time period t, respectively; and subscript i refers to an industry. For each industry (at the four-digit NAICS level) within a county, we calculate the share of total county employment in the beginning of a three-year period ($IndShare_{ci\tau-3}$), multiply it by the national growth rate in corresponding industries over the three-year period ($NatGr_{i\text{-}3,\tau}$), and sum over all the county's industries. In equation (1), the coefficient β_1 is the local employment multiplier associated with economic shocks due to having different industry composition; that is, it shows how many jobs are created in a county for each job that is expected to be created exogenously. If the coefficient is, for instance, 1.5, it means that there are positive spillovers of 0.5 jobs because per each one job added as a direct result of the exogenous shock, 0.5 jobs are created by the county itself. In contrast, if the coefficient is 0.8, it indicates crowding out because one job that is created as a result of exogenous economic changes translates into only 0.8 jobs in a county, suggesting that 0.2 jobs were destroyed. In the analysis presented in the article, however, an average composition of the industry mix variable (self-employment vs. wage and salary employment) needs to be accounted for when interpreting estimation coefficients.

Notes

1. A micropolitan area is a principal "city" of between 10,000 and 50,000 people along with the county(s) that include the principal city and any other counties with tight commuting links to this city.

2. See http://www.pewresearch.org/fact-tank/2015/09/10/how-the-geography-of-u-s-poverty-has-shifted-since-1960/.

3. The new economic geography (NEG) models build upon the urban hierarchy conceptualization of CPT and emphasize the role of agglomeration in the formation of different tier cities. However, NEG models have not been particularly effective in explaining more recent evolutions of U.S. settlement patterns (Glaeser and Kohlhase 2004; Partridge 2010).

4. We use paid employment and wage and salary employment interchangeably.

5. In equation (1), $\Delta Y_{ict} = Y_{ic\tau} - Y_{ic\tau-3}$ is a three-year difference in county self-employment or wage and salary employment growth calculated with total county employment serving as the base (τ stands for a year within a time period considered, whereas all other subscripts have meaning identical to the one described following equation [1] in the main body of the article): $Y_{ic\tau} = \left(Emp_{ic\tau} - Emp_{ic\tau-3} \right) / TotEmp_{c\tau-3}$.

6. Since we report estimation results for counties in small and medium MSAs only, the actual number of counties used to estimate our models in metropolitan subsample is 703.

7. See http://www.economicmodeling.com.

8. See http://www.economicmodeling.com/2012/07/09/emsi-data-update-four-new-categories/.

9. The advantage of using a proprietary dataset that does not have suppressed values is that our sample includes smaller counties, which would be omitted from the analysis should we rely on the publicly available data only. Thus, our results are generalizable to the universe of counties regardless of their size.

10. This is in line with the observation that self-employment formation rates are down after the Great Recession. See, for example, http://www.forbes.com/sites/jacquelynsmith/2014/02/06/self-employment-has-declined-since-the-recession-but-it-may-be-on-the-rise-again-soon/#19cc4d897e56.

11. There is a high correlation between road travel time and straight-line distance in advanced economies with developed road systems. For instance, Combes and Lafourcade (2005) find that the correlation between straight-line distances and French transport costs is .97.

12. See note 1.

References

Audretsch, David, and Max Keilbach. 2004a. Entrepreneurship and regional growth: An evolutionary interpretation. *Journal of Evolutionary Economics* 14:605–16.

Audretsch, David, and Max Keilbach. 2004b. Entrepreneurship capital and economic performance. *Regional Studies* 38 (8): 949–59.

Bartik, Timothy J. 1991. *Who benefits from state and local economic development policies?* Kalamazoo, MI: W.E. Upjohn Institute for Employment Research.

Berdegué, Julio A., Fernando Carriazo, Benjamín Jara, Félix Modrego, and Isidro Soloaga. 2015. Cities, territories, and inclusive growth: Unraveling urban–rural linkages in Chile, Colombia, and Mexico. *World Development* 73:56–71.

Betz, Michael R., Michael Farren, Linda Lobao, and Mark Partridge. 2015. Coal mining, economic development, and the natural resource curse. *Energy Economics* 50:105–16.

Birch, David. 1979. The job generation process. Unpublished manuscript. MIT Program on Neighborhood and Regional Change for the Economic Development Administration, U.S. Department of Commerce.

Blanchard, Olivier Jean, Lawrence F. Katz, Robert E. Hall, and Barry Eichengreen. 1992. Regional evolutions. *Brookings Papers on Economic Activity* 1992 (1): 1–75.

Boarnet, Marlon G. 1994. An empirical model of intrametropolitan population and employment growth. *Papers in Regional Science* 73 (2): 135–52.

Carree, Martin, Emilio Congregado, Antonio Golpe, and André van Stel. 2015. Self-employment and job generation in metropolitan areas, 1969–2009. *Entrepreneurship & Regional Development* 27 (3–4): 181–201.

Christiaensen, Luc, Joachim Weerdt, and Yasuyuki Todo. 2013. Urbanization and poverty reduction: The role of rural diversification and secondary towns. *Agricultural Economics* 44 (4–5): 435–47.

Combes, Pierre-Philippe, and Miren Lafourcade. 2005. Transport costs: Measures, determinants, and regional policy implications for France. *Journal of Economic Geography* 5 (3): 319–49.

Dijkstra, Lewis, Enrique Garcilazo, and Philip McCann. 2013. The economic performance of European cities and city regions: Myths and realities. *European Planning Studies* 21 (3): 334–54.

Dijkstra, Lewis, Enrique Garcilazo, and Philip McCann. 2015. The effects of the global financial crisis on European regions and cities. *Journal of Economic Geography* 15 (5): 935–49.

Dobkins, Linda Harris, and Yannis M. Ioannides. 2001. Spatial interactions among U.S. cities: 1900–1990. *Regional Science and Urban Economics* 31 (6): 701–31.

Domina, Thurston. 2006. What clean break? Education and nonmetropolitan migration patterns, 1989–2004. *Rural Sociology* 71 (3): 373–98.

Farber, Henry S. 2011. Job loss in the Great Recession: Historical perspective from the displaced workers survey, 1984–2010. National Bureau of Economic Research Working Paper 17040, Cambridge, MA.

Ferré, Céline, Francisco H. G. Ferreira, and Peter Lanjouw. 2012. Is there a metropolitan bias? The relationship between poverty and city size in a selection of developing countries. *The World Bank Economic Review* 26 (3): 351–82.

Gereffi, Gary, John Humphrey, and Raphael Kaplinsky. 2001. Introduction: Globalisation, value chains and development. *IDS Bulletin* 32 (3): 1–8.

Glaeser, Edward L., Sari Pekkala Kerr, and William R. Kerr. 2015. Entrepreneurship and urban growth: An empirical assessment with historical mines. *Review of Economics and Statistics* 97 (2): 498–520.

Glaeser, Edward L., and Janet E. Kohlhase. 2004. Cities, regions and the decline of transport costs. *Papers in Regional Science* 83 (1): 197–228.

Goetz, Stephan, David A. Fleming, and Anil Rupasingha. 2012. The economic impacts of self-employment. *Journal of Agricultural and Applied Economics* 44 (3): 315–21.

Helsley, Robert W., and William C Strange. 2011. Entrepreneurs and cities: Complexity, thickness and balance. *Regional Science and Urban Economics* 41 (6): 550–59.

Henderson, J. Vernon. 1997. Medium size cities. *Regional Science and Urban Economics* 27 (6): 583–612.

Henry, Mark S., David L. Barkley, and Shuming Bao. 1997. The hinterland's stake in metropolitan growth: Evidence from selected southern regions. *Journal of Regional Science* 37 (3): 479–501.

Henry, Mark S., Bertrand Schmitt, Knud Kristensen, David L. Barkley, and Shuming Bao. 1999. Extending Carlino-Mills models to examine urban size and growth impacts on proximate rural areas. *Growth and Change* 30 (4): 526–48.

Henry, Mark S., Bertrand Schmitt, and Virginie Piguet. 2001. Spatial econometric models for simultaneous systems: Application to rural community growth in France. *International Regional Science Review* 24 (2): 171–93.

Irwin, Elena G., Andrew M. Isserman, Maureen Kilkenny, and Mark D. Partridge. 2010. A century of research on rural development and regional issues. *American Journal of Agricultural Economics* 92 (2): 522–53.

Isserman, Andrew M. 2005. In the national interest: Defining rural and urban correctly in research and public policy. *International Regional Science Review* 28 (4): 465–99.

Krugman, Paul. 1991. Increasing returns and economic geography. *Journal of Political Economy* 99 (3): 483–99.

Lichter, Daniel T., and David L. Brown. 2011. Rural America in an urban society: Changing spatial and social boundaries. *Annual Review of Sociology* 37:565–92.

Lichter, Daniel T., Diane K. McLaughlin, and Gretchen T. Cornwell. 1995. Migration and the loss of human resources in rural America. In *Investing in people: The human capital needs of rural America*, eds. Lionel J. Beaulieu and David Mulkey, 235–56. Boulder, CO: Westview Press.

Low, Sarah, Jason Henderson, and Stephan Weiler. 2005. Gauging a region's entrepreneurial potential. *Economic Review-Federal Reserve Bank of Kansas City* 90 (3): 61–89.

Malecki, Edward. 1994. Entrepreneurship in regional and local development. *International Regional Science Review* 16 (1&2): 119–53.

Myrdar, Gunnar. 1963. *Economic theory and underdeveloped regions*. London: Methuen and Co., Ltd.

Partridge, Mark. 2010. The duelling models: NEG vs amenity migration in explaining U.S. engines of growth. *Papers in Regional Science* 89 (3): 513–36.

Partridge, Mark, Ray D. Bollman, M. Rose Olfert, and Alessandro Alasia. 2007. Riding the wave of urban growth in the countryside: Spread, backwash, or stagnation? *Land Economics* 83 (2): 128–52.

Partridge, Mark, Dan S. Rickman, Kamar Ali, and M. Rose Olfert. 2008. Lost in space: Population growth in the American hinterlands and small cities. *Journal of Economic Geography* 8 (6): 727–57.

Partridge, Mark, Dan S. Rickman, Kamar Ali, and M. Rose Olfert. 2009. Do new economic geography agglomeration shadows underlie current population dynamics across the urban hierarchy? *Papers in Regional Science* 88 (2): 445–66.

Partridge, Mark D., Dan S. Rickman, Kamar Ali, and M. Rose Olfert. 2010. The spatial dynamics of factor price differentials: Productivity or consumer amenity driven? *Regional Science and Urban Economics* 40:440–52.

Rupasingha, Anil, and Stephan Goetz. 2013. Self-employment and local economic performance: Evidence from U.S. counties. *Papers in Regional Science* 92 (1): 141–61.

Schaeffer, Peter V., Mulugeta S. Kahsai, and Randall W. Jackson. 2013. Beyond the rural-urban dichotomy: Essay in honor of Professor A. M. Isserman. *International Regional Science Review* 36 (1): 81–96.

Schmitt, Bertrand, and Mark S. Henry. 2000. Size and growth of urban centers in French labor market areas: Consequences for rural population and employment. *Regional Science and Urban Economics* 30 (1): 1–21.

Stephens, Heather M., and Mark Partridge. 2011. Do entrepreneurs enhance economic growth in lagging regions? *Growth and Change* 42 (4): 431–65.

Stephens, Heather M., Mark D. Partridge, and Alessandra Faggian. 2013. Innovation, entrepreneurship and economic growth in lagging regions. *Journal of Regional Science* 53 (5): 778–812.

Tsvetkova, Alexandra, and Mark Partridge. 2016. Economics of modern energy boomtowns: Do oil and gas shocks differ from shocks in the rest of the economy? *Energy Economics* 59 (1): 81–95.

van Praag, C. Mirjam, and Peter H. Versloot. 2007. What is the value of entrepreneurship? A review of recent research. *Small Business Economics* 29:351–82.

Upward Mobility of Low-Income Youth in Metropolitan, Micropolitan, and Rural America

We analyze county-level social, demographic, and economic data in U.S. counties to explore how economic mobility in the United States varies across the geography of the rural-urban interface. We reveal that micropolitan areas—small and medium urban centers—appear to play a unique role in the geography of intergenerational economic mobility. Micropolitan areas help to define the blurred boundaries of the new rural-urban interface, and play a unique and potentially powerful role in supporting the upward mobility of low-income youth. In some geographic areas, micropolitan counties serve as cores of nonmetropolitan America, supporting upward mobility in ways that take advantage of their density and scale. In other domains, they are relatively low-density transition zones between remote noncore rural counties and metropolitan America, supporting upward mobility of low-income youth in ways that exploit the opportunities and reveal weaknesses associated with nonmetropolitan small size, lack of density, and limited technological capacity.

Keywords: micropolitan; intergenerational mobility; rural-urban interface; low-income; rural; metropolitan

Stagnation in the earnings of middle- and low-income households over the past several decades has generated increased concern

By
BRUCE A. WEBER,
J. MATTHEW FANNIN,
SAM M. CORDES,
and
THOMAS G. JOHNSON

Bruce A. Weber is professor emeritus of applied economics at Oregon State University, former codirector of RUPRI Rural Poverty Research Center, and director emeritus of the OSU Rural Studies Program. His current research focuses on economic mobility and social safety net programs. He coedited Frontiers in Resource and Rural Economics *(Routledge 2008) and* Rural Wealth Creation *(Routledge 2014).*

J. Matthew Fannin is the William H. Alexander Professor of agricultural economics and agribusiness at Louisiana State University. He serves as associate director of analytic and academic programs at the Rural Policy Research Institute. His current research focuses on the functional characteristics of micropolitan areas. He coedited Rural Wealth Creation *(Routledge 2014).*

Correspondence: bruce.weber@oregonstate.edu

DOI: 10.1177/0002716217713477

about the economic prospects of young people. This concern has led to heightened interest in intergenerational upward mobility in the United States and other countries. Because of the paucity of multigenerational panel data needed for studies of intergenerational income mobility, there have been relatively few studies of this issue. Of those that do exist, almost all have been national and cross-national analyses (Aaronson and Mazumder 2008; Auten and Gee 2009; Corak 2013). A recent breakthrough in the analysis of economic mobility by Chetty et al. (2014), however, permits such analysis at a much finer level of geography. With access to a very large dataset of intergenerationally linked U.S. income tax records, they have estimated intergenerational income mobility at the commuting zone and county level. In their study, Chetty et al. provide conclusive evidence that that there is enormous variation in upward mobility across localities in the United States, and they examine the local factors correlated with this intergenerational upward economic mobility.[1]

Here, we extend this analysis by exploring how mobility and its correlates vary across a geography that reflects the new rural-urban interface. We examine mobility in a tripartite classification that enriches the standard metropolitan-nonmetropolitan dichotomy by recognizing the role of micropolitan counties as intermediate urban cores in nonmetropolitan America. It is our contention that the simplification of spatial dynamics into rural and urban has missed the fundamental spatial role of intermediate urban places that are characterized by modest agglomeration economies and relatively significant economies of scale that support concentrations of shopping, healthcare, and educational services and, often, are endowed with rich natural resources and recreational amenities. While overall costs of distance are declining globally, still-significant costs of distance in some sectors can confer an economic benefit to remote intermediate urban places, making them competitive in production of certain goods and in supplying intermediate inputs and essential services. Our working hypothesis is that a focus on these intermediate "micropolitan" centers will sharpen our understanding of the new rural America characterized by increasing rural-urban interdependence and the blurring of boundaries between rural and urban noted by Lichter and Brown (2011).

In this article, we seek evidence for this idea that micropolitan counties play a unique role in the geography of the rural-urban interface by exploring the geography of upward mobility. The central questions addressed in this article are, Do

Sam M. Cordes is a professor emeritus of agricultural economics at Purdue University, where he served as founder and codirector of the Purdue Center for Regional Development, associate vice provost for engagement, and assistant director of cooperative extension. He currently serves as chair of the Rural Policy Research Institute's spatial analytics group.

Thomas G. Johnson is a professor emeritus of applied economics and public affairs at the University of Missouri. He is coeditor of Rural Wealth Creation *(Routledge 2014),* Towards Sustainable Rural Regions in Europe *(Routledge 2011),* Community Policy Analysis Modeling *(Wiley 2006), and* Microcomputer Based Input Output Modeling *(Westview Press 1993).*

NOTE: The Rural Policy Research Institute at the University of Iowa provided impetus and support for this article through its Micropolitan Initiative.

micropolitan counties constitute a unique economic and social environment for supporting upward mobility of low-income youth? Are the correlates of upward mobility different for micropolitan counties than for metropolitan and rural counties? If we find evidence of a different environment with different relationships between correlates and upward mobility in micropolitan counties, this may reveal new contours in the blurred rural-urban boundaries and an opportunity to shift our conception of how to define the geography of the rural-urban interface.

Our article is the first to use these data to explore the variation in the absolute upward mobility measures of Chetty et al. (2014) in metropolitan, micropolitan, and rural (noncore nonmetropolitan) counties and the first to determine the extent to which the factors associated with upward mobility of low-income youth are different across metropolitan, micropolitan, and rural counties. We explore how correlations between absolute upward mobility and race, commuting patterns, social capital, inequality, educational attainment, and family structures differ across these areas. We seek to develop some stylized facts that can point to local characteristics of places that expand or inhibit intergenerational economic mobility in the United States. Through this exploration, we also seek to discover whether the introduction of boundaries between micropolitan and noncore counties in the geography of rural America provides new insights into the social and economic interdependence of rural and urban places and the increasingly blurred rural-urban landscape.

The remainder of the article is organized into four parts. We first summarize what has been learned about the geography of intergenerational upward mobility in the work of Chetty et al. (2014). Then in the Data and Methods section, we define upward mobility and explain how the data were obtained, describe the Core-Based Statistical Area classification that created the micropolitan area designation, define and justify the correlates selected for analysis, and describe our analytic methods. In the Results section, we present the findings from the correlation and regression analysis about how correlates of upward mobility vary across types of counties. We end by summarizing what we learned about the role of micropolitan areas in the rural-urban interface and draw some implications for future research.

The Geography of U.S. Intergenerational Economic Mobility

In a path-breaking analysis of intergenerational economic mobility, Chetty et al. (2014) found very extensive cross-sectional variation in upward mobility across localities in the United States. With de-identified federal income tax data, they developed estimates of the extent to which the income rank of adult children corresponded to the income rank of their parents at both the multicounty commuting zone and the county level. The federal income tax data allowed them to link the 2011–2012 incomes of people born in 1980–1982 with the 1996–2000 incomes of their parents (during the time period when the children were in their late teens). They measured the 2011 and 2012 mean total family incomes of the "children's" cohort and placed each child in a national ranking of 2011–2012 incomes in this children's cohort. They then placed the parents in a national ranking based on data on the mean total family income of the parent family in 1996–2000. By linking the child income ranking with the parent income ranking, they were able to determine the upward mobility of the children. Based on the residence of parents when these children were teenagers, they estimate the average mobility for each county in the United States with at least 250 children in the core sample.

Chetty et al. (2014) first estimate the commonly used measure of relative economic mobility—the intergenerational elasticity of income, which they find to be unstable and nonlinear. For both empirical and conceptual reasons, they prefer a rank-rank correlation of parent and child income, which they estimate as their relative measure of mobility. They then use this "rank-rank slope" to develop a unique measure of intergenerational upward mobility that they term "absolute upward mobility."

Chetty et al. (2014) focused on both the variation across U.S. commuting zones in absolute upward mobility and the social, demographic, and economic correlates of cross-commuting-zone upward mobility in the United States.[2] They found very large regional variations in mobility with concentrations of low-mobility areas in the southern United States and concentrations of high-mobility areas in the Upper Great Plains. They also noted that low-income children growing up in rural commuting zones are more likely to be upwardly mobile than children growing up in urban commuting zones: "Urban areas tend to exhibit lower levels of intergenerational mobility than rural areas on average" (pp. 1593–95). They explored many economic and social variables hypothesized to affect economic mobility in their article and found variables in six domains to be very highly correlated with upward mobility in their cross-commuting-zone analysis. These six domains were race, job segregation (or alternatively, quality of spatial job matching), income inequality, school quality, social capital, and family structure. They selected for each of these domains the variable most highly correlated with upward mobility (with the largest simple correlation coefficients) for further analysis in a multivariate regression. The Chetty et al. analysis focused on six variables: the share of households that were African American; the share of households with less than a 15-minute commute (a measure of segregation of work from residence capturing the quality of spatial job matching), the Gini ratio (a measure of income inequality), the high school dropout rate (a measure of school quality), an index of social capital, and the fraction of families with a single mother (a measure of family structure). Chetty et al. found fraction black alone, income inequality, high school dropout rate, and fraction single female–headed households negatively correlated with upward mobility, and the fraction with short commutes and social capital positively correlated with upward mobility. Chetty et al. concluded their article by suggesting that, since upward mobility varies greatly across localities in the United States, the level of mobility is a local issue, and local place-based policies may have a role in supporting upward mobility.

The current article extends the work of Chetty et al. (2014) in three ways. First, by analyzing county-level rather than commuting zone data, we examine the patterns of upward mobility at a more local level that better corresponds to government decision-making authority. Second, we extend earlier research that examines metropolitan and nonmetropolitan differences in mobility by disaggregating nonmetropolitan into its micropolitan and noncore components. Finally, we develop a new analysis of ways that race and family structure interact in determining upward mobility of low-income youth.

Data and Methods

Absolute upward mobility

We use the public use county-level data on absolute upward mobility from the Equality of Opportunity website[3] as our mobility measure. Absolute economic mobility is defined as the "expected [income] rank of children whose parents are at the 25th percentile of the national income distribution based on the rank-rank regression." A higher rank indicates greater upward mobility of low-income youth (i.e., youth whose parents were at the 25th percentile of the national distribution).[4]

These data are mapped in Figure 1, which shows the significant variation in absolute mobility across counties in the United States. Figure 1 shows for each county the mean 2011–2012 income percentile rank for children who grew up in the county whose parents were at the 25th percentile of the 1996–2000 income distribution. Note that the county designation indicates where the child grew up, not where they live as an adult. For a county with an absolute mobility score of 43 (about average for the U.S.), the expected adult (2011–2012) income rank for a person who grew up there in a household at the 25th percentile is the 43rd percentile.

Counties for which there are no data are not shaded. It is clear from Figure 1 that there are many sparsely populated counties for which there are no data because of their small population size. Of the 395 counties with missing data, 336 are noncore counties. Since the counties with missing data are disproportionately noncore counties, this may introduce some bias into our analysis.

Micropolitan statistical areas as nonmetropolitan core regions

In the late 1940s the predecessor of the current Office of Management and Budget (OMB) developed a classification of counties designed to both capture the interdependence of major cities with their emerging suburbs, and distinguish the counties in the nation that were not linked to these cities through commuting of workers.[5] The OMB scheme placed each of the nation's counties into one of two categories: metropolitan (metro) or nonmetropolitan (nonmetro). A "core" metropolitan county or set of counties contained an urban area with 50,000 or more inhabitants. Adjacent counties exhibiting a high degree of social and

FIGURE 1
Geography of Absolute Upward Mobility in United States' Counties

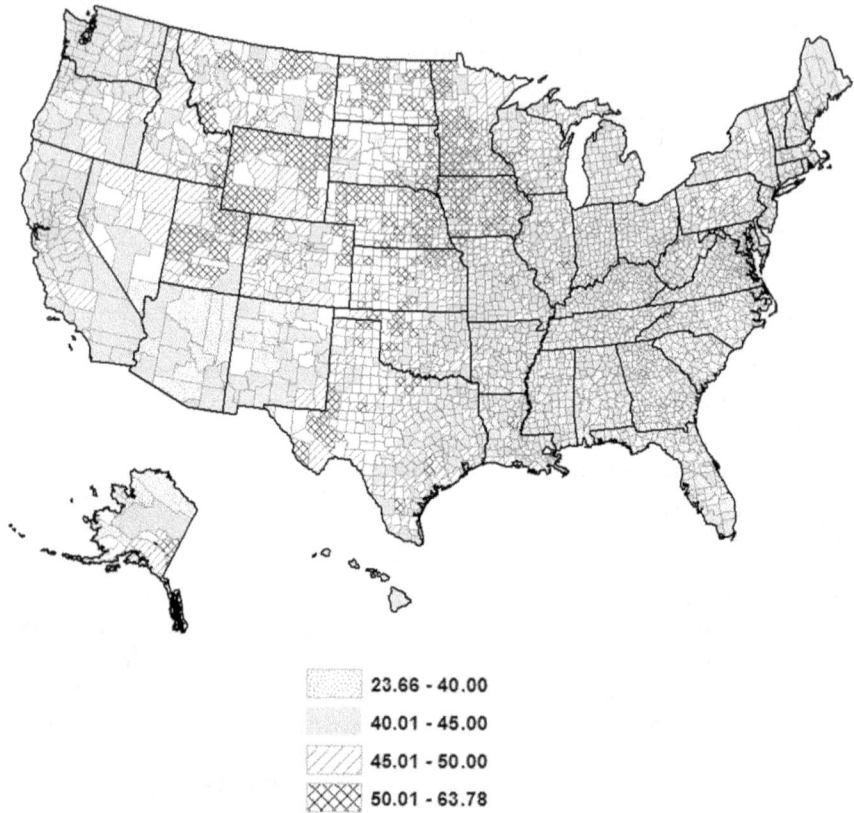

23.66 - 40.00
40.01 - 45.00
45.01 - 50.00
50.01 - 63.78

economic integration with the core metropolitan counties were also categorized as metropolitan.[6] All other counties in the United States were categorized as nonmetropolitan (OMB 2015).

Many have recognized that the metro and nonmetro areas are not two neatly separable geographies. Lichter and Brown (2011), for example, have argued that "social and spatial boundaries that have divided rural from urban America histori-cally are rapidly shifting, blurring, and being crossed" (p. 584). And in 2003, the OMB, recognizing that the nonmetro category did not capture the enormous diversity in population size and economic function of counties in this category, developed Core-Based Statistical Areas (CBSAs), which separated nonmetropoli-tan counties into "micropolitan" (micro) and "noncore" counties. A "central" micropolitan county has at least one "urban cluster" of at least 10,000 but less than 50,000 population. As in the metropolitan classification, adjacent counties with a high degree of social and economic integration with the urban cluster are categorized as "outlying" micropolitan counties.[7] Counties that are not part of either a metropolitan or micropolitan area are referred to as "noncore" counties.

FIGURE 2
Micropolitan Statistical Areas of the United States, 2013

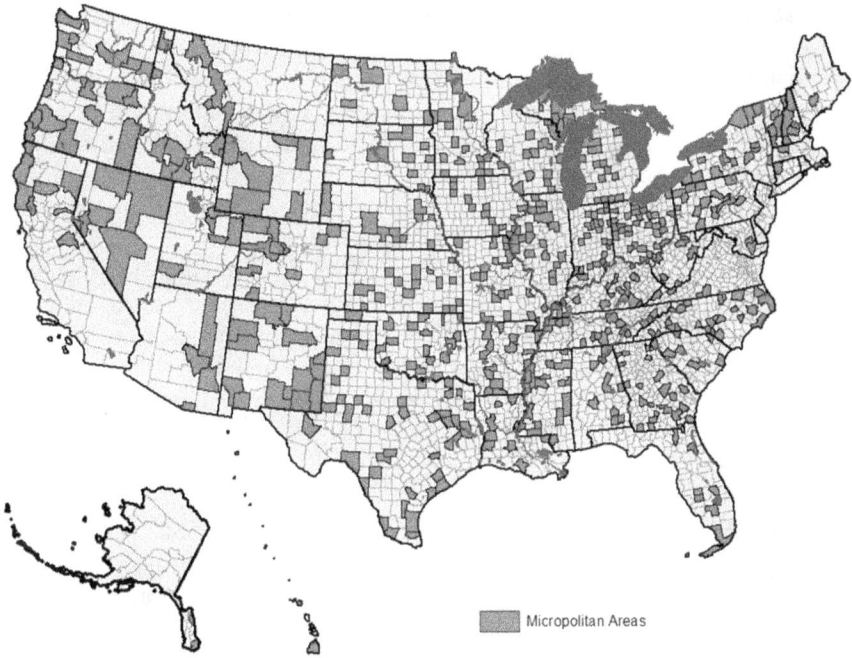

SOURCE: Cordes and Fannin (2015).

Of 3,142 counties in the United States, the 37 percent (1,167 counties) in the 382 metropolitan statistical areas contain about 85 percent of the U.S. population. The 21 percent of counties (658 counties) in the 551 micropolitan statistical areas contain about 9 percent of the population. The remaining 6 percent of the population live in the 1,317 counties that are "noncore nonmetropolitan counties," what we call "rural" (OMB 2015).

Some micropolitan counties are located at the far edges of metropolitan areas, while others serve as midsize urban hubs for sparsely settled nonmetropolitan areas. Figure 2 identifies the current micropolitan counties in the United States.[8] Micropolitan areas recognize the boundary shifting in nonmetropolitan space, by drawing new boundaries within nonmetropolitan areas that separate counties with small and midsized cities of 10,000 to 50,000 people (plus adjacent counties with strong commuting ties) from counties with no town of 10,000 people or more. By drawing new lines, micropolitan areas, in a sense, convert the blurred line between large urban centers and small towns into a transition zone between metro and noncore counties.

Micropolitan areas provide some of the economic functions of cities for the towns and open country in their hinterlands, and they provide some of the natural resources and amenities of rural places for the metropolitan centers. There is extensive interdependency and interconnectedness across this entire landscape.

People in the nation's remote towns and villages depend on the largest cities to provide them with global news, manufactured products, and a variety of other goods and services. Businesses in these rural towns often also depend on more proximate intermediate-size micropolitan areas for production inputs and consumer items. Conversely, people in the large metropolitan concentrations depend on the micropolitan and noncore areas to provide them with food, energy, water, many recreational opportunities, environmental and ecosystem services such as carbon sinks/sequestration, and much more. Globalization and technological advances in communication, transportation, and production have altered these geographic interdependencies and will continue to shape, blur, and shift the boundaries (Weber and Freshwater 2016).

Since we seek to explore the extent to which micropolitan areas create a unique environment supporting upward mobility, we use the metropolitan and micropolitan definitions for the year 2000. This enables us to represent more closely the geography where the children lived when they were teenagers and it is consistent with the time period when the correlates were measured.[9]

Correlates of upward mobility

In this article, we examine six county-level social, demographic, and economic variables as potential correlates of average absolute upward mobility in U.S. counties. We obtained county-level data for four of the six variables from the Equality of Opportunity website and the U.S. Census Bureau: fraction of population that is black alone,[10] fraction of workers with less than a 15 minute commute, Gini coefficient for parent family income within county using parents in core sample, and the fraction of households that are female-headed with children.[11] We use the county-level social capital index for 1990 developed by Rupasingha, Goetz, and Freshwater (2006) as our social capital variable.[12] We obtained the data from Northeast Center for Rural Development,[13] which indicates that the social capital index for 1990 was created using principal components analysis. The variables used in the principal components analysis are: total associations per 10,000 people; number of not-for-profit organizations per 10,000 people; census mail response rate for 1990; and votes cast for president in 1988 divided by total population of age 18 and over in 1990. We obtained our human capital variable "fraction of adults without a high school degree" from the U.S. census. Table 1 contains the list of variables that we examine and the data sources for each of the variables.

Each of these variables may affect upward mobility by either reducing opportunity for parents or children or by creating barriers to success in work or community environments. In communities with large shares of African Americans, discrimination in school and work can reduce opportunities for learning and earnings. Low commuting times imply a better spatial match between jobs and workers, which can reduce family expenses and stress and enhance skills of children by increasing the opportunities for parent-child interaction. Income inequality may lead to unequal investments in young people and create barriers to upward mobility. A larger share of the population with low education may signal

TABLE 1
Variable Definitions and Data Sources

Variable Name	Description	Data Source
Absolute mobility	Absolute upward mobility	Equality-of-Opportunty.org website
Fraction black alone	Fraction of the population that is black alone	U. S. Census Bureau, 2000 Decennial Census
Fraction with short commute (< 15 minutes)	Fraction of workers commuting less than 15 minutes from residence to place of work	U.S. Census Bureau, 2000 Decennial Census
Gini index	Gini coefficient for parent family income within county using parents in core sample	Equality-of-Opportunty.org website
Fraction of adults < HS diploma	Fraction of adults age 25 and over without a high school degree	U.S. Census Bureau, 2000 Decennial Census
Social capital index	Social capital index (1990 base) developed by Rupasingha, Goetz, and Freshwater (2006)	Northeast Regional Center for Rural Development website
Fraction single mother households	Fraction of households that are female headed with children under 18 years of age	U.S. Census Bureau, 2000 Decennial Census

an environment in which formal education is less valued, and it may lead to less support for schools and higher education, which could lower upward mobility. Social capital in a county may provide personal, social, and community linkages that increase upward mobility. A high share of female-headed households in a county may reduce the average investments parents can make in their children. As Chetty et al. (2014) point out, these variables are community characteristics and operate at the place level not just the individual level. A high negative correlation between the share of female-headed households in a county and upward mobility, for example, characterizes an environment affecting all children in the county, not just the children in the female-headed households.

Table 2 contains the descriptive statistics for the variables used in this analysis. Noncore counties have the lowest scores on variables that are expected to be negatively related to upward mobility, and with one exception (fraction with short commute), the highest scores on variables expected to be positively correlated with upward mobility. The mean values for micropolitan counties of each of these variables falls between the values for metropolitan and noncore counties, except in two cases. For the fraction of single-mother families, the mean value for micropolitan counties is slightly greater than the value for metropolitan counties. For

TABLE 2
Descriptive Statistics: Absolute Mobility and Its Correlates

Variable		Metropolitan County N = 1,061	Micropolitan County N = 644	Rural (Noncore) County N = 1042
Absolute mobility	Mean	42.14	43.00	45.08
	(Std Dev)	(4.39)	(5.08)	(6.17)
Fraction black alone	Mean	.1052	.0903	.0878
	(Std Dev)	(.1361)	(.1480)	(.1607)
Fraction with short commute	Mean	.3076	.4417	.4366
(< 15 minutes)	(Std Dev)	(.0910)	(.1123)	(.1272)
Gini index	Mean	.3975	.3876	.3681
	(Std Dev)	(.0936)	(.0810)	(.0783)
Fraction of adults < HS	Mean	.1976	.2295	.2555
diploma	(Std Dev)	(.0745)	(.0836)	(.0900)
Social capital index	Mean	−.3539	−.0615	.1060
	(Std Dev)	(1.1066)	(1.2494)	(1.3460)
Fraction single mother	Mean	.0926	.0934	.0842
households	(Std Dev)	(.0319)	(.0316)	(.0347)

the fraction with short commutes, the mean value for micropolitan counties is slightly larger than for noncore counties.

Correlation and regression analysis

Our analysis explores the extent to which the factors associated with upward mobility in micropolitan counties are different from those associated with mobility in metro and noncore counties. We examine how the size and strength of the correlations between mobility and six local social and economic characteristics differ across metropolitan, micropolitan, and noncore counties. We first explore the simple correlations between mobility and each of the correlates. Our correlation coefficient estimates are the standardized regression coefficients from unweighted univariate ordinary least squares (OLS) regressions of absolute mobility on the selected local socioeconomic correlates, normalizing all variables to have a mean of zero and a standard deviation of one.

Variables with the largest simple correlation coefficients may not be the most important factors affecting upward mobility. We consider the possibility that these socioeconomic variables may be correlated with one another and interact in ways that affect their overall predictive power. Using multiple regression analysis, we seek to understand which variables are the strongest predictors of absolute upward mobility in metropolitan, micropolitan, and noncore counties, controlling for other covariates. We run an OLS regression in which dependent and independent variables are normalized to have a mean of zero and a standard deviation of one. Our research strategy for exploring the extent to which the predictors of upward mobility are different in metropolitan, micropolitan, and noncore areas is to analyze all the data in a single regression model and introduce categorical (dummy) variables for metropolitan and for noncore counties, with micropolitan counties as the omitted category. By assessing the statistical significance of the categorical variables we can discover whether there are significant differences in expected mobility between micropolitan counties and metropolitan and noncore counties, controlling for the other covariates, and capture any unmeasured characteristics of each type of county that may be affecting upward mobility of low-income youth. And by interacting the metropolitan and noncore dummy variables with each of the correlates, we can discover whether the associations between each of these correlates and upward mobility differ across county type.

Results

Absolute upward mobility across metro/micro/noncore counties

Prior research has shown that nonmetropolitan areas have been more successful on average than metropolitan areas in generating upward mobility for low-income children. As shown in Table 2, the mean value of absolute upward mobility is lowest in metropolitan counties, higher in micropolitan counties, and highest in the noncore nonmetropolitan counties. A *t*-test for equivalence of means shows that the mean values of absolute mobility in metropolitan, micropolitan, and noncore counties are all statistically different from each other. Micropolitan areas appear to be a unique boundary-spanning environment for upward mobility on the rural-urban interface.

Correlates of absolute upward mobility across metro/micro/noncore counties

Our analysis explores the extent to which the factors that contribute to upward mobility in micropolitan counties are different from those that contribute to mobility in metro and noncore counties. Table 3 reports the simple correlations of upward mobility with each of the six correlates identified in Table 2.

Counties with high shares of black population have low upward mobility. The largest simple correlation in Table 3 is between race and upward mobility. For noncore counties, the simple correlation is –.884; and for metro and micro counties, it is –.628 and –.612, respectively. Counties with large shares of single-mother families also have low upward mobility. The simple correlation between the fraction of single mothers and upward mobility is also very strong ranging from a low of –.608 for micropolitan counties to –.653 for noncore counties.

For metro counties, the third strongest correlation (–.548) is with inequality, as measured by the Gini coefficient. This suggests a type of Great Gatsby curve relationship, in which counties with high inequality also tend to have low upward mobility. For micropolitan and noncore counties, the third strongest correlation is with the social capital index, consistent with the notion that social capital is

TABLE 3
Correlates of Absolute Upward Mobility: Unweighted Standardized Correlations of
Upward Mobility with Selected Variables

Local Characteristic	Metropolitan County $N = 1,061$	Micropolitan County $N = 644$	Noncore County $N = 1,042$
Fraction black alone	−.628	−.612	−.884
Fraction with short commute (< 15 minutes)	.176	.485	.530
Gini index	−.508	−.525	−.506
Fraction of adults < HS diploma	−.396	−.466	−.563
Social capital index	.409	.530	.644
Fraction of children with single mother	−.624	−.608	−.653

generally stronger in nonmetropolitan places and that it is more powerful in producing good social and economic outcomes.

As noted in the previous section, simple correlations may not reveal the complex interactions of variables associated with upward mobility. Thus, we use OLS multiple regression on the county-level data to explore which of these factors are the strongest predictors of absolute upward mobility, controlling for the other factors.

Table 4 reports the coefficients and standard errors from the baseline model and a model that adds a set of variables to capture any interactions between race and single-mother households. In the baseline model, we include standardized covariates for all six of the correlates in Table 1 and include dummy variables for metro and noncore counties as well as interaction terms between each of the correlates and each of the county type dummy variables. The dependent variable in the OLS regressions for both models is the county-level measure of "absolute upward mobility" from the Equality of Opportunity website. As in the simple regressions that produced the correlation coefficients reported above, all the continuous variables are normalized to have a mean of zero and a standard deviation of one.

Because the micropolitan counties are the omitted category for the dummy variables, the coefficients reported for each of the correlates captures the relationship of that correlate to upward mobility in micropolitan counties. Significant coefficients for the interaction terms between the metro and noncore dummy variables and each of the correlates indicate that the relationship between the correlate and upward mobility is different for metro or noncore counties.

The R^2 reported in Table 4 suggests that the baseline model of six correlates and their interactions with metro and noncore county types explains about two-thirds of the variation in upward mobility across U.S. counties.

Other things equal, expected upward mobility is greater in both noncore and metro counties than in micropolitan counties. The coefficients on the county type

TABLE 4
OLS Regression Results: Correlates of Intergenerational Mobility

	Baseline Model	Interaction Model
	Coefficient (Standard Error)	Coefficient (Standard Error)
Fraction black	.061	−.085
	(.040)	(.055)
Interaction of fraction black × metro	−.231°°°	−.239°°°
	(.058)	(.067)
Interaction of fraction black × noncore	−.041	−.047
	(.055)	(.064)
Fraction single mother	−.486°°°	−.547°°°
	(.049)	(.050)
Interaction of fraction single mother × metro	.212°°°	.192°°°
	(.060)	(.060)
Interaction of fraction single mother × noncore	−.019	.008
	(.057)	(.057)
Interaction of fraction black × fraction single mother		.086°°°
		(.017)
Interaction of fraction black × fraction single mother × metro		.031
		(.023)
Interaction of fraction black × fraction single mother × noncore		.009
		(.021)
Fraction with short commute	.450°°°	.443°°°
	(.032)	(0.031)
Interaction of fraction with short commute × metro	−.350°°°	−.327°°°
	(.043)	(.042)
Interaction of fraction with short commute × noncore	−.084°°	−.085°°
	(.039)	(.038)
Gini index	−.209°°°	−.180°°°
	(.031)	(.031)
Interaction of Gini index × metro	.088°°	.090°°
	(.037)	(.037)
Interaction of Gini index × noncore	−.002	−.017
	(.039)	(.038)
Fraction of adults < HS diploma	.026	.030
	(.032)	(.031)
Interaction of fraction of adults < HS diploma × metro	−.129°°°	−.142°°°
	(.041)	(.040)
Interaction of fraction of adults < HS diploma × noncore	.007	.006
	(.041)	(.040)
Social capital index	.115°°°	.091°°°
	(.031)	(.031)
Interaction of social capital index × metro	.019	.003
	(.041)	(.040)
Interaction of social capital index × noncore	.143°°°	.140°°°
	(.040)	(.039)
Metro	.079°°	.075°
	(.038)	(.040)
Noncore	.194°°°	.171°°°
	(.036)	(.039)
Constant	−.211°°°	−.275°°°
	(.026)	(.029)
Number of Observations	2,747	2,747
Adjusted R^2	.652	.671

°p < .10. °°p < .05. °°°p <.01.

dummy variables indicate that, relative to growing up in a micropolitan county, growing up in a noncore county is associated with a 0.2 standard deviation higher upward mobility score, and being raised in metro counties is associated with a 0.1 standard deviation increase in mobility.

For micropolitan counties (the omitted category for the county type dummy), all of the correlates, except the human capital and percent black variables, are significant at the .01 level. The strongest predictors of upward mobility in micropolitan counties are the fraction of single-mother households and the fraction of workers with less than a 15 minute commute. The fraction of single-mother households in the county is very strongly and negatively related to the upward mobility of low-income children, and short commutes for workers are strongly and positively related. High levels of income inequality are also negatively correlated with upward mobility, but higher levels of social capital are positively associated with mobility.

In this baseline model, the fraction of single mothers is very highly correlated with upward mobility in micropolitan and noncore counties. Other things equal, a one standard deviation higher fraction of single mothers in micropolitan counties is associated with a –.486 lower upward mobility score, and the relationship is not statistically different in noncore counties. The share of single mothers has a much smaller negative effect in metropolitan counties: a one standard deviation increase in the fraction of single mothers is associated with only a .274 lower level of upward mobility. (The F-test of the null hypothesis that the sum of the coefficients for the various correlates and interaction terms is equal to zero is rejected at the .001 level of significance for all the results reported below, except as otherwise noted.[14]) A greater set of work support systems in metropolitan areas might be one of the possible reasons why the fraction of single mothers is less negatively related to mobility in metro counties.

The prevalence of short commuting times, which is so strongly and positively related to upward mobility in micropolitan areas, is not so strongly related in either noncore or metro areas. Short commutes appear to have a stronger association with upward mobility in micropolitan areas than in other types of counties. Whereas a one standard deviation increase in short commutes increases mobility by 0.450 standard deviations in micro areas, the same increase in noncore counties is associated with a 0.366 (0.450 – 0.084) standard deviation increase in mobility. In metro areas, it is associated with only a 0.100 (0.450 – 0.350) standard deviation increase. The link between mobility and short commute times for parents may operate through the level and quality of work supports for families or through the amount of time that parents who do not have long commutes have for community or family or home-related activity.

Inequality, as measured by the Gini index, is higher in metropolitan counties than in micropolitan or noncore counties, but the association between inequality and upward mobility is almost twice as strong in the nonmetropolitan counties as it is in metro counties. For micropolitan counties, a one standard deviation higher level of inequality is associated with a 0.209 standard deviation lower level of upward mobility, and the relationship is not statistically different in noncore counties. For metropolitan counties, however, a one standard deviation higher level of inequality is associated with a 0.121 standard deviation lower level of upward mobility.

Social capital is strongest and most strongly related to upward mobility in noncore counties. The link between social capital and upward mobility is significantly larger for noncore counties than for micropolitan counties. In the baseline model, a one standard deviation higher level of social capital in micropolitan areas is associated with a 0.115 standard deviation higher average level of upward mobility of low-income youth. In noncore counties, however, a one standard deviation higher value of the social capital index is associated with a 0.258 (0.115 + 0.143) standard deviation higher level of upward mobility. This stronger relationship of upward mobility with social capital is consistent with the perception that the social networks and organizations in rural communities benefit young people growing up in these communities. The relationship is not significantly different for metro counties relative to micro counties.

Low human capital (as measured by the fraction of adults without a high school diploma) does not appear to be associated with upward mobility of low-income youth in micropolitan and noncore counties, but it is associated with lower upward mobility in metro counties. This may be related to the historical industrial structure of metro and nonmetro areas and the educational requirements of the basic industries in metro and nonmetro areas.

The fraction black has no significant association with upward mobility in either micropolitan or noncore counties. The coefficient on the fraction black variable is insignificant, suggesting no relationship in micropolitan counties. The joint test of significance for the fraction black variable combined with the interaction of the fraction black variable and the noncore county dummy suggests that there is also no significant relationship between the fraction black population and upward mobility in noncore counties. In metropolitan counties, however, there is a negative relationship between the fraction black and upward mobility. The coefficients for the fraction black and interaction of fraction black × metro variables suggest that for a one standard deviation increase in the fraction black variable, there is a –0.170 standard deviation decrease (0.061 – 0.231) in upward mobility of children from households originating in metropolitan counties.

Untangling the roles of single-mother families and race

In their analysis of upward mobility, Chetty et al. (2014) found that "the correlation of upward mobility with black shares is slightly *positive* and statistically significant when we include controls for all five explanatory factors"[15] (p. 1619). This finding and some other analyses in their article led them to conclude that "these results support the view that the strong correlation of upward mobility with race operates through channels beyond the direct effect of race on mobility" (p. 1619). Given the strong simple correlation between race and mobility, some have questioned whether their analysis is capturing the complexities of the relationship between race and mobility. And given the strong correlation between race and fraction single mothers ($r = .76$) within the counties, it seems important to better untangle the relationship among race, single-mother fraction, and mobility.

We explore the roles of single-mother families and race by introducing variables indicating metropolitan/noncore status and an interaction term between fraction black and fraction single mother. The results for the interaction model in the final column of Table 4 provide further evidence of a strong negative association between fraction black and upward mobility in metropolitan counties. They also provide new evidence about a strong interaction between fraction black and single-mother families across all county types. The results from the interaction model for the other correlates (short commutes, inequality, human capital, and social capital) are very similar to the baseline results, so we do not discuss these further. We discuss the new results only for the fraction black, fraction single mother, and their interaction.

In both our baseline and interaction models, there is no significant relationship between percent black and upward mobility for micropolitan areas, although, in metro areas, the association is significant and negative. For micropolitan counties, in the interaction model, the fraction black coefficient is −.085, the fraction single mother is −.547, and the interaction term (fraction black × fraction single mother) is .086. This positive interaction term indicates that higher levels of either factor blunt the negative effects of the other factor on mobility. In micropolitan counties with one standard deviation higher fraction black residents, the marginal effect of higher single mothers estimated in the interaction model is reduced by about 16 percent from the estimate in the baseline model (to −.461). In micropolitan counties with one standard deviation higher levels of single mothers, the marginal impact of higher fraction black residents is not different than zero (.001) as the combined interaction term value of .086 offsets the coefficient on fraction black of .085. This suggests that there is little impact of additional black populations on upward mobility in micropolitan counties with high fractions of single mothers.

For noncore counties, the relationships are similar. For noncore counties with large black populations (one standard deviation above the mean), the marginal effect of a one standard deviation greater level of single mothers is −.444, an 18 percent reduction from the effect estimated in the baseline model. For noncore counties with large single mother populations (one standard deviation above the mean), the estimated marginal effect of one standard deviation greater black population is reduced by 72 percent from the estimate in the baseline model and is not statistically different than zero.

In metropolitan counties the reduction in the marginal effect of additional black populations in the presence of large single-mother fractions is smaller, and the marginal effect of additional single-mother populations in the presence of high fractions of black populations is greater. This is because the negative effect of black populations on upward mobility is greater in metropolitan areas than in micropolitan areas, and the negative effect of single-mother populations on upward mobility is less in metro areas than in micropolitan areas. The coefficient for fraction black in metro counties is −.324 (−.085 + −.239), and for fraction single mothers it is −.355 (−.547 + .192). The coefficient for the black × single-mother interaction term is .117 (.086 + .031). In metropolitan counties with one standard deviation higher fraction black, the marginal effect of a one standard deviation higher proportion of single mothers is −.238, a reduction of 33 percent.

In metropolitan counties with one standard deviation higher levels of single mothers, the marginal impact of higher fraction black residents, is −.207, a reduction of 36 percent.

Our overall conclusion from the exploration of the association of race and family structure with upward mobility is that the relationship depends on both metropolitan status and the interaction between fraction black and fraction single-mother family. In metropolitan counties, both fraction black and fraction single mother are strongly and negatively associated with upward mobility, whereas in both nonmetropolitan categories, the single-mother fraction is negatively associated with upward mobility but the fraction black is not, ceteris paribus. In all county types, however, the size of the association of both fraction black and fraction single-mother families with upward mobility depends on the level of each variable. Where high concentrations of both blacks and single mothers are found together, their interaction can offset the negative individual relationship with mobility for both variables. These new findings about differences across the rural-urban interface in the relationship of race and mobility and about the interaction of race and single-mother families provide impetus for a continued reexamination of the role of race and channels of influence of race in the analysis of upward mobility.

The analysis of intergenerational upward mobility in this article has some clear limitations. The analysis explores correlations and is not a test of a causal model. All of the variables in the model are endogenous. The analysis is based on variables that were available and there are certainly omitted variables whose omission may be biasing the coefficients of included variables. As noted above, there may also be a systematic sample bias in that most of the missing observations are for noncore counties. The analysis is also only for a single age cohort, and the conclusions drawn from this analysis may not hold for those in more recent cohorts. Nonetheless, patterns observed in different types of counties do indicate that different processes seem to be at work in different places, and these appear to be systematically related to the size and density of the population and commuting links that determine where a county fits in the metro/micro/noncore classification.

It also is important to emphasize that the data we have used in our analysis do not reveal where the young adults are living in 2011–2012. We do not know what proportion of young adults who achieved upward mobility have migrated from noncore to micro or to metro counties and what proportion have attained upward mobility by staying in noncore counties. We do not know what proportion of young adults attain upward mobility by migrating from metro or micro counties to one of the other two county types. Answers to these questions might attenuate or enhance the significance placed on the community characteristics where the young adults were living when they were children.

Conclusion

We have explored the hypothesis that micropolitan areas can play a unique role in the geography of economic and social development in the new rural-urban interface. We examined this by exploring the geography of intergenerational mobility through a core-based statistical area lens in which micropolitan counties serve as cores of nonmetropolitan America and transition zones between remote noncore rural counties and metropolitan America.

Based on the results of the final interaction model in Table 4, we can draw some preliminary conclusions about how micropolitan counties might constitute a unique geography in the rural-urban interface. In some ways, micropolitan counties appear to function much like metropolitan areas in their support of upward mobility, revealing a blurred border between metro and micro areas and a bright boundary between the noncore and the metro and micro counties. Social capital, for example, is positively associated with upward mobility in all types of counties, but the association is more than twice as large in noncore counties than it is in micropolitan and metropolitan counties. To the extent that social capital relies on strong networks and social ties, metropolitan and micropolitan counties may be sufficiently large that the social capital does not work as effectively as in noncore counties to provide support for low-income youth.

In other domains, micropolitan counties appear to function more like noncore areas and the bright boundaries are between metro and nonmetro (micro/noncore) counties (the blurred boundaries are between micro and noncore). The relationships between upward mobility and fraction black, fraction single mother, inequality, and educational attainment are significantly different in metro counties than in nonmetro (micro and noncore) counties. Growing up in a county with large fractions of single mothers is strongly associated with low economic mobility for low-income youth, but this relationship is much weaker in metro counties than in nonmetro counties. Growing up in a county with large fractions of blacks, however, is associated with worse upward mobility outcomes, but only if that county is metro. And the size of the relationship in all counties depends on the levels of both fraction black and fraction single mother. Lack of education is also more detrimental in metro areas than in either nonmetropolitan category. The negative relationship between a large fraction of adults without a high school diploma and upward mobility of low-income youth is larger in metro counties than in nonmetro counties. On the other hand, increased income inequality appears to be less detrimental to upward mobility in metro counties compared to micro and noncore counties. The social structures and economic structures of nonmetropolitan counties may present barriers to upward mobility that are not found in the more populous and technologically intensive urban environments.

But there are also domains in which micropolitan counties appear to function very differently from both metropolitan and noncore counties, in which there is a fairly bright border between micropolitan counties and both metropolitan and noncore counties. Micropolitan counties, for example, have the largest fraction of short commutes. And these short commutes are very strongly and positively associated with upward mobility of low-income youth. The associations between short commutes and upward mobility are significantly smaller for both noncore counties and for metropolitan counties. The additional time and resources associated with short commutes may be more effectively leveraged for the benefit of youth in micropolitan counties. There may be sufficiently higher density and scale in micro counties relative to noncore counties to permit the development of supportive activities and sufficiently lower congestion costs relative to metro counties to permit more efficient use of the supporting structures.

Micropolitan areas appear to play a unique role in the geography of intergenerational economic mobility. As small and medium urban centers, they help to define the blurred boundaries of the new rural-urban interface. In some domains, micropolitan counties serve as small urban cores in nonmetropolitan America, supporting upward mobility in ways that take advantage of their density and scale. In other domains, they are relatively low-density transition zones between remote noncore rural counties and metropolitan America, supporting upward mobility of low-income youth in ways that both exploit the opportunities and reveal weaknesses associated with small size, lack of density, and limited technological capacity in nonmetropolitan communities. We conclude that micropolitan areas do have a unique and potentially powerful role in supporting the upward mobility of low-income youth. While the relationships uncovered in this article are not necessarily causal, they are suggestive of underlying determinants that can be examined in future research.

Notes

1. Intergenerational economic mobility can be measured in terms of earnings, income, and wealth. As noted below, economic mobility can be conceptualized as absolute or relative. And mobility can be upward or downward. This article focuses on absolute upward income mobility, and except as otherwise noted, we use the terms absolute upward mobility, absolute mobility, economic mobility, income mobility, and upward mobility interchangeably.

2. Though they develop county-level mobility estimates, their analysis uses commuting zone data.

3. See http://www.equality-of-opportunity.org/index.php/data.

4. This absolute income mobility measure can be constructed to estimate mobility at any percentile of the parent income distribution. It is derived from the "rank-rank slope" measure of relative income mobility used by Chetty et al. (2014): the "slope from the OLS regression of child [income] rank on parent [income] rank." Larger values for this slope indicate that child rank is closer to parent rank, so higher values of the slope indicate lower economic mobility and a more rigid class structure. Since our interest is in the upward mobility of low-income youth, we examine only the absolute mobility measure estimated at the 25th percentile of the parents' income distribution. See Chetty et al. for more detail about the derivation of these measures.

5. See https://www.whitehouse.gov/sites/default/files/omb/fedreg/msa.html.

6. This definition continues to be used to identify metropolitan areas.

7. See http://www.census.gov/population/metro/about/.

8. For those wishing to see a map of both metropolitan and micropolitan areas to understand the geographic proximity of micropolitan to metropolitan counties, see the map of current metropolitan and micropolitan areas on the U.S. Census website: https://www.census.gov/population/metro/fil2013.pdfes/metro_micro_Feb2012.pdf.

9. Since the counties are sorted into categories based on their 2000 metro, micro, and noncore status, counties that would have been noncore in 1970 if those categories had existed, and then grew into the next larger category in subsequent decades, are not included in the 2000 noncore counties. Counties that would have been micro counties include the noncore counties that grew into micro counties and exclude the micro counties that grew into metro counties.

10. The 2000 U.S. Census allowed respondents to self-identify either as being of one race alone, or as being of two or more races. The fraction black variable that we use is the fraction who reported their race as black alone.

11. Chetty et al. (2014) identify this variable as the "fraction of children being raised by single mothers." In the online data Table IX available on the Equality of Opportunity website, they define the variable as the "number of single female households with children divided by total number of households with children."

12. This is consistent with the analysis done by Chetty et al. (2014).

13. See http://aese.psu.edu/nercrd/community/social-capital-resources/social-capital-variables-for-1990-1997-and-2005.

14. Results available on request from the authors.

15. Three of the five explanatory factors in Chetty et al. (2014) were the same variables as in our analysis and similar to our variables for the other two: "the fraction of working individuals who commute less than 15 minutes to work (segregation), the bottom 99% Gini coefficient (inequality), high school dropout rates adjusted for income differences (school quality), the social capital index, and the fraction of children with single parents (family structure)" (p. 1617). Their regression model did not include an interaction between fraction black and fraction single mother or control for metropolitan and micropolitan status.

References

Aaronson, Daniel, and Bhashkar Mazumder. 2008. Intergenerational economic mobility in the U.S., 1940 to 2000. *Journal of Human Resources* 43 (1): 138–72.

Auten, Gerald, and Geoffrey Gee. 2009. Income mobility in the United States: New evidence from income tax data. *National Tax Journal* 62 (2): 301–28.

Chetty, Raj, Nathaniel Hendren, Patrick Kline, and Emmanuel Saez. 2014. Where is the land of opportunity? The geography of intergenerational mobility in the United States. *Quarterly Journal of Economics* 129 (4): 1553–1623.

Corak, Miles. 2013. Income inequality, equality of opportunity, and intergenerational mobility. *Journal of Economic Perspectives* 27 (3): 79–102.

Cordes, Sam M., and J. Matthew Fannin. 2015. *Micropolitan America: A new and critical part of the nation's geography*. Rural Policy Research Institute Policy Brief. Columbia, MO: Rural Policy Research Institute.

Lichter, Daniel T., and David L. Brown. 2011. Rural America in an urban society: Changing spatial and social boundaries. *Annual Review of Sociology* 37:565–92.

Office of Management and Budget (OMB), Executive Office of the President. 2015. *Revised delineations of metropolitan statistical areas, micropolitan statistical areas, and combined statistical areas, and guidance on uses of the delineations of these areas*. OMB Bulletin No. 15-01. Washington, DC: OMB.

Rupasingha, Anil, Stephan J. Goetz, and David Freshwater. 2006. The production of social capital in U.S. counties. *Journal of Socio-Economics* 35:83–101.

Weber, Bruce A., and David Freshwater. 2016. The death of distance? Networks, the costs of distance and urban-rural interdependence. In *International handbook of rural studies*, eds. Mark Shucksmith and David L. Brown, 154–64. New York, NY: Taylor and Francis.

Long-Term Trends in Rural and Urban Poverty: New Insights Using a Historical Supplemental Poverty Measure

By
LAURA B. NOLAN,
JANE WALDFOGEL,
and
CHRISTOPHER WIMER

Poverty has a strong relationship to geography in the United States. Previous research has found that rural areas have higher average poverty rates than urban areas, but the new supplemental poverty measure (SPM) has shown in recent years that urban areas have higher average poverty. In this article, we analyze poverty trends from 1967 to 2014 in rural and urban America, using the improved SPM metrics. We find a dramatic decline in poverty in rural areas, and also show that the geographic adjustment of the poverty threshold in the SPM (which lowers poverty thresholds in less expensive areas and raises them in more expensive areas) is an important explanatory factor. We also find that changes in the demographic and economic characteristics of rural and urban residents help to explain the decline. Last, we investigate whether migration of the poor between rural and urban areas helps to account for differential poverty trends, but we find little evidence in support of that hypothesis.

Keywords: rural-urban poverty; inequality; demographic change; economic well-being

The United States has steadily become more urban over time, and rural and urban areas have become more integrated than they were in the past (Schaeffer, Loveridge, and Weiler

Laura B. Nolan is a demographer and a health researcher at Mathematica Policy Research. Her work focuses on the measurement of latent constructs such as poverty and health and the impact of social policy on vulnerable populations, particularly children. Her work has been published in Social Science & Medicine, Survey Research Methods, *and the* Journal of Economic and Social Measurement.

Jane Waldfogel is Compton Foundation Centennial Professor for the Prevention of Children and Youth Problems at the Columbia University School of Social Work and codirector of the Columbia Population Research Center. She has written extensively on the impact of public policies on poverty, inequality, and child and family well-being as well as paid family leave and inequality in achievement.

Correspondence: LNolan@mathematica-mpr.com

DOI: 10.1177/0002716217713174

2014). While the number of rural residents in the United States has hovered between 50 and 60 million since the early twentieth century, rural people and places have often been overlooked and even ignored in the scholarly literature and public policy discourse (Lichter and Brown 2011). It is not possible, however, to understand important aspects of American life, including the nation's political and economic systems, ongoing demographic trends, and economic hardship, without reliable information on the economic well-being of both rural and urban residents (Castle, Wu, and Weber 2011). This also holds true for the study of poverty—an important indicator of economic well-being.

Poverty has a strong geographic dimension in the United States (Glaeser, Kahn, and Rappaport 2008). Previous research on the geographic distribution of poverty in the United States has found higher poverty rates in rural versus urban areas (Albrecht and Albrecht 2000). But rural poverty is often not a focus of study (Gurley 2016); the vast majority of poverty studies either discuss national trends (e.g., Fox et al. 2015) or delve into the plight of the inner-city poor (e.g., Wilson 1987, 1996; Massey and Denton 1993). Rural sociology, however, has a strong tradition of research on poverty, particularly long-term poverty, historically poor areas, and concentrated poverty (Lobao 2004; Swanstrom, Dreier, and Mollenkopf 2002; Snyder and McLaughlin 2004). The Rural Sociological Society Task Force on Persistent Rural Poverty moved this research agenda forward in 1993 with their report, *Persistent Poverty in Rural America*.

This smaller body of literature that focuses on rural poverty finds that America's rural poor have some unique challenges, such as lack of transportation, affordable daycare, and other social services such as job training (Lichter and Brown 2011). But the economic well-being of the rural and urban United States should not be investigated in isolation; their increasing spatial and economic dependence requires a global approach. While some studies have investigated the migration of the poor between rural and urban areas (Foulkes and Schafft 2010), a comprehensive evaluation of trends in poverty in rural and urban areas has not previously been undertaken.

A second limitation of research on geographic variation in poverty is its use of the official poverty measure (OPM), which was developed in the 1960s and has

Chris Wimer is codirector of the Center on Poverty and Social Policy at Columbia University. He conducts research on the measurement of poverty and disadvantage both locally and nationally, as well as historical trends in poverty and the impacts of social policies on the poverty rate. His research also investigates how families cope with poverty and insecurity and the role of government policies and programs to reduce disadvantage.

NOTE: We thank Liana Fox for her work on the SPM time series. We also thank Jim Ziliak, Dan Lichter, our anonymous reviewers, and the participants of the Urban-Rural Interface conference for their comments and suggestions. This work was supported by the Annie E. Casey Foundation and the JPB Foundation. This work was also supported by the Columbia Population Research Center, which receives funding from the Eunice Kennedy Shriver National Institute of Child Health & Human Development of the National Institutes of Health under award number P2CHD058486.

remained largely unchanged since then (Citro and Michael 1995). In 1995, a panel of the National Academy of Sciences (NAS) recommended that a new measure of poverty be developed in the United States, which eventually led to the creation of the supplemental poverty measure (SPM). The SPM improves upon the OPM by taking into account posttax income, in-kind benefits, and non-discretionary expenses such as out-of-pocket medical expenditures and work/child care expenses, and defines the household unit more broadly to include cohabiters and unrelated children living in the home. A further advantage of the SPM is that it adjusts the poverty thresholds of households according to their geographic location—that is, it accounts for relative cost of living in a given area, compared to the national average. These adjustments in the SPM do not change the poverty threshold of the nation on the whole but become very important when investigating poverty in rural versus urban areas (Zimmerman, Ham, and Frank 2008).

The decision to geographically adjust poverty thresholds is not without controversy. Some have argued against adjusting poverty thresholds for price differences because they believe these differences will be offset by income differences—employers in more expensive areas will need to pay their employees more to keep them. Another argument against geographic adjustment is that people can move to better (i.e., less expensive) areas if they so desire (Roback 1982). A final argument is that cost of living reflects quality of life, with higher-cost areas reflecting "indirect purchases of non-market amenities" like proximity to the beach, low crime, or economic opportunity (Albouy 2011; Hirsch 2011).

In response to these critiques, the NAS panel and other experts have argued that poverty spells are often of short duration, and families cannot be expected to move each time they experience a decline in economic resources. Further, the "movement" argument may not be relevant when characterizing the economic well-being of the worst off given this population's limited mobility due to moving costs, which include removal from locally based social networks and other important sources of support (Rosenthal 2011). Both the NAS panel and a research forum convened to discuss the cost of living in the SPM (Ziliak 2011) and ultimately recommended adjusting the poverty threshold for cost of living differentials. This more nuanced, geographically adjusted measure of poverty is essential for understanding not just pretax income differentials in rural versus urban areas, but also the differential effects that taxes and transfers have on poverty reduction in those areas.

The methodological contribution of this article is to implement a geographical adjustment for cost of living in an SPM time series dating back to 1967. The time series we present here is substantially longer than has ever been presented before. The substantive contribution of this article is to reassess long-term trends in poverty in rural and urban areas. In doing so, we aim to answer the following research question: What do trends in SPM poverty in rural and urban areas look like over time, and what explains the particularly dramatic decline in poverty in rural areas since the 1960s? We find that, according to the SPM, poverty has declined dramatically in both rural and urban areas, but that the decline has been largest in rural areas, ultimately resulting in higher average poverty rates in urban areas (than in rural areas) at the end of the time series. We then explore a number of hypothesized reasons for this differential poverty decline, particularly the dramatic reduction in poverty in rural areas:

(1) changing demographic composition of rural and urban areas, i.e., "boundary blurring";
(2) differential safety net robustness in the two areas;
(3) differential cost of living (levels and trends); and
(4) differential migration (i.e., by poverty status) in/out of rural and urban areas, or "boundary crossing."

In the final section of the article, we conduct a simulation exercise to explore demographic and economic changes simultaneously. Doing so allows us to undertake the following thought experiments: what would poverty be over the course of our time series if (1) the demographic composition of rural and urban areas had stayed as they were in 1970, and (2) the economic characteristics of rural and urban areas had stayed as they were in 1970. The simulation highlights the relative importance of select demographic and economic factors in explaining the differential poverty trends in rural and urban areas.

Data and Methods

Data

We compute an SPM time series back to 1967, only a few years after Lyndon B. Johnson declared a War on Poverty. We make use of historical data from the Annual Social and Economic Supplement to the Current Population Survey (March CPS) and the Consumer Expenditure Survey (CEX) for the period 1967 to 2009. We use the Census Bureau's SPM Research Data Files for the years 2009 to 2014.

The methodology that we use to compute resources and thresholds for our SPM time series follows that used by Fox et al. (2015) and replicates as faithfully as possible the methodology used by the Census Bureau and the Bureau of Labor Statistics to calculate SPM poverty (Short 2012, 2015). Like most poverty measures, the SPM compares a household's resources to its needs, as defined by a threshold; a household whose resources fall below the relevant threshold is considered poor. Briefly, *resources* in the SPM is the sum of cash income, plus in-kind benefits that families use to meet their food, clothing, shelter, and utilities needs, minus taxes (and/or plus credits), minus work expenses and out-of-pocket medical expenses. In this article we also use *resources pre–taxes and transfers*, which is defined by the Census Bureau in the CPS as including fifteen items: earnings, interest and investment income, child support, alimony, and nongovernmental educational assistance, among others (U.S. Census Bureau 2016a).

Our methodology differs from the Census Bureau's and the Bureau of Labor Statistics' in one main respect: instead of using a poverty threshold that is recalculated over time, we use today's SPM threshold and carry it back histori-cally by adjusting it for inflation using the Consumer Price Index Research Series Using Current Methods (CPI-U-RS). Because this alternative measure is anchored with today's SPM threshold, we refer to it as an *anchored supplemental poverty measure*, or *anchored SPM* for short (Wimer et al. 2016). An advantage of an anchored SPM is that poverty trends resulting from such a measure can be explained only by changes in income and net transfer payments (cash or in kind). Trends in poverty based on a relative measure (i.e., SPM poverty), on the other hand, could be due to changes over time in thresholds. Thus, an anchored SPM arguably provides a cleaner measure of how changes in income and net transfer payments have affected poverty historically (Wimer et al. 2016). Anchoring the poverty threshold implicitly asks the question: How well were families in years past able to meet today's living standards?

A detailed description of the steps required to compute the SPM is available in the online appendix (see the online version of the article for the appendix). In brief, thresholds are set using the 2012 SPM public use research files, which are constructed by the Census Bureau and the Bureau of Labor Statistics. These thresholds are adjusted for cost of living using the average rent of a standard two-bedroom apartment, obtained from the best available data source in each year—census data from 1967 to 1984, the Department of Housing and Urban Development's Fair Market Rents (FMR) from 1985 to 2008 and the SPM Public Use Research Files from 2009 on.

The demographic variables that we use from the CPS in our analyses are for family structure (whether the head of the SPM unit is single, married, or living with a cohabiting partner), race/ethnicity (non-Hispanic white, non-Hispanic black, and Latino[1]), and age group (<18, 18–24, 25–34, 35–44, 45–54, 55–64, 65+). The economic variables that we use are employment status (all adults in the SPM unit employed full time, all adults employed at least part time, at least one adult not employed, no adults employed, no adults in unit) and percentage of full-time work (denominator is 52 and numerator is one of seven bins used in the CPS prior to 1974 when number of weeks worked started to be reported: 0, 1–13, 14–26, 27–39, 40–47, 48–49, 50 and over). Finally, we use a number of migration variables in a secondary investigation into individuals who move between rural and urban areas: we look at both urban to rural migrants as well as migrants from rural to urban areas.

The CPS data contain an indicator of metropolitan/nonmetropolitan area des-ignations. We have redefined the small proportion of "not identified" households as urban residents given the large uptick in the urban population in the mid-1980s when the "not identified" population declines to almost zero (see Figure A1 in the online appendix). We use metropolitan/nonmetropolitan as a proxy for rural/urban as Integrated Public Use Microdata Series (IPUMS) data do not contain the rural/urban indicator variable; this is standard in the rural sociology and rural economics literature. Metro/nonmetro designation—henceforth referred to as "rural/urban"—is assigned to each housing unit, and not collected from survey participants.

It is important to note that rural/urban designation is dynamic over time; many areas that were rural in 1970 transition to being urban by the end of the time series. This can be due to redesignation or being incorporated into a larger urban area. Unfortunately, the rural/urban designation in our data is operationalized at the household level—the census allocates geographic status to households by census block after the survey is completed. This precludes our ability to look at changes in specific geographic areas' status over time. Further, since the CPS is not longitudinal, we are unable to investigate whether households' geographic designation changed over time.

Method

We first present rural/urban trends in anchored SPM poverty, and compare them to trends in OPM poverty. We then investigate the four hypotheses (specified above) for why rural SPM poverty rates declined faster than urban poverty rates during our time series. Then, to assess the role of both demographic and economic factors simultaneously, we provide both nonparametric graphs as well as a parametric approach that can be characterized as a combination of standardization and simulation (and henceforth referred to as a "simulation"). In this simulation, we undertake the following thought experiments: what would anchored SPM poverty be over the course of our time series if (1) the demographic composition of rural and urban areas had stayed as they were in 1970, and (2) the economic characteristics of rural and urban areas had stayed as they were in 1970? A formal description of the methods used to undertake these thought experiments are available in the online appendix.

Results

Trends over time in rural and urban poverty

To address our first research question, we begin by presenting trends in the proportion poor in rural and urban areas using the OPM versus the SPM. When using the OPM (Figure 1, left panel), about 20 percent of rural residents are poor at the start of the time series; the corresponding proportion of urban residents is 11 percent. OPM poverty increased over time among metro residents but decreased among nonmetro residents over the course of the time series. By the end of the time series, it still remains the case that a larger percent of rural residents is poor (about 16 percent) than urban residents (about 14 percent). When using the SPM (Figure 1, right panel), more than 30 percent of rural residents are poor at the start of the time series, compared to just over 20 percent of urban residents. SPM poverty declined dramatically over time in both areas, but much more dramatically in rural areas, which by the end of the time series had a lower poverty rate than urban areas. In sum, rural/urban poverty trends are substantially different when using the OPM versus the SPM. OPM poverty rates start lower and urban areas actually become poorer over time (although not as poor as

FIGURE 1
Poverty Rates in Rural and Urban Areas

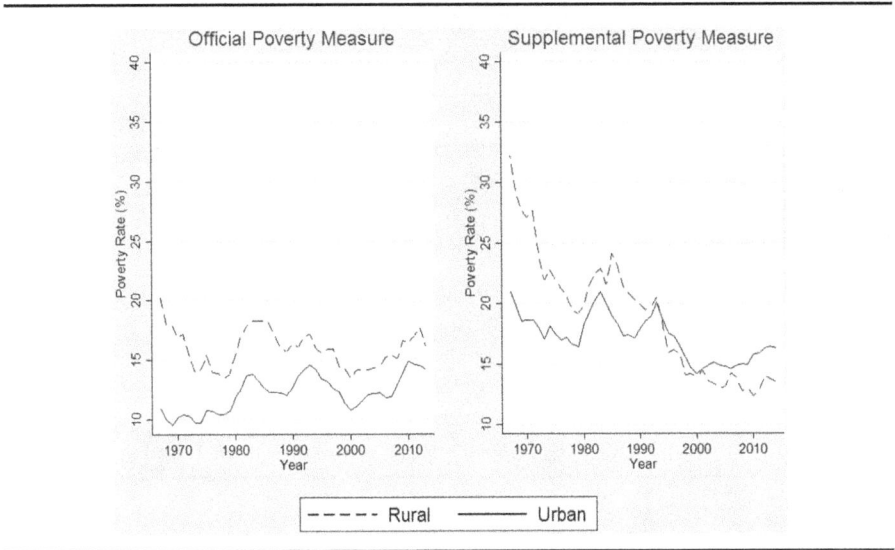

rural areas); SPM poverty rates begin the time series quite high and urban areas end the time series poorer than rural areas. We next explore possible explanations for the differential trends in SPM poverty in rural and urban areas, particularly the dramatic decline in poverty in rural areas.[2]

Explaining differential poverty trends in rural versus urban areas

What explains the dramatic decline in SPM poverty in rural areas that we see in the right-side panel of Figure 1? To address our second research question, we investigate four (among many possible) hypotheses for this differential poverty decline:

Changing demographic composition of rural and urban areas: "Boundary blurring." Changing demographic composition in rural and urban areas—or "boundary blurring"—may help to explain differential trends in SPM poverty rates in rural and urban areas as shown in Figure 1 because important subgroups of the U.S. population have very different poverty rates. If changes in the concentration of these populations in rural and urban areas depends on demographic or other characteristics that are correlated with poverty, then this process might help to explain differential poverty trends in the two areas. It is a well-known fact that there has been a substantial decline in the proportion of the population living in rural areas over the course of the time series (see Figure A4 in the online appendix).[3]

While the proportion of the U.S. population living in urban areas has increased across all demographic groups, the composition *within* urban and rural areas has

TABLE 1
Demographic Distribution in Rural and Urban Areas at the Beginning
and End of the Time Series

| | Age Group | | |
	Children (%)	Working-age (%)	Elderly (%)
Rural, beginning	34.0	54.9	11.1
Rural, end	23.2	59.7	17.1
Rural difference	−10.8	4.8	6.0
Urban, beginning	32.7	58.1	9.2
Urban, end	24.0	62.8	13.2
Urban difference	−8.7	4.7	4.0

| | Race/ethnicity | | |
	White, Non-Hispanic (%)	Black, Non-Hispanic (%)	Latino (%)
Rural, beginning	87.5	8.9	2.9
Rural, end	79.0	8.1	7.8
Rural difference	−8.4	−0.8	4.9
Urban, beginning	80.2	12.3	6.0
Urban, end	60.1	12.8	18.7
Urban difference	−20.1	0.5	12.6

| | Family structure | | |
	Single (%)	Cohabiting (%)	Married (%)
Rural, beginning	14.9	0.6	84.5
Rural, end	28.7	7.6	63.7
Rural difference	13.8	7.0	−20.8
Urban, beginning	19.4	0.8	79.8
Urban, end	30.8	6.5	62.7
Urban difference	11.4	5.7	−17.1

also changed. Table 1 compares the population distribution across age group, race/ethnicity, and family structure within rural and urban areas for the first five years of the time series (1970–1974)[4] and the last five years (2011–2015). The proportion elderly in rural areas has increased more than it has in urban areas. The proportion of white, non-Hispanics has declined in both rural and urban areas; this decline has been particularly steep in urban areas. Notably, the proportion of urban residents who are Latino has increased substantially (from 6 percent to almost 19 percent) while the proportion of urban residents who are white, non-Hispanic has declined by 20 percent. This suggests that in urban areas in particular, there has been a substantial shift toward racial and ethnic diversity.

FIGURE 2
Poverty Rates before and after Taxes and Transfers

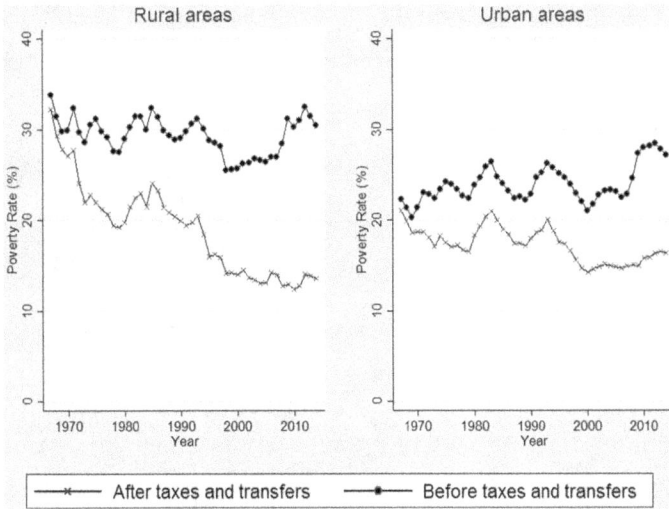

Immigrants, particularly those from Mexico and Central America, tend to be poorer than the average American and have less access to the social safety net; this may contribute to the lesser declines in poverty in urban as compared to rural areas over the course of our time series. It may be the case, for example, that immigrants are unable to take advantage of one of the most successful anti-poverty programs available in the United States—Social Security—if they did not work enough years or in the formal labor market.

Is the safety net more robust in rural areas? A second hypothesis that we investigate to explain the differential poverty trends in rural and urban areas is the possibility that the safety net has become more robust in rural areas than in urban areas (or less robust in urban areas relative to rural areas). A less robust safety net over time in urban areas as compared to rural areas could be correlated with the less pronounced decline in poverty among urban residents. This change could be due to more stigma and discrimination against the racially and ethnically diverse urban population, distinctive eligibility profiles in the two areas, or other differences. We thus first looked at whether pre–taxes and transfers poverty and resources-to-needs ratios showed the same pattern over time as post–taxes and transfers poverty and resources-to-needs ratios.

In the left panel of Figure 2, we can see that before taxes and transfers are taken into account, poverty declined slightly in rural areas. Pre–tax and transfers poverty actually *increased* in urban areas (right panel of Figure 2), however, over the course of the time series. Further, the safety net appears to be less robust in urban than in rural areas—at the end of the time series, poverty rates were

FIGURE 3
Poverty Rate in Rural and Urban Areas

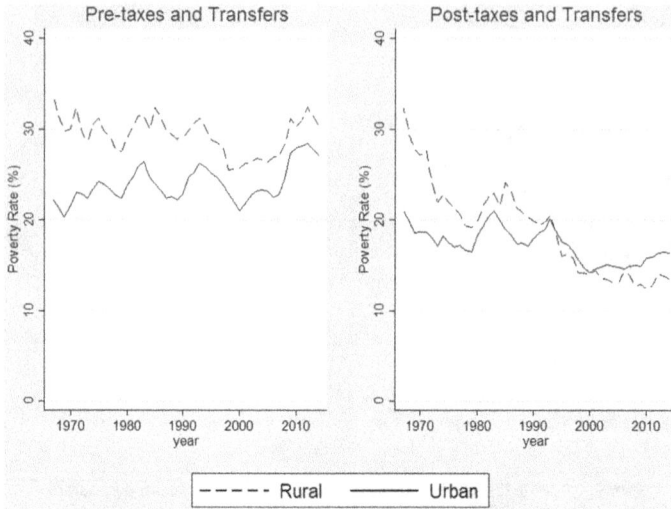

brought down by 55.5 percent (16.9 percentage points) in rural areas and 39.9 percent (10.8 percentage points) in urban areas. Figure 2 thus suggests a divergence in rural and urban areas in both pre–taxes and transfers income as well as in the effectiveness of the safety net.

We explore restricting Figure 2 to only individuals within 200 percent of the poverty line to focus in on those most likely to be receiving net benefits from taxes and transfers (see Figure A14 in the online appendix). Before the safety net is taken into account, the median resources-to-needs ratio in 2014 is lower in rural than in urban areas. However, rural residents with resources-to-needs under 200 percent of the poverty line experience a 96.2 percent increase in their resources to needs when the safety net is taken into account. The corresponding number for urban residents is 47.1 percent. This suggests that the safety net is doing more to increase resources-to-needs in rural areas than in urban areas. Thus, while rural residents below 200 percent of the poverty line have lower pretax income than their urban counterparts in 2014, rural residents end up with higher resources-to-needs once the safety net is taken into account.

This leads us to Figure 3, which juxtaposes more directly poverty rates in the two areas—while pre–tax and transfers poverty remains lower in urban areas, it is in post–tax and transfers poverty that we see the crossover with rural areas.

Figure 4 shows the proportion of people under 200 percent of the poverty line (who we might classify as roughly "eligible" for various benefits) who receive a variety of benefits in rural and urban areas.[5] These graphs are very similar when using a poverty threshold that is unadjusted for relative cost of living differences (see Figure A15 in the online appendix).

A higher proportion of rural residents receives assistance from the Supplemental Nutrition Assistance Program (SNAP) (food stamps), heating subsidies, and

FIGURE 4
**Proportion of Rural/Urban within 200 Percent of Adjusted Poverty
Line Receiving Benefits**

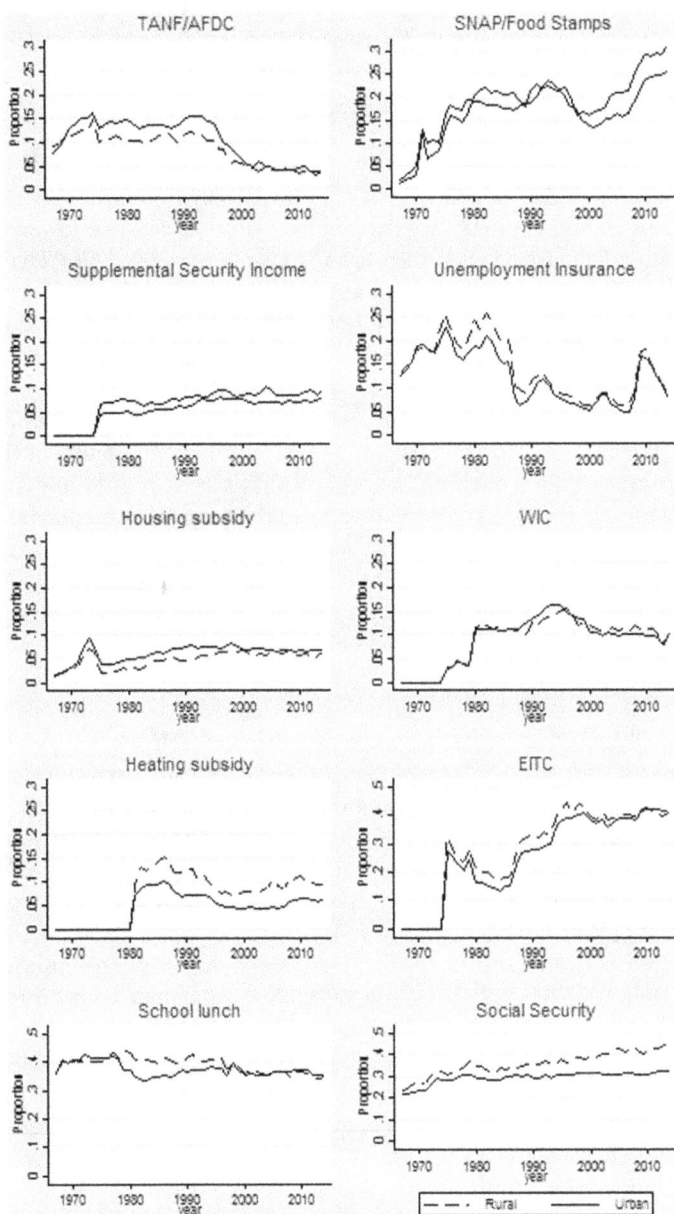

Social Security than urban residents. Note that the y-axes in these graphs vary somewhat by benefit—there are many more people receiving the Earned Income Tax Credit (EITC) than Supplemental Security Income, for example, regardless of residence. While we hypothesized that immigrants might have lower levels of attachment to the formal labor market and thus be driving the increasingly larger proportion of rural as compared to urban residents receiving Social Security, we find no evidence of racial/ethnic disparities in the rural/urban differential in the receipt of Social Security.

Further, there is a crossover in rural versus urban poverty rates in all age groups (children, adults, and the elderly), so while differentials in Social Security coverage are striking, these do not explain why rural areas have lower SPM poverty at the end of the time series than urban areas at the population level. In sum, it appears that the safety net is indeed more robust in rural than in urban areas— bringing about larger increases in resources-to-needs in the former—but we are unable to determine to which program we may attribute this difference.

Cost of living divergence between rural and urban areas over time and the geographic adjustment. An essential component of the computation of the SPM is adjusting the poverty threshold (or "needs" to which resources are compared to compute the poverty rate) for cost of living relative to the national average. The use of the SPM (as compared to the OPM), and the geographic adjustment in particular, has previously been found to substantially affect statistics on the geographic distribution of poverty (U.S. Department of Agriculture [USDA] Economic Research Service 2016). SPM poverty thresholds are generally lower than OPM thresholds in rural areas, so fewer rural residents have resources below the SPM thresholds than have resources below the OPM thresholds (Council of Economic Advisers, Domestic Policy Council, and Office of Management and Budget 2015).

The impact of using the SPM and geographically adjusting poverty thresholds in particular has only been illustrated using data from recent years (USDA Economic Research Service 2016); the impact over time of this aspect of the SPM methodology has not been previously investigated because implementing the geographic adjustment consistently over time has been a challenge (Fox et al. 2015). We have implemented this adjustment throughout our time series and are thus able to evaluate whether there has been a substantial divergence in the relative cost of living in rural and urban areas, and to what extent the geographic adjustment can explain the differential SPM poverty trends that we see in rural and urban areas.

Figure 5 presents average geographic adjustments over time in rural and urban areas. Rural areas have a lower average cost of living than urban areas throughout the time series and have become somewhat relatively less expensive (than the national average) over time. There are some very small breaks in the geographic adjustments time series when we change data sources; we see a similar pattern when using just one data source—Fair Market Rents, from 1985 to 2014 (see Figure A16 in the online appendix). Overall, there is a divergence in relative cost of living in rural and urban areas in the mid-2000s, followed by a slight reduction in the differential in the final years of the time series.

FIGURE 5
Average Geographic Adjustments in Rural and Urban Areas

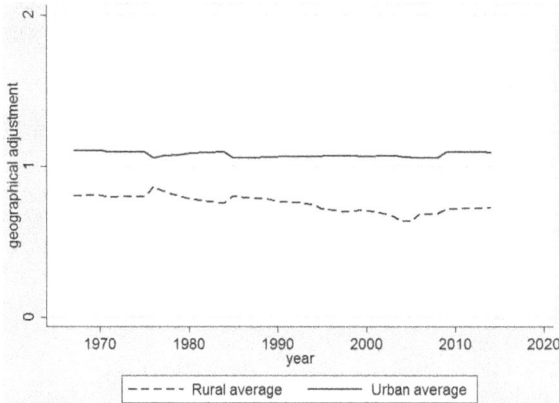

One way to investigate the "importance" of the geographic adjustment in explaining the convergence and crossover in poverty rates in rural and urban areas is to redo the figures of trends in poverty and resources-to-needs using a geographically unadjusted poverty threshold—what the poverty rates would be if the SPM did not take relative cost of living into account. Figure 6 displays poverty rates in rural and urban areas using a geographically unadjusted threshold (before and after taking the safety net into account) and juxtaposes them with the geographically adjusted poverty rates from Figure 3.

Before taking taxes and transfers into account, the difference between geographically unadjusted poverty rates in rural and urban areas is larger than the difference between geographically adjusted poverty rates (Figure 6). Further, there is no crossover in poverty rates in rural and urban areas (i.e., rural areas begin and end the time series with higher poverty rates than urban areas) when using a geographically unadjusted threshold and taking the safety net into account. This is consistent with previous cross-sectional research that has found the geographic adjustment to be extremely important in determining rural/urban poverty differentials (Council of Economic Advisers, Domestic Policy Council, and Office of Management and Budget 2015; Jolliffe 2006). When comparing the geographically adjusted and unadjusted trends in pre– and post–taxes and transfers resources-to-needs, the conclusion is the same (see Figure A17 in the online appendix).

"Boundary crossing": Are poor people moving from rural to urban areas? A fourth hypothesized explanation for the larger declines in rural than in urban SPM poverty over time from Figure 1 is that poor people may be moving from rural to *urban areas.* There are unfortunately relatively few migrants between rural and urban areas in the CPS sample—there are about 1,000 sampled individuals who migrate from urban to rural and rural to urban areas, respectively, in each year. Each group

FIGURE 6
Geographically Adjusted and Unadjusted Poverty Rates in Rural and Urban Areas

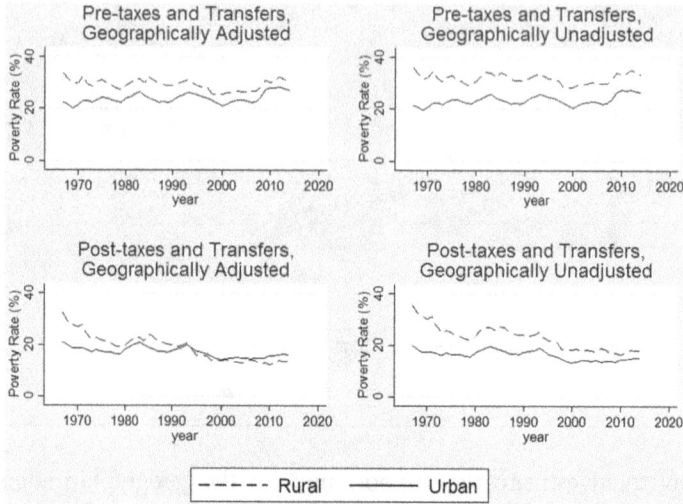

constitutes less than 1 percent of the CPS sample in each year. Since the sample is somewhat limited, we combine these migration data across years and present descriptive statistics from 1985 to 1999 and 2000 to 2014 to investigate whether relative poverty rates among movers and stayers have changed appreciably over time. These year groupings highlight a further limitation of the data—migration information is available beginning only in 1985. We can, however, evaluate whether higher poverty among people who have moved to urban areas from rural areas may help to explain the differential average poverty trajectories.

We find that migrants both to and from rural areas are poorer, on average, than those who stay in either urban or rural areas. In 1985–1999, urban stayers had the lowest poverty rates, on average, followed by rural stayers, then urban to rural movers, and finally rural to urban movers (Figure 7). By 2000–2014, rural stayers have the lowest poverty rates on average, followed by urban stayers, urban to rural movers, and rural to urban movers. Urban areas appear to have been receiving some of the poorest Americans in each period, and possibly slightly more so in the second period. This suggests that migration of the poor to urban areas may be contributing to persistently high poverty rates in urban areas, although the effect is likely to be relatively small given the size of the migrant population relative to the stayers, and the relatively small difference in poverty rates between rural to urban movers versus urban to rural movers.[6]

Decomposing urban and rural poverty trends

To investigate the relative contribution of different factors to explaining the convergence in pre–taxes and transfers poverty and the crossover of post–taxes

FIGURE 7
Poverty Rates by Migration Status

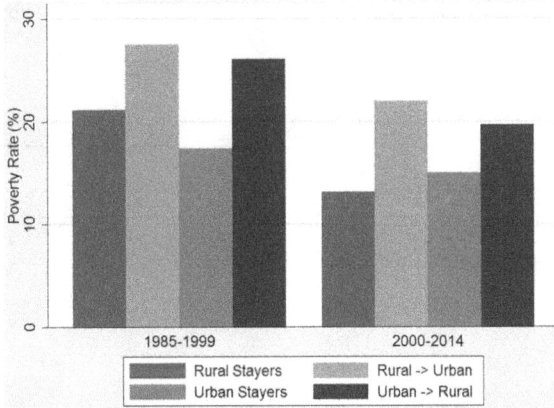

and transfers poverty in rural and urban areas shown in Figure 6, we implement a simulation approach. This approach addresses the following two questions: What would the average poverty rates in rural and urban areas be if (1) the demographic composition of rural and urban areas had stayed as they were in 1970, and (2) the economic characteristics of rural and urban areas had stayed as they were in 1970? We find that holding demographics constant slightly reduces the convergence in pre–taxes and transfers poverty rates between the two areas, but that holding employment constant, the convergence is accentuated (Figure 8). This suggests that both demographics and economic conditions contribute to patterns in pre–taxes and transfers poverty rates. Increased demographic diversity in urban areas appears to slightly increase poverty rates in urban areas (relative to the counterfactual), while changes in the economy over time appear to have resulted in poverty reductions in urban areas.

We find a similar pattern when looking at post–tax and transfers poverty—the crossover in poverty rates between the two areas is minimized when holding demographics constant but accentuated when holding employment characteristics constant (Figure 9). Again, the increased diversity in urban areas appears to contribute to its elevated poverty levels even after accounting for the safety net, but changes in employment again appear to have been particularly good for urban areas, where poverty would have been higher had individuals' employment characteristics stayed constant.

Limitations

There are a number of limitations to these analyses. First, as previously mentioned, the FMR data used to create the geographic adjustments from 1985 to

FIGURE 8
Pre–Taxes and Transfers Poverty Rate

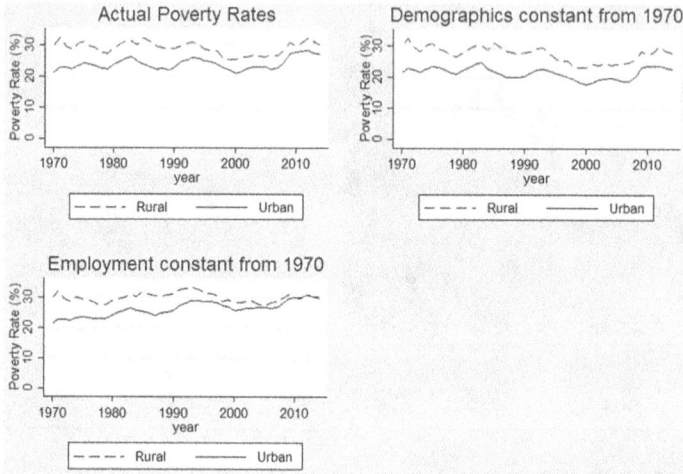

NOTE: Demographics and employment constant graphs are counterfactuals.

2008 unfortunately do not contain median rents for "not identified" areas.[7] Any household in our historic SPM time series not matched to a metropolitan statistical area (MSA) or rural area is considered to be "not identified" and assigned the average geographic adjustment factor from the years in which we have that information. A further challenge is that the MSA codes change over time in the FMR data; for 2004 and 2005, we add the metro variable from the IPUMS CPS data to our historic SPM time series to combine our time series with the geographic adjustments from the FMRs. Further limitations of the geographic adjustments include the need to interpolate between decennial census years and the grouping of states before 1976 in the CPS.

Second, the parametric models used in our simulation procedures may suffer from omitted variables, and this may affect the predictions obtained from them. For example, housing is only one part of families' costs. Further, it may not always be the case that rural areas are less expensive than urban areas when expenses other than housing are taken into account. Food may be more expensive in rural areas because there are fewer grocery stores with lower purchasing power; transportation costs can be higher because of the longer distances to traverse (Zimmerman, Ham, and Frank 2008). However, housing is a very large proportion of a family's budget, and it has been steadily growing over time; housing costs are unlikely to be outweighed by other expenses.

A third limitation is that the U.S. Census Bureau has changed the definition of what constitutes a rural and urban area over time. For example, in the 1990 Census, the Census Bureau defined *urban* as territory, persons, and housing units in (1) places of 2,500 or more persons incorporated as cities, villages, boroughs (except in Alaska and New York), and towns (except in the six New England States, New York, and Wisconsin), but excluding the rural portions of "extended cities"; (2) census designated places of 2,500 or more persons; or (3)

FIGURE 9
Post–Taxes and Transfers Poverty Rate

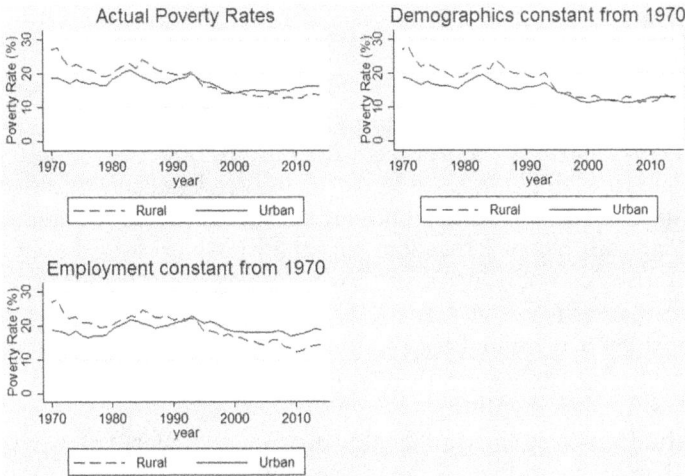

NOTE: Demographics and employment constant graphs are counterfactuals.

other territory, incorporated or unincorporated, included in urbanized areas (U.S. Census Bureau 2016b). By 2000, the Census Bureau added a density criterion for some types of urban territory, and by 2010, it began delineating urban areas at the tract level. Aside from obtaining a sensitive data contract at a secure research data center, we are not able to address this data challenge; we use the available rural/urban definition in each year of our time series.

Fourth, we are unable to evaluate the impact of shifting rural/urban boundaries over time. This is an important area of future research as rural areas that become metro may be different from those that stay rural (Artz and Orazem 2006; Isserman 2001). Unfortunately, it is not possible to investigate shifting rural/urban boundaries over time. The census designates rural/urban status for each household at the census block level. Further, the CPS is not longitudinal, so it is not possible to identify households that were previously rural and transitioned to urban. Future research should endeavor to investigate the impact of shifting boundaries on poverty by, for example, holding original rural/urban designation constant and comparing the counterfactual poverty rates to the poverty rates when areas' designation is allowed to change. This will highlight the impact of areas whose designation changes over time.

Discussion and Conclusion

Notwithstanding the technical limitations, this article contributes to the study of poverty in rural and urban areas, showing that rural poverty has indeed declined relative to urban poverty over time. We provide an accounting of the factors underlying this trend, and demonstrate the extent to which geographic adjustment of economic well-being in the United States influences the measurement of poverty.

Our findings are based on analyses of an improved poverty measure (the SPM) and show that poverty has declined more—and from a higher initial level—in rural areas than in urban areas. Further, poverty was higher, on average, in urban areas than in rural areas by the end of our time series in 2014. These findings appear to be in contrast with previous work on this topic that showed that rural residents (and rural single mothers in particular) are less likely to escape poverty than their urban counterparts (Lichter and Jensen 2000). However, these results are consistent with recent indications that the SPM's use of geographic adjustment for relative costs of living plays a large role in explaining the higher poverty rates in urban areas in recent years (USDA Economic Research Service 2016). Indeed, we show that throughout the time frame of our analyses, poverty rates would be higher in rural areas than in urban centers were it not for the geographic adjustment of the SPM.

We also find a more robust antipoverty effect of the safety net in rural as compared to urban areas, and this is the case in both geographically unadjusted and adjusted measures of poverty. We find that rural residents below 200 percent of the poverty line are more likely to receive support from one of the most effective antipoverty programs—Social Security—than their urban counterparts, and that this is the case across racial/ethnic groups. Simulation analyses reveal that in terms of pretax income, poverty would have been higher in urban areas by the end of the time series if employment conditions remained as they were in 1970. In terms of post–tax and transfers poverty, we find that poverty would have been lower in rural and urban areas if demographics had remained constant from 1970. This effect is larger in urban areas, suggesting that diversification by race/ethnicity, family structure, and age distribution may be keeping urban poverty rates elevated compared to rural poverty rates. Finally, we find little evidence of an exodus of poor people from rural to urban areas, although the sample of migrants in the CPS is disappointingly small.

Notes

1. We do not include Asian or other race/ethnicity categories as these are not available for the entirety of our time series.

2. While the trends are similar, they are less dramatic when looking at a continuous resources-to-needs measure—the ratio of SPM resources-to-needs (see appendix Figure A2). The 10th percentile of the resources-to-needs ratio has a pattern similar to that of the median, although the levels are naturally much lower and the variation somewhat less as well (see appendix Figure A3).

3. In supplementary analyses (available in the online appendix), we found that this pattern was widely shared among different race/ethnicity, family structure, and age groups (see appendix Figures A5–A13). In these online appendix figures, we also provide anchored SPM poverty rates for these groups, which again show similar results to the overall trends—a convergence or crossover in poverty rates in rural and urban areas by the end of the time series.

4. All analyses using race/ethnicity are presented starting in 1970, which was the first year that Hispanics were recorded separately.

5. We did not find substantially different levels of underreporting of benefits in rural and urban areas. When comparing the Transfer Income Model (TRIM) to the CPS, we find that underreporting of SNAP is almost half the size in rural areas ($21.80 on average) than it is in urban areas ($49.93 on average). While the difference between rural and urban areas in underreporting of supplemental security income is smaller, the magnitude of the underreporting is larger—$111.81 in rural areas and $120.85 in urban areas. We do not think these differences are large enough to affect our results.

6. When using a continuous measure—ratio of resources-to-needs—rather than the dichotomous poverty indicator, we do not see much of a difference between median resources-to-needs in urban to rural and rural to urban movers in the first time period, although both are substantially less well off than urban and rural stayers (see appendix Figure A18). We do, however, see somewhat higher median resources-to-needs among urban to rural movers as compared to rural to urban movers in the second time period, providing tentative support for the idea that rural to urban movers may be somewhat worse off than urban to rural movers.

7. Other limitations of the use of FMRs can be found in Renwick (2011).

References

Albouy, David. 2011. *Report for cost of living and the supplemental poverty measure*. Report submitted to the Office of the Assistant Secretary for Planning and Evaluation, U.S. Department of Health and Human Services. Available from http://citeseerx.ist.psu.edu/viewdoc/download?doi=10.1.1.422.4303& rep=rep1&type=pdf.

Albrecht, Don E., and Stan L. Albrecht. 2000. Poverty in nonmetropolitan America: Impacts of industrial, employment, and family structure variables. *Rural Sociology* 65 (1): 87–103.

Artz, Georgeanne M., and Peter F. Orazem. 2006. Reexamining rural decline: How changing rural classifications affect perceived growth. *Review of Regional Studies* 35 (2): 161–91.

Castle, Emery N., Junjie Wu, and Bruce A. Weber. 2011. Place orientation and rural-urban interdependence. *Applied Economic Perspectives and Policy* 33 (2): 179–204.

Citro, Constance F., and Robert T. Michael, eds. 1995. *Measuring poverty: A new approach*. Washington, DC: National Academy Press.

Council of Economic Advisers, Domestic Policy Council, and Office of Management and Budget. 2015. *Opportunity for all: Fighting rural child poverty*. Washington, DC: OMB. Available from https://www. whitehouse.gov/sites/default/files/docs/rural_child_poverty_report_final_no n-embargoed.pdf.

Foulkes, Matt, and Kai A. Schafft. 2010. The impact of migration on poverty concentrations in the United States, 1995–2000. *Rural Sociology* 75:90–110.

Fox, Liana, Chris Wimer, Irwin Garfinkel, Neeraj Kaushal, and Jane Waldfogel. 2015. Waging war on poverty: Poverty trends using a historical supplemental poverty measure. *Journal of Policy Analysis and Management* 34 (3): 567–92.

Glaeser, Edward L., Matthew E. Kahn, and Jordan Rappaport. 2008. Why do the poor live in cities? The role of public transportation. *Journal of Urban Economics* 63 (1): 1–24.

Gurley, Lauren. 2016. Who's afraid of rural poverty? The story behind America's invisible poor. *Economics and Sociology* 75 (3): 589–604.

Hirsch, Barry. 2011. *Adjusting poverty thresholds when area prices differ: Labor market evidence*. Report submitted to the Office of the Assistant Secretary for Planning and Evaluation, U.S. Department of Health and Human Services. Washington, DC: U.S. Department of Health and Human Services.

Isserman, Andrew M. 2001. Competitive advantages of rural America in the next century. *International Regional Science Review* 42 (1): 38–58.

Jolliffe, Dean. 2006. Poverty, prices, and place: How sensitive is the spatial distribution of poverty to cost of living adjustments? *Economic Inquiry* 44 (2): 296–310.

Lichter, Daniel T., and David L. Brown. 2011. Rural America in an urban society: Changing spatial and social boundaries. *Annual Review of Sociology* 37:565–92.

Lichter, Daniel T., and Leif Jensen. 2000. Rural poverty and welfare before and after PRWORA. Paper presented at Rural Dimensions of Welfare Reform: A Research Conference on Poverty, Welfare, and Food Assistance, May, Washington, DC.

Lobao, Linda. 2004. Continuity and change in place stratification: Spatial inequality and middle-range territorial units. *Rural Sociology* 69 (1): 1–30.

Massey, Doug, and Nancy Denton. 1993. *American apartheid: Segregation and the making of the underclass*. Cambridge, MA: Harvard University Press.

Renwick, Trudi. 2011. *Geographic adjustments of supplemental poverty measure thresholds: Using the American Community Survey five-year data on housing costs*. Washington, DC: U.S. Census Bureau. Available from https://www.census.gov/hhes/povmeas/methodology/supplemental/research/Renwick_SG E2011.pdf.

Roback, Jennifer. 1982. Wages, rents, and the quality of life. *Journal of Political Economy* 90 (6): 1257–78.

Rosenthal, Stuart. 2011. *Comments on the U.S. Census Bureau and Interagency Technical Working Group supplemental poverty measure*. Report submitted to the Office of the Assistant Secretary for Planning and Evaluation, U.S. Department of Health and Human Services. Washington, DC: U.S. Department of Health and Human Services.

Rural Sociological Society Task Force on Persistent Rural Poverty. 1993. *Persistent poverty in rural America*. Boulder, CO: Westview Press.

Schaeffer, Peter, Scott Loveridge, and Stephen Weiler. 2014. Urban and rural: Opposites no more! *Economic Development Quarterly* 28 (1): 3–4.

Short, Kathleen. 2012. *The research supplemental poverty measure: 2011*. Current Population Reports P60-244. Washington, DC: U.S. Census Bureau.

Short, Kathleen. 2015. *The supplemental poverty measure: 2014*. Current Population Reports P60-254. Washington, DC: U.S. Census Bureau.

Snyder, Anastasia R., and Diane K. McLaughlin. 2004. Female-headed families and poverty in rural America. *Rural Sociology* 69 (1): 127–49.

Swanstrom, Todd, Peter Dreier, and John Mollenkopf. 2002. Economic inequality and public policy: The power of place. *City & Community* 1 (4): 349–72.

U.S. Census Bureau. 2016a. Current Population Survey (CPS) income definitions. Available from http://www.census.gov/cps/data/incdef.html.

U.S. Census Bureau. 2016b. Urban and rural classification. Available from https://www.census.gov/geo/reference/urban-rural.html.

U.S. USDA Economic Research Service. 2016. *Rural poverty & wellbeing poverty overview: A note about the data sources*. Available from http://www.ers.usda.gov/topics/rural-economy-population/rural-poverty-well-being/poverty-overview.aspx.

Wilson, William Julius. 1987. *The truly disadvantaged: The inner city, the underclass, and public policy*. Chicago, IL: The University of Chicago Press.

Wilson, William Julius. 1996. *When work disappears: The world of the new urban poor*. New York, NY: Alfred A. Knopf.

Wimer, Chris, Liana Fox, Irwin Garfinkel, Neeraj Kaushal, and Jane Waldfogel. 2016. Progress on poverty? New estimates of historical trends using an anchored supplemental poverty measure. *Demography* 53 (4): 1207–18.

Ziliak, James P. 2011. *Cost of living and the supplemental poverty measure*. A Research Forum Report Submitted to the Office of the Assistant Secretary for Planning and Evaluation, U.S. Department of Health and Human Services. Available from http://www.ukcpr.org/sites/www.ukcpr.org/files/documents/UKCPR_COL%26SPM_For um_withAppendices%20(1).pdf.

Zimmerman, Julie N., Sunny Ham, and Sarah Michelle Frank. 2008. Does it or doesn't it? Geographic differences in the costs of living. *Rural Sociology* 73 (3): 463–86.

A Qualitative Census of Rural and Urban Poverty

If we want to build authentic evidence-based policy, we need a strong descriptive foundation of evidence on the everyday experience of poverty. The National Poverty Study (NPS), which is currently in development, provides this foundation with a new "qualitative census" of the everyday conditions of poverty in rural, suburban, and urban sites. The NPS will allow us to build new evidence-based theories of poverty, evaluate and improve existing place-based antipoverty policies, validate official poverty measures, and assist local communities in improving the safety net for vulnerable populations.

Keywords: poverty; qualitative research; everyday life; census

By
J. TRENT ALEXANDER,
ROBERT ANDERSEN,
PETER W. COOKSON JR.,
KATHRYN EDIN,
JONATHAN FISHER,
DAVID B. GRUSKY,
MARYBETH MATTINGLY,
and
CHARLES VARNER

In the United States, our survey-based infrastructure for *counting* the number of people in poverty is very sophisticated (U.S. Census Bureau 2017), whereas our capacity to monitor the *everyday conditions* of poverty is less

J. Trent Alexander is an assistant center chief in the Center for Administrative Records Research and Applications at the U.S. Census Bureau. His team uses administrative records to enhance Census Bureau programs and to produce new social and economic statistics.

Robert Andersen is a professor of sociology and dean of social science at the University of Western Ontario. He is also cross-appointed in the departments of Statistics and Political Science. Most of his recent research explores how individual-level economic position—measured by social class or income—interacts with national economic conditions to influence social and political outcomes considered important to the health of democracy.

Peter W. Cookson Jr. is a principal researcher at the American Institutes for Research. He also teaches sociology at Georgetown University. His 2013 book, Class Rules: Exposing Inequality in American High Schools *(Teachers College Press) was chosen by the Society of Professors of Education as a best book of 2014.*

Correspondence: grusky@stanford.edu

DOI: 10.1177/0002716217714156

well-developed. The National Poverty Study (NPS), currently slated to launch in 2019, addresses this problem with an innovative approach to monitoring the everyday conditions of poverty in rural, suburban, and urban sites. This article reviews the rationale for the NPS and discusses how it can inform research and policy on poverty across America's small towns, suburban communities, and inner-city neighborhoods.

The NPS is a joint research initiative of the Stanford Center on Poverty and Inequality, Johns Hopkins University, and the American Institutes for Research. The NPS planning committee, many members of which are serving as authors of this article, is currently involved in fund-raising for the NPS rollout and developing the protocol, sampling design, and possible forms of collaboration with the U.S. Census Bureau. This article provides a report on the NPS with due attention to the still-unresolved issues.

The objective of the NPS is to provide a systematic understanding of the everyday lives of the poor and near poor in the United States. The NPS is founded on three premises: (1) that existing quantitative protocols for measuring poverty, although immensely useful, tell us relatively little about the day-to-day experience of poverty; (2) that existing qualitative studies, although also immensely

Kathryn Edin is the Bloomberg Distinguished Professor in the Department of Sociology, Zanvyl Krieger School of Arts and Sciences and Department of Population, Family, and Reproductive Health, Bloomberg School of Public Health. She is a member of the National Academy of Sciences and a fellow of the American Academy of Political and Social Science.

Jonathan Fisher is an applied micro-economist who studies inequality, poverty, mobility, and personal bankruptcy. He is a research scholar at the Stanford Center on Poverty and Inequality and a senior researcher on the American Opportunity Study, a joint project between Stanford University, the National Academies, and the Census Bureau.

David B. Grusky is Barbara Kimball Browning Professor in the School of Humanities and Sciences, a professor of sociology, director of the Stanford Center on Poverty and Inequality, and coeditor of Pathways Magazine. His research addresses the changing structure of late-industrial poverty, mobility, and inequality.

Marybeth (Beth) Mattingly is a research consultant for the Stanford Center on Poverty and Inequality and director of research on vulnerable families at the Carsey School of Public Policy, University of New Hampshire. Her research addresses family well-being, obstacles to stability in family life, how state and federal policies may better support children and families, and Hispanic poverty and inequality.

Charles Varner is associate director of the Center on Poverty and Inequality at Stanford University. He studies mechanisms of economic, geographic, and social mobility, and their implications for government policy. His current research integrates census, tax, program, and qualitative data for the study of poverty and opportunity.

NOTE: We are grateful for support from the Russell Sage Foundation, the James Irvine Foundation, the Annie E. Casey Foundation, the American Institutes for Research, the Stanford Center on Poverty and Inequality, Stanford University, and the Successful Societies Program of the Canadian Institute for Advanced Research. The opinions expressed herein are those of the authors and not necessarily those of the U.S. Census Bureau or any of the institutes, universities, or foundations funding this research.

useful, do not allow for systematic comparison across different types and levels of poverty; and (3) that a new hybrid form that blends the best of qualitative and quantitative approaches is therefore needed. We refer to this new hybrid form as a "qualitative census."

We make the case that a qualitative census will allow us to better understand the conditions, causes, and effects of poverty and thereby strengthen the country's basic science on poverty. We also show that a qualitative census will support the development of authentic evidence-based policy on poverty. Because a qualitative census of this kind is not currently available, the country has tended to default to one-size-fits-all policy without, in most cases, strong evidence in support of this approach.

The NPS, once fielded, will allow us to better address many of the issues and themes raised in this volume. It will most obviously serve to repair the long-standing urban bias in our country's poverty policy. Although there is of course much research on rural poverty, the singular image of poverty that informs our one-size-fits-all policy is that of urban poverty in its most racialized and concentrated form (e.g., Chicago, Philadelphia, Atlanta). This image of poverty provides a misleading portrait of the everyday experience of low-income populations in rural areas (and likewise in urban areas that do not take on a stereotypical racialized form).

But in what ways does it mislead? We do not know as much as we should on this point. To be sure, there have been many important qualitative studies of rural poverty (e.g., Duncan 2000; Vance 2016; Hochschild 2016b), but these have not typically involved *systematic comparison* of the many different expressions of poverty from one place to another. We are left, then, with many questions. Is rural poverty truly as distinctive—and dysfunctional—as some commentators (e.g., Vance 2016) have argued? Or is rural poverty becoming less distinctive as the rural-urban divide fades in response to the growing "back and forth of people, money, and culture" (Lichter and Ziliak, this volume)? Is the opioid epidemic, coupled with rising rates of disability insurance, fundamentally changing the experience of poverty in hard-hit regions? Or is this story overblown? The NPS will allow for systematic cross-site comparisons that can better address questions of this sort.

The NPS will also allow for new insights into the *types* of spatial boundaries that matter. When urban, rural, and suburban poverty are studied, it is typically taken for granted that this tripartite categorization captures the main spatial distinctions of interest. But does it indeed "draw the lines" in ways that best highlight the differing day-to-day experiences of people living in the many forms of poverty that have emerged within this urban-to-rural continuum? Are the new "interstitial zones" (Lichter and Ziliak, this volume) between urban and rural yielding a qualitatively new form of poverty experience? Or are they just a midpoint on an underlying rural-urban continuum (as expressed, for example, in the U.S. Department of Agriculture [USDA] Economic Research Service's Rural-Urban Continuum Codes)? Is the everyday experience of poverty in the nation's largest cities (e.g., New York, Los Angeles, Chicago) fundamentally different from the experience in smaller—but still very urban—locales (e.g., Pittsburgh,

Portland, Kansas City)? Are highly isolated forms of poverty, as found in Appalachia and the Delta, just a more extreme version of poverty in more densely settled rural areas? The NPS, by providing evidence from 5,000 households in 100 sites varying across the rural-urban continuum, will allow us to (1) put the tripartite scheme to test, (2) determine whether qualitatively new "interstitial forms" of poverty are emerging, and (3) discover other—perhaps new—forms of poverty that are not represented with the standard tripartite characterization.

The NPS will, relatedly, allow us to better capture the seemingly substantial heterogeneity within the rural poverty form. Is "deindustrializing poverty," as experienced throughout the Midwest, marked by an overwhelming sense of abandonment, hopelessness, and dependency (see Seefeldt 2016)? Has the "postextractive" form of poverty, a form that emerged long ago as coal mining faded, settled into a more sustainable equilibrium than the newer "deindustrializing" forms (see Duncan 2000)? Are the "new immigrant" communities of the rural South experiencing a standard first-generation form of poverty (see Waters and Pineau 2016)? Is the "border community" poverty of California, Arizona, New Mexico, and Texas fundamentally different from immigrant poverty elsewhere? Is reservation poverty an especially dysfunctional form (see Miller 2013; Sprague 2004; Pickering 2000; Biolsi 1998)? And how does poverty play out within rural communities (e.g., Big Sur, California) that are experiencing unusually sharp increases in housing costs (see Sherman 2009)? Although these types of questions have been addressed in some qualitative studies, the NPS will allow us to pursue them more systematically.

The foregoing discussion indicates some of the ways in which NPS-based research could speak to the themes of this volume. As our description of the NPS unfolds, we develop some of these themes in more detail, and we raise additional questions about rural and suburban poverty that have not been as directly taken up in other articles presented in this collection. Before turning to these substantive issues, we set the stage by describing (1) the NPS sampling design, (2) our approach to fielding the NPS, and (3) our infrastructure for delivering the data to a wide range of researchers and policy analysts. After the NPS methodology is laid out, we will then be in a position to discuss its payoff for developing a stronger basic science of poverty and a stronger understanding of poverty policy.

Designing a Qualitative Census

The NPS has been developed in a series of planning sessions at Stanford University, Johns Hopkins University, Western University, the Russell Sage Foundation, and the American Institutes for Research. It has required a relatively lengthy planning and testing period because it rests on a new approach to qualitative research.

The study innovates by (1) administering a common protocol across different types of poverty, (2) drawing a sample large enough to allow for precise estimates of key poverty parameters, (3) relying on a representative sample that allows for generalizations to a known population, (4) allowing for comparisons across different poverty levels (e.g., extreme poor, deep poor, near poor), (5) allowing for comparisons across different types of poverty (e.g., urban, suburban, immigrant, reservation), (6) anchoring all inferences against a middle-class comparison group, (7) linking the qualitative transcripts to the American Community Survey (ACS) and other quantitative administrative data (subject to approval from the Census Bureau), and (8) allowing all authorized researchers to analyze and reanalyze the qualitative and quantitative data within a Federal Statistical Research Data Center (again subject to approval from the Census Bureau). These innovations, each of which is discussed in more detail here, are intended to advance a new type of qualitative analysis that is systematic, replicable, and representative (see Sánchez-Jankowski 2002; Dohan and Sanchez-Jankowski 1998; Abramson 2011).

The main purpose of the NPS is to understand how the low-income population lives in the context of stress, disruption, and deprivation. We take on this task by exploiting the "Making Ends Meet" protocol as devised by Edin and Lein (1997) and then adapted by Edin and Shaefer (2015). This protocol, which has been used more extensively within the low-income population than any other qualitative protocol, has been modified modestly for the purposes of the NPS and pretested in both San Francisco, CA, and Tucson, AZ. The modifications entail, most notably, a new set of prompts intended to elicit reflections and commentary on matters of identity and civic participation. Although the standard Making Ends Meet protocol already often elicits just such material (e.g., Edin and Shaefer 2015), the growing worries about populism and disaffected rural populations (e.g., Hochschild 2016b; Vance 2016) led us to introduce modifications that will allow us to address these matters more directly.

The resulting protocol is based on modules eliciting (1) a short life history and defining life-course events; (2) the rhythm of everyday life; (3) important relationships with family, friends, coworkers, and relatives; (4) the main sources of income and detailed expenses; (5) the formal and informal jobs held by household members; (6) the extent of economic hardship (e.g., difficulties in paying bills) and characteristic reactions to such hardship; (7) mental health, drug use, anxiety, and stress; (8) political beliefs, civic engagement, and participation; and (9) key identities and sources of meaning. Because the interview is long and typically intense, it delivers a rich and deep portrait of the respondents and their everyday lives.

The NPS, unlike most qualitative studies, will be based on a sample large enough to provide precise estimates with acceptably small margins of error (i.e., confidence intervals). There is of course nothing intrinsic to the qualitative form that requires defaulting to a small-sample approach. Given how influential qualitative studies of poverty have become (e.g., Hochschild 2016b; Edin and Shaefer 2015; Duncan 2000; Seefeldt 2016; Desmond 2016), it is surely appropriate to turn now to the task of building a big-science version of the qualitative form, a version that is consistent with its growing influence on poverty policy (without gainsaying the continuing importance of conventional qualitative studies).

We have thus developed a plan to deliver the largest qualitative study in the United States. The target sample size—5,000 households—makes it as large as the initial sample for the Panel Study of Income Dynamics (PSID), the country's go-to panel study for quantitative research on the labor market.[1] The key technical challenge, one to which we will return, is that of carrying out a large-scale qualitative study of this sort at an affordable price.

The NPS, unlike most qualitative studies, will also be based on a representative sample. There is again nothing intrinsic to the qualitative form that requires us to eschew the benefits of generalizing to a known population. For reasons laid out below, we have decided to target the population of low-income and middle-income households, where the upper threshold for "middle income" is defined to be 250 percent of the supplemental poverty measure (SPM) threshold. By using the previous year's ACS sample frame (pending permission from the Census Bureau),[2] we will be able to (1) draw the NPS sample efficiently (by minimizing the amount of household filtering) and (2) supplement the qualitative responses with quantitative data on income, earnings, housing conditions, poverty status, health, and other relevant items.[3] It may also be possible to link to other administrative data (such as social program data).[4] The payoff to combining qualitative and quantitative data in this way is, as we discuss subsequently, quite substantial.

The NPS sampling design is place-based. Because there is growing evidence of profound neighborhood differences in poverty and labor market outcomes (e.g., Chetty et al. 2014; Sampson 2012; Sharkey 2013), the NPS design makes it at once possible to generalize to the U.S. population (of lower-income and middle-income households) and to compare the experience of poverty across different settings, each of which has enough cases to be treated as a bona fide site. We have opted for a three-stage design much like that of the Fragile Families and Child Wellbeing Study (e.g., Reichman et al. 2001).[5] The first stage entails stratifying counties on three key characteristics (i.e., urbanization, race and ethnicity, reservation status) and then oversampling on combinations of county characteristics that, based on prior research and theory, are likely to produce distinctive poverty experiences.[6] We list the resulting county-level strata in Table 1.[7] The twofold rationale for this county-based approach is that it lowers interviewing costs (as our interviewers can be assigned to counties and thereby minimize travel time) and, just as importantly, it allows each county to serve as a standalone ethnographic site.[8] The second sampling stage entails subdividing each county into census block groups (and then oversampling on high-poverty block groups), and the third stage entails sampling households within the selected block groups.[9] In Figure 1, we have provided an example of how Beattyville, an especially poor city in Lee County (Kentucky), was divided into blocks and block groups for the 2010 Census. The block groups are defined by blocks starting with the same first digit.

We can assess this design by using it to draw 1,000 samples after coding each of the 3,144 counties and 693 reservations in the United States on the variables of Table 1. This simulation allows us to gauge whether the drawn samples reliably represent the wide range of poverty experiences in the United States. The results have been encouraging. The regional distribution of counties comes close, for example, to replicating the regional distribution of U.S. poverty. Across the 1,000 draws, 16.1 percent of the counties were (on average) in the Northeast, 20.4

TABLE 1
County-Level Strata for First Stage of NPS Design

Stratum	% Full Population	% Poverty Population	Mean Pov. % (county avg.)	# Selected Counties
Rural				
Concentrated black	3.3	4.8	22.7	10
Concentrated Hispanic	2.3	2.7	17.2	10
All others	9.0	9.2	15.5	10
Suburban				
Concentrated black	10.7	11.3	15.7	10
Concentrated Hispanic	18.3	17.2	13.7	10
All others	25.8	20.8	12.0	10
Urban				
Concentrated black	2.7	3.9	21.8	10
Concentrated Hispanic	8.3	9.3	16.0	10
All others	11.6	11.2	14.0	10
Superurban	8.0	9.5	17.6	5
Reservation	1.5	2.1	20.0	5

NOTE: The "concentrated black" stratum includes the top quintile of counties when arrayed by the proportion of the population that is black. The "concentrated Hispanic" stratum is defined analogously. The counties that fall into the top stratum on both distributions are assigned to the "concentrated black" stratum. The "superurban" category refers to New York, Chicago, Los Angeles, San Francisco, and Washington, D.C. We use the term "reservation" colloquially to refer to American Indian Areas, Alaska Native Areas, Hawaiian Home Lands, and American Indian Tribal Subdivisions. The totals in columns 1 and 2 do not sum to 100 because the reservation population has not been excluded from the other ten strata.

percent were in the Midwest, 40.4 percent in the South, and 23.1 percent in the West. These results compare satisfactorily to the corresponding percentages of the country's poverty population in these regions.[10] We have also examined whether, after stratifying on the variables of Table 1, other features of U.S. poverty are adequately represented. The results on the various dimensions we considered were again encouraging: We found, for example, that the samples typically included an ample number of counties with (1) deindustrializing economies, (2) formerly extractive economies, (3) high real estate or rental prices, (4) rapidly increasing immigrant populations, or (5) high income inequality. These results make it clear that the most distinctive types of rural and urban poverty will appear within the sampled NPS sites.[11] In the appendix (see the online version of the article), we have listed the 100 counties selected in one of our experimental draws, with each of the counties coded on variables that may affect the experience of poverty. The appendix table reveals the wide range of "poverty types" that are likely to appear under our design.

FIGURE 1
Census Blocks and Block Groups in Beattyville, Kentucky

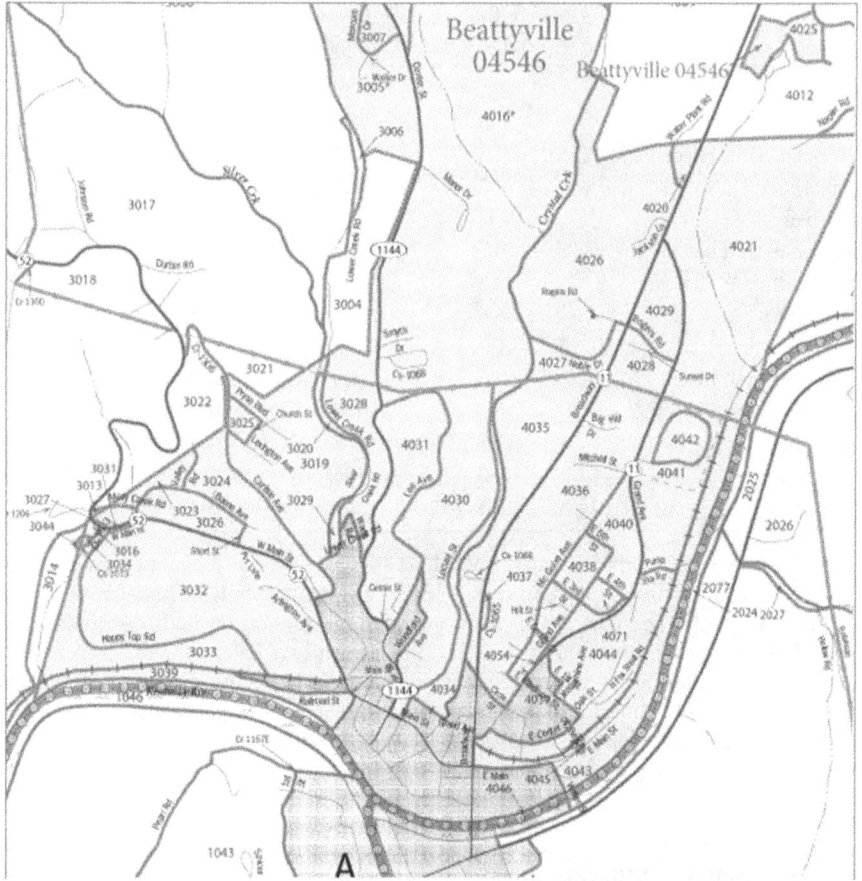

SOURCE: U.S. Census Bureau County Block Maps; see http://www2.census.gov/geo/maps/pl10map/cou_blk/st21_ky/c21129_lee/PL10BLK_C21129_006.pdf.

The selected sites may also be supplemented with additional locally funded ones that will not be used to generalize to the U.S. population (see Reichman et al. [2001] for a discussion of similar supplementary sites within the Fragile Families and Child Wellbeing Study). These additional sites, although not part of the NPS national sample, will provide valuable further evidence on variability in U.S. poverty. This supplementary-sample approach thus allows us to extend the reach of the NPS by partnering with additional cities or counties that wish to join the NPS and have the funding to do so. By using our standardized protocol within these supplementary sites, not only are design costs reduced but the results can then be compared to those of other NPS sites, thus making it possible for local leaders to discover—and learn from—other communities facing similar problems. We are currently discussing the selection of several possible supplementary sites with local universities and funders.

Within each of the NPS sites, we will be able to compare across the full range of different income and poverty levels, although we will be particularly interested in the validity of three conventional cut-points within this range (i.e., 50 percent, 100 percent, and 125 percent of the SPM threshold). Because this cross-group comparison is an important NPS objective, an equal number of respondents will be drawn from each of the four categories defined by these three cut-points (i.e., deep poverty, middle poverty, near poverty), thus maximizing the power of our cross-group comparisons.[12] The highest income category, bracketed by 125 percent and 250 percent of the SPM threshold, will serve as our "middle-class" comparison group. In most qualitative studies of poverty, a middle-class comparison group is not drawn (cf. Lareau 2011), thus making it difficult to speak to the distinctiveness of the poverty experience. Without a comparison group, we run the risk, for example, of treating some experiences as distinctive to poverty when in fact they are also widespread among the middle class.

Fielding the NPS

The balance of the NPS planning work is being carried out by a partnership comprising the Stanford Center on Poverty and Inequality, Johns Hopkins University, and the American Institutes for Research. The purpose of this partnership is to raise the balance of funds needed to field the NPS, to finalize the study design, and to continue discussions with the Census Bureau about possible protocols for sampling and fielding the NPS.

The distinctive features of the NPS (e.g., representativeness, large sample size, explicit comparison group) of course make it expensive. It is precisely such concerns with cost that presumably account for the design compromises that many qualitative scholars have been obliged to make. It is fair to ask why qualitative research has not been funded well enough to allow standard scientific practice to be followed even as, by contrast, quantitative research has been. This question is all the more legitimate given that much of our current poverty policy now draws so heavily and productively on qualitative research.

It is likely that this asymmetry is partly a practical response to the high cost of adapting conventional science to the qualitative case. Moreover, most of the recent cost-saving inventions have been on the quantitative side (e.g., Internet-based interviewing), thus making the cost gap even more troubling. There is, then, a special pressure to find ways to efficiently field the NPS by developing cost-saving methods for qualitative data collection.

This issue informed a series of NPS planning meetings and conferences at the Russell Sage Foundation, Stanford University, and the American Institutes for Research. The approach upon which we have settled, the establishment of the U.S. Poverty Corps, capitalizes on the substantial savings that arise by (1) centralizing the training process, (2) using predoctoral fellows as interviewers, and (3) reducing the number of interviewers (and thus training costs) by rotating each predoctoral fellow through six county sites. This design not only reduces costs but also introduces an important new form of intensive and hands-on training for the young talent needed to take on the country's persistent poverty problem.

The Poverty Corps will be staffed through a national competition held in spring 2019. The competition, which will be open to all college graduates and graduating seniors, will be widely publicized and advertised via relevant feeder schools and nonprofits, with a focus on identifying and drawing diverse applicants. If the Census Bureau approves the Poverty Corps plan, the selected participants will be reviewed for security clearance, as they will be serving as Special Sworn Census Bureau employees for the purpose of the NPS interviewing. In early summer, the participants will undergo intensive training, with this training taking the form of (1) a boot camp on the economics, sociology, psychology, and political science of poverty; (2) a comprehensive introduction to qualitative interviewing; and (3) specialized training in the NPS protocol. The local site coordinators (one for each of the 100 sites) will also come to Johns Hopkins University and participate in all training sessions. This training program will be adapted from Kathy Edin's existing protocol developed to staff her many large-scale qualitative projects.

The predoctoral fellows will then be divided into approximately twenty two-person teams, with each team assigned to a site, and each student within each team expected to complete approximately twenty interviews per site (i.e., approximately 2.5 interviews/week). This level of productivity is consistent with past experience with protocols similar to that of the NPS (e.g., Edin and Shaefer 2015). There will be a full support staff at each local site (comprising one coordinator and one local social service expert) as well as centralized oversight. After two months at the first site, the teams will be reformed with new partners, and each team will move on to a second site. The interviews for the remaining sites will be completed under the same format.

After the final round of interviewing is completed, the full Poverty Corps will reassemble at one of the affiliated universities, where they will be introduced to methods for analyzing quantitative census data and qualitative transcript data. This intensive training will introduce students to natural language processing, mixed methods, qualitative methods, and other approaches to analyzing the NPS data. During the course of this training, all students will be expected to complete a report for each of the sites at which they were located, with these reports then forming the basis of the NPS site descriptions (which will be published as a user's guide on the NPS website). We expect that many of these site reports will become major poverty studies as NPS students continue to work on them as graduate students or in other capacities.[13] The NPS staff will also assist all students during this period with the application process for graduate school or other poverty-relevant jobs in the public, nonprofit, or private sectors.

This approach to NPS data collection will reduce costs substantially[14] and, just as importantly, provide a new training pipeline for young adults interested in issues of poverty. By reaching out to HBCUs (historically black colleges and universities) and HSIs (Hispanic-serving institutions) and advertising very aggressively, we will make the Poverty Corps one of the nation's premier training regimens for future scholars of color. The experience will give corps participants an unrivaled understanding of the experience of U.S. poverty that then prepares them to lead in academia, government, and the nonprofit sector. Although obviously not for the faint of heart, the Poverty Corps experience will only require that same level of commitment that we now routinely demand for those training in medicine (e.g., the residency), private sector consulting (e.g., a McKinsey consultant), or teaching (e.g., Teach for America). By establishing an analogous high-expectations track in the poverty sector, we can instill considerable prestige in the sector, raise its profile, ramp up the caliber of recruits, and provide rite-of-passage training of unparalleled quality.

Delivering the NPS

The NPS data will take the form of de-identified ACS items (conditional on approval to link from the Census Bureau), de-identified interview transcripts, and county and block-group metadata for the 100 sites (collected by the interviewers as well as drawn from other sources).[15] In some cases, other administrative data (e.g., program data) may be important for the analyses, and analysts may be able to link them to the NPS.[16]

How will these data be made available for research purposes? The objective is of course to ensure that the NPS provides a strong foundation for a cumulative qualitative science of poverty. In many qualitative studies, only the team that originally collected the data is allowed to analyze it, and the data may even be destroyed immediately after the study is completed. In effect, this approach trusts the scholars who collected the original data but refuses to extend that same trust to other scholars who might carry out a secondary analysis of the data. This approach reduces the value of the data, makes replication and cumulation difficult, and has led to "a hundred years of debate" about the method's reliability (Lewis-Kraus 2016). By discarding the data after a single use, we are also failing to properly honor the real contributions of those who gave their time and energy to be interviewed.

The solution to this problem, and indeed the centerpiece of our approach, is to borrow from and develop practices similar to those used for census data, tax data, program data, and other highly sensitive quantitative records. As it stands, the convention within qualitative scholarship is to rely wholly on Institutional Review Boards (IRBs), with the presumption that those analyzing the data will adhere to IRB strictures about protecting data and maintaining confidentiality. Although this trust-based approach has worked relatively well to date and can serve as an important first line of defense, it can and should be coupled with the use of formal institutions that control data access and use. The Federal Statistical Research Data Centers (FSRDCs) are precisely institutions of this sort. These facilities, which are overseen by the Census Bureau, have been established for the purpose of ensuring that sensitive quantitative data are secure and that respondent confidentiality is maintained.

If the Census Bureau approves our request to link the NPS qualitative data with ACS items, all analyses would then have to be completed within an FSRDC, a constraint that would serve to protect the data. To access the NPS, qualified researchers would need to submit a research proposal, have it approved by a Census Bureau proposal review process, and acquire appropriate security clearance. If these steps were successfully completed, the analyses could then be carried out within an FSRDC. Before any output could leave the FSRDC, it would be subjected to output review for disclosure risk, a review process that would have to be extended to address complications that arise when qualitative and quantitative data are linked. This approach would establish a high level of security while also making it possible for secondary researchers to carry out formal replications, extend the research of others, and compare results across sites and over time. It would allow the NPS, like the PSID, the Survey of Income and Program Participation (SIPP), and similar high-use surveys, to become an ongoing resource that justifies the investment on the part of funding agencies, interviewers, and respondents.

It is accordingly important to deliver a website that makes high-quality secondary analysis possible. The NPS will, again like other public-use datasets, come with a full-service website that provides a codebook, the interview protocol, a data viewing and selection utility, information about sampling and weights, a discussion of the county sites and site metadata, and a guide to tools for analysis (e.g., natural language processing, multilevel analysis). The website will allow users to share information about the data, their code, and their documentation and will thus explicitly crowd-source user expertise. We will also support the development of new analytic tools that exploit the opportunities that open up when both quantitative and qualitative data are available for the *same* respondent. In most mixed-method projects, the qualitative and quantitative analyses tend to stand side by side, with little in the way of true integration. The NPS will, by contrast, allow for an organic combination of qualitative and quantitative data, a point to which we return in the following sections.

The Payoff to the NPS

The NPS is clearly an ambitious effort. Does the expected payoff warrant the cost? The purpose of this section is to lay out some of the immediate and long-term benefits of the NPS for basic research and policy on rural, suburban, and urban poverty.

Unmediated experience of poverty

The most obvious payoff is the large body of evidence that the NPS will provide on the everyday experience of poverty. This evidence is an important complement to existing qualitative research that typically takes the form of an organized narrative prosecuting a thesis or dispelling a stereotype. The consumers of these narratives have no alternative but to accept them given that the underlying data are unavailable. The NPS, by contrast, will provide 5,000 transcripts, making it possible to *directly listen* to the voices of a rigorously representative sample of the country's poverty population. These transcripts can be used to develop new bottom-up accounts of poverty, test existing theories of poverty, and assess whether new policy proposals are responding to real needs. The NPS will thus provide a fact-checking resource of undisputed integrity that allows for rigorous assessments of the steady stream of claims—by politicians, scholars, and journalists—about the everyday experience of poverty. By serving as the country's go-to resource for evaluating claims about the everyday lives of low-income populations, the NPS will become our qualitative analogue to the PSID, SIPP, or Current Population Survey (CPS).

The diversity of experience

The NPS will be especially valuable in representing the wide diversity of experiences within the country's low-income populations. Because the same protocol will be delivered to all 100 sites, and because a representative sample will be drawn from each, it becomes possible to assess whether the everyday experience of poverty differs fundamentally across (1) urban, suburban, and rural communities; (2) different economies and labor markets; and (3) different regions. There is of course much important qualitative research on different types of poverty. The NPS will allow us to examine the heterogeneity of experience more systematically by virtue of its standardized protocol, large and representative samples, middle-class comparison group, and comprehensive range of poverty settings.

An early warning system

The low-income population is facing new challenges as prime-age employment continues to decline (e.g., Hout 2016); automation, robotics, and autonomous systems spread (e.g., Acemoglu and Restrepo 2017); rates of opiate addiction and disability insurance continue to rise (e.g., Case and Deaton 2017); highly concentrated forms of poverty spread (Kneebone and Holmes 2016); manufacturing and union jobs disappear (e.g., Rosenfeld 2010); the "gig economy" grows (Katz and Krueger 2016); and disaffection and disconnection become more prominent (Hochschild 2016a, 2016b). These and other changes, many of which may fundamentally transform the low-income population, make it especially pressing to establish the NPS as one of the country's early-warning systems. If the NPS had been available in the past, we might not have been taken by surprise by the rise of deep poverty (Edin and Shaefer 2015), the takeoff in disability claims (e.g., Case and Deaton 2017), or the growing disaffection of the white low-income population (e.g., Hochschild 2016b). Although it is difficult to estimate the cost of defaulting to "catch-up policy" in addressing these and other developments (see Holzer et al. 2007), it is likely extremely high in terms of lives lost, increased program spending, and income and gross national product (GNP) forgone. The cost of the NPS, as high as it is, pales in comparison to the costs of operating in the blind.

One-size-fits-all policy

The United States has defaulted to one-size-fits-all policy on poverty without any strong evidence in favor of this approach. Although there are of course some local variations in policy, they are only rarely based on a considered assessment of what types of policy work best for a given type or form of poverty. To the contrary, when a state exercises some discretion in its poverty programming (e.g., state-specific decisions on Medicaid expansion), it appears to reflect the prevailing political discourse within that state rather than any state-specific assessment of the facts. The conceit of the NPS is that, if ever the United States were to decide to build its poverty policy wholly around the facts, it would help first to establish them. Over the next several decades, the United States will likely be making major policy decisions on the safety net and labor market, decisions that should be informed by the actual experience of poverty rather than some stereotypical image of it.

Local poverty policy

In some cases, the local NPS sites may also be used to carry out field experiments on local poverty interventions, a cost-effective approach because the NPS interviews can serve as a baseline measurement. This approach may be used, for example, to evaluate local experiments with basic income, the minimum wage, and many other poverty policies. We have held discussions with many local communities interested in hosting add-on NPS sites that would allow for field experiments of this sort.

Validating poverty measures

We have made much of the importance of not just counting the number of people in poverty but also better understanding their everyday lives. The NPS, although clearly focused on the latter objective, can equally assist with the former by validating the "poverty thresholds" defined by the supplemental poverty measure (SPM), official poverty measure (OPM), and other poverty measures. The NPS transcripts can be used to examine whether these thresholds capture the key qualitative differences in deprivation, disruption, and stress for the full poverty population, for different types of poverty (e.g., rural, urban), for demographic subgroups (e.g., racial groups), and for different multiples of the thresholds (referring to extreme, deep, middle, and near poverty). We can examine, for example, whether the "poor" and "near poor" lead qualitatively different lives or whether the distinction between "deep poverty" and "middle poverty" is likewise a fundamental one (see Newman and Massengill 2006). There has of course been much research seeking to validate the main poverty thresholds (e.g., Meyer and Sullivan 2012). However, because the most critical criterion variables (e.g., deprivation, stress, disruption, disorder) have gone unmeasured, such efforts have not been entirely satisfactory. This validation exercise is arguably important enough to itself justify an investment in the NPS. If we do not know where the key thresholds lie, it is difficult, after all, to tailor the safety net well.

The latter set of analyses speak to the potential benefits of blending qualitative transcripts with micro-level ACS, program, and other administrative data. It is not merely that blending in this way allows us to validate conventional poverty measures. As important as that validation is, the NPS also opens up a new form of mixed-methods research that, unlike the usual "stapling together" of two distinct projects, now allows qualitative and quantitative data to be brought together at the microlevel.

Hidden poverty populations

Within the qualitative tradition, much of the research has understandably focused on the largest poverty subpopulations, such as young men (e.g., Edin and Nelson 2013), young women with children (e.g., Edin and Kefalas 2011), the homeless (e.g., Russell 2013), and relatively big racial and ethnic groups. Although some smaller subpopulations have also been studied, it is difficult to draw strong conclusions from these studies in the absence of comparative data. Because the NPS sample is very large, it can provide new comparative evidence on subpopulations that have to date remained largely hidden, including childless women, foster children, small ethnic or immigrant groups, middle-aged adults, the elderly, and doubled-up families.

Conclusion

The foregoing list makes it clear that the NPS will provide important information on how low-income populations are making ends meet, dealing with stress and adversity, and reacting to government programs. At present, we are left to try to set policy with incomplete evidence on the low-income population, a task that may become more difficult with increasingly rapid changes in prime-age employment, precarious work, automation-induced displacement, and opiate addiction and disaffection. Because our current policy is tailored to a stereotypical image of poverty, it seems unlikely that our responses to these threats will—absent the NPS—take into account how the low-income population is actually trying to meet them.

If we want to build authentic evidence-based policy, we need a strong descriptive foundation of evidence on the everyday experience of poverty. This in turn means moving beyond our currently antiquated infrastructure for garnering evidence on poverty. The NPS will modernize this infrastructure with a new "qualitative census" that allows for systematic, representative, and large-scale qualitative analysis. It is intended as a qualitative analogue to the country's go-to surveys, such as the PSID, CPS, or SIPP, that now regularly provide quantitative evidence on poverty. The payoff is likely to be substantial: The NPS will allow us to build new evidence-based theories of poverty, evaluate and improve existing place-based antipoverty policies, validate official poverty measures, and assist local communities in improving the safety net for vulnerable populations.

Can the country afford the NPS? It is conventional to argue, as indeed we would, that investing in the evidence needed to reduce poverty can be justified in economic terms alone. There is nonetheless the seemingly intractable problem of converting such future savings into present-day capital.[17] We have thus worked hard to reduce costs to the point that the NPS becomes too attractive to pass up. The key formula that ensures its cost-effectiveness—the establishment of a U.S. Poverty Corps—will not just deliver the NPS at an affordable price but also energize a new cohort of adults and prepare them to lead in government, academia, and the nonprofit sector.

Notes

1. The NPS sample size is also similar to that of the Fragile Families and Child Wellbeing Study (approximately 4,900 families).

2. The ACS sampling frame is derived from the Census Bureau's Master Address File. There is limited precedent for using the ACS as a frame for other surveys (see National Research Council 2011). If the NPS is not given approval to draw a sample from the ACS frame, it will become necessary to supplement the NPS protocol with items that replicate the poverty-relevant measures in the ACS (e.g., income). We have developed—and pretested—a modified NPS protocol of precisely this sort. Although we would obviously prefer to link to the ACS data, this modified protocol proves to be a very acceptable fallback. If it is necessary to resort to this fallback, the Census Bureau might still agree to develop and provide a set of Master Address File (MAF) flags identifying housing units *likely* to contain the target population.

3. The ACS frame likely performs less adequately at the very bottom of the income distribution. We will address this concern by carrying out supplementary interviews of transient respondents who are likely to have a reduced probability of appearing in the ACS frame.

4. The NPS respondents would of course have to provide consent before any such linkages could be made.

5. We are grateful to Greg Duncan for suggesting this design and to Christopher Jencks and others for gently noting the various problems with some of our earlier design proposals. We have considered, for example, the possibility of delivering the NPS as an add-on module to the SIPP. Although this design would have many attractive features, it would be unwise to add such a demanding module to an already demanding protocol. It would also be difficult to prevail upon the SIPP advisory board to allow this add-on module.

6. We define "reservations" in the note to Table 1. The counties will be sampled with probabilities proportional to population size.

7. We have found it necessary to introduce four regional substrata (Northeast, South, West, Midwest) within the "concentrated black" stratum. This is necessary because otherwise the vast majority of selected counties are in the South. We will likewise select one reservation in the Northeast, West, and Midwest and two in the South (as 74 percent of the reservation population is in the South). We will of course have to eliminate from the sample any reservations with populations that are too small to preserve confidentiality.

8. The sample for each county, approximately fifty households, is larger than that of most single-site qualitative studies. Although we considered using commuting zones instead of counties, it should be borne

in mind that there are just 709 commuting zones and 3,144 counties, with each commuting zone an aggregation of counties. This means that commuting zones are more heterogeneous than counties and, in particular, are more likely to blur the distinction between urban, suburban, and rural forms of poverty.

9. The typical census block group contains approximately 1,500 individuals (but block groups vary widely in size). The sampling of block groups will again be proportional to population.

10. The corresponding percentage of the country's poverty population in each of the regions is 12.9 (Northeast), 20.3 (Midwest), 42.4 (South), and 24.5 (West). The poverty statistics provided here and throughout pertain to the Official Poverty Measure (OPM).

11. How should we proceed, it might be asked, if our draw happens to yield a very unattractive collection of counties (in the sense that it fails to represent the types of poverty that we deem to be important but on which we have not directly stratified)? Although our illustrative draws demonstrate that this happens only rarely, we cannot rule out that it will happen when we turn to the actual draw that determines our selection of counties. The advice of R.A. Fisher on this point is instructive. As reported by Cox (2016), R.A. Fisher was in fact quite surprised by a question on this point when it was posed to him, as his view was that, obviously, one should just draw again in the unlikely event of securing a sample with just such "undesirable features." This advice of course only holds insofar as one has verified in advance, as we have, that the design itself throws up such undesirable draws but rarely.

12. We rely throughout on the supplemental poverty measure. We use conventional definitions of deep poverty (i.e., income below 50 percent of the poverty threshold), middle poverty (i.e., income between 50 and 100 percent of the threshold), and near poverty (i.e., income between 100 and 125 percent of the threshold). The "middle class" category will refer to households with an income between 125 and 250 percent of the threshold.

13. These reports are of course important because they represent and preserve the very special insights that accrue to those who complete the interviewing and develop a rapport with the respondents.

14. We do not yet have final budget estimates because they depend on the outcome of ongoing discussions with the Census Bureau about the sampling design and frame.

15. It is possible that audio transcripts could be "de-identified" and thus provided within the FSRDC without compromising confidentiality. If the Census Bureau were to allow access to audio transcripts (within an FSRDC), it would of course only be with respondent consent and with assurance that reidentification was impossible.

16. These linkages will of course require respondent consent.

17. Although this problem can in principle be addressed with social impact bonds (and related approaches), the appetite for these vehicles has to date proven to be limited.

References

Abramson, Corey M. 2011. Qualitative research in the positivist-behavioral tradition. *The QDA Newsletter* 3:5–9. Available from http://cmabramson.com/uploads/CMA-ATLASti_Newsletter_2011-03.pdf.

Acemoglu, Daron, and Pascual Restrepo. 2017. Robots and jobs: Evidence from U.S. labor markets. NBER Working Paper No. 23285, National Bureau of Economic Research, Cambridge, MA.

Biolsi, Thomas. 1998. *Organizing the Lakota: The political economy of the New Deal on the Pine Ridge and Rosebud Reservations*. Tucson, AZ: University of Arizona Press.

Case, Anne, and Angus Deaton. 2017. *Mortality and morbidity in the 21st century*. Washington, DC: Brookings Institution.

Chetty, Raj, Nathaniel Hendren, Patrick Kline, and Emmanuel Saez. 2014. Where is the land of opportunity? The geography of intergenerational mobility in the United States. *Quarterly Journal of Economics* 129 (4): 1553–1623.

Cox, David R. 2016. The design of empirical studies: Towards a unified view. *European Journal of Epidemiology* 31:217–28.

Desmond, M. 2016. *Evicted: Poverty and profit in the American city*. New York, NY: Crown.

Dohan, Daniel, and Martin Sanchez-Jankowski. 1998. Using computers to analyze ethnographic field data: Theoretical and practical considerations. *Annual Review of Sociology* 24:477–98.

Duncan, Cynthia M. 2000. *Worlds apart: Why poverty persists in rural America*. New Haven, CT: Yale University Press.

Edin, Kathryn, and Maria Kefalas. 2011. *Promises I can keep: Why poor women put motherhood before marriage*. Berkeley, CA: University of California Press.

Edin, Kathryn, and Laura Lein. 1997. *Making ends meet: How single mothers survive welfare and low-wage work*. New York, NY: Russell Sage Foundation.

Edin, Kathryn, and Timothy J. Nelson. 2013. *Doing the best I can: Fatherhood in the inner city*. Berkeley, CA: University of California Press.

Edin, Kathryn, and Luke Shaefer. 2015. *$2 a day: The art of living on virtually nothing in America*. Boston, MA: Houghton-Mifflin Harcourt.

Hochschild, A. R. 2016a. I spent 5 years with some of Trump's biggest fans. Here's what they won't tell you. *Mother Jones*. Available from http://www.motherjones.com/politics/2016/08/trump-white-blue-collar-supporters.

Hochschild, A. R. 2016b. *Strangers in their own land. Anger and mourning on the American Right*. Berkeley, CA: University of California Press.

Holzer, Harry, Diane Whitmore Schanzenbach, Greg J. Duncan, and Jens Ludwig. 2007. *The economic costs of poverty: Subsequent effects of growing up poor*. Washington, DC: Center for American Progress.

Hout, Michael. 2016. Labor markets. In *Pathways: State of the Union*. Special issue 2016. Stanford Center on Poverty and Inequality. Available from http://inequality.stanford.edu/sites/default/files/Pathways-SOTU-2016.pdf.

Katz, Lawrence F., and Alan B. Krueger. 2016. The rise and nature of alternative work arrangements in the United States, 1995–2015. NBER Working Paper No. 22667, National Bureau of Economic Research, Cambridge, MA.

Kneebone, Elizabeth, and Natalie Holmes. 2016. *U.S. concentrated poverty in the wake of the Great Recession*. Washington, DC: Brookings Institution. Available from https://www.brookings.edu/research/u-s-concentrated-poverty-in-the-wake-of-the-great-recession/.

Lareau, Annette. 2011. *Unequal childhoods: Class, race and family life*. Berkeley, CA: University of California Press.

Lewis-Kraus, Gideon. 12 January 2016. The trials of Alice Goffman. *New York Times Magazine*. Available from https://www.nytimes.com/2016/01/17/magazine/the-trials-of-alice-goffman.html.

Lichter, Daniel T., and James P. Ziliak. 2017. The rural-urban interface: New patterns of spatial interdependence and inequality in America. *The ANNALS of the American Academy of Political and Social Science* (this volume).

Meyer, Bruce D., and James X. Sullivan. 2012. Identifying the disadvantaged: Official poverty, consumption poverty, and the new supplemental poverty measure. *Journal of Economic Perspectives* 26 (3): 111–35.

Miller, Robert J. 2013. *Reservation "capitalism."* Santa Barbara, CA: Praeger.

National Research Council. 2011. *The future of federal household surveys: Summary of a workshop*. K. Marton and J.C. Karberg, rapporteurs. Committee on National Statistics, Division of Behavioral and Social Sciences and Education. Washington, DC: National Academies Press.

Newman, Katherine, and Rebekah Peeples Massengill. 2006. The texture of hardship: Qualitative sociology of poverty, 1995–2005. *Annual Review of Sociology* 32:423–46.

Pickering, Kathleen. 2000. Alternative economic strategies in low-income rural communities: TANF, labor migration, and the case of the Pine Ridge Indian Reservation. *Rural Sociology* 65 (1): 158–67.

Reichman, Nancy E., Julien O. Teitler, Irwin Garfinkel, and Sara S. McLanahan. 2001. Fragile families: Sample and design. *Children and Youth Services Review* 23 (4/5): 303–26.

Rosenfeld, Jake. 2010. Little labor: How union decline is changing the American landscape. *Pathways* (Spring): 3–6.

Russell, Betty G. 2013. *Silent sisters: An ethnography of homeless women*. New York, NY: Routledge.

Sampson, Robert J. 2012. *Great American city: Chicago and the enduring neighborhood effect*. Chicago, IL: University of Chicago Press.

Sánchez-Jankowski, Martin. 2002. Representation, responsibility, and reliability in participant-observation. In *Qualitative research in action*, ed. Tim May, 144–61. London: Sage Publications.

Seefeldt, Kristin S. 2016. *Abandoned families: Social isolation in the twenty-first century*. New York, NY: Russell Sage Foundation.

Sharkey, Patrick. 2013. *Stuck in place: Urban neighborhoods and the end of progress toward racial equality*. Chicago, IL: University of Chicago Press.

Sherman, Jennifer. 2009. *Those who work, those who don't: Why poverty persists in rural America*. Minneapolis, MN: University of Minnesota Press.

Sprague, Donovin Arleigh. 2004. *Pine Ridge Reservation*. Charleston, SC: Arcadia Publishing.

U.S. Census Bureau. 2017. Poverty. Available from https://www.census.gov/topics/income-poverty/poverty.html.

Vance, J. D. 2016. *Hillbilly elegy*. New York, NY: HarperCollins.

Waters, Mary C., and Marisa Gerstein Pineau. 2016. *The integration of immigrants into American society*. Washington, DC: National Academies Press.

Political Polarization along the Rural-Urban Continuum? The Geography of the Presidential Vote, 2000–2016

This article documents the diversity of political attitudes and voting patterns along the urban-rural continuum of the United States. We find that America's rural and urban interface, in terms of political attitudes and voting patterns, is just beyond the outer edges of large urban areas and through the suburban counties of smaller metropolitan areas. Both Barack Obama and Hillary Clinton performed well in densely populated areas on the urban side of the interface, but they faced increasingly difficult political climates and sharply diminished voter support on the rural side of the interface. The reduction in support for Clinton in 2016 in rural areas was particularly pronounced. Even after controlling for demographic, social, and economic factors (including geographic region, education, income, age, race, and religious affiliation) in a spatial regression, we find that a county's position in the urban-rural continuum remained statistically significant in the estimation of voting patterns in presidential elections.

Keywords: urban America; suburban America; rural America; urban-rural continuum; regional voting; migration; presidential elections

The 2016 presidential election will be remembered as the year the white rural voter roared. Despite weak support in urban America, Donald Trump became the forty-fifth president by outperforming previous Republican nominees in rural areas of crucial "swing states," such as Florida,

By
DANTE J. SCALA
and
KENNETH M. JOHNSON

Dante J. Scala is an associate professor of political science at the University of New Hampshire. His work focuses on voter demographics, as well as campaigns and elections in the United States, particularly the presidential nomination process.

Kenneth M. Johnson is a professor of sociology and senior demographer at the Carsey School of Public Policy at the University of New Hampshire, as well as an Andrew Carnegie Fellow. His research examines national and regional population redistribution, rural and urban demographic change, the growing racial diversity of the U.S. population, and the implications of demographic change for public policy.

Correspondence: dante.scala@unh.edu

DOI: 10.1177/0002716217712696

North Carolina, Michigan, Wisconsin, and Pennsylvania. Journalists and scholars focused their attention on the sources of white rural resentment (for one outstanding example, see Cramer 2016). Although the political divisions between "red" America and "blue" America were already well known, the polarization of urban and rural seemed especially stark in the wake of the 2016 campaigns.

Even after accounting for sex, race, and ideology, place itself is political. Liberals prefer living in areas where people live closer to one another and can walk to stores and other amenities. Conservatives, on the other hand, prefer living farther apart from their neighbors, even if that means they have to drive significant distances to reach schools and restaurants (Pew Research Center 2014). Wrote one journalist, "The new political divide is a stark division between cities and what remains of the countryside. The difference is no longer about *where* people live, it's about *how* people live: in spread-out, open, low-density privacy—or amid rough-and-tumble, in-your-face population density and diverse communities that enforce a lower-common denominator of tolerance among inhabitants" (Kron 2012). The differences between urban life and rural life, and the feeling among rural residents that their areas are often neglected by political elites, lead to resentment among those who live in areas peripheral to metropolitan areas (Cramer 2016).

However, merely defining the 2016 elections as the tale of two Americas—one urban, one rural—is an obstacle to a nuanced understanding of the country's political geography. We argue here that it is better to think of urban-rural differences in terms of a continuum, not as a dichotomy. Our previous research demonstrates that political commentators mistakenly caricature rural America as a single entity (Scala, Johnson, and Rogers 2015). In fact, rural America is a deceptively simple term describing a remarkably diverse collection of places. It encompasses more than 70 percent of the land area of the United States and 46 million people (Johnson 2017). Both demographic and voting trends in this vast area are far from monolithic. Republican presidential candidates have generally done well in rural America, but there are also important enclaves of Democratic strength there. Voters who reside in the most remote rural places, especially if they are dominated by farming, typically favor Republicans. Yet Democrats find electorally important pockets of strength among voters residing in rural areas dominated by recreational amenities and services. In fact, Barack Obama's support in rural recreational counties was greater than in any other part of rural America, except in counties with a significant number of African American voters (Scala, Johnson, and Rogers 2015).

Why is there more political diversity in rural America than we might expect? Migration is one factor. Some argue that migration has driven a significant portion of the polarization that we see today along the urban-rural continuum. The "big sort" argument that Americans are self-segregating into "ideologically inbred

NOTE: The second author's work on this project was supported in part by his Andrew Carnegie Fellowship. The views expressed here are his and do not represent the official views of the Carnegie Corporation. Barb Cook and Andrew Schaefer provided valuable research support for this article.

… pockets of like-minded citizens" has become received wisdom among the commentariat (Bishop and Cushing 2008; also see McDonald 2011), although scholars have raised important qualifications to this argument (Abrams and Fiorina 2012; Hui 2013). Regardless of whether residents actually influence their neighbors' political views and behavior (Cho, Gimpel, and Dyck 2006; Gimpel, Dyck, and Shaw 2004; McKee and Teigen 2009), migration does have significant effects on local political environments (Gimpel and Schuknecht 2001; Frendreis and Tatalovich 2013). Migration has helped to diversify some parts of rural America politically, while it has diminished political diversity elsewhere (Scala, Johnson, and Rogers 2015). "Old rural" politics centered on farmers, whose ideological conservatism and civic apathy were occasionally awakened by radical movements (Knoke and Henry 1977; also see Buttel and Flinn 1975; Glenn and Hill 1977). But for decades now, social scientists also have noted changes in rural life due to migration and technological innovation, specifically, the homogenization of rural life (Drury and Tweeten 1997; Knoke and Henry 1977; Lewis-Beck 1977).

One of the greatest changes in American rural politics has been the transformation of the "solid South"—a Democratic fortress for a century after the Civil War—into an equally strong source of Republican votes (McKee 2008; Black 2004; Hayes and McKee 2008). Republican success in rural America is also evident in much of the Midwest (Frank 2004; Bartels 2006; Francia and Baumgartner 2005; McVeigh and Diaz 2009; Monson and Mertens 2011; Gimpel and Karnes 2006). However, the Republican Party's dominance in rural America has not been uniform. Pockets of relative Democratic strength have emerged in areas dominated by the "new rural" economy of amenities and recreation. These areas have enjoyed demographic growth trends distinctive from those seen in "old rural" territory, especially in the Northeast and the West. The drivers of this growth have been twofold: older adults in search of an attractive place to retire and family-age migrants in pursuit of economic and employment opportunities (Johnson, Winkler, and Rogers 2013; Johnson et al. 2005; Robinson and Noriega 2010; Morrill, Knopp, and Brown 2007).

When we turn our attention to metropolitan areas, there is also evidence of a continuum between urban and rural, rather than stark division. Democrats' greatest political strength lies in the urban core counties of the nation's largest metropolitan areas. Their support decreases in smaller metro areas and disappears altogether in a key interface between urban and rural: the suburbs of small metropolitan areas, which bear a striking resemblance to rural America, and the nonmetropolitan counties adjacent to the urban edge. The political trends at this urban-rural interface are especially concerning for Democrats, because the largest urban cores where they dominate are growing relatively slowly. In contrast, politically competitive areas—metropolitan suburban counties and rural counties just beyond the sprawling urban fringe—historically enjoy faster rates of population increase (Johnson 2012).

"Swing states" in American politics have less political polarization between their urban and rural areas (McKee 2008). In other words, there is less of an urban-rural dichotomy and more of a continuum. In New Hampshire, for example, the in-migration to the state's northern rural recreational counties was a significant factor in the state's political shift from solidly Republican to slightly Democratic over the past two decades (Scala 2011). But in 2016, rural and exurban New Hampshire supported Donald Trump much more strongly than previous Republican nominees, and Trump nearly carried the state for the GOP for the first time since 2000. The situation in New Hampshire and numerous other swing states illustrates a crucial point: the future of American politics depends in part on what happens along the blurry interface between urban and rural America.

Objectives

In this article, our objectives are to (1) delineate a rural-urban continuum that differentiates U.S. counties based on size, location, and proximity; (2) determine whether this rural-urban continuum has utility for understanding voting patterns in recent presidential elections, controlling for important demographic, social, and religious factors, and for region; and (3) determine where along this rural-urban continuum the interface between rural and urban America exists.

We address these objectives by using a combination of survey and election data to examine political diversity along a rural-urban continuum. Our goal is to ascertain whether a linkage exists between where a county is situated along this continuum and its voting behavior in presidential elections. If successful, this will provide a better, nuanced understanding of political trends among the more than 3,100 counties in the United States.

Methods and Data

We examine political data along the rural-urban continuum at two levels. First, we consider opinion data to identify voting patterns and attitudes of individuals along the rural-urban continuum. Second, we examine aggregate voting trends in U.S. counties, both in a bivariate and a multivariate framework, to determine whether position along the rural-urban continuum matters when other variables are taken into account, and to identify where the interface between rural and urban is.

The Cooperative Congressional Election Study (CCES) is a national stratified sample survey of more than 54,000 respondents that asks a battery of questions about demographic characteristics and political attitudes (Ansolabehere and Schaffner 2012). We classify these respondents into groups based on where their county fits along the rural-urban continuum, using criteria outlined below. Because of difficulties with boundary changes in Alaska's boroughs, we excluded respondents from that state from our analysis.

A major concern for any researcher examining rural and urban areas is the definition of *rural* and *urban*. For our analysis, we use counties as the unit of analysis. U.S. counties are the basis for much of the research on rural and urban areas. This is appropriate because in much of the United States counties are important units of local government with broad authority over elections, law enforcement, health, and taxes—especially in rural areas, where fewer municipal governments exist. They also have historically stable boundaries, and are a basic unit for reporting political, economic, and demographic data. New England county equivalents are included, as well as the independent cities in Virginia and elsewhere.

We classified counties as metropolitan or nonmetropolitan, using the 2013 Office of Management and Budget definition (Office of Management and Budget 2015). Metropolitan areas include counties containing an urban core of a population of 50,000 or more (central city), along with adjacent counties that are highly integrated with the core county as measured by commuting patterns. There are 1,163 metro counties and 1,949 counties classified as rural or nonmetropolitan. We use the terms *rural* and *nonmetropolitan* interchangeably here, as we do the terms *urban* and *metropolitan*. We also examined subsets of nonmetropolitan counties representing farm-dependent and recreation-dependent counties using the Economic Research Service, U.S. Department of Agriculture county typology from 2015.[1]

To characterize the rural-urban continuum, we subdivided the counties into eight categories that represent population concentration, from the densely settled large cities to the most remote rural periphery.[2] The sixty-seven *large urban core* metropolitan counties include the major city (or twin cities) of metropolitan areas containing more than 1 million people in 2010 (Figure 1). More than 98.5 million people resided in these counties in 2015, representing 32 percent of the U.S. population (see Table 2). Most of these large urban core counties contain both the central city and some of the older, inner suburbs. An additional 365 large metropolitan counties adjoin these large core counties. These *large metro suburban* counties include 79.3 million residents, which is 25 percent of the U.S. population. They encompass newer suburban areas and the periphery of large metropolitan areas. Metropolitan counties containing the urban core (central city) in metropolitan areas of less than 1 million were classified as *small metro core*. The 78.9 million residents living in these 339 counties were another quarter of the population. These core counties generally contain both the central city and a larger proportion of the suburban population of the metropolitan area than is the case in the large metro cores. The 392 counties in metropolitan areas of less than a million that were outside the core county were classified as *small metro suburban*. The 18.6 million residents living in these areas represent 6 percent of the U.S. population. Suburban counties in smaller metropolitan areas tend to contain some suburban areas as well as the sparsely settled urban periphery and have significantly fewer residents than other metropolitan counties.

The remaining 1,949 counties are outside of metropolitan areas. These rural (or nonmetropolitan) counties contain just 46 million people (15 percent of the U.S. population), but approximately 70 percent of the land area of the United States. We subdivided nonmetropolitan counties into four groups. Those that were outside metropolitan areas but contiguous with them were classified as

FIGURE 1
Counties by Rural-Urban Continuum Status

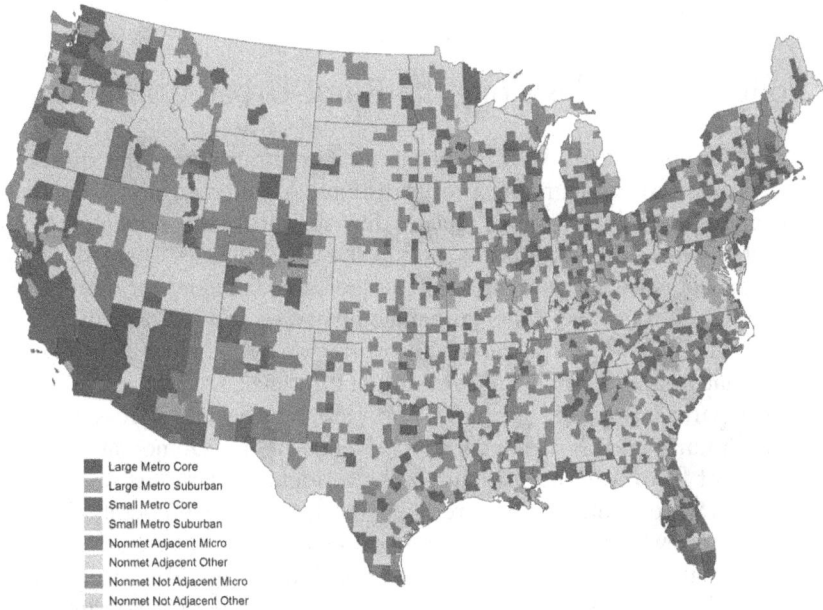

Large Metro Core
Large Metro Suburban
Small Metro Core
Small Metro Suburban
Nonmet Adjacent Micro
Nonmet Adjacent Other
Nonmet Not Adjacent Micro
Nonmet Not Adjacent Other

adjacent nonmetropolitan counties. Those that did not share a boundary with a metropolitan area were classified as *nonadjacent*. We further subdivided the nonmetropolitan counties into those that had a town with a population between 10,000 and 50,000 (micropolitan counties) and those with no town of more than 10,000 in 2010 (other counties). There were 372 *adjacent micropolitan* counties with 18.4 million residents in 2010 and 654 *adjacent other* counties with 12.0 million residents. Among the more remote rural counties, 269 were *nonadjacent micropolitan* counties with 8.9 million residents and the remaining 679 counties were *nonadjacent other* with 6.9 million residents.

Much of our data are from U.S. Census Bureau sources. Information about the proportion of the population age 18 to 29, percentage of the population who were black and non-Hispanic, and the percentage who were Hispanic are from the 2010 decennial Census of Population. From the American Community Survey for 2007 to 2011, we obtained median family income, and the percentage of the population 25 and older with a college degree.[3] We also used the Census Bureau regional classification system to assign each county to one of the four census regions (Northeast, Midwest, South, and West).

Electoral data were obtained from an online atlas (Leip 2016). The 2016 presidential election counts were not officially certified in every state at the time that this analysis was completed, so there may be very minor differences in vote totals.

We also included data on the distribution of religious groups within U.S. counties for two major religious clusters that have received attention in political research: white Evangelical Christians and Catholics (Campbell, Green, and Layman 2011; McDaniel and Ellison 2008).[4] We calculated the percentage of adherents/population in 2010.

Political Attitudes along the Rural-Urban Continuum

Survey data from the 2012 CCES indicate that counties across the rural-urban continuum possess a demographic profile distinctive from their peers. Population concentrations were larger, more racially diverse, and better educated in large metropolitan cores, in their suburbs, and in the core counties of smaller metropolitan areas than elsewhere in the country (see Table 5, below, for more details). The gap between these three most urban county types and the remainder of the country is evident both in the survey and voting analysis below. It is along this boundary that we see the political rural-urban interface.

Political partisanship and attitudes also vary significantly across the rural-urban continuum, and illustrate the dependence of the Democratic Party on strong support from America's urban cores. Residents of large urban cores and their suburbs were significantly more likely to identify as Democrats than their counterparts elsewhere (Table 1). Rural residents and those who lived in the suburbs of small metropolitan areas were considerably less likely to identify as Democrat. This pattern persisted in measures of respondents' support for President Obama.[5]

Residents of densely populated urban areas also differed significantly from their peers in terms of their religious adherence and cultural conservatism. They were less likely to report that they often prayed or attended church, and they less frequently reported that religion was an important factor in their lives. The percentage of "born again" Christians also was much lower in the urban cores than elsewhere. Residents of urban areas also were more likely to take liberal positions on so-called moral issues, such as abortion and gay marriage.

Race, ethnicity, and immigration were a prominent part of the 2016 presidential campaign. In the 2012 CCES, residents of the metropolitan cores were significantly more willing to grant legal status to illegal immigrants, provided that they were employed and paid their taxes. They also were less likely to favor raising the number of patrols on the U. S.-Mexico border and less willing to allow police to question anyone suspected of being in the United States illegally, to punish American businesses that hired illegal immigrants, and to deny citizenship rights to children of illegal immigrants born in the United States. Metropolitan residents also were more willing to support affirmative action than their peers elsewhere.

Gun control is an issue that clearly demarcates residents along the urban-rural continuum. Residents of the urban cores were significantly more likely to desire stronger gun control laws than their counterparts in rural areas. On the rural outskirts of the continuum, only three of ten respondents reported support for tighter gun control. On the environment, residents of the urban cores were more

TABLE 1
Political Attitudes along the Rural-Urban Continuum (in percentages)

Survey Question	Metropolitan				Nonmetropolitan			
	Large Core	Large Suburbs	Small Core	Small Suburbs	Adjacent Micro	Adjacent Other	Non-Adj Micro	Non-Adj Other
Democratic Party identification	41	33	31	25	27	30	28	27
Obama job approval	62	52	50	39	45	44	40	41
Voted for Obama in 2012	63	52	49	39	47	45	42	40
Religion important factor in life	65	68	70	74	73	79	73	74
Pray daily	44	47	49	54	52	57	50	54
Born-again Christian	28	31	36	45	41	47	41	42
Attend church at least once a week	26	28	31	34	32	35	30	33
Pro-choice on abortion	56	52	46	38	40	38	43	40
Approve of same-sex marriage	60	55	51	41	46	41	45	42
Pro-affirmative action	48	29	37	28	31	29	31	26
Pro-legal status for illegal immigrants	55	48	46	41	40	40	43	42
Increase border patrols	50	56	56	62	62	59	58	60
Expand police powers on immigration	30	38	39	47	46	47	45	46
Fine businesses hiring illegal immigrants	56	62	63	68	69	63	66	64
Deny automatic citizenship	28	34	35	40	38	40	39	35
In favor of stricter gun control	56	50	44	36	37	33	33	30
Environment higher priority than jobs	32	29	30	26	29	28	25	22
Believe climate change is real	65	60	57	52	55	53	52	54

likely to acknowledge climate change as a significant problem and favor policies that prioritized environmental protection over job creation.

To summarize, survey data reflect sharp political distinctions between urban and rural America, with important qualifications. First, metropolitan areas vary significantly in terms of their partisanship: larger, more diverse urban cores are friendlier to Democrats than smaller urban cores. Second, the interface or "tipping point" between urban and rural actually occurs in the suburbs of small metropolitan areas. Residents there closely resemble rural Americans in their conservative ideology and Republican partisanship. The nuanced political distinctions between urban and rural in these survey data are better understood as a continuum, rather than as stark division.

Democratic Presidential Performance along the Rural-Urban Continuum, 2000–2016

The rural-urban continuum variable that we developed delineates a clear and consistent pattern of support for presidential candidates between 2000 and 2016. Democrats did best in large city counties at the core of the nation's biggest metropolitan areas (Figure 2). In fact, these large urban cores are the only place along the rural-urban continuum where Democrats received a majority of the votes. Democratic support has also increased modestly in suburbs of large metropolitan areas and in small urban core counties over the last several elections. And in all four groupings of counties (large metro, small metro, adjacent nonmetro, and nonadjacent nonmetro), Democrats consistently received a larger percentage of votes in the counties containing larger population centers (large urban core, small urban core, micropolitan) than in other counties (large urban suburbs, small metro suburban, other).

Outside of the urban cores, Republican presidential candidates enjoyed geographically widespread support. They consistently received the majority of votes in all but the large metro cores in each of the last five presidential elections. They also consistently performed better in the suburban counties of metropolitan areas and in nonmetropolitan counties that did not have large towns.

However, despite a clear gradient along the rural-urban continuum, Republican support has increased significantly at the boundary between the three most urban types and smaller metropolitan suburban counties and nonmetropolitan counties in each of the last five elections. It is here that the rural-urban interface occurs. As we see, small suburban counties are more like rural counties than the other metropolitan counties. The striking decline in Democratic support in 2016 in nonmetropolitan counties and the suburbs of small urban areas is also starkly evident at this rural-urban interface. Hillary Clinton's percent of the vote matched Obama's in large urban cores and diminished very modestly in large suburban and smaller urban core counties. But her support declined sharply in rural and small suburban counties.

FIGURE 2

Percent of the Vote for Democratic Presidential Candidates along the
Rural-Urban Continuum, 2000 to 2016

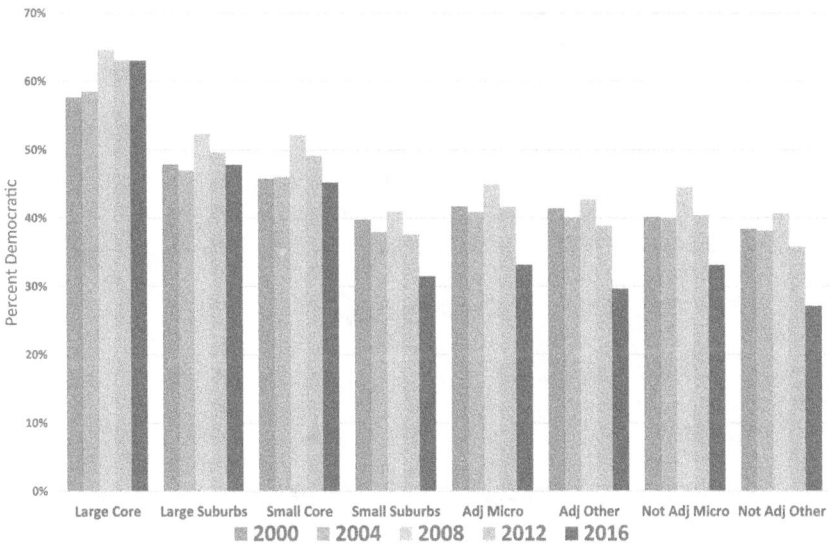

Democrats received their greatest support in the urban core counties of the largest metropolitan areas in each of the last five presidential elections. Gore and Kerry averaged slightly less than 60 percent of the vote in these areas in 2000 and 2004. Obama received 65 and 63 percent of the vote in 2008 and 2012, respectively, and Clinton also received 63 percent. Obama and Clinton won majorities in nearly 90 percent of the large urban core counties. (Table 2). Democrats were weaker in the suburban areas of these large metropolitan areas: in 2012, Obama received 49.6 percent of the vote there and Clinton received 47.8 percent. A similar pattern was evident in metropolitan areas of less than 1 million. Democratic presidential candidates always did better in the core counties of these smaller metropolitan areas than in their suburban counties. In 2012, Obama received 49.2 percent of the vote in the smaller core counties, but 37.6 percent in their suburban counties. Four years later, Clinton received 45.2 percent of the small core vote, but only 31.5 percent of the small suburban vote. The steep drop-off in Democratic support in "small suburbia" mirrors our findings in individual-level survey data.

In nonmetropolitan areas, a similar pattern is evident. Democratic presidential candidates' performance was consistently poorer in rural counties without large towns than in those with a town of 10,000 to 50,000. Democratic support was also always greater in counties adjacent to metropolitan areas than among those that were not adjacent. Though the pattern of where Democrats do best in rural areas remains consistent across the five elections, the substantial decline in support for Clinton across all rural counties is clearly evident. In rural counties adjacent to

TABLE 2
Vote for Democratic Presidential Candidate along the Rural-Urban
Continuum, 2012 and 2016

	2016 Election				2012 Election			
	Total Vote ('000s)	Clinton Vote ('000s)	Clinton Vote Percent	Percent Counties Won	Total Vote ('000s)	Obama Vote ('000s)	Obama Vote Percent	Percent Counties Won
Large core	37,795	23,823	63.0	89.6	36,048	22,770	63.2	89.6
Large fringe	35,947	17,185	47.8	26.0	33,952	16,851	49.6	28.8
Small core	32,993	14,927	45.2	34.8	31,596	15,530	49.2	42.8
Small fringe	8,297	2,613	31.5	7.4	7,852	2,954	37.6	14.8
Adjacent micro	7,785	2,578	33.1	12.9	7,629	3,173	41.6	21.0
Adjacent other	5,241	1,555	29.7	8.9	5,136	1,998	38.9	17.0
Not adjacent micro	3,616	1,197	33.1	13.9	3,555	1,437	40.4	19.1
Not adjacent other	3,045	826	27.1	6.7	3,009	1,079	35.8	12.8
Total	134,718	64,703	48.0	15.7	128,776	65,790	51.1	22.2

metropolitan areas, Obama received 41.6 percent of the vote in those that were micropolitan and 38.9 percent in those that were not. Clinton received just 33.1 percent in these adjacent large town counties and 29.7 percent in other adjacent counties.

The pattern is similar in rural counties that are not adjacent to metropolitan areas. In these more remote areas, Obama received 40.4 percent of the vote in large town counties and 35.8 percent in those without a town. In contrast, Clinton received just 33.1 percent in the large-town remote counties and 27.1 percent of the vote in remote counties without a town. In total, Clinton received 2.1 million fewer votes than Obama did four years earlier in nonmetropolitan counties, even though 531,000 more votes were cast there in 2016. She also received 338,000 fewer votes in the suburban counties of small metro areas, even though 450,000 more were cast.

In sum, through the last five presidential elections, voting patterns were consistent along our rural-urban continuum. Democratic presidential candidates did best in large metropolitan areas, next best in small metropolitan areas, not as well in adjacent nonmetropolitan areas, and least well in nonadjacent counties. Within each of these four groupings, Democrats did better in counties containing the largest city or town. In each election, there was also a distinct drop-off in Democratic support between small metro cores and small metro suburban areas, leading us to conclude that the rural-urban interface runs along this boundary, at

FIGURE 3
Percentage of Democratic Vote in 2016 Presidential Election

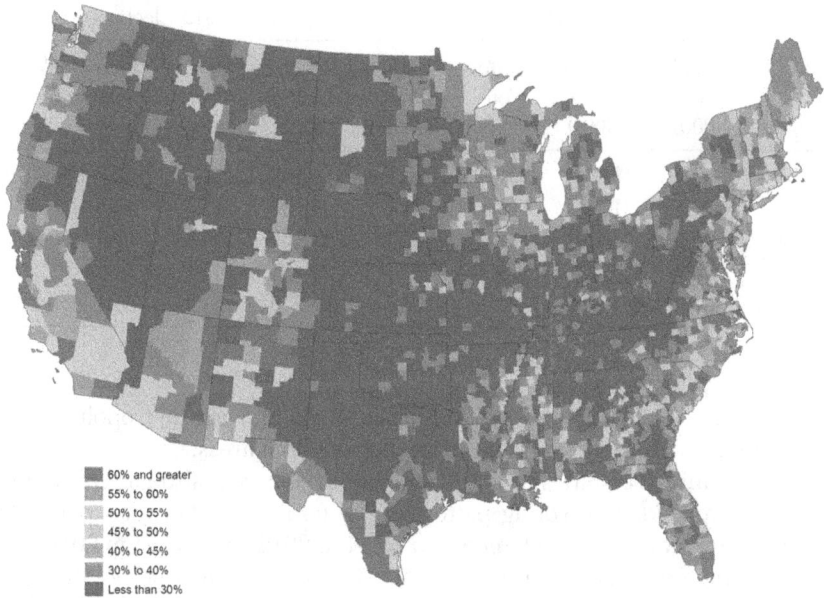

60% and greater
55% to 60%
50% to 55%
45% to 50%
40% to 45%
30% to 40%
Less than 30%

least in the political sphere. This difference was pronounced in the 2016 election.

Factors Influencing Presidential Voting Patterns

Position along the rural-urban continuum is certainly not alone in influencing presidential voting patterns (Scala, Johnson, and Rogers 2015). Figure 3 demonstrates distinct regional differences in voting patterns. In both 2012 and 2016, Democratic presidential support was weakest in the South, except in areas with substantial black populations, and in the largely rural areas of the central and southern Great Plains. In many counties in these regions, Donald Trump received more than 70 percent of the vote. In contrast, Democratic support was greatest in the Northeast, along much of the East and West Coasts, in the urban cores of the Great Lakes, and in minority areas of the Southeast and Southwest. Support for Clinton was less than that for Obama in all four major regions, with a notable fall-off in support for her in the Midwest (Table 3). A critical question here is whether our rural-urban continuum remains viable across regions. Though regional voting differences were substantial in both 2016 and 2012, the pattern along the rural-urban continuum remains consistent in each region with only minor exceptions (data not shown). Democratic presidential candidates did best in large metropolitan areas and small metropolitan cores in all regions, with

TABLE 3
Votes for Democratic Presidential Candidate by Region, 2012 and 2016

	2016 Election				2012 Election			
	Total Vote ('000s)	Clinton Vote ('000s)	Clinton Vote Percent	Counties Won Percent	Total Vote ('000s)	Obama Vote ('000s)	Obama Vote Percent	Counties Won Percent
Northeast	24,260	13,178	54.3	40.1	23,359	13,677	58.6	57.6
South	49,905	21,917	43.9	15.3	46,792	21,407	45.8	17.8
Midwest	31,576	14,151	44.8	7.0	31,161	15,788	50.7	18.2
West	28,976	15,458	53.3	26.3	27,465	14,917	54.3	29.2
Total	134,718	64,703	47.8	15.7	128,776	65,790	51.1	22.2

support falling off in small metro suburban areas and nonmetropolitan areas, particularly those that were distant from metropolitan areas.

The racial mix of counties in both rural and urban areas also has considerable relevance to presidential voting patterns. The correlation between percentage black and percentage voting Democrat ($r = .41$ in 2012 and $r = .51$ in 2016) is the largest bivariate correlation in our analysis (Table 4). Though not as strong, the correlations for Hispanics ($r = .10$ in 2012 and $r = .20$ in 2016) are also significant. It is widely recognized that one reason Democratic presidential candidates do so well in the large urban cores is because minority voters are a larger share of the voting pool in these areas. In the average large urban core county, 21 percent of the population was black and 18 percent was Hispanic in 2010 (Table 5). In contrast, in nonmetropolitan nonadjacent counties with no large town, 5 percent of the population was African American and 8 percent was Hispanic. Such racial diversity crosscuts the rural-urban continuum in complex spatial patterns because the minority population is unevenly distributed (Figure 4). There are enclaves of Democratic support in the largely Republican South, in areas with significant minority populations, including in battleground states such as North Carolina and Virginia, as well as in the Mississippi Delta and along the border between Texas and Mexico. Farther west in New Mexico, Colorado, and California, many counties with significant minority populations straddle the Democrat-Republican divide. In the Great Lakes region and the Northeast, both large and small urban cores are centers of diversity as well as Democratic strength.

Religion has also been a critical factor in the past several elections, especially the influence of white Evangelicals (Campbell, Green, and Layman 2011; McDaniel and Ellison 2008). There was a strong negative bivariate correlation between the percentage white Evangelical and support for Democrats ($r = -.39$ in 2012; $r = -.34$ in 2016). In contrast, the percentage Catholic had a moderately strong positive correlation with Democratic support ($r = .28$ in 2012; $r = .24$ in 2016). There is considerable variation along the rural-urban continuum in the distribution of these two groups. The smallest percentage of white Evangelicals

TABLE 4

Univariate Statistics for Selected Characteristics and Bivariate Correlation with
Percentage of Vote for Democratic Presidential Candidate, 2012 and 2016

| | | | Bivariate Correlation | |
Variable	Mean	Standard Deviation	Obama Percent	Clinton Percent
Percent voting for Obama	38.49	14.77		
Percent voting for Clinton	31.52	15.19		
Northeast region, dummy	.07	.25	.23	.21
Southern region, dummy	.46	.50	−.13	−.01
Midwest region, dummy	.34	.47	.00	−.15
West region, dummy	.13	.34	.01	.05
Large urban core, dummy	.02	.14	.24	.30
Large urban suburban, dummy	.12	.32	.08	.14
Small urban core, dummy	.11	.31	.19	.25
Small urban suburban, dummy	.13	.33	−.07	−.06
Adjacent micropolitan, dummy	.12	.33	.04	.02
Adjacent other, dummy	.21	.41	−.04	−.09
Not adjacent micropolitan, dummy	.09	.28	−.02	−.03
Not adjacent other, dummy	.21	.41	−.23	−.26
Farm county, dummy	.14	.35	−.24	−.28
Recreation county, dummy	.10	.29	.06	.05
Percent age 18 to 29, 2010	14.59	4.34	.29	.37
BA or higher, 2010	18.62	8.46	.30	.44
Median family income (in thousands)	55.47	13.27	.12	.20
Non-Hispanic black, percent, 2010	8.75	14.43	.41	.51
Hispanic, percent, 2010	8.32	13.24	.10	.20
Evangelical, percent, 2010	22.88	16.88	−.39	−.34
Catholic, percent, 2010	13.71	14.87	.28	.24

and the largest percentage of Catholics are in the cores of large urban areas. In contrast, white Evangelicals constitute the greatest share of the population and Catholics the smallest in nonmetropolitan counties. The difference between the religious concentrations in large cores, large suburbs, and small cores, on one hand, and the remaining counties, on the other, is evident here, as it was in the survey data, and underscores this as the likely rural-urban interface.

Religion and race are not the only factors related to voting with substantial disparities along the rural-urban continuum. Education has been widely discussed with reference to the 2016 election (Tyson and Maniam 2016). The correlation between percentage college graduate and Democratic voting is the second largest bivariate association in our analysis (r = .44 in 2016; up from .30 in 2012). Though income is not as closely related, it also had a modest correlation with Democratic support (r = .12 in 2012; .20 in 2016). Both education and

TABLE 5
Demographic Characteristics along the Rural-Urban Continuum

	Population					Characteristics				
	Population 2015	Mean Population	Change 2010–2015 Percent	College Grad Percent	Family Income (dollars)	White Evangelical Percent	Catholic Percent	Age 18–29 Percent	Black Percent	Hispanic Percent
Large core	98,573,202	1,471,242	5.9	31.8	$65,329	11.4	23.2	19.0	20.5	18.1
Large fringe	79,252,761	217,131	5.1	25.1	$72,489	17.5	16.8	14.3	10.4	8.3
Small core	78,863,066	231,270	3.9	25.1	$60,035	17.9	17.0	18.6	10.9	11.9
Small fringe	18,563,188	47,235	3.1	17.6	$56,949	22.4	10.4	14.1	8.4	9.5
Adjacent micro	18,379,158	49,406	0.1	17.4	$52,845	22.4	12.8	15.9	8.4	9.5
Adjacent other	11,951,861	18,275	-1.2	14.3	$49,659	26.8	10.9	13.4	10.5	6.5
Not adjacent micro	8,881,459	33,017	1.1	18.8	$53,386	23.4	14.0	15.8	7.4	9.3
Not adjacent other	6,931,633	10,209	-1.3	16.1	$50,279	24.7	14.6	12.5	4.6	8.0
Total	321,396,328	102,356	4.1	18.7	$55,554	22.8	13.7	14.6	8.8	8.3

FIGURE 4
Percentage Democratic Vote in Presidential Election in Counties with Minority
Population Greater than 20 Percent, 2016

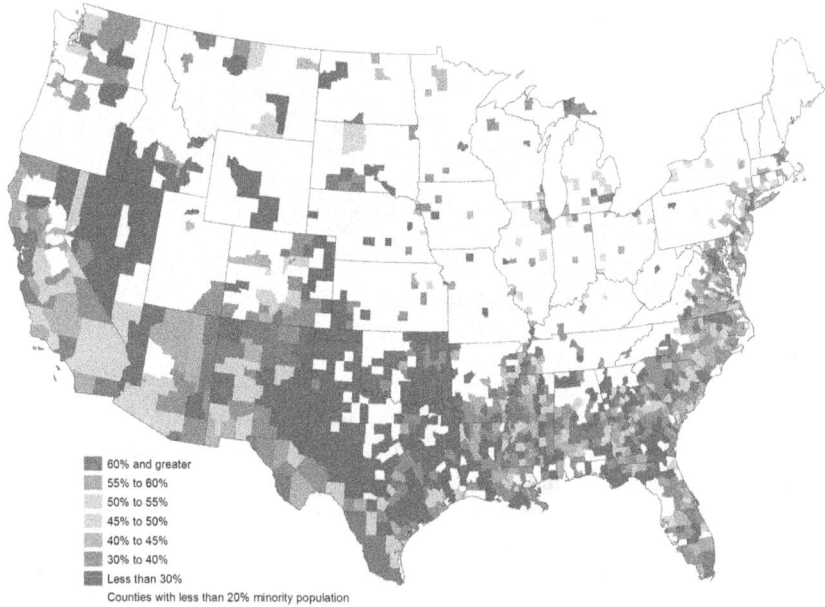

60% and greater
55% to 60%
50% to 55%
45% to 50%
40% to 45%
30% to 40%
Less than 30%
Counties with less than 20% minority population

income are unevenly distributed across the rural-urban continuum, with a familiar point of disjuncture. The percentage of the population with a college degree and higher median family income is considerably greater in large urban cores, their suburbs, and smaller urban cores than they are in the rest of the country.

Areas with higher education and incomes are also attractive to young adults, a group of considerable interest in recent elections. In both 2012 and 2016, counties with a larger proportion of young adults tended to vote more Democrat ($r = .29$ in 2012 and $.37$ in 2016). Here again, there are distinct differences in how young people are distributed along the rural urban-continuum. The proportion of the population between the ages of 18 and 29 was greatest in both large and small urban cores and lowest in the most remote rural counties. The age disparities are less pronounced along the rural-urban continuum than for some of the other variables considered here, though the urban cores certainly stand out.

There are also distinct differences in the scale of counties along the continuum. The large urban cores average nearly 1.5 million residents and grew by 5.9 percent between 2010 and 2015. The large suburban and small core counties average well over 200,000 residents and are also growing at a faster pace. In contrast, smaller suburban counties and rural counties with large towns in close proximity to metropolitan areas have roughly 50,000 residents on average. The other types of rural counties are far smaller and none have experienced much growth since 2010. Here again the break between the three most urban groups on the continuum and the remaining five is quite distinct.

Multivariate Spatial Analysis

Presidential voting patterns are the consequence of a myriad of demographic, economic, geographic, and social phenomena including, but certainly not limited to, the rural-urban continuum. We use multivariate spatial error regression models to represent the combined influence of these factors.[6] The models include measures of the rural-urban continuum, region, education, income, age, race, religious affiliation, and selected nonmetropolitan economic types. The models examine the impact of these independent variables on the percentage of the vote for Democrats in the 2012 and 2016 presidential elections in counties in the forty-eight continental states (Table 6).[7]

An important finding that supports our expectations of differences along the rural-urban continuum is the significance of the dummy variables representing the continuum. Being a large urban core county increased support for both Obama and Clinton considerably, even when controlling for a host of other variables. The predicted increase in support for the Democrat diminishes as one moves down the rural-urban continuum as expected, with a considerable disparity at the rural-urban interface. Counties that are in large metro areas or small core areas provide considerably more advantage to the Democratic candidate. Differences among nonmetropolitan county types are modest once we control for other variables; these differences are not statistically significant (nonadjacent other is the reference category). Overall, the dummy variables representing the rural-urban continuum provide unique explanatory power even in the complex multivariate environment represented in this model (data not shown), a finding consistent with our expectations.

The regional variables were also influential even when other variables were controlled. Support for both Obama and Clinton was greatest in the Northeast and least in the South, with the West (reference category) and Midwest in the middle. Education, income, and the proportion of young adults also had statistically significant impacts on county voting patterns. In this multivariate environment, the influence of education is positive, suggesting that both Obama and Clinton did better in counties where a larger proportion of the adult population graduated from college. The influence of education was considerably stronger for Clinton than it was for Obama. The presence of a significant number of young adults in the county also increased support for the Democratic candidate in 2012 and 2016. In contrast, in the multivariate environment, support for the Democratic nominee diminished as median family incomes increased.

The percentage of African Americans and Hispanics in a county also had a significant influence on the percentage voting Democrat in each election, with both variables producing a larger positive effect in 2016 than in 2012.[8] These findings are consistent with prior research that documented the extremely large

TABLE 6
Spatial Error Regression of Percentage Vote for Democratic Presidential
Candidate, 2012 and 2016

	Obama 2012				Clinton 2016			
	Coeff.	SE	Z-Value	Sig.	Coeff.	SE	Z-Value	Sig.
Constant	37.293	1.815	20.547	.000	20.462	1.518	13.478	.000
Northeast	5.313	2.255	2.356	.018	6.039	1.830	3.300	.001
South	–4.617	1.542	–2.993	.003	–4.215	1.260	–3.346	.001
Midwest	–0.191	1.485	–0.129	.898	–0.435	1.219	–0.356	.722
Big metro core	4.886	0.993	4.919	.000	5.573	0.905	6.161	.000
Big metro sub	2.102	0.680	3.094	.002	2.293	0.616	3.724	.000
Small metro core	1.056	0.578	1.826	.068	1.622	0.526	3.081	.002
Small metro sub	0.691	0.528	1.309	.190	0.777	0.480	1.618	.106
Nonmetro adj micro	0.555	0.476	1.165	.244	0.347	0.435	0.799	.424
Nonmetro adj nonmicro	0.551	0.401	1.373	.170	0.440	0.365	1.205	.228
Nonmetro nonadjacent micro	0.107	0.451	0.236	.813	0.121	0.415	0.291	.771
Nonmetro farm	–1.599	0.393	–4.074	.000	–1.480	0.360	–4.105	.000
Nonmetro recreation	0.955	0.459	2.080	.038	1.486	0.422	3.523	.000
College grad, percent	0.377	0.027	14.201	.000	0.637	0.024	26.196	.000
Median family income '000s	–0.244	0.020	–12.311	.000	–0.197	0.018	–10.906	.000
Age 18 to 29, percent	0.196	0.031	6.419	.000	0.190	0.028	6.766	.000
Non-Hispanic black, percent	0.716	0.018	40.827	.000	0.772	0.016	49.007	.000
Hispanic, percent	0.251	0.019	13.350	.000	0.338	0.017	20.012	.000
Evangelical percent	–0.108	0.013	–8.025	.000	–0.081	0.012	–6.618	.000
Catholic percent	0.093	0.012	7.583	.000	0.090	0.011	8.074	.000
Lambda	0.858	0.010	82.874	.000	0.817	0.012	67.409	.000
Number of cases	3,106				3,106			
Variables	20				20			
Degrees of freedom	3,086				3,086			
Pseudo R-squared	.84				.87			
Sigma-square	35.22				29.59			
Standard error of regression	5.93				5.44			
Log likelihood	–10,249				9,936			
Akaike information criterion	20,539				19,912			
Schwarz criterion	20,659				20,033			

proportion of the black population that supported Democrats in recent elections (Abrajano and Burnett 2012; Sullivan and Johnson 2008).

Religion also had a significant influence on voting patterns. Holding all other variables constant, as the percentage of the county population that were adherents of white Evangelical churches increased, support for the Democratic candidate diminished.[9] In contrast, the percentage Catholic had a positive impact on the percentage of voters supporting Democrats. The influence of Evangelicals, even after accounting for so many other factors, supports other scholarly research highlighting the importance of white Evangelicals to the Republican voter base (Campbell, Green, and Layman 2011; McDaniel and Ellison 2008).

Previous research concluded that the type of economy that dominates a particular rural county affects its partisan tilt even after taking into account other important factors (Scala, Johnson, and Rogers 2015). To address this, we included a dummy variable identifying the 296 nonmetropolitan recreational counties where natural and built amenities, as well as the provision of services to residents and visitors, were the basis for the local economy. A second dummy identified the 443 nonmetropolitan counties dominated by farming that are heavily concentrated in the Great Plains. The influence of farming and recreation is not limited to these counties, but it is more dominant there. Both variables had a significant though modest influence, even after controlling for other variables. The Democrats' performance tended to improve in recreational counties and diminish in counties dominated by farming. This finding is consistent with earlier research on rural counties (Scala, Johnson, and Rogers 2015).

A spatial error term (lambda) was included in the model to adjust for spatial autocorrelation. It diminishes in size as relevant independent variables, which reflect the underlying factors that produce spatial correlation, are introduced to the model. Nonetheless, the statistical significance of the lambda coefficient demonstrates that spatial autocorrelation still exists even when all the independent variables are included. The spatial coefficient removes this spatial bias from the standard errors associated with the estimated regression parameters, making the multivariate analysis statistically efficient and inferences from the model valid (Anselin 2005).

In sum, our model accounts for a substantial proportion of the variability in county-level voting patterns. It also underscores the political importance of where a county is located along the rural-urban continuum. It suggests that the percentage voting Democrat was greatest in large urban cores and smallest in remote nonmetropolitan counties, even holding other variables constant. It also suggests that a number of other factors also influence voting. Democrats did better in the Northeast, in counties with large young adult populations, in counties with more well-educated populations, in counties that had larger black and Hispanic populations, and in counties with fewer white Evangelicals and more Catholics. Republicans did best in counties at the other end of the rural-urban continuum. They performed better in remote nonmetropolitan counties, especially those in the South; with relatively few college graduates; higher incomes; dominated by farming; with fewer young adults; few Hispanics and blacks; and a larger percentage of white Evangelical adherents.

Conclusion

In the aftermath of the 2016 presidential election, commentators focused on the political polarization separating residents of urban and rural America. Yet both survey data and county-level voting data indicate that variations in voting patterns and political attitudes exist along a continuum. The residents of large metropolitan cores and surrounding suburbs are the base of the Democratic Party: they are the most likely to identify as Democrat, vote Democrat, and hold liberal attitudes on a host of social and political issues. Democrats enjoy considerable support in the suburbs of these large urban areas and in the cores of smaller metropolitan areas, though they received less than 50 percent of the vote in each. Outside of these areas, Democrats face a slippery slope. Smaller, less diverse suburbs of small metropolitan areas are less friendly to Democrats, as are rural counties. Politically speaking, the urban-rural interface lies in the suburbs of smaller metropolitan cores and at the outer edge of larger metropolitan areas. At this tipping point, where the suburbs start to resemble rural exurbia, and in the vast rural regions beyond, Republicans find much friendlier territory.

As we have shown, Hillary Clinton nearly matched Barack Obama's performance in the most populous areas of America. But her campaign faced defeat by a thousand cuts on the other end of the urban-rural continuum. From the "small suburbs" to the most far-flung rural areas, Clinton's inability to match Obama's performance led to defeat in crucial swing states such as Florida, Michigan, North Carolina, Pennsylvania, and Wisconsin. Given the faster rates of population growth and growing diversity on the urban side of the urban-rural interface, Democrats would appear to have a significant advantage over the long term. However, although the voting power of rural America is limited, the 2016 election demonstrated that what happens on the rural side of the interface remains important in future elections.

Notes

1. Detailed information about the Economic Research Service, U.S. Department of Agriculture (USDA) 2015 County Typology is available from https://www.ers.usda.gov/data-products/county-typology-codes/documentation/.

2. Any rural-urban classification system is a compromise between detail and summary. We tested a number of other rural-urban classification systems including the USDA Economic Research Service's Urban-Rural Continuum typology and Urban Influence typology. The classification we settled on was less detailed than either of the USDA systems, but produces a better voting gradient across the rural-urban continuum.

3. To obtain the median family income, annual data for each of the five years are adjusted for inflation so that all incomes are in 2011 dollars; then the five years of income data are averaged to estimate median income.

4. The data were downloaded from the Association of Religion Data Archives, www.TheARDA.com, and were collected by Grammich et al. (2012). The measure of "adherents" offers a consistent measure of religious affiliation across denominations and allows for meaningful comparisons between groups (Grammich et al. 2012). The dataset includes 151 million religious adherents, or 49 percent of the U.S. population at the time of the survey. An estimated 31 million additional individuals who are religious

adherents are not included in the database. For the first time in 2010, an effort was made to estimate adherents to historically African American denominations; however, the enumeration was incomplete and historically African American denominations were reported separately. Because almost all these historically African American denominations are Evangelical, the measure of Evangelicals that we use actually reflects the percentage of the county population that is white Evangelicals (Finke and Scheitle 2005).

5. The comprehensive survey data we required for this analysis are not available yet for the 2016 election.

6. Because spatial autocorrelation is present in both 2012 and 2016, ordinary least squares (OLS) regression is not appropriate (Anselin 2002). The spatial error model selected assumes that spatial heterogeneity exists among the independent variables and corrects for it by adding a spatial error coefficient (lambda). This removes spatial bias from the standard errors associated with the estimated regression parameters. Incorporating a spatial error coefficient and using maximum likelihood to estimate model parameters make the multivariate analysis statistically efficient and inferences from the model valid (Anselin 2005). The spatial "neighborhood" for each county was all contiguous counties—a first order queen neighborhood. The spatial error model was selected in preference to the spatial lag model based on comparisons of LaGrange multipliers for the spatial lag and spatial error models (Anselin 2002, 2005).

7. In this model, the reference category would be a county that is not adjacent to a metro area, has no large town, is neither a farm nor a recreational county, and is in the West.

8. We represent race and Hispanic origin with measures of the proportion of the population in the county that was Hispanic and the proportion that was non-Hispanic black in 2010.

9. The Evangelical variable included in this model represents white Evangelical churches. Black Evangelical adherents are not included (Finke and Scheitle 2005).

References

Abrajano, Marisa, and Craig M. Burnett. 2012. Polls and elections: Do blacks and whites see Obama through race-tinted glasses? A comparison of Obama's and Clinton's approval ratings. *Presidential Studies Quarterly* 42 (2): 363–75.

Abrams, Samuel J., and Morris P. Fiorina. 2012. "The big sort" that wasn't: A skeptical reexamination. *PS: Political Science & Politics* 45 (2): 203–10.

Anselin, Luc. 2002. Under the hood: Issues in the specification and interpretation of spatial regression models. *Agricultural Economics* 27:247–67.

Anselin, Luc. 2005. *Exploring spatial data with GeoDa*. Urbana-Champaign, IL: Spatial Analysis Lab, Department of Agricultural and Consumer Economics, University of Illinois.

Ansolabehere, Stephen, and Brian Schaffner. 2012. CCES Common Content, 2012. Version 5. Available from http://hdl.handle.net/1902.1/21447UNF:5:mMbfa1Vn45NxO7I6aZPicg== CCES.

Bartels, Larry M. 2006. What's the matter with *What's the matter with Kansas?* *Quarterly Journal of Political Science* 1 (2): 201–26.

Bishop, Bill, and Robert Cushing. 2008. *The big sort: Why the clustering of like-minded America is tearing us apart*. Boston, MA: Houghton Mifflin.

Black, Merle. 2004. The transformation of the Southern Democratic Party. *Journal of Politics* 66 (4): 1001–17.

Buttel, Frederick, and William Flinn. 1975. Sources and consequences of agrarian values in American society. *Rural Sociology* 40 (2): 134–51.

Campbell, David E., John C. Green, and Geoffrey C. Layman. 2011. The party faithful: Partisan images, candidate religion, and the electoral impact of party identification. *American Journal of Political Science* 55 (1): 42–58.

Cho, Wendy K. T., James G. Gimpel, and Joshua J. Dyck. 2006. Residential concentration, political socialization, and voter turnout. *Journal of Politics* 68 (1): 156–67.

Cramer, Katherine J. 2016. *The politics of resentment: Rural consciousness in Wisconsin and the rise of Scott Walker*. Chicago, IL: University of Chicago Press.

Drury, Renée, and Luther Tweeten. 1997. Have farmers lost their uniqueness? *Review of Agricultural Economics* 19 (1): 58–90.

Finke, Roger, and Christopher P. Scheitle. 2005. Accounting for the uncounted: Computing correctives for the 2000 RCMS data. *Review of Religious Research* 47 (1): 5–22.

Francia, Peter L., and Jody Baumgartner. 2005. Victim or victor of the "culture war"? How cultural issues affect support for George W. Bush in rural America. *American Review of Politics* 26:349–67.

Frank, Thomas. 2004. *What's the matter with Kansas? How conservatives won the heart of America*. New York, NY: Metropolitan Books.

Frendreis, John, and Raymond Tatalovich. 2013. Secularization, modernization, or population change: Explaining the decline of Prohibition in the United States. *Social Science Quarterly* 94 (2): 379–94.

Gimpel, James G., Joshua Dyck, and Daron Shaw. 2004. Registrants, voters, and turnout variability across neighborhoods. *Political Behavior* 26 (4): 343–75.

Gimpel, James G., and Kimberly A. Karnes. 2006. The rural side of the urban-rural gap. *PS: Political Science & Politics* 39 (3): 467–72.

Gimpel, James G., and Jason E. Schuknecht. 2001. Interstate migration and electoral politics. *Journal of Politics* 63 (1): 207–31.

Glenn, Norval D., and Lester Hill. 1977. Rural-urban differences in attitudes and behavior in the United States. *The ANNALS of the American Academy of Political and Social Science* 429:36–50.

Grammich, Clifford, Kirk Hadaway, Richard Houseal, Dale E. Jones, Alexei Krindatch, Richie Stanley, and Richard H. Taylor. 2012. *2010 U.S. Religion Census: Religious congregations & membership study*. Lenexa, KS: Association of Statisticians of American Religious Bodies.

Hayes, Danny, and Seth C. McKee. 2008. Toward a one-party South? *American Politics Research* 36 (1): 3–32.

Hui, Iris. 2013. Who is your preferred neighbor? Partisan residential preferences and neighborhood satisfaction. *American Politics Research* 41 (6): 997–1021.

Johnson, Kenneth M. 2012. *Rural demographic change in the new century: Slower growth, increased diversity*. Issue Brief No. 44. Durham, NH: Carsey Institute, University of New Hampshire.

Johnson, Kenneth M. 20 February 2017. Where is "rural America" and what does it look like? *The Conversation*. Available from https://theconversation.com.

Johnson, Kenneth M., Paul R. Voss, Roger B. Hammer, Glenn V. Fuguitt, and Scott McNiven. 2005. Temporal and spatial variation in age-specific net migration in the United States. *Demography* 42 (4): 791–812.

Johnson, Kenneth M., Richelle L. Winkler, and Luke T. Rogers. 2013. *Age and lifecycle patterns driving U.S. migration shifts*. Carsey Institute Issue Brief 62. Durham, NH: Carsey Institute, University of New Hampshire.

Knoke, David, and Constance Henry. 1977. Political structure of rural America. *The ANNALS of the American Academy of Political and Social Science* 429:51–62.

Kron, Josh. 30 November 2012. Red state, blue city: How the urban-rural divide is splitting America. *The Atlantic*. Available from www.theatlantic.com (accessed 8 December 2016).

Leip, Dave. 2016. *Atlas of U.S. presidential elections*. Available from uselectionatlas.org.

Lewis-Beck, M. 1977. Agrarian political behavior in the United States. *American Journal of Political Science* 21 (3): 543–65.

McDaniel, Eric L., and Christopher G. Ellison. 2008. God's party? Race, religion, and partisanship over time. *Political Research Quarterly* 61 (2): 180–91.

McDonald, Ian. 2011. Migration and sorting in the American electorate: Evidence from the 2006 Cooperative Congressional Election Study. *American Politics Research* 39 (3): 512–33.

McKee, Seth C. 2008. Rural voters and the polarization of American presidential elections. *PS: Political Science & Politics* 41 (1): 101–8.

McKee, Seth C., and Jeremy M. Teigen. 2009. Probing the reds and blues: Sectionalism and voter location in the 2000 and 2004 U. S. presidential elections. *Political Geography* 28 (8): 484–95.

McVeigh, Rory, and Maria-Elena D. Diaz. 2009. Voting to ban same-sex marriage: Interests, values, and communities. *American Sociological Review* 74:891–915.

Monson, Renée A., and Jo Beth Mertens. 2011. All in the family: Red states, blue states, and postmodern family patterns, 2000 and 2004. *Sociological Quarterly* 52 (2): 244–67.

Morrill, Richard, Larry Knopp, and Michael Brown. 2007. Anomalies in red and blue: Exceptionalism in American electoral geography. *Political Geography* 26 (5): 525–53.

Office of Management and Budget. 2015. *Revised delineations of metropolitan statistical areas, micropo-litan statistical areas and combined statistical areas and guidance on uses of the delineation of these areas*. OMB Bulletin 15-01. Washington, DC: U.S. Government Printing Office.

Pew Research Center. 2014. *Political polarization in the American public: How increasing ideological uniformity and partisan antipathy affect politics, compromise and everyday life*. Washington, DC: Pew Research Center. Available from pewresearch.org.

Robinson, Tony, and Stephen Noriega. 2010. Voter migration as a source of electoral change in the Rocky Mountain West. *Political Geography* 29 (1): 28–39.

Scala, Dante. 2011. *Changes in New Hampshire's Republican Party: Evolving footprint in presidential politics, 1960–2008*. New England Issue Brief 30. Durham, NH: Carsey Institute, University of New Hampshire.

Scala, Dante, Kenneth M. Johnson, and Luke T. Rogers. 2015. Red rural, blue rural? Presidential voting patterns in a changing rural America. *Political Geography* 48:108–18.

Sullivan, Jas M., and Melanie S. Johnson. 2008. Race is on my mind: Explaining black voters' political attraction to Barack Obama. *Race, Gender & Class* 15 (3–4): 51–64.

Tyson, Alec, and Shiva Maniam. 2016. *Behind Trump's victory: Divisions by race, gender, education*. Washington, DC: Pew Research Center. Available from www.pewresearch.org (accessed 6 December 2016).

Schools at the Rural-Urban Boundary: Blurring the Divide?

By
JULIA BURDICK-WILL
and
JOHN R. LOGAN

Schools often mirror the communities in which they are located. Research on rural-urban school inequality tends to focus on the contrast among urban, suburban, and rural schools, glossing over the variation and similarities within these areas. We provide a richer description of the spatial distribution of educational inequality by examining school composition, achievement, and resources in all U.S. public elementary schools in 2010–2011. We take the traditional census categories derived from residential and commuting patterns, and apply them to schools across the country in analyses that reveal gradual transitions and blurry boundaries among the traditional zones. The results show high levels of variation within the suburbs and substantial commonality between rural and urban areas and suggest that census-defined metropolitan areas are not ideal when considering the geography of educational opportunity.

Keywords: education; inequality; geography; race; performance; resources

Schools vary widely in racial/ethnic composition, poverty concentration, student performance, and organizational resources. It is well known that these differences have a spatial pattern, especially pronounced in the disparities between many central city school districts and those in the surrounding suburbs. Urban

Julia Burdick-Will is an assistant professor in the Department of Sociology and in the School of Education at Johns Hopkins University. She is the author of "School Violent Crime and Academic Achievement in Chicago," published in Sociology of Education *(2013).*

John R. Logan is a professor of sociology at Brown University. He is coauthor, along with Harvey Molotch, of Urban Fortunes: The Political Economy of Place *(1987). His most recent edited book,* Diversity and Disparities, *was published by Russell Sage Foundation in 2015.*

Correspondence: jburdickwill@jhu.edu

DOI: 10.1177/0002716217707176

schools tend to have much larger proportions of minority students, higher poverty rates, and lower achievement than do suburban schools (Orfield and Lee 2005; Logan, Minca, and Adar 2012). However, many studies of school segregation and educational inequality are limited to metropolitan regions (Reardon and Owens 2014). In this study, we extend analysis to rural schools, and we examine variation within urban, suburban, and rural areas as well as the similarities among them.

Much research on the rural-urban interface, including studies of rural schools, focuses on the simple dichotomy between nonmetropolitan and metropolitan locations, ignoring differences between cities and suburbs (Lichter and Brown 2011). Other studies add dummy variables (simple yes/no categorical indicators) for urban, suburban, and rural locations to test whether rural schools are distinctive, but they do not examine variation within each of these categories (Fan and Chen 1999). We believe that variation within and commonalities across these locations are important for two reasons. First, boundaries are arbitrary and changing; for example, the Census Bureau uses set population density cut-offs to define urban and rural areas, and what counted as rural at one time might well be suburban at another (Taylor 2011; Ratcliffe et al. 2016). Second, people are also in flux. In recent decades, net migration flows between central cities and the suburbs have strongly favored suburban areas, as has migration from rural to suburban areas. Suburbanites now account for more than half of the U.S. population (Lichter and Brown 2011). As populations have grown and farmland has been converted into residential developments, many metropolitan areas have also expanded and been redefined to include areas previously marked by a rural settlement pattern (see the introduction to this volume for more detail).

These growing suburban populations are not homogeneous, and different locations within the suburban ring vary greatly from others. On the outer edge of metropolitan areas, the incorporation of new counties is likely to include some rural communities that maintain a traditional rural settlement pattern despite the new suburban designation (Taylor 2011). Closer to the cities, poor and minority families are moving into inner suburban neighborhoods at increasing rates (Allard 2008; Murphy 2007). By 2008, the poor population in the suburbs was growing faster than in the cities or rural areas (Kneebone and Garr 2010). New immigrants are also moving directly to suburban and rural areas without stopping in traditional urban ethnic enclaves (Ehrenhalt 2012; Lichter and Brown 2011; see also García and Schmalzbauer, this volume).

The heterogeneity of schools located in each part of the metropolis is reflected in the fact that when analysts seek to sort schools into clusters with similar characteristics, these clusters do not neatly divide into urban, suburban, and rural categories. Logan, Minca, and Adar (2012) analyzed all U.S. public elementary schools in 2000 and reported one cluster that seems to represent typical suburban characteristics, with a large number of white students (87 percent on

NOTE: This project was made possible with indirect support from the Population Studies and Training Center at Brown University and the Hopkins Population Center.

average), low levels of free and reduced lunch eligibility (21 percent on average), and highly ranked schools (averaging at the 68th percentile on test scores compared with others in the same state). However, only 71 percent of schools in this cluster are in the suburbs. The others are split evenly between cities and rural areas. Two clusters have a plurality of schools located in central cities, and their characteristics approximate the city stereotype: they have high shares of minority children, around two-thirds of students are free-lunch eligible, and they are also the poorest performing schools on standardized tests. Yet both suburban and nonmetro schools are well represented in these clusters. Even the cluster that was most likely to be found in rural areas (distinguished partly by overrepresentation of Native American students) included just as many suburban and central city schools as it did nonmetro schools. Hence there is much overlap in characteristics across these three kinds of locations. Research that only taps the average differences among them risks reifying the boundaries among urban, suburban, and rural locations and ignoring the transitional zones among them.

Research Design

Our purpose is to provide an assessment of variation in schools within and among these locations for all public schools in the United States in 2010–2011. Our research design incorporates two critical choices: (1) we identify school locations based on the boundaries of the school district that administers them, and (2) we examine only public elementary schools.

There are several reasons to focus on school districts for our main classification of schools. Most students attend a school in the district where they reside, and many families, both rich and poor, make housing decisions based on the perceived quality of the public schools in each district (Lareau and Goyette 2014). Research on school segregation also shows that there are larger racial and economic differences between districts than among schools within the same district (Reardon and Owens 2014). School funding is generally allocated at the district level, as are decisions about instruction and staffing. While the relationship between expenditures and achievement is complicated and more money does not tend to lead directly to higher achievement, when resources are used appropriately, both scholars and parents expect them to lead to better schooling outcomes and more educational opportunity (Morgan and Jung 2016).

In most of the country school districts are smaller than the counties used by the U.S. Census Bureau to delineate metropolitan location and to distinguish cities, suburbs, and rural areas. Therefore, districts allow for the division of large county-based regions into more finely grained categories. We define a locational gradient from the central city to the suburban fringe and then beyond to rural areas, using school district boundaries as dividing lines to distinguish schools in the largest cities; schools in smaller cities within large metropolitan areas; inner suburban, core suburban, and outer suburban schools; and finally rural schools close to the metropolitan boundary and those that are more distant. We also undertake a systematic comparison of pairs of schools that lie near one another on either side of each of these regions to test the salience of the boundaries between locational categories. We do find important differences between large and small city schools, suburban schools, and rural schools. But we also show that the boundaries between these types are blurred rather than sharply divided. Schools near one another on either side of each of these boundaries are rather similar, creating gradients where we might have found large differences. The inner and outer edges of suburbia look a lot like the urban and rural areas on the other side. Further, many schools in rural districts have more in common in terms of composition, resources, and achievement with many smaller city districts than with the privileged middle suburban areas that lie between them. By examining the composition of schools along the rural-urban interface, we expose the rather thin line that separates the rural from the urban.

Our second major choice is to focus on public elementary schools. The vast majority of students attend public schools. These schools are likely to draw students from a smaller catchment area than schools of different types or grade levels, and the quality of those schools often reflects residential patterns and influences housing prices (Downes and Zabel 2002).[1] Because grade ranges in schools vary greatly across districts, we define an "elementary school" here as one that includes at least one grade between kindergarten and sixth grade. Where possible we consider data only for elementary grade children. We use fourth graders to represent the achievement levels of elementary students because this is the elementary grade level for which test scores are most often available. When test score data are not available for fourth graders, we use scores from fifth graders. If there are no fourth or fifth graders, we take the scores of third graders.

Data

Data on all public schools in 2010–2011 are provided by the National Center for Education Statistics (NCES). NCES provides data on the student body of each school through its Common Core of Data (NCES 2012b). Race/ethnicity is reported in the following categories: non-Hispanic white, black, Hispanic, Asian, Native American, and other races. NCES also reports for most schools the number of students who are eligible for free or reduced price lunches, which we use as an indicator of poverty. Eligibility for reduced price lunches is reported for the entire school. We assume that free/reduced price lunch eligibility of students in each grade mirrors that of the whole school. The Common Core of Data also includes the total number of students, student-teacher ratio, and the precise geographic location of each school.[2]

The Common Core of Data also provides information on school district finances (NCES 2012a). School-level funding is not available, but we use the district-level measure of instructional salary per student (total district expenditures on salaries for teachers divided by total number of students in the district) to capture an approximation of the educationally relevant expenditures in each school. It is important to note that while equity of funding is important in and of itself, numerous studies have found that financial resources alone are not related to student achievement (see Morgan and Jung [2016] for a recent analysis of the different ways to measure school financial resources and its relationship with achievement test scores).

Testing data are calculated from the percent of students who meet state proficiency levels in reading and mathematics on tests administered by each state, reported to and made available by NCES (EDFacts 2013a, 2013b). The content and scoring of these tests vary widely across states. However, these are the most comprehensive testing data. The National Assessment of Educational Progress (NAEP) provides scores that are comparable across states, but these are available only for a sample of students within a small sample of U.S. schools. To make the state test scores more meaningful, we have recalibrated the percent passing scores as percentiles of school performance within the state (following the approach by Logan, Minca, and Adar [2012] and Logan and Burdick-Will [2016]). A complication in using these scores is that in many cases NCES reported a score range (sometimes a range as large as 15 or 20 percentage points) rather than a specific score. For each reported range, we determine the average score among schools in the nation with reported specific scores in that range. We then use the imputed precise scores to calculate a percentile within each state. This creates a rank ordering within every state. From the perspective of a parent who is considering a range of school options, almost always within a state, these percentiles are meaningful. A school at the 20th percentile is much worse than one at the 50th percentile in any state, regardless of differences in the states' test content or proficiency cutoffs that we suspect are considerable.

Table 1 shows the means of each school measure using the traditional urban-suburban-rural categories. Suburban schools educate the largest number of elementary school students. Approximately half of the 25.8 million elementary school students go to school in the suburbs. A little under one third attend urban schools, and 15 percent attend schools in a rural area.

Unsurprisingly, there are stark differences among these groups. Overall, student populations get substantially whiter as schools get farther from the urban core. There is a steep urban-to-rural decrease in black and Hispanic students and a sharp increase in Native American students. Free and reduced lunch eligibility, on the other hand, is lowest in suburban areas (42.8 percent) and only slightly lower in rural areas (58.0 percent) than urban ones (62.5 percent). The achievement measures follow the inverse trend, with suburban schools scoring approximately 12 percentage points higher than urban schools and 8 percentage points higher than rural schools, on average. The ratio of students to teachers is substantially lower in rural schools (30) than urban or suburban (36). Instructional salary expenditure per student is somewhat higher in urban areas than in rural areas, and suburbs fall in between.

Methods of Analysis

The focus of this analysis is to understand the differentiation along the boundaries between the traditional large census categories of urban, suburban, and

TABLE 1
Average Characteristics of Schools by Metropolitan Location,
Public Elementary Schools, 2010–2011

	All	Urban	Suburban	Rural
Percent white	51.3	30.3	58.1	70.6
Percent black	15.6	24.2	11.9	10.8
Percent Hispanic	24.3	35.1	21.5	12.0
Percent Asian	4.7	6.4	4.7	1.0
Percent Native American	1.1	0.8	0.7	3.1
Free or reduced lunch	51.5	62.5	42.9	58.0
Reading	45.0	37.4	50.7	41.4
Math	44.7	38.0	49.7	41.7
Student-teacher ratio	35.7	37.1	36.8	29.6
Instructional salary per student	$4,262	$4,388	$4,275	$3,968
Sample sizes:				
N students (1,000s)	25,760	8,102	13,540	4,118
N schools	67,977	19,339	32,529	16,109
N districts	12,842	1,045	6,316	6,291

SOURCE: Authors' calculations based on data from the U.S. Census Bureau and the National Center for Education Statistics.

rural. To do this we code every school based on its location and the boundaries of its school district using the school's geographic coordinates (reported by NCES) and maps of school district boundaries provided by the Census Bureau. Geographic information systems (GIS) procedures were used to locate schools within principal cities of metropolitan statistical areas (MSAs), the suburban remainder of the MSA, or outside of an MSA using the Census Bureau's geographic definitions as of 2010. The geographic boundaries of elementary school districts (or unified districts including elementary schools) were then used to determine if the district touched the boundary of a metropolitan area or a principal city. Since the MSAs are defined by county boundaries and school districts do not always align with county boundaries, there are some districts that cross both boundaries. This is especially true in the Southwest. This means that schools in the same district may be placed in different categories.

Every school was given one of the following mutually exclusive codes. All categories are defined by location, and all suburban and rural categories are based entirely on adjacency. The distinction between schools in large and smaller city districts is based on their elementary enrollment.

(A) Large urban: schools located in the largest city in a multicity metropolitan areas. There are 136 cities that fit this category, including the ten largest cities in terms of student population and most of the top twenty.

(B) Small urban: schools located within any other principal city, including cities in single city metropolitan areas.
(C) Inner suburban: suburban schools in a district that touches or crosses the city limit.
(D) Middle suburban: suburban schools in a district that does not touch or cross the city limit or the MSA boundary.
(E) Outer suburban: suburban schools in a district that touches a rural district, but not the city limit.[3]
(F) Inner rural: rural schools in a district that touches or crosses the MSA boundary.
(G) Middle rural: rural schools in a district that touches an inner rural district.
(H) Outer rural: rural schools in a district that does not touch an inner rural district.

These definitions rely on the adjacency of city, metro, and district boundaries rather than arbitrary distance or density cut-offs. Since these boundaries are socially constructed, they often are influenced by political and demographic differences between residents, making them likely to represent real social distinctions. If we relied on distance or density criteria, we would have to treat rural districts in the Southwest, where districts are especially large and transportation relies on major highways, as "more isolated" than those in the denser and more politically fragmented Northeast. Our view is that the important distinctions along the rural-urban interface are not based solely on proximity but also on social differentiation and differences in resources (Hiner 2016).

A map of the continental United States using these location categories can be found in Figure 1. These categories of schools are not evenly distributed across the country. Table 2 shows the relative frequency of each category in four major census regions. Here we follow the census designation of regions except for Texas, which we place in the West rather than the South due to its large Hispanic population. In the Northeast, due to the high density of adjacent metropolitan areas and fragmentation of districts, nearly one third of all schools are middle suburban (that is, in the suburbs but not adjacent either to the central city limits or the outer metropolitan boundary). Despite high population density, many schools in this region are also outer rural. In the South and the West, where districts are much larger, there are fewer metropolitan areas, and city districts are quite large, many fewer schools are middle suburban. The largest number of inner rural schools are in the South, while middle and outer rural schools are most common in the Midwest.

Schools and districts vary in different areas of the country in ways other than their locational category. For example, districts in the Northeast and rustbelt are much smaller and more densely populated, and districts on the coasts tend to have more wealthy residents. To remove these overall regional differences, we will make comparisons only between schools in the general area. We do this by creating what we call *metro-plus zones*—metropolitan regions plus the rural schools nearest to them. We define *nearest* by using GIS software to find the nearest metropolitan principal city to every rural school. Rural schools are then

FIGURE 1
Detailed Locational Categories in the Continental United States

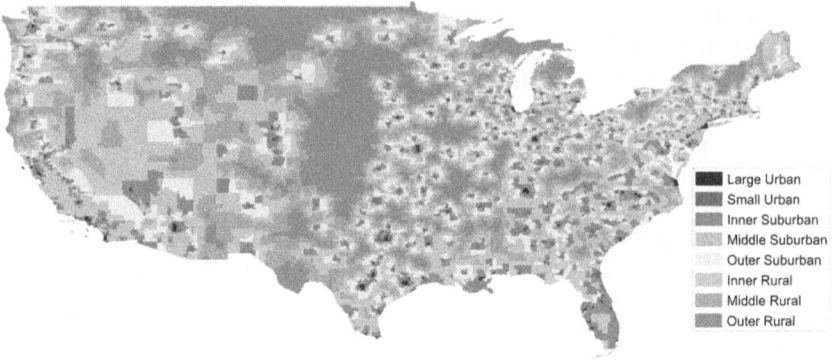

SOURCE: Authors' calculations based on data from the U.S. Census Bureau and the National Center for Education Statistics.

considered to be part of that nearest principal city's metro-plus area. In our multivariate analyses, we calculate the differences between locational categories in the same metro area using regressions with fixed effects for each metro-plus area. Since many metropolitan areas cross state lines, we also include indicators for each state. The results are weighted by the number of students in each metro-plus area. The general approach is represented in the following equation, where Y_{ij} is the proportion of non-Hispanic white students in the school:

$$Y_{ij} = \beta_0 + \beta_1 SmallUrban_{ij} + \beta_2 InnerSuburban_{ij}$$
$$+ \beta_3 MiddleSubruban_{ij} + \beta_4 OuterSuburban_{ij}$$
$$+ \beta_5 InnerRural_{ij} + \beta_6 MiddleRural_{ij} + \beta_7 OuterRural_{ij}$$
$$+ State_{ij} + MetroPlusArea_i + e_{ij}.$$

By comparing categories within the same metro-plus zones, the focus becomes the relative difference in racial composition among urban, suburban, and rural areas rather than the absolute proportions. For example, in the small metropolitan areas in the Midwest that tend to have very high proportions of white residents, the model is focused on differences within them rather than the relatively high proportions in all the area's schools. Note that not all metro-plus areas include every category. Some MSAs have only one city and therefore are not included in the large urban category. Some MSAs do not include enough suburban districts to have middle or outer suburban areas. Many MSAs do not include middle or outer rural areas and some have no rural or outer suburban areas at all because they are completely surrounded by other metropolitan areas. When an MSA does not include a category, its schools do not contribute to the estimate of the relative difference. Predicted means for each category are reported in Table 3.

TABLE 2
Regional Location of Schools by Metropolitan Category

	Total	Northeast	Midwest	South	West
Total schools	67,977	11,310	17,177	17,836	21,654
Large urban	52.2%	40.9%	54.1%	53.9%	55.1%
Urban	7.1%	4.2%	7.6%	8.2%	7.2%
Inner suburban	18.8%	14.1%	13.0%	22.4%	22.9%
Middle suburban	11.5%	30.0%	13.3%	2.6%	7.6%
Outer suburban	3.5%	3.0%	3.9%	4.5%	2.5%
Inner rural	3.8%	3.2%	3.6%	5.6%	2.7%
Middle rural	2.1%	2.4%	3.1%	1.9%	1.4%
Outer rural	1.1%	2.1%	1.5%	0.8%	0.5%

SOURCE: Authors' calculations based on data from the U.S. Census Bureau and the National Center for Education Statistics.

These means do not represent the characteristics of any specific metro-plus area but, rather, the national average of each category controlling for differences in metro area and state.

To examine variations right at the boundaries between location categories, we carry out another series of analyses based on selected pairs of schools on either side of the boundary. Using ArcGIS 10.4, all schools were matched to the closest school in a different locational category within the same metro-plus area, regardless of distance. Since we only want schools that fall as close as possible to the locational boundary, pairs of matching schools were included in the analysis if they represent the closest cross-location match for both schools. Therefore, one school may not be a match for multiple schools even if they are in different locational categories. These pairs represent as closely as possible the idea of adjacency using points that take into account the density of schools, rather than arbitrary distance bands.

For these analyses, we do not consider the boundary between the two urban categories (large urban and small urban) because there are very few MSAs with adjacent large and small urban cities. Not all potential cross-boundary pairs exist in every MSA. For example, in MSAs with no middle suburban area, inner suburban schools are paired with outer suburban or even inner rural schools. There are approximately 13,000 schools included in these edge analyses. The average distance between schools in a pair is three miles. The average distance is smallest at the urban boundary (1.5 miles) and largest at the rural boundary (7.5 miles) due to the differences in density between urban and rural areas.[4]

The average value for category edges is then calculated using a regression that includes all cases where one of the pairs forms the edge of a given category and includes a fixed effect for each pair of schools. This means that we estimate the relative difference between schools on either side of the boundary rather than the absolute value. We also control for the category of the school that falls on the

TABLE 3
Predicted Average Characteristics of Schools by Detailed Location Category, Based on
Fixed-Effects Model Controlling for Metro-Plus Location

	Large Urban	Inner Urban	Middle Suburban	Outer Suburban	Inner Suburban	Inner Rural	Middle Rural	Outer Rural
Percent white	14.8	32.4	42.7	59.2	68.2	58.1	54.6	56.0
Percent black	35.3	23.8	16.4	8.3	3.5	9.3	10.8	10.0
Percent Hispanic	41.2	31.3	29.3	24.5	21.9	24.0	25.0	25.0
Percent Asian	6.2	9.2	8.3	4.7	3.6	4.8	4.9	4.7
Percent Native American	0.7	0.4	0.6	0.7	0.9	2.0	2.8	2.1
Free or reduced lunch	73.4	55.9	45.4	33.6	43.8	54.1	56.0	55.4
Reading	30.5	42.5	50.7	55.8	49.8	43.1	42.3	41.5
Math	32.5	42.2	50.1	52.7	48.6	42.5	40.7	41.5
Student-teacher ratio	33.4	35.9	36.7	33.8	29.1	26.9	26.3	26.0
Instructional salary per student	$4,914	$5,420	$5,218	$5,311	$4,936	$5,211	$5,402	$5,452
Sample sizes								
N students (1000s)	3,715	4,387	8,118	3,845	1,576	2,182	1,244	693
N schools	8,853	10,486	17,746	9,900	4,883	7,663	5,055	3,391
N districts	280	765	2,138	2,575	1,603	2,365	2,124	1,802

SOURCE: Authors' calculations based on data from the U.S. Census Bureau and the National
Center for Education Statistics.

other side of the boundary because not all metro areas have all the middle and
outer categories, and therefore pairs of schools contain different combinations of
categories.

For example, the predicted mean of the outer most edge of inner suburban is
the intercept of the following equation, estimated with all pairs of schools in
which one of the schools is on that edge:

$$Y_{ij} = \alpha_0 + \alpha_1 \text{MiddleSuburban}_{ij} + \alpha_2 \text{OuterSuburban}_{ij} +$$
$$\alpha_3 \text{InnerRural}_{ij} + \alpha_4 \text{MiddleRural}_{ij} +$$
$$\alpha_5 \text{OuterRural}_{ij} + \text{Pair}_i + e_{ij}.$$

Instead of reporting the coefficients of these models, we present results for
predicted means in graphical form (Figures 2–3). In these figures the line from
one edge to the mean of all nonedge schools to the other edge is then drawn for
each category along the same y-axis with the label for each category in the middle
of the line. These graphs show the slope of change within each category as well

FIGURE 2
Category Edges for Racial Composition

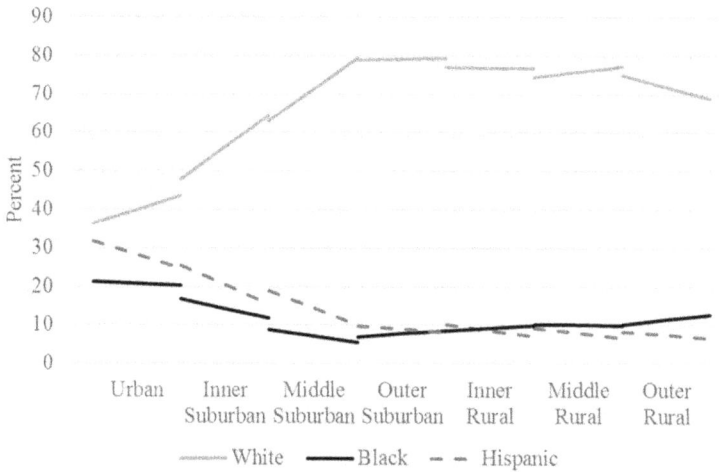

SOURCE: Authors' calculations based on data from the U.S. Census Bureau and the National Center for Education Statistics.

as any gaps or jumps between categories. If there is a smooth gradient in our measure, the lines will all connect; but if there are clear categorical differences, the lines for each area will appear disconnected.

Results

Table 3 shows the results of the metro-plus fixed-effects regressions and reports the school means in each detailed category (controlling for differences across metropolitan areas and regions of the country).[5] Any factors that are constant across a metropolitan area are therefore removed from the estimates as schools are compared only to the other schools in their general areas.[6]

Overall, most variables show a steady gradient across categories, rather than clear-cut differences between urban, suburban, and rural schools. There are only small differences among inner, middle, and outer rural schools, but there are dramatic differences between large and small urban areas and inner, middle, and outer suburbs. The average proportion of white students in a school increases rapidly from large urban (14.8) through the outer suburbs (68.2) and then declines somewhat in rural areas to about the share found in middle suburban schools. The average proportion of black students shows an inverse trend, with a dramatic decline from 35.2 percent in the large urban areas to 3.5 percent in the outer suburbs, but then a substantial jump to around 10 percent in rural areas. The decline in Hispanic residents is less dramatic and is found mainly in declines

FIGURE 3
Category Edges for Math Achievement and Free and Reduced Lunch Eligibility

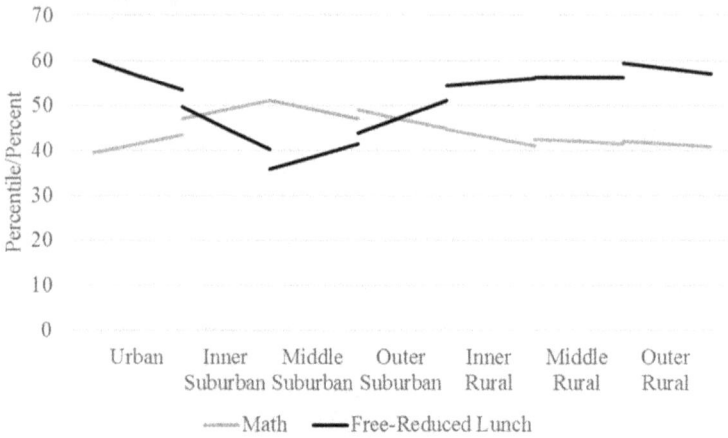

SOURCE: Authors' calculations based on data from the U.S. Census Bureau and the National Center for Education Statistics.

from the very high shares in large urban, urban, and inner suburban schools. Large central city schools are approximately 41.2 percent Hispanic, on average, and the middle suburbs through the outer rural areas have schools with an average of around 25 percent Hispanic students. Asian students are most likely to be concentrated in small cities (9.2) and inner suburbs (8.3), but they have similar shares in other areas. Native American students have small shares in every zone at a national level because they are so concentrated in specific regions of the country. However, they are clearly overrepresented in all rural areas.

Free and reduced lunch status and achievement scores all follow a somewhat different pattern than this. Disadvantage is highest and achievement is lowest in large urban areas (73.4 percent are eligible for free and reduced lunch and schools have an average reading percentile of 30.5). These shares reach their minimum in the middle suburbs (33.6 eligible and 55.8 reading percentile), but then rise again in the outer suburbs and rural areas. The suburbs are relatively advantaged, but this conclusion does not hold equally for all suburbs; it is the middle suburbs that are adjacent neither to the city nor to rural areas that are most advantaged. Levels of free and reduced lunch eligible students and achievement are similar in rural areas to those found in smaller urban areas.

One might expect to find urban and rural areas to be similarly disadvantaged in terms of student-teacher ratios and spending. This is not the case. Student-teacher ratios are quite similar in large urban and other urban areas, inner suburbs, and middle suburbs. It is in the outlying school districts that we find evidence of smaller class sizes. Also, aside from the somewhat lower expenditures on instructional salary in large urban districts, we find only small differences in spending between the other categories of schools. These results point us away from staffing and spending as major differences among schools in different zones.

Table 3 shows that there are important differences among suburban schools' racial composition, class composition, and test performance. Those closer to the city line are more like city schools, and those nearer the metropolitan periphery are more like rural schools. We can measure these differences more precisely by analyzing cross-boundary pairs of schools. Are schools near the edge of categories more similar to those in the adjacent category? Figures 2 and 3 address this question directly. The x-axis represents each category in descending degrees of urbanicity from left to right. The combined urban category comes first and is represented by a line between the mean for all nonedge urban schools and then the outer urban edge. (Since there is nothing adjacent to the middle of urban there is no point for an inner edge.) Inner suburban through middle rural are all represented by a line between two points: the inner edge (i.e., the mean of schools adjacent to a more urban category) and the outer edge (i.e., the mean of schools adjacent to a less urban category). Outer rural is represented by a line between the inner edge and the mean of nonedge schools because it is the most rural category. If there is a smooth gradient from urban to rural, the start of one line should connect with the end of the next. However, if there are clear changes at the edge of a category, there will be vertical gaps between the categories. The slope of the line for a specific category provides an indication of the geographic variability within that category. Flat lines represent relatively smooth geographic distributions and steep slopes represent dramatic change from one side of the category to the other.

Figure 2 shows the geographic gradient for percent white, black, and Hispanic. Predicted percentages of Asian and Native American students are not shown because the absolute changes across categories are very small. The highest line represents the average percent of white students at the edge of each category. The line starts on the left at approximately 36 percent, the mean value of nonedge urban schools, and increases slightly to 43 percent at the edge of urban areas. In other words, on average, there is some, but not much, spatial change in the percent of white students near the edge of cities. To be clear, this does not mean that city schools are not segregated. It just means that the geographic edge of the city is not, on average, much different from the rest of the city. The start of the next section of the line represents the urban edge of the inner suburbs. Here the grey line representing percent white jumps to 47 percent, indicating a moderate change in racial composition at the edge of the city. Larger change in the proportion of white students comes within the inner and middle suburbs. By the outer edge of middle suburbs, schools are, on average, 79 percent white. The lines then remain relatively flat with only a slight decline within the outer rural schools.

The proportion of Hispanic residents (dashed line) is also relatively smooth and follows the inverse pattern to that of whites. The line starts in nonedge urban schools at approximately 32 percent and declines steadily to just 10 percent in the outer edge of middle suburban. It remains relatively flat through the rest of the categories. Proportions of black students (black line) also decline substantially within the inner and middle suburbs (from 21 percent to just 5 percent);

however, these lines are somewhat flatter with slightly larger jumps between categories, suggesting a less smooth geographic gradient when it comes to black students. The proportion of black students is also relatively flat after the outer edge of the middle suburbs. Overall, it appears that from the outer edge of middle suburbs through all the rural categories, the racial composition is relatively stable with no clear geographic patterns. The major racial changes happen within the inner and middle suburbs. Note, however, that the discontinuities at the edges of each location are fairly modest compared to the differences within each one.

Figure 3 shows the trends for Math achievement (Reading is almost identical) and the percent free and reduced lunch. These lines are almost the exact inverse of one another. They form a curve with urban and rural at very similar levels of high eligibility and low achievement, with the outer edge of inner suburbs being the least disadvantaged and the highest achieving. Compared to the racial composition there are larger discontinuities between categories, especially between the urban and suburban categories suggesting that these categories represent more consequential social boundaries. Nevertheless, the major share of change occurs within each category, especially in the suburbs. There also appears to be a sharp increase in the proportion of free and reduced lunch eligible students between middle and outer rural areas.

Figures for student-teacher ratio and district-level funding are not shown because both mirror the results shown in Table 3. Student-teacher ratio shows a very smooth, slow, and steady decrease from urban to outer rural. Instructional salary per student is measured at the district level and therefore just represents differences across districts rather than schools that are adjacent to one another. Since district boundaries are used to define the categories and many categories are only one district wide, these lines are quite flat within categories with clear jumps between them. The one exception is middle suburban, which often contains many districts in adjacent metropolitan areas. In this category, there is a steep decline in expenditures from the inner to outer edge.

Discussion and Conclusion

This study has taken the traditional census categories derived from residential and commuting patterns and applied them to the schooling landscape across the country. We have compared the educational characteristics and opportunities for students in urban, suburban, and rural areas, finding stark contrasts in demographics and school quality across these areas. The main contribution of this article, however, is that we looked within census categories at the spatially patterned differences within the larger geographic areas.

First, we divided the three traditional census categories into smaller ones based on the spatial pattern of the school districts within them. Within the same metro areas, we examined whether smaller urban areas differ from larger ones, whether the suburbs that are adjacent to urban areas are different from those adjacent to rural ones, and whether rural areas on the edge of the suburbs are different from those farther away from an urban center. While there are some breaks between the large categories, particularly in racial composition, we find that there is much variation within each of the traditional census categories. This variation is not due to regional differences in the fragmentation of school districts since we compare categories only within the same extended metropolitan area.

We then broke each category down further to examine schools that fall on the more urban versus more rural edges of each zone. Overall, we find that much of the demographic and educational change that exists between suburban and rural schools occurs within the inner and middle suburbs. While there are small breaks between categories, these areas change dramatically from one end to another. In terms of racial composition, the suburban areas serve as a tipping point compared to the relative flat spatial trends in urban and rural areas. Therefore, we find that it will be useful to expand the existing literature on urban segregation patterns to explicitly examine the role of inner ring suburbs as tipping points for racial composition and concentration. In the case of funding, achievement, and free and reduced lunch levels, this change is u-shaped, with a peak at the inner-middle suburban boundary and the urban and rural schools ending up at quite similar levels. While inner suburban schools are somewhat more advantaged than nearby urban ones, that advantage increases dramatically as schools move farther from the urban core. Middle suburban schools, in turn, become more disadvantaged as they approach rural areas. In other words, it is a relatively narrow band of schools in the middle suburbs that are the most advantaged in terms of demographics and resources. This means that privilege is far more concentrated and spatially isolated than the large category of suburban would suggest. Understanding the sources of this advantage and its geographic isolation from both urban and rural disadvantage is important for understanding the extent of inequality in the educational landscape. (See Bischoff and Reardon [2014] for more on trends in socioeconomic segregation.)

In contrast, the outer suburbs look a lot like nearby rural areas. The suburban-rural boundary is barely noticeable in many of the figures and tends to be dwarfed by the variation within suburban areas. Together this suggests that perhaps the census defined metropolitan areas are not ideal when considering the geography of educational opportunity because they exaggerate the differences between suburban and rural areas in some parts and mask variability within categories in others.

While large cities stand apart in their disadvantage, the results show that the issues faced by smaller urban areas and rural public schools may be more similar than previously noticed. Urban public schools are more racially diverse, but rural public schools experience just as much economic disadvantage and low achievement and have comparable levels of instructional salaries per student. Though it is beyond the scope of these data, other research suggests that poor urban neighborhoods and some rural areas may be experiencing other similarities in disadvantage that have implications for schools. For example, as the suburban population grows at the expense of urban and rural areas, uneven population decline becomes a serious problem in many neighborhoods of Chicago, Baltimore, or Detroit, but also in rural areas. When enrollments decline, schools are forced to make hard decisions about what to do with the physical and social infrastructure of schooling, and this can lead to a sense of lost community in both metropolitan locations (Bard, Gardener, and Wieland 2006; Burdick-Will, Keels, and Schuble 2013; Lipman 2011). Similarly, brain drain and the difficulties youth face when they must leave their community to pursue higher education have been documented in both locations (Carr and Kefalas 2009; Wilkins 2014). Highlighting these similarities has important implications for how we think about urban and rural disadvantage and may provide some common ground to pursue policies that equalize educational opportunity regardless of location.

Finally, our approach to understanding the spatial gradient of educational opportunity is only a first step in analyzing spatial patterns. Our fine-grained categories and the differences between their edges show that there is a linear spatial component to school composition, but these measures do not capture the full extent of segregation within and between different metropolitan locations. Schools may be segregated on a scale that does not fit neatly into the transitional zones between categories. More research is needed to address the extent to which overall segregation patterns are similar or different across the rural-urban interface.

Notes

1. It should be noted that a substantial minority of students attend private rather than public schools (around 15 percent), and private school students are twice as likely to live in a city than in a suburban or rural area (Grady and Beilick 2010, 11). Unfortunately, there is very little reliable data on private schools, making it difficult to include them in an analysis of spatial inequality.

2. Student-teacher ratios were inexplicably missing for the entire state of California in the 2010–2011 Common Core data, but were supplemented with values from the California State Board of Education (http://www.ed-data.org).

3. Not all suburban districts at the edge of their metropolitan area are outer suburban since they are adjacent to another metropolitan area, not a rural district. Suburban districts that touch both rural districts and the city limit are considered inner suburbs.

4. Ninety-nine percent of pairs are less than 18 miles apart. In Alaska, however, due to extremely low density, some pairs are as much as 50 miles apart.

5. The standard deviations in each category are quite similar with no clear trend across categories and will not be discussed in detail.

6. The differences between categories are remarkably similar to the means without any controls for metropolitan area (not shown). The similarity between the raw means and the predicted estimates from the fixed-effects models suggests that the differences along the urban-rural continuum are not driven solely by regional differences in the prevalence of each category.

References

Allard, Scott W. 2008. *Out of reach: Place, poverty, and the new American welfare state*. New Haven, CT: Yale University Press.

Bard, Joe, Clark Gardener, and Regi Wieland. 2006. Rural school consolidation: history, research summary, conclusions, and recommendations. *Rural Educator* 27 (2): 40–48.

Bischoff, Kendra, and Sean F. Reardon. 2014. Residential segregation by income, 1970–2009. In *Diversity and disparities: America enters a new century*, ed. John Logan, 208–34. New York, NY: Russell Sage Foundation.

Burdick-Will, Julia, Micere Keels, and Todd Schuble. 2013. Closing and opening schools: The association between neighborhood characteristics and the location of new educational opportunities in a large urban district. *Journal of Urban Affairs* 35 (1): 59–80.

Carr, Patrick J., and Maria J. Kefalas. 2009. *Hollowing out the middle: The rural brain drain and what it means for America*. Boston, MA: Beacon Press.

Downes, Thomas A., and Jeffrey E. Zabel. 2002. The impact of school characteristics on house prices: Chicago 1987–1991. *Journal of Urban Economics* 52 (1): 1–25.

EDFacts. 2013a. *Achievement results for state assessments in mathematics: School year 2010–11*. Washington, DC: U.S. Department of Education. Available from https://explore.data.gov/Education.

EDFacts. 2013b. *Achievement results for state assessments in reading/language arts: School year 2010–11*. Washington, DC: U.S. Department of Education. Available from https://explore.data.gov/Education.

Ehrenhalt, Alan. 2012. *The great inversion and the future of the American city*. New York, NY: Alfred A. Knopf.

Fan, Xitao, and Michael J. Chen. 1999. Academic achievement of rural school students: A multi-year comparison with their peers in suburban and urban schools. *Journal of Research in Rural Education* 15 (1): 31–46.

García, Angela S., and Leah Schmalzbauer. 2017. Placing assimilation theory: Mexican immigrants in urban and rural America. *The ANNALS of the American Academy of Political and Social Science* (this volume).

Grady, Sarah, and Stacey Bielick. 2010. *Trends in the use of school choice, 1993 to 2007*. Washington, DC: U.S. Department of Education.

Hiner, Colleen C. 2016. Beyond the edge and in between: (Re)conceptualizing the rural-urban interface as meaning-model-metaphor. *The Professional Geographer* 68 (4): 520–32.

Kneebone, Elizabeth, and Emily Garr. 2010. *The suburbanization of poverty*. Washington, DC: Brookings Institution.

Kneebone, Elizabeth, and Kimberly Goyette, eds. 2014. *Choosing homes, choosing schools*. New York, NY: Russell Sage Foundation.

Lichter, Daniel T., and David L. Brown. 2011. Rural America in an urban society: Changing spatial and social boundaries. *Annual Review of Sociology* 37:565–92.

Lipman, Pauline. 2011. *The new political economy of urban education: Neoliberalism, race, and the right to the city*. New York, NY: Taylor & Francis.

Logan, John, and Julia Burdick-Will. 2016. School segregation, charter schools, and access to quality education. *Journal of Urban Affairs* 38 (3): 323–43.

Logan, John R., Elisabeta Minca, and Sinem Adar. 2012. The geography of inequality: Why separate means unequal in American public schools. *Sociology of Education* 85 (3): 287–301.

Morgan, Stephen L., and Sol Be Jung. 2016. Still no effect of resources? Even in the new gilded age? *Russell Sage Foundation Journal of the Social Sciences* 2 (5): 83–116.

Murphy, Alexandra K. 2007. The suburban ghetto: The legacy of Herbert Gans in understanding the experience of poverty in recently impoverished American suburbs. *City & Community* 6 (1): 21–37.

National Center for Education Statistics (NCES). 2012a. *Local education agency (school district) finance survey 2010–11*. Washington, DC: U.S. Department of Education. Available from http://nces.ed.gov/ccd/f33agency.asp.

National Center for Education Statistics (NCES). 2012b. *Public elementary/secondary school universe survey data 2010–11*. Washington, DC: U.S. Department of Education. Available from http://nces.ed.gov/ccd/pubschuniv.asp.

Orfield, Gary, and Chungmei Lee. 2005. *Why segregation matters: Poverty and educational inequality*. Cambridge, MA: The Civil Rights Project, Harvard University.

Ratcliffe, Michael, Charlynn Burd, Kelly Holder, and Alison Fields. 2016. *Defining rural at the U.S. Census Bureau*. Washington, DC: U.S. Department of Commerce. Available from https://www2.census.gov/geo/pdfs/reference/ua/Defining_Rural.pdf.

Reardon, Sean F., and Ann Owens. 2014. 60 years after Brown: Trends and consequences of school segregation. *Annual Review of Sociology* 40:199–218.

Taylor, L. 2011. No boundaries: Exurbia and the study of contemporary urban dispersion. *GeoJournal* 76:323–39.

Wilkins, Amy C. 2014. Race, age, and identity transformations in the transition from high school to college for black and first-generation white men. *Sociology of Education* 87 (3): 171–87.

Mass Imprisonment across the Rural-Urban Interface

Academic work on crime and punishment has focused mostly on urban centers, leaving rural communities understudied, except for acknowledgement that rural communities warehouse a large number of prisoners and that rural prisons provide jobs and economic development for some struggling communities. This study uses a novel dataset that includes information on the home addresses of all prisoners in Arkansas from 1993 to 2003 to document imprisonment rates and racial disparities in imprisonment rates across metropolitan and nonmetropolitan counties. We show how rural communities both *receive* and *produce* prisoners and that imprisonment and racial disparities in imprisonment vary more *within* different types of communities than *across* different types of communities. Further, we find that nonmetropolitan rates of imprisonment are *higher* than would be expected, based on observed local risk factors such as poverty rate. We close with a discussion of what these findings illustrate about concentrated disadvantage across the rural-urban interface.

Keywords: mass incarceration; prisons; race; disproportionate minority contact; rural; urban

By
JOHN M. EASON,
DANIELLE ZUCKER,
and
CHRISTOPHER WILDEMAN

In 1973, rates of imprisonment in the United States did not merit much attention, except for the massive racial disparities that have been a feature of imprisonment since the first statistics on the American criminal justice system

John M. Eason is an assistant professor in the Department of Sociology at Texas A&M University, author of Big House on the Prairie: Rise of the Rural Ghetto and Prison Proliferation *(University of Chicago Press 2017), and recipient of the 2012 Rural Sociological Society Young Scholar Award. His research examines crime, health, and punishment in relation to spatial demographics.*

Danielle Zucker is a research assistant on a project for the Bureau of Justice Statistics at Cornell University. Her interests include racial inequality and childhood maltreatment risks, particularly with respect to the criminal justice and the foster care systems.

Correspondence: eason@tamu.edu

DOI: 10.1177/0002716217705357

were recorded (e.g., Cahalan 1984; Muller 2012; Pettit and Western 2004). Although the U.S. imprisonment rate was high relative to other developed democracies, the United States was not an extreme outlier. If the rate of imprisonment was unexceptional, the rate of change in imprisonment in the United States was downright boring, as it had hovered between 75 per 100,000 and 125 per 100,000 for 50 years. Indeed, the imprisonment rate in the United States seemed so impervious to change that some criminologists speculated that almost no social change could happen that would dramatically change its imprisonment rate (Blumstein and Cohen 1973).

This prediction, it turns out, was dead wrong. The 1970s, 1980s, 1990s, and 2000s were all decades characterized by extreme increases in the imprisonment rate. Despite a recent slowdown (and even a slight decline) in the last five years (e.g., Carson and Golinelli 2014), the American imprisonment rate remains both historically novel and comparatively extreme. It currently stands at around 500 per 100,000 (e.g., Carson and Golinelli 2014), with a total incarceration rate— including prison and jail inmates—of 750 per 100,000 (e.g., Pettit 2012; Western 2006). Compared to the 100 per 100,000 rate the United States had grown accustomed to, this increase was novel to say the least. Because no other country experienced such an increase (e.g., Cahalan 1984), the United States also became comparatively extreme in terms of incarceration in a way that no other country had ever been. As the imprisonment rate increased over this 40-year period, the combination of high rates of imprisonment and (relatively) stable racial disparities in incarceration led to incarceration becoming a common experience for African Americans (e.g., Bonczar 2003; Pettit and Western 2004; Western 2006).

These two features—historically and comparatively extreme rates of imprisonment that led to astonishingly high rates of imprisonment for the most marginalized men—form the core of what has come to be called "mass imprisonment" (e.g., Garland 2001) or "hyperincarceration" (e.g., Wacquant 2010). Yet while the evidence building the case for extreme cumulative risks of imprisonment for African Americans tended to be made using nationally representative data (which by definition would include a combination of rural, suburban, and urban individuals), the theoretical literature on mass incarceration has taken on an almost exclusively urban flare, with the most prominent accounts focusing heavily on African American offenders from the poorest inner-city neighborhoods (e.g., Garland 2001; Wacquant 2001). Sociologist David Garland perhaps states the case most clearly: "imprisonment becomes *mass imprisonment* when it ceases to be the incarceration of individual offenders and

Christopher Wildeman is an associate professor of policy analysis and management at Cornell University and a senior researcher at the Rockwool Foundation Research Unit in Copenhagen, Denmark. His research and teaching interests revolve around the consequences of mass imprisonment for inequality, families, health, and children. He is also interested in child welfare, especially as it relates to child maltreatment and the foster care system. He is the 2013 recipient of the Ruth Shonle Cavan Young Scholar Award from the American Society of Criminology.

NOTE: A portion of this research was funded by a theme project grant from the Institute for the Social Sciences at Cornell University to the third author. We are especially grateful to Youngmin Yi for research assistance and to the external reviewers for helpful comments.

becomes the systematic imprisonment of whole groups of the population. In the case of the USA, the group concerned is, of course, young black males in large urban centres" (Garland 2001, 2, emphasis in original). Although rarely stated as boldly in other work, the idea that mass incarceration is completely—or at least primarily—an issue faced by those living in the very poorest neighborhoods in large cities pervades current research.

This is not to say, of course, that rural or sparsely populated areas have received no attention from those interested in the problems of crime and punishment. Criminality and the problems of crime have not bypassed rural areas, which makes the lack of emphasis on imprisonment in these spaces somewhat surprising. Indeed, roughly half of all U.S. counties with the highest homicide rates are classified as nonmetropolitan (Weisheit, Falcone, and Wells 2006), and there is little variation within counties in the violent crime rate across the rural-urban interface (e.g. Lee and Ousey 2001; Light and Harris 2012). Despite similarities in rural and urban imprisonment, rural crime and punishment is much less studied (Simes 2016). The dearth of research on rural crime and punishment is in part due to data limitations since most of the core surveys used to study imprisonment focus heavily on urban samples. Research on rural crime and punishment has also failed to develop in part because of the lack of a unified theoretical approach to understanding how context shapes crime and punishment in rural communities (Donnermeyer and DeKeseredy 2008; Eason 2012). Given the attention to urban neighborhood crime along with the dearth of studies on rural community crime, how can a spatially inclusive approach to these issues be established?

Although the literature on imprisonment in rural spaces has tended to be underdeveloped, some recent research has considered how rural communities might simultaneously *produce* prisoners and *receive* them (e.g., Eason 2012, 2017a). In one recent effort to provide a more complete picture of how crime and punishment are linked across the rural-urban continuum, Eason and colleagues (forthcoming) show that a multitude of crime and punishment outcomes are linked to concentrated disadvantage in urban and rural communities. Specifically, they demonstrate that concentrated disadvantage is positively correlated with murder rates, imprisonment rates, prisoner reentry rates, and prison building in rural spaces, suggesting a more nuanced relationship between disadvantage and punishment than is usually noted in the literature (Eason et al., forthcoming).

This study offers an empirical analysis that builds toward a spatially inclusive approach to crime and punishment across the rural-urban continuum. We argue that the fates of rural and urban people and places are inextricably linked through crime and punishment. We consider how concentrated disadvantage in Arkansas predicts both prisoner reentry and prison building across the rural-urban interface. Lichter and Brown (2011, 20) describe the new rural-urban interface as "an interstitial zone that is dense in social, political and economic relationships," bringing people "together in intense interaction and durable social and economic relationships." This interstitial zone is defined by activities that blur and cross traditional rural-urban boundaries. Prisoner reentry and prison building both blur and cross boundaries.

On one hand, the flow of prisoners and correctional officers demonstrates a new type of rural-urban boundary crossing. Because the U.S. Census Bureau officially designates prisoners as part of the population of the locale or county where the prison resides (and not the offender's last known address), the entry and exit of prisoners represent the back-and-forth flows of populations across the rural-urban interface. The atypical flow of prisoners in Arkansas not only exemplifies the movement across boundaries, but also speaks to how some populations are unwillingly crossing rural-urban boundaries. Furthermore, as corrections officers travel to work, they cross economic boundaries. On the other hand, prison building also blurs the lines between rural and urban communities. Because prisons are often built outside of rural towns that annex the land the prison is built on, prison building is not only the flow of labor and capital across these places, but also the result of difficult, contested political processes. These trends speak to the economic and social interdependence of rural and urban communities.

This article advances the idea that rural communities—across the size-of-place hierarchy—are both places of prisoner *reception* and places of prisoner *production*. To address this issue, we use a novel dataset that includes information on the home addresses of all prisoners in Arkansas from 1993 to 2003. After showing that prisons in Arkansas, unlike in the rest of the country, are evenly divided between metropolitan and nonmetropolitan locales, our analysis proceeds in two stages. First, we show that imprisonment rates and racial disparities in imprisonment rates do not vary as much as suggested in most of the literature on mass imprisonment. Metropolitan areas may produce a larger *number* of prisoners than nonmetropolitan areas, but the actual *rate* of imprisonment and racial disparities in imprisonment in many of these communities is comparably high. Second, we show that after adjusting for observed county-level attributes (e.g., poverty rate, racial composition), the rates of imprisonment and racial disparities in imprisonment are even *higher* in many nonmetropolitan areas than would be expected based on observed local area risk factors. This suggests, maybe most provocatively, that some small communities of concentrated disadvantage may suffer more imprisonment than the metropolitan spaces that receive so much more attention in the literature and media. Having incorporated nonmetropolitan spaces as producers of prisoners into the empirical work on mass incarceration, we close with a discussion of what these findings illustrate about concentrated disadvantage across the rural-urban interface.

Data and Analytic Strategy

Data

The data for the prison analyses come from the Prison Proliferation Project.[1] These data were collected as part of a larger research project and to test theories of rural-urban interdependence in that project (see Eason 2017a, 2017b). Because prisons and prisoners are disproportionately in the South, Arkansas nicely characterizes current and recent historical trends in punishment. However, unlike other southern states, such as Florida, Georgia, Louisiana, or Texas, Arkansas is not a leader in rates of imprisonment or prison building. The primary sources of the prison data are the *2010 Directory of Adult and Juvenile Correctional Departments, Institutions, Agencies, and Probation and Parole Authorities* (2010; hereafter, the ACA directory) and the Inter-University Consortium for Political and Social Research (ICPSR) data holdings for the 2005 Census of State and Federal Adult Correctional Facilities (CSFACF). The latter includes a listing of the 1,600-plus U.S. prison facilities by latitude and longitude coordinates, U.S. Census place, name of facility, year of facility construction, and a limited sample of facility renovations by year.

Our analyses are also based on a novel administrative dataset of all prisoners in Arkansas from 1993 to 2003 that was made available through a cooperative agreement with the Arkansas Department of Correction. These data provide information on the latitude and longitude of each inmate's home address, which allows us to ascertain which of the seventy-five counties in Arkansas is listed as their home address. We rely on these county-level indicators because they provide a stable yet textured portrait of imprisonment rates across urban and rural spaces. The stability of the estimates is especially important because estimates of rates of imprisonment at lower levels of aggregation are bound to be sufficiently noisy that they could provide a very specific yet also very imprecise portrait of imprisonment rates across locales.[2]

In addition to drawing information on the home address of prisoners in these data, we also rely on information on each inmate's race/ethnicity to construct county-level measures of the imprisonment rate, the white imprisonment rate, and the black imprisonment rate. Because the population of Arkansas is well over 90 percent white and black, we could only produce stable estimates of the imprisonment rate for these two populations for most counties in Arkansas. Given the dramatic influx of Hispanics into many other new immigrant destinations in the last 20 years (e.g., Lichter 2012; Waters and Jiménez 2005), estimates for other states should also include estimates of the imprisonment rate for Hispanics.

To produce estimates of imprisonment rates, we used an average of the 1990 and 2006 National Center for Health Statistics county measurements, which range from one to six (e.g., U.S. Department of Health and Human Services 2012). Parallel analyses using the Rural-Urban Continuum Codes, which range from one to nine, produced analyses that were substantively similar to our results (U.S. Department of Agriculture 2004). We coded counties as rural if they were classified as six (noncore), which represents communities outside the urban core. We coded counties as urban if they were classified as one (large central metro), two (large fringe metro), or three (medium metro). We coded counties as intermediate if they were classified as four (small metro) or five (micropolitan). Coding counties in this way left us with nine metropolitan counties and sixty-six nonmetropolitan counties, thirty of which classify as intermediate counties and thirty-six of which we classify as rural counties. Because of the relatively small number of metropolitan counties, we treated each yearly observation as unique to provide the most complete distributions possible for the analyses we present later in this article.

For some analyses, we also consider county-level characteristics, such as the violent crime rate, poverty rate, unemployment rate, fertility rate, age distribution, racial distribution, share of the population that is married, and other characteristics of places. We focus on the violent crime rate rather than the total crime rate or some components of the nonviolent crime rate since many nonviolent crimes (e.g., drug crimes) are as much a function of police regimes as they are reflections of actual crime rates (for an extended discussion of this issue, see Western 2006). All of these data are drawn from the 1990 U.S. Census, the 2000 U.S. Census, and the 2005 American Community Survey. We linearly interpolate between 1990, 2000, and 2005 to produce yearly estimates. This leads to a total of 825 county-year observations, including 99 urban county-year observations and 726 nonmetropolitan county-year observations, of which 330 county-year observations we classify as intermediate, with the remaining counties considered rural.

Analytic strategy

Our analysis proceeds in two stages. In the first stage, we present information on the black, white, and total imprisonment rates and black-white disparities in imprisonment rates for each county-year from 1993 to 2003 (Figures 1–3). We do this both through providing maps showing both how counties fit on the rural-urban continuum and how they fit in terms of imprisonment and by showing how the distribution of these imprisonment rates and ratios of these rates vary across the rural-urban continuum. To be clear, the disparities represent the ratio of black-to-white imprisonment rates. By providing this information, we provide valuable insight into whether there are great differences in these rates and ratios across urban, intermediate, and rural areas.

In the second stage, we seek to see how much of the differences in these rates across the rural-urban continuum are due to differences in community characteristics (Figures 4 and 5). To do so, we first run a basic ordinary least squares (OLS) regression, including both dummy variables for each county in Arkansas and a host of observed community-level factors predicting (1) the total imprisonment rate, (2) the black imprisonment rate, (3) the white imprisonment rate, and (4) the black-white disparity in the imprisonment rate (measured as a ratio). To be clear, although we include county dummy variables, we are not running a "true" fixed effects model in which we try to tease out causal relationships between some time-varying dependent and explanatory variables; instead, we merely try to descriptively map how much variation in imprisonment is driven by unobserved factors taking place at the county level. Although we cluster our standard errors to account for the correlated error structure in our data (due to the repeated observations on each county), our descriptive analyses do not include bounds on any of the point estimates in the figures that represent the core of our analyses. Based on the results from these simple OLS models, we then hold all community-level factors at their mean for the entire state and then predict what (1) the total imprisonment rate, (2) the black imprisonment rate, (3) the white imprisonment rate, and (4) the black-white disparity in the imprisonment rate would be for each of the counties we consider, holding all other variables at their mean. In so doing, we demonstrate how much county-level differences in other observed characteristics explain urban-rural distinctions in the imprisonment rate.

Results

Prison placement across the rural-urban continuum

In 2010, Arkansas was home to twenty-eight prisons—twenty-one state, five private, and two federal facilities. Prior to 1970, Arkansas had two prisons, with the last being constructed in 1916. During the 1970s, the state added three facilities. However, the 1980s and 1990s witnessed a sharp increase in prisons with six and twelve new facilities opening, respectively. Since 2000, the state has built five new prisons. The timing of the peak of prison building during the 1990s in Arkansas is consistent with national trends, but the spatial patterning of prison placement in Arkansas was inconsistent with national patterns.

Nationally, nearly 70 percent of all prisons were built in nonmetropolitan communities. Arkansas bucks this trend as 50 percent of its prisons are in urban areas. One contributing factor to this may be that the population of Arkansas is distributed very differently from most other states. While less than 20 percent of U.S. residents in 2010 lived in rural communities, roughly 45 percent of Arkansas' residents live in rural places. Fourteen facilities were in U.S. Census places designated as *urban cores*. However, while Pine Bluff housed four facilities and Tucker housed two, every other urban core in Arkansas housed only one prison. This includes Benton, Little Rock, Springdale, Texarkana, and Wrightsville. There are other key variations in facilities across metropolitan and nonmetropolitan places in Arkansas. The average facility cost of care per day per inmate in 2010 was $49, and the average daily population (ADP) across all twenty-eight facilities was 520 with 485 males and 35 females guarded by an average of 138 corrections officers. The ADP for prison facilities outside the urban core was 655 while the ADP inside the core was 384. This means that in 2010, urban communities in Arkansas were transferring citizens through imprisonment at nearly twice the rate as nonmetropolitan communities were sending them into the core. Nonmetropolitan communities also have larger correctional staff on average, employing 161 officers versus 114 in metropolitan places. The cost of care per day per inmate was also $8 more expensive in metropolitan areas, far lower than the difference would be in other states.

Differences in imprisonment across the rural-urban continuum

Figures 2 and 3 present information on the spatial distribution of imprisonment rates and inequality in imprisonment rates in Arkansas to demonstrate whether suburban and rural counties are both consumers of prisoners and producers of prisoners. The spatial concentration of imprisonment for the total

FIGURE 1
Total Imprisonment Rate by County, 1993–2003

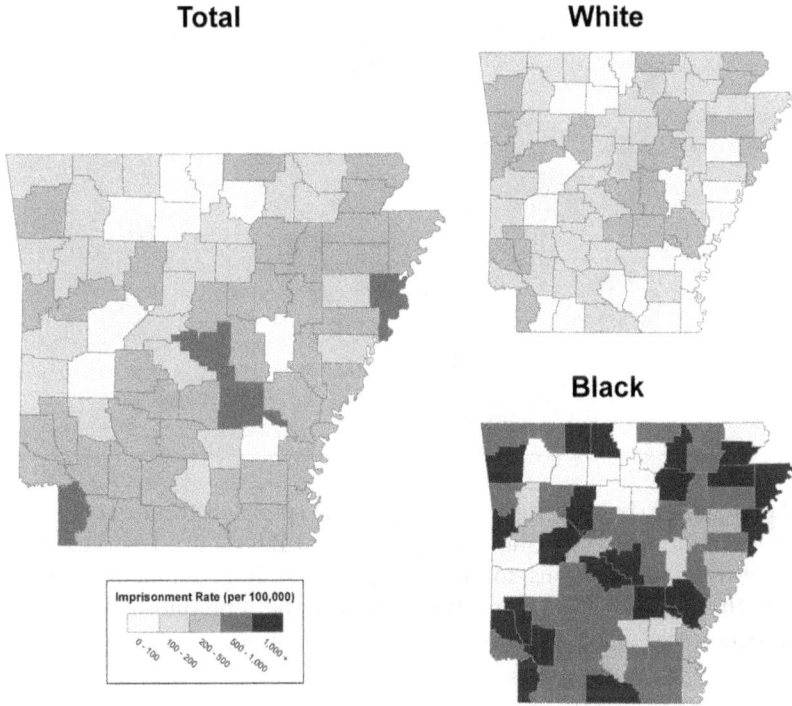

imprisonment rate, as shown in Figure 1, is weighted toward the urban centers in the state—specifically in the northeast and central portion of the state—but there are also high imprisonment rates in intermediate and rural sections of the state. The same is the case for the white imprisonment rate, where, as Figure 1 shows, there is very little obvious difference in white imprisonment rates across the rural-urban continuum. For African Americans, there are two features of the imprisonment rate that bear mentioning in Figure 1. First, twenty-one of the seventy-five counties in Arkansas had imprisonment rates for African Americans over 1,000 per 100,000. Second, although some of the very high African American imprisonment rates are concentrated in urban centers, many of them are not. And, indeed, there appears to be relatively little difference across the rural-urban continuum in the imprisonment rates of African Americans.

There is even less patterning in terms of racial inequality in the imprisonment rate, as Figure 2 illustrates. None of the counties with the highest level of inequality in the imprisonment rate was located in (or even near) urban centers, with the highest levels of inequality in the imprisonment rate clustered around the northern border of the state. The major urban centers still tended to have high levels of inequality in imprisonment at between 5:1 and 10:1, but the counties with racial inequality in imprisonment in excess of 10:1 were not located near cities.

FIGURE 2
Black-White Inequality in Imprisonment Rates by County, 1993–2003

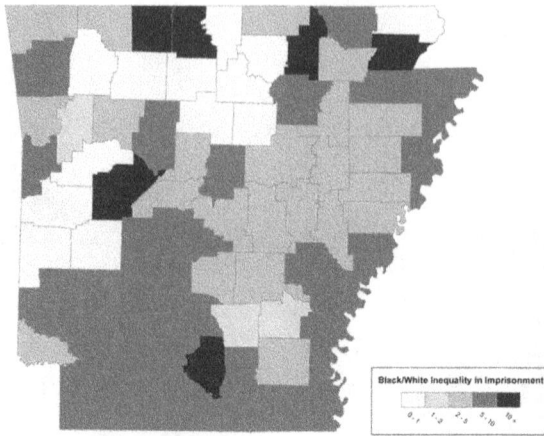

Taken together, the descriptive analysis of the spatial distribution of imprisonment rates and racial disparities in imprisonment rates—two key dimensions of mass imprisonment—seems to suggest that mass imprisonment is occurring across both rural and urban areas. Rural areas are both producers of prisoners as well as consumers of prisoners (i.e., places of reception).

How much of these differences are driven by other observed differences?

Figure 3 starts a more formal analysis of just how different rural, intermediate, and urban areas are when it comes to imprisonment rates and inequality in imprisonment rates in Arkansas. The top panels plot the distribution of total, white, and black imprisonment rates across the rural-urban continuum; the bottom panels plot racial inequality in the imprisonment rate across the rural-urban continuum. The mean for each distribution is also indicated by a line to make it easy to compare across figures. Differences in the total and white imprisonment rates across urban, intermediate, and rural areas are relatively muted, although, as the mean lines indicate, rates tend to be higher in urban areas than in intermediate or rural areas. Regardless, the distribution for the total and white imprisonment rate tends to be relatively compressed regardless of how urban or rural a county is.

The black imprisonment rate varies somewhat more across the rural-urban continuum. Two features in particular bear mentioning. First, the average black imprisonment rate is higher in urban counties (at around 1,100 per 100,000) than it is in intermediate (at around 900 per 100,000) or rural (at around 700 per 100,000) counties. Second, although the *average* black imprisonment rate is higher in urban counties, the highest black imprisonment rates were actually in rural and intermediate counties. There were a handful of rural and intermediate counties with even higher black imprisonment rates than those in urban counties—a finding that seems to run counter to much existing research.

FIGURE 3
Arkansas Imprisonment Rate by County, 1993–2003

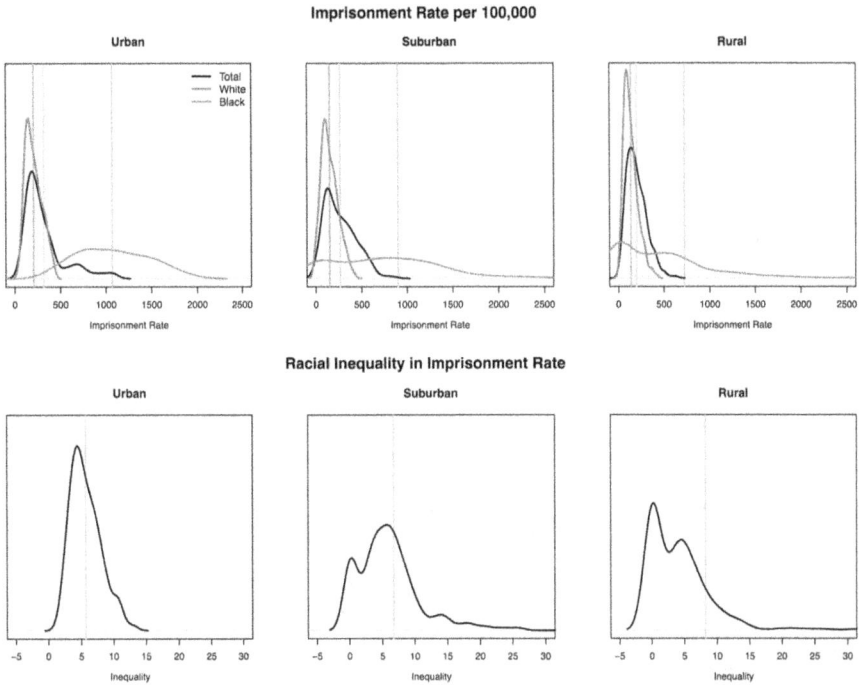

Average levels of inequality in the imprisonment rate were also somewhat higher in rural (8:1) and intermediate (7:1) counties than they were in urban (5:1) counties, although these differences were relatively muted. The highest levels of racial inequality in imprisonment rates could also be found in rural and suburban counties, with disparities approaching 30:1 in some counties. Thus, inequality in imprisonment is certainly not an exclusively urban phenomenon.

Figures 4 and 5 provide an alternate way to think through the degree to which differences in imprisonment rates and disparities in imprisonment rates are attributable to other, observable county-level factors (e.g., county-level poverty rates). To do this, we ran two sets of the models. The first included only a series of county fixed effects (which, as mentioned earlier, are just county-level dummy variables). The second included a series of county fixed effects and a host of other county-level covariates that could partially explain why some counties have higher imprisonment rates or racial disparities in imprisonment than do others. If the distributions shift significantly between the first and second models, that would suggest that other county-level differences explain some share of the relationship; if the distributions do not shift, that would suggest that other factors unique to the counties, but unmeasured, explain the differences.

Figure 4, which focuses on imprisonment rates, indicates that adjusting for county-level differences in observed characteristics does little to explain the

FIGURE 4
Adjusted and Unadjusted County-Level Fixed Effects for Imprisonment Rates

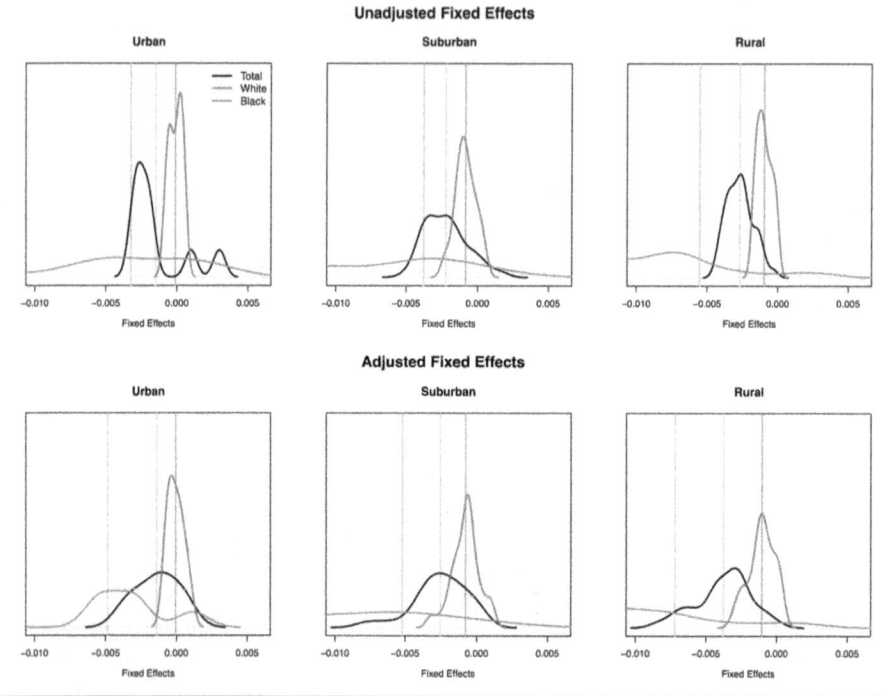

imprisonment rates of urban, intermediate, and rural counties. The one exception to this rule comes for urban counties, where the few high-end outliers for
the black imprisonment rate seem to be at least partially explained by adjusting
for other observed differences between counties. Yet with this one exception it
appears that differences in imprisonment rates across the rural-urban continuum
are driven primarily not by other observed differences between counties but
instead by other social forces.

As Figure 5 illustrates, the same is very much the case for county-level inequality in imprisonment, as adjusting for other county-level differences explains
relatively little of the county-level variations in inequality in imprisonment across
the rural-urban continuum.

Taken together, these results indicate that high imprisonment rates and vast
racial disparities in imprisonment rates are not as highly concentrated in the most
densely populated urban areas as has historically been argued in the literature on
mass imprisonment and that observed differences between counties do little to
change this story. This suggests, as we discuss more below, that differences *within*
the rural-urban continuum are far more important for understanding which
places produce prisoners than are differences *along* the rural-urban continuum.
Future research on mass imprisonment should therefore devote attention to
thinking about the myriad ways in which urban, suburban, and rural disadvantage

FIGURE 5
Adjusted and Unadjusted County-Level Fixed Effects for Inequality
in Imprisonment Rates

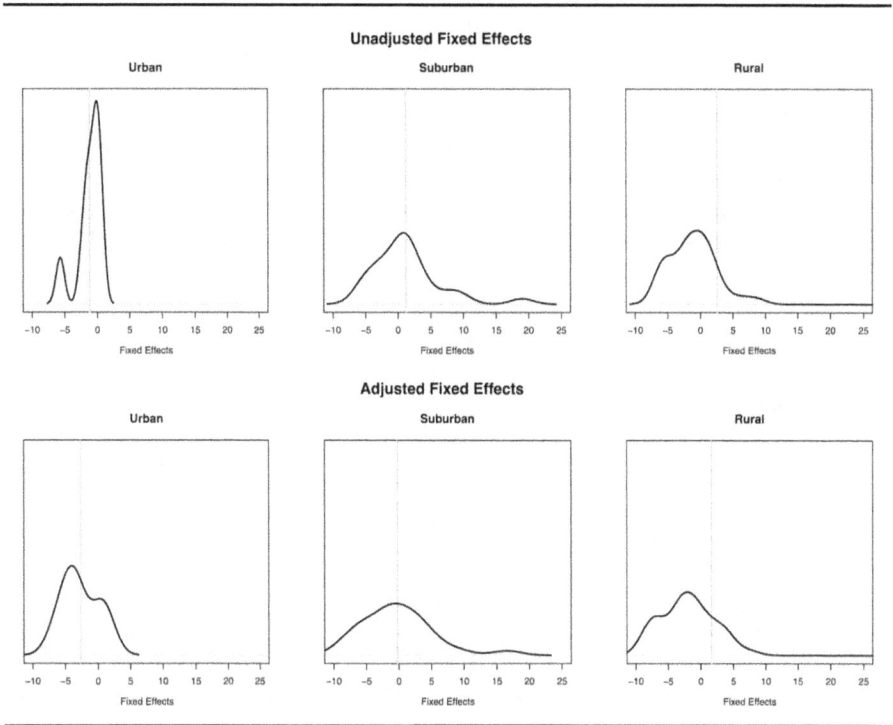

work in similar (and different) ways to produce the extreme imprisonment rates
characteristic of mass imprisonment.

Conclusion

This article shows how mass imprisonment plays out across the rural-urban interface. Unlike most research in this literature on nonmetropolitan spaces, our focus
is on imprisonment rates rather than prison placement rates. The results from
our analyses suggest that rural places do not only *receive* prisoners, but they also
produce prisoners. As evidence of this, consider that the average black imprisonment rate is higher in metropolitan communities (1,100 per 100,000) than it is
across nonmetropolitan communities that range from the most rural areas (700
per 100,000) to intermediate areas (900 per 100,000), yet the highest black
imprisonment rates in Arkansas (in excess of 2,500 per 100,000) are not found in
urban centers but in intermediate and rural counties. Thus, it appears that mass
imprisonment is something that exists across the rural-urban continuum in a
significantly more complex and nuanced way than is typically noted in research.

This suggests that mass imprisonment constitutes a blurring of the rural-urban interface in a way that researchers of crime and punishment had mostly missed until recently. According to the traditional narrative, mass imprisonment increased rural-urban interaction by moving primarily urban populations (many of whom were people of color) to primarily rural locations (where they would primarily be guarded by poor whites). If this perspective were correct in fact, mass imprisonment would exist across the rural-urban interface in such a way that it would provide rural working-class whites an opportunity to maintain their socioeconomic dominance over poorer, urban African Americans. Instead, this analysis suggests that the prison system in Arkansas may be placing bodies from rural areas in urban industries while exporting urban workers to rural places. These findings speak to the importance of spatial inequality across rural and urban places as a central mechanism in determining racial variation in punishment outcomes such as mass imprisonment.

Our findings suggest a complex narrative, and one that should push our thinking in at least two new ways. First, total imprisonment rates, black imprisonment rates, white imprisonment rates, and racial inequality in imprisonment rates do not differ markedly across urban and rural spaces—at least in Arkansas, the site for our study. This suggests, as we mention above, that the emphasis on mass imprisonment as a primarily urban phenomenon that affects less urban spaces in only positive ways (through job creation), if it affects them at all, is inaccurate. Second, and maybe even more importantly, there is far more variation *within* rural and urban areas when it comes to imprisonment than there is *between* these areas when it comes to imprisonment. And, as such, it may be reasonable to assume that mass imprisonment should be seen as something that affects socially marginalized spaces across the rural-urban interface.

Although the practical application of our findings is limited because our study focused only on Arkansas, the theoretical implications for future research on mass imprisonment are maybe even more important. As we noted above, most of the studies that are used to consider the consequences of imprisonment for individuals, families, and communities are situated in urban centers. The Fragile Families and Child Wellbeing Study, for instance, which includes an extensive battery of questions on criminal justice contact, is based exclusively on a sample of cities of at least 200,000 inhabitants (see Wildeman 2009; Wildeman and Muller 2012; Wildeman 2016). Future studies of mass imprisonment must seek to break out of this mold, focusing not only on major urban centers where imprisonment is, of course, still common, but also on a host of different types of spaces across the rural-urban interface, as it is only by focusing too on these areas that we will get a comprehensive portrait of what mass imprisonment's harms are.

Notes

1. Given the high potential for error in most prison-building data, we compiled, cleaned, and geocoded the Prison Proliferation Project data from several sources over a five-year period. The ACA directory is a compilation of data on institutions throughout the United States, its territories, and military

facilities overseas. The directory includes data on facility name, street and mailing addresses, opening date, capacity, security level, average daily population, gender of population, adult or juvenile indicators, number of full-time and part-time staff, cost of care per day, and other information. This source was recommended as the "gold standard" of prison locations by a contact at the U.S. Bureau of Prisons. Even so, its use of mailing addresses introduces potential error. ACA data alone cannot be used to geocode prisons because more than 150 prisons list addresses located five or more miles from the actual prison facility. The lead author has improved on the ACA and CSFACF data by using an extensive verification process assigning each prison to the U.S. census place identified by the Bureau of Prisons or state department of corrections. Entries from the ACA directory and CSFACF holdings were reviewed by trained coders and entered into a database. The current data include adult facilities operated by federal and state governments, Native American governments, and private contract facilities. The database entries were then checked in their entirety for errors and duplicate entries. Due to differences in record keeping across jurisdictions, entries in the ACA directory exhibit some inconsistencies with respect to the types of data provided and the format of those data. Where data were missing, researchers contacted either the facility itself or the state department of correction to attempt to obtain proper figures. We also used the CSFACF data to reconcile some latitude/longitude coordinates and used Google Maps to obtain the latitude and longitude coordinates for facilities with adequate information and checked street addresses again. For those ACA entries that provided only a mailing address or P.O. Box, researchers again used Google Maps with satellite view to obtain visual confirmation of the facility and to collect the latitude and longitude coordinates. The location of each facility was then verified using the Coding Accuracy Support System, a location verification system used by institutions like the United States Postal Service, and each case was reconciled a third and final time. These data were augmented and merged with Geolytics' decennial U.S. census demographic and economic data using GIS software. To date, this process has resulted in a dataset that includes every U.S. census place from 1970 to 2000, normalized to 2000 decennial boundaries ($N = 25,150$) and 1,663 prisons spread across all fifty states. Unlike most data on prisons, these data are not a sample of prisons or towns—the dataset includes every adult prison facility in the United States. These data were merged with files containing U.S. state-level economic and program transfer data covering the years 1980–2011, as maintained by the University of Kentucky Center for Poverty Research (UKCPR).

2. The initial dataset included 34,462. The final dataset includes 28,566 observations, representing 83 percent of the initial data. The change in observations is mostly driven by cases where the inmate's release date is before their intake date (4,563 observations); we also lose some observations because of missing or implausible location information.

References

American Correctional Association. 2010. *2010 directory of adult and juvenile correctional departments, institutions, agencies, and probation and parole authorities*. Alexandria, VA: American Correctional Association.

Blumstein, Alfred, and Jacqueline Cohen. 1973. A theory of the stability of punishment. *Journal of Criminal Law and Criminology* 64 (2): 198–207.

Bonczar, Thomas P. 2003. *Prevalence of imprisonment in the U.S. population, 1974–2001*. Washington, DC: U.S. Department of Justice, Bureau of Justice Statistics. Available from www.bjs.gov.

Cahalan, Margaret. 1984. Exploration of the stability of institutionalization hypothesis: 1850–1980. Paper delivered at the Law and Society Meeting, June, Boston, MA.

Carson, E. Ann, and Daniela Golinelli. 2013/2014. *Prisoners in 2012: Trends in admissions and releases, 1991–2012*. Washington, DC: U.S. Department of Justice, Bureau of Justice Statistics. Available from www.bjs.gov.

Donnermeyer, Joseph F., and Walter DeKeseredy. 2008. Toward a rural critical criminology. *Southern Rural Sociology* 23 (2): 4–28.

Eason, John M. 2012. Extending the hyperghetto: Toward a theory of punishment, race, and rural disadvantage. *Journal of Poverty* 16 (3): 274–95.

Eason, John M. 2017a. *Big house on the prairie: Rise of the rural ghetto and prison proliferation*. Chicago, IL: University of Chicago Press.

Eason, John M. 2017b. Prisons as panacea or pariah? The countervailing consequences of the prison boom on the political economy of rural towns. *Sociology* 6 (1): 1–23.

Eason, John M., Jason Greenberg, Richard Abel, and Corey Sparks. Forthcoming. Crime, punishment, and spatial inequality. In *Rural poverty in the US*, eds. Jennifer Sherman, Ann Tickamyer, and Jennifer Warlick. New York, NY: Columbia University Press.

Garland, David. 2001. *The culture of control: Crime and social control in contemporary society*. Chicago, IL: University of Chicago Press.

Lee, Matthew R., and Graham C. Ousey. 2001. Size matters: Examining the link between small manufacturing, socioeconomic deprivation, and crime rates in nonmetropolitan communities. *Sociological Quarterly* 42 (4): 581–602.

Lichter, Daniel T. 2012. Immigration and the new racial diversity in rural America. *Rural Sociology* 77:1–34.

Lichter, Daniel T., and David L. Brown. 2011. Rural America in an urban society: Changing spatial and social boundaries. *Annual Review of Sociology* 37:565–92.

Light, Michael T., and Casey T. Harris. 2012. Race, space, and violence: Exploring spatial dependence in structural covariates of white and black violent crime in U.S. counties. *Journal of Quantitative Criminology* 28 (4): 559–86.

Muller, Christopher. 2012. Northward migration and the rise of racial disparities in American incarceration, 1880-1950. *American Journal of Sociology* 118:281–326.

Pettit, Becky. 2012. *Invisible men: Mass incarceration and the myth of black progress*. New York, NY: Russell Sage Foundation.

Pettit, Becky, and Bruce Western. 2004. Mass imprisonment and the life course: Race and class inequality in U.S. incarceration. *American Sociological Review* 69 (2): 151–69.

Simes, Jessica Tayloe. 2016. Essays on place and punishment in America. PhD diss., Harvard University, Cambridge, MA.

U.S. Department of Agriculture. 2004. *Rural-Urban Continuum Codes*. Washington, DC: Economic Research Service, U.S. Department of Agriculture. Available from http://www.ers.usda.gov/data-products/rural-urban-continuum-codes/.aspx.

U.S. Department of Health and Human Services. 2012. *NCHS urban-rural classification scheme for counties*. Available from http://www.cdc.gov/nchs/data/series/sr_02/sr02_154.pdf.

Wacquant, Loïc. 2001. Deadly symbiosis: When ghetto and prison meet and mesh. *Punishment & Society* 3:95–133.

Wacquant, Loïc. 2010. Class, race, and hyperincarceration in revanchist America. *Daedalus* 139 (3): 74–90.

Waters, Mary, and Tomás R. Jiménez. 2005. Assessing immigrant assimilation: New empirical and theoretical challenges. *Annual Review of Sociology* 31:105–25.

Weisheit, Ralph A., David N. Falcone, and L. Edward Wells. 2006. *Crime and policing in rural and small-town America: An overview of the issues*. Long Grove, IL: Waveland Press.

Western, Bruce. 2006. *Punishment and inequality in America*. New York, NY: Russell Sage Foundation.

Wildeman, Christopher. 2009. Parental imprisonment, the prison boom, and the concentration of childhood advantage. *Demography* 46 (2): 265–80.

Wildeman, Christopher. 2016. Is it better to sit on our hands or just dive in? Cultivating family-friendly criminal justice policy in the contemporary era. *Criminology & Public Policy* 15:497–502.

Wildeman, Christopher, and Christopher Muller. 2012. Mass imprisonment and inequality in health and family life. *Annual Review of Law and Social Science* 8 (1): 11–30.

An extensive literature has described U.S. food insecurity and its determinants, but there has been little work
on the geographic distribution of food insecurity and no
work on the distribution of private food assistance by
geography. To study the former, we use data from the
Map the Meal Gap (MMG) project, which is broken
down by Rural-Urban Continuum Codes. For the latter, we combine MMG data with data from the Hunger
in America 2014 (HIA 2014) survey to determine the
geographic distribution of charitable food assistance. At
the national level, we find few differences across the
rural-urban interface, but we do find differences within
and across regions. We also find that regardless of how
it is measured, the distribution of charitable food assistance is directed more toward counties with smaller
populations—a finding that holds even after controlling
for factors that influence the distribution of charitable
assistance.

Keywords: food insecurity; Rural-Urban Continuum
Codes; Map the Meal Gap; Hunger in
America; rural; nonmetro

Food Insecurity across the Rural-Urban Divide: Are Counties in Need Being Reached by Charitable Food Assistance?

By
CRAIG GUNDERSEN,
ADAM DEWEY,
MONICA HAKE,
EMILY ENGELHARD,
and
AMY S. CRUMBAUGH

Food insecurity has become a leading health
and nutrition issue in the United States.
The magnitude of the problem is staggering: in
2014, more than 48 million Americans (15.4
percent) were food insecure (Coleman-Jensen

*Craig Gundersen is the Soybean Industry Endowed
Professor in Agricultural Strategy in the Department of
Agricultural and Consumer Economics at the University
of Illinois. He is on the Feeding America Technical
Advisory Group. His research concentrates on the
causes and consequences of food insecurity and the
evaluation of food assistance programs.*

*Adam Dewey is a research analyst at Feeding America,
where he manages the Map the Meal Gap project, including the most recent Map the Meal Gap 2016 study.*

*Monica Hake is a manager of social policy research and
analysis at Feeding America, where she has contributed to
numerous studies about food insecurity and the charitable
feeding sector, including Hunger in America 2014.*

Correspondence: cggunder@illinois.edu

DOI: 10.1177/0002716217710172

et al. 2015). About one-third of these individuals experienced a more serious level of food insecurity: very low food security. A vast literature has also demonstrated that numerous negative health consequences are associated with food insecurity (see Gundersen and Ziliak [2015] for a review). As might be expected, these negative health consequences are also associated with higher health care costs (Tarasuk et al. 2015).

The probability of being food insecure is not evenly distributed across the U.S. population, but research in this field has not shown that the uneven distribution correlates to whether one lives in a metropolitan or nonmetropolitan area. Since 2009, for example, the food insecurity rates in nonmetro areas have been only 1.1 percentage points higher, on average, than in metro areas. This is perhaps surprising given other work that has shown worse conditions in rural areas over dimensions such as poverty (see, e.g., Lichter et al. 2008; Peters 2012) and health (see, e.g., Auchincloss and Hadden 2002; Burton et al. 2013; Simmons et al. 2008; Vargas, Ronzio, and Hayes 2003). One reason why research has shown such small differences in food insecurity across the rural-urban divide is that studies have generally relied on the coarse, standard nonmetro/metro designations found in datasets such as the Current Population Survey (CPS).

To address food insecurity, the federal government uses multiple food assistance programs. Particularly important is the Supplemental Nutrition Assistance Program (SNAP; formerly known as the Food Stamp Program). The program is large both in terms of number of people reached (about 47 million people in 2014) and the maximum benefit levels (almost $650 for a family of four); it has proven to be an enormously successful program across numerous dimensions. In particular, research has demonstrated that SNAP recipients are upwards of 20 percent less likely to be food insecure than eligible nonrecipients (Kreider et al. 2012; for more on SNAP, see Bartfeld et al. 2015). The majority of food banks engage in SNAP application outreach and assistance, and food banks that serve rural counties may prioritize these efforts since the benefits allow low-income residents to access food through existing retail outlets that they are likely to visit.

While SNAP is the largest component of the social safety net against food insecurity, charitable food assistance programs also play a critical role in helping to relieve food insecurity. However, whether these charitable food assistance programs are truly directed toward areas in need remains an open question. There is evidence that rural areas are less well-served with respect to some services such as health care (see Aday, Quill, and Reyes-Gibby 2001; Fields, Bigbee, and Bell 2016; Kaufman et al. 2016) and banking (see Tolbert et al. 2014). The most common charitable feeding programs operating in rural areas are traditional food pantries and mobile food pantries. The latter model often involves

Emily Engelhard is managing director of research and evaluation at Feeding America, where she leads the organization's research and evaluation work related to food insecurity and charitable feeding, including Hunger in America and Map the Meal Gap.

Amy S. Crumbaugh is the director of social policy research and analysis at Feeding America, where she oversees a number of research initiatives, including Hunger in America and Map the Meal Gap.

delivering grocery products to temporary, but central, locations for direct distribution to clients and can be particularly suitable in rural areas. Nevertheless,
many food banks report that serving rural counties involves operational and logis-
tical challenges and can require substantial resources.

In this article, we use results from Map the Meal Gap (MMG)—a project of
the nonprofit organization Feeding America—to address the following unan-
swered question: How do food insecurity rates differ by Rural-Urban Continuum
Codes[1] across the United States? We also use data from MMG combined with
data from the Agency and Program Surveys of the Hunger in America 2014 (HIA
2014) study to analyze the distribution of charitable food by Rural-Urban
Continuum Codes across the United States.

Methods and Data

To address our first question of how food insecurity differs across the rural-urban
continuum, we use data from Feeding America's MMG project (described
below). First, we analyze the data using the nine Rural-Urban Continuum Codes,
and because there may be differences by region of the country, we further break
things down into the four standard regions—South, West, Midwest, and
Northeast.[2] We then move on to our second question: How does charitable food
distribution differ across the rural urban continuum? First we provide descriptive
information at the county level, using three measures of food bank coverage
(described below). We then use a multivariate framework to consider the relative
roles of population, food insecurity, Rural-Urban Continuum Codes, region, and
size in determining food bank coverage by county. The distribution of the rural-
urban continuum, along with food bank locations, is found in Figure 1.

Background: Measuring food insecurity

The Core Food Security Module (CFSM) was established in 1996 as a means
of establishing the food insecurity status of a household. The measure is based on
a set of eighteen questions for households with children and ten questions for
households without children. Examples of questions include: "I worried whether
our food would run out before we got money to buy more" (the least severe
item); "Did you or the other adults in your household ever cut the size of your
meals or skip meals because there wasn't enough money for food?" "Were you
ever hungry but did not eat because you couldn't afford enough food?" and "Did
a child in the household ever not eat for a full day because you couldn't afford
enough food?" (the most severe item for households with children). (A complete
list of questions can be found in Coleman-Jensen et al. 2015.) Each question is
qualified by the stipulation that the outcomes are due to financial issues.

Based on criteria established by the U.S. Department of Agriculture (USDA),
households are then delineated into official food insecurity categories based on
responses from the CFSM. This is under the assumption that the number of

FIGURE 1
Counties by Rural Urban Continuum Code

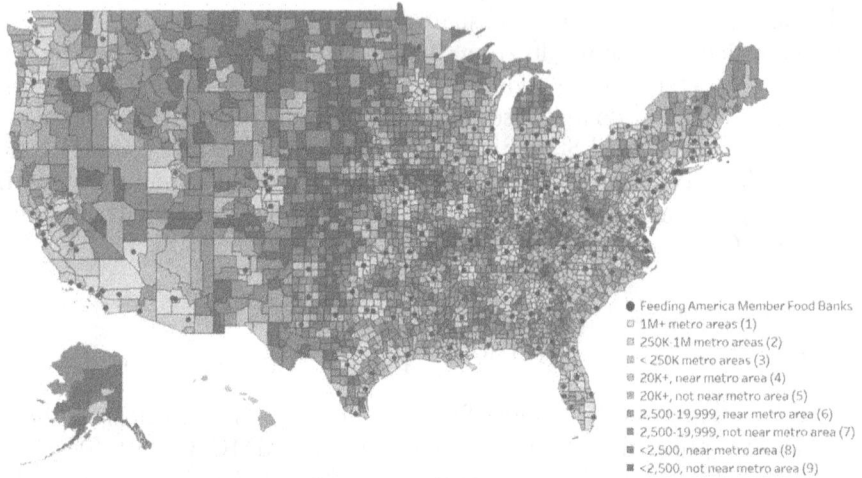

SOURCE: Rural-Urban Continuum Codes (https://www.ers.usda.gov/data-products/rural-urban-continuum-codes/).

affirmative responses reflects the level of food hardship experienced by the family.[3] The following thresholds are established: (1) food security (all household members had access at all times to enough food for an active, healthy life); (2) low food security (at least some household members were uncertain of having enough food, because they had insufficient money and other resources for food); and (3) very low food security (one or more household members were hungry, at least some time during the year, because they could not afford enough food). A household is said to be food insecure if they fall into the second or third category.

Map the Meal Gap

While the food insecurity rates for some counties can be calculated directly using information from the Current Population Survey (CPS), in most cases, either a county is not identified in the CPS or the sample size is too small to provide meaningful food insecurity rates. To obtain estimates of food insecurity rates for all counties in the United States, then, Feeding America conducts an analysis as part of its annual MMG study. This is done through a two-step process, which is described in the appendix.

A map of MMG results can be found in Figure 2. As seen, there is enormous geographic variation in food insecurity rates across the United States. For example, rates range from relatively low in the upper Midwest to quite high in the Mississippi Delta, Appalachia, and on American Indian reservations.

FIGURE 2
Percentage of People per County Who Are Food Insecure, 2014

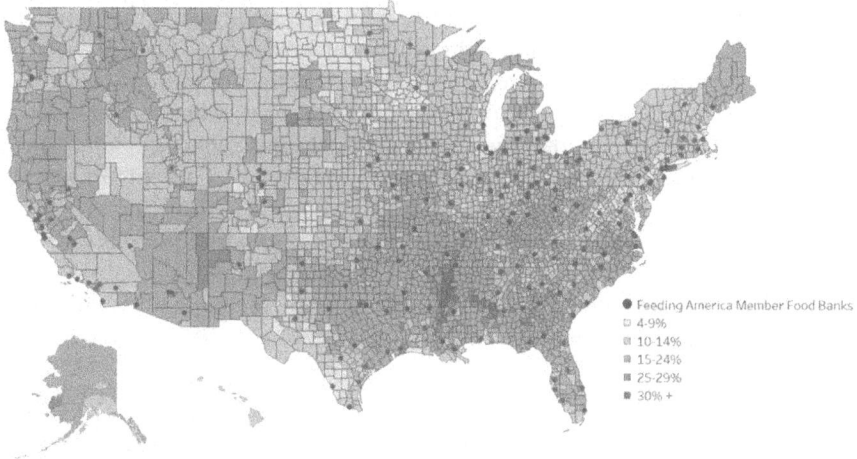

SOURCE: Map the Meal Gap 2016 (http://map.feedingamerica.org/).

Hunger in America

HIA 2014 is the latest in a series of quadrennial studies that provides comprehensive, nationally representative demographic profiles of people seeking food assistance through the charitable sector and in-depth analyses of partner agencies in the Feeding America network.[4] There are three components to HIA 2014. There is a client survey, which is based on a nationally representative sample of clients who use Feeding America food banks. There is also an agency survey and a program survey. The former is a census of all the partner agencies of all participating food banks, and the latter is a census of all programs in all participating food banks. More than 32,000 partner agencies completed the agency survey, which asked detailed questions about partner agencies' services, capacity, and food distribution, including a specific set of additional questions about each meal, grocery, and food-related benefit program operated by the partner agency. The program-specific questions that were asked covered topics including schedule of operations, volunteer utilization, sources of food, intake procedures, and program facilities, among others. These additional questions are what are used to establish the information in the program survey.

Based on information from HIA 2014, we define three measures of service by food banks and their partner agencies. The first is the number of food-providing locations per person in the county.[5] Under this definition, a location providing food for, say, one day per month is treated the same as a location providing food five days per week, every week. To address this differential access, which may influence the ability to procure food, our second measure is the number of days that food programs are open. Responding agencies are asked about the number of days they are open and, in some instances, this yields a specific number that can be aggregated to the annual level (e.g., open once a week). In other cases, the responses are in categories and, in those instances, we assign the number of days per year as roughly the midpoint of these categories (e.g., open certain days each month).[6] Our third measure considers the number of pounds available in food bank agencies.[7] Unlike the previous two measures, which are defined by programs, this one is defined at the agency level. Because agencies do not get all of their food from food banks, this is adjusted by the proportion of food supplied from other sources by agency. For example, if an agency reports that they get 50 percent of their food from the food bank, the total number of pounds said to be supplied from that agency is doubled. In an effort to compare across counties of different sizes, we normalize these three measures by the population and by the food insecure population in those counties.

Results

Our central findings are threefold. First, at the national level, food insecurity rates are relatively similar across rural and urban areas. While this is true at the national level, when we break things down by region, there are differences across the rural-urban divide. Third, and perhaps contrary to expectations, the distribution of charitable food assistance is, on average, actually more directed toward counties with smaller populations. This holds even after controlling for other factors that influence the distribution of charitable assistance.

Distribution of food insecurity by Rural-Urban Continuum Codes

In Table 1, we display average food insecurity rates by Rural-Urban Continuum Codes. To give some context for the distribution of counties, the number of counties within each category is found in the first column. Nonmetro counties containing between 2,500 and 20,000 people, adjacent to a metro area, have the largest number of counties (593), while nonmetro counties containing 20,000 or more people, not adjacent to a metro area, have the smallest (92). In the second column, the average population for each category is displayed. These decrease monotonically in size. In counties in metro areas containing 1 million or more people, the average population is almost 400,000, while completely rural counties or those with an urban population of less than 2,500 and not adjacent to a metro area have an average population of 6,125. In the next column, the average size of the counties is displayed in square miles. Here, there is no clear relationship across the rural-urban divide. Instead, the largest counties are those with an urban population of 2,500 to 19,999 people, not adjacent to a metro area (1,777 square miles) and the smallest are those in metro areas with at least 1 million residents (653 square miles).

TABLE 1
Descriptive Statistics and Food Insecurity Rates by Rural-Urban Continuum Codes

Rural-Urban Continuum Codes	Description	Number of Counties	Population (SD)	Size in Square Miles (SD)	Food Insecurity Rate (SD)
1	Counties in metro areas with a population of 1 million or more	432	399,192 (765,014)	652.66 (1,268.09)	.131 (.039)
2	Counties in metro areas with a population of 250,000 to 1 million	378	176,577 (194,967)	939.93 (1,627.29)	.145 (.033)
3	Counties in metro areas with a population of fewer than 250,000	356	80,509 (61,499)	955.42 (1,514.18)	.147 (.037)
4	Urban population of 20,000 or more, adjacent to a metro area	214	63,342 (24,453)	1022.27 (1,595.65)	.152 (.036)
5	Urban population of 20,000 or more, not adjacent to a metro area	92	54,321 (24,010)	1,652.11 (2,321.14)	.153 (.048)
6	Urban population of 2,500 to 19,999, adjacent to a metro area	593	24,838 (12,658)	849.79 (990.21)	.156 (.042)
7	Urban population of 2,500 to 19,999, not adjacent to a metro area	433	19,011 (11,161)	1,776.57 (5,281.18)	.150 (.044)
8	Completely rural or with an urban population of fewer than 2,500, adjacent to a metro area	220	9,731 (6,311)	846.60 (1,256.24)	.154 (.049)
9	Completely rural or with an urban population of fewer than 2,500, not adjacent to a metro area	424	6,125 (5,078)	1,706.14 (7,520.89)	.139 (.041)
	Total	3,142	99,970 (319,922)	1,123.74 (3,611.42)	.147 (.041)

In the final column we consider the food insecurity rates. The highest are found in counties with an urban population of 2,500 to 19,999, adjacent to a metro area. However, the rate there (15.6 percent) is not that much higher than the lowest—counties in metro areas with a population of 1 million or more (13.1 percent).[8]

In Table 2, we break things down by region. As seen in the first four columns, there is substantial variation in the average population of counties. For example, in counties in metro areas of 250,000 to 1 million people, that are in the South, the average population is 133,685; while for those in the West it is 326,620. In looking at the overall averages, the final row, the Northeast has by far the highest (257,171), while the South has the smallest (82,504).

Turning to the final four columns where the food insecurity rates are displayed, the overall rates are higher in the South and West (16.7 percent and 14.4 percent) versus the Midwest and Northeast (12.6 percent and 12.2 percent). Within these areas, the highest average rate (19.1 percent) is found in the South in counties in nonmetro areas with an urban population of 20,000 or more, not adjacent to a metro area. This is substantially higher than the lowest (11.4 percent), in Northeast counties in metro areas with a population of at least 1 million. Within regions, the highest average food insecurity rates in the South are in counties in metro areas with an urban population of 20,000 or more, not adjacent to a metro area (19.1 percent); the highest are found in counties in nonmetro areas with urban populations of 20,000 or more, adjacent to a metro area in both the West (15.8 percent) and Midwest (13.4 percent); and in the Northeast, the highest rate is found in counties in nonmetro areas that are completely rural or have an urban population of fewer than 2,500, not adjacent to a metro area (13.7 percent). Consistent with what we find at the national level, the lowest food insecurity rates are found in counties in metro areas with populations of at least 1 million in the South (14.0 percent), West (13.0 percent), and Northeast (11.4 percent). In the Midwest, in contrast to the Northeast, counties in nonmetro areas that are completely rural or have an urban population of fewer than 2,500 and not adjacent to a metro area have the lowest rate (12.0 percent).

Locations of food pantries

A central goal of the Feeding America network is to provide services that reach all Americans in need, irrespective of where they reside. This often entails trade-offs between having enough resources in areas of high population density while also being able to reach less densely populated areas. In Table 3, we consider this issue based on our first two measures—the number of food service providers per capita and the number of days that food providers are open per capita. Before turning to the results, three caveats are in order. First, food banks had the option of participating or not participating in HIA 2014. As a consequence, not all counties are represented in the data, and the number of counties is fewer than found in MMG. However, more than 90 percent of Feeding America member food banks did participate. The number of counties included in each Rural-Urban Continuum Code is found in column (1). Second, there are

TABLE 2
Food Insecurity Rates by Rural-Urban Continuum Codes and Region of Country

Rural-Urban Continuum Codes	Description	Population (SD)				Food Insecurity Rates (SD)			
		South	West	Midwest	Northeast	South	West	Midwest	Northeast
1	Counties in metro areas of 1 million population or more	268,305 (486,795)	1,100,325 (1,719,572)	292,247 (586,605)	573,540 (539,416)	.140 (.043)	.130 (.019)	.125 (.035)	.114 (.032)
2	Counties in metro areas of 250,000 to 1 million population	133,685 (151,569)	326,620 (279,297)	147,282 (159,426)	274,803 (218,079)	.159 (.036)	.139 (.019)	.128 (.024)	.120 (.015)
3	Counties in metro areas of fewer than 250,000 population	68,031 (56,848)	113,690 (65,708)	75,991 (60,721)	115,088 (50,555)	.163 (.038)	.149 (.025)	.128 (.031)	.125 (.018)
4	Urban population of 20,000 or more, adjacent to a metro area	60,484 (19,951)	58,136 (20,711)	60,607 (21,475)	83,783 (35,533)	.176 (.038)	.158 (.027)	.134 (.026)	.125 (.012)
5	Urban population of 20,000 or more, not adjacent to a metro area	53,503 (14,155)	68,735 (34,004)	42,630 (14,410)	85,595 (5,325)	.191 (.054)	.139 (.034)	.131 (.030)	.118 (.014)
6	Urban population of 2,500 to 19,999, adjacent to a metro area	24,089 (12,213)	22,648 (12,613)	24,117 (11,784)	43,069 (10,706)	.176 (.044)	.150 (.031)	.131 (.025)	.126 (.018)
7	Urban population of 2,500 to 19,999, not adjacent to a metro area	20,171 (10,639)	15,952 (8,991)	17,202 (9,519)	38,434 (16,614)	.180 (.049)	.142 (.027)	.126 (.028)	.129 (.020)
8	Completely rural or less than 2,500 urban population, adjacent to a metro area	11,214 (6,500)	8,972 (4,090)	8,329 (4,927)	17,047 (11,184)	.177 (.053)	.147 (.019)	.123 (.031)	.131 (.022)
9	Completely rural or less than 2,500 urban population, not adjacent to a metro area	8,429 (5,519)	4,092 (3,147)	5,366 (4,626)	15,065 (10,502)	.169 (.040)	.142 (.030)	.120 (.033)	.137 (.016)
	All Counties	82,504 (218,673)	164,347 (609,418)	63,842 (211,680)	257,171 (380,444)	.167 (.045)	.144 (.027)	.126 (.030)	.122 (.023)

TABLE 3
Coverage of Feeding America Food Provision Services by Rural-Urban Continuum
Codes: Information at the Program Level

Rural-Urban Continuum Codes	Description	Number of Counties	Number of Locations per 1,000 Persons (SD)	Number of Days Open of Location per Person (SD)	Number of Locations per 1,000 Food Insecure Person (SD)	Number of Days Open of Location per Food Insecure Person (SD)
		(1)	(2)	(3)	(4)	(5)
1	Counties in metro areas of 1 million population or more	416	0.14 (0.12)	0.022 (0.030)	1.07 (0.86)	0.167 (0.209)
2	Counties in metro areas of 250,000 to 1 million population	361	0.18 (0.12)	0.028 (0.036)	1.28 (0.96)	0.207 (0.309)
3	Counties in metro areas of fewer than 250,000 population	319	0.21 (0.18)	0.030 (0.035)	1.54 (1.52)	0.218 (0.275)
4	Urban population of 20,000 or more, adjacent to a metro area	203	0.18 (0.11)	0.025 (0.023)	1.26 (0.84)	0.179 (0.173)
5	Urban population of 20,000 or more, not adjacent to a metro area	84	0.19 (0.13)	0.032 (0.030)	1.36 (0.98)	0.241 (0.257)
6	Urban population of 2,500 to 19,999, adjacent to a metro area	552	0.21 (0.16)	0.026 (0.036)	1.42 (1.19)	0.179 (0.279)
7	Urban population of 2,500 to 19,999, not adjacent to a metro area	402	0.22 (0.18)	0.026 (0.033)	1.56 (1.38)	0.194 (0.254)
8	Completely rural or less than 2,500 urban population, adjacent to a metro area	191	0.27 (0.29)	0.034 (0.058)	2.02 (2.43)	0.262 (0.546)
9	Completely rural or less than 2,500 urban population, not adjacent to a metro area	382	0.27 (0.36)	0.025 (0.047)	2.24 (3.46)	0.195 (0.366)
	Total	2,910	0.21 (0.21)	0.027 (0.037)	1.52 (1.78)	0.197 (0.304)

NOTE: The number of counties includes all counties in the Hunger in America survey minus counties with implausible estimates of coverage. These implausible estimates occur when the number of locations per person exceeds 0.002 and where the number of days open per location exceeds 0.4.

some counties where, despite their inclusion in HIA 2014, no food was provided under the definitions discussed above. There are several possible reasons for this. Among them, some counties may not be home to a food-providing program but residents of those counties may visit programs in neighboring counties or be served by mobile distributions that originate in other counties. Alternatively, some counties may be unrepresented due to agency/program nonresponse. Third, our measures at the county level are aggregate measures. As such, they cannot account for factors such as distance to services, disproportionate distribution of food within a county, transportation barriers, and whether participants' schedules allow them to visit the program(s) during the hours that they are open. While the simple existence of food programs is important, the extent to which people can and do access those programs is an important aspect that needs to be considered as well.

In columns (2) and (3), we portray the measures for which the denominator is the population of the county. Perhaps contrary to expectations, we find that more rural counties have higher coverage rates than more urban counties. For example, consider a comparison of counties in metro areas with a population of 1 million or more (the lowest) with counties in rural areas with a population of fewer than 2,500 that are not adjacent to a metro area (the highest). There are 1.4 locations for every 10,000 people in the former versus 2.7 locations in the latter. When we consider this comparison for number of days open per county, things change slightly. Metro areas with a population of 1 million or more still have the lowest degree of coverage—22 days for every 10,000 people; but this is only slightly different than counties in rural areas with an urban population of fewer than 2,500 and that are not adjacent to a metro area—25 days for every 10,000 people (p-value of .057). Under this measure, counties in completely rural areas or less than 2,500 urban population, adjacent to a metro area, have the highest—34 days for every 10,000 people.

In columns (5) and (6), we consider a different denominator, the number of food insecure persons. When looking at either metric of service, the ordering is roughly the same as when the denominator is the number of persons.

In Table 4, we consider the distribution of pounds of food per county. The results largely mimic Table 3 in terms of the distribution found there by number of days of service albeit the relative difference between the counties with the least coverage and the counties with the most coverage is smaller. Namely, counties in metro areas with a population of 1 million or more have the lowest number of pounds distributed per person (10.33), and counties in rural areas with an urban population of fewer than 2,500 that are not adjacent to a metro area have the highest (13.27).

We now turn to our multivariate results in Tables 5 through 7. In each table we consider in the first column the impact of total population and the number of food insecure persons, both in logs. In the second column, we add in category variables for each of the Rural-Urban Continuum Codes, with counties in metro areas with a population of 1 million or more as the omitted group. In the third column we add in two other factors that may influence the outcome—the region of the country (South is the omitted category) and the size of the county in logs.

TABLE 4
Coverage of Feeding America Food Provision Services by Rural-Urban Continuum
Codes: Information at the Agency Level

Rural-Urban Continuum Codes	Description	Number of Counties	Number of Pounds per Person (SD)	Number of Pounds per Food Insecure Person (SD)
1	Counties in metro areas of 1 million population or more	412	10.33 (8.28)	82.13 (69.53)
2	Counties in metro areas of 250,000 to 1 million population	356	12.20 (10.06)	85.09 (70.82)
3	Counties in metro areas of fewer than 250,000 population	310	11.42 (10.24)	80.07 (75.37)
4	Urban population of 20,000 or more, adjacent to a metro area	202	11.86 (9.08)	80.06 (60.94)
5	Urban population of 20,000 or more, not adjacent to a metro area	83	11.25 (8.99)	73.88 (49.84)
6	Urban population of 2,500 to 19,999, adjacent to a metro area	534	11.75 (9.36)	78.92 (67.08)
7	Urban population of 2,500 to 19,999, not adjacent to a metro area	387	11.43 (11.27)	78.97 (80.23)
8	Completely rural or less than 2,500 urban population, adjacent to a metro area	173	12.52 (10.98)	85.74 (77.57)
9	Completely rural or less than 2,500 urban population, not adjacent to a metro area	301	13.27 (14.41)	96.52 (100.75)
	Total	2,758	11.72 (10.43)	82.61 (75.02)

NOTE: The number of counties includes all counties in the Hunger in America survey that reported pounds distributed to agencies minus counties with implausible estimates of coverage. These implausible estimates occur when the number of pounds per person exceeds 90.

In Table 5, the outcome is the number of Feeding America food-providing locations. As expected, population size is positively related to the number of locations, as is, in two of the three specifications, the number of food insecure persons.[9] The latter is evidence that resources, at least over this dimension, are effectively directed. All else equal, counties that are completely rural or have an urban population of fewer than 2,500, adjacent to a metro area and counties that are completely rural or have an urban population of fewer than 2,500, not adjacent to a metro area have more locations than other counties. While these two

TABLE 5
Determinants of Number of Feeding America Food-Providing Locations

	(1)	(2)	(3)
Total population (log)	11.149°°	11.437°°	4.584°
	(1.861)	(1.895)	(2.126)
Number of food insecure persons (log)	2.849	6.109°°	12.626°°
	(1.822)	(1.785)	(1.995)
Counties in metro areas of 250,000 to 1 million population		−5.295°°	−6.098°°
		(1.943)	(1.955)
Counties in metro areas of fewer than 250,000 population		−9.841°°	−11.907°°
		(2.063)	(2.080)
Urban population of 20,000 or more, adjacent to a metro area		−16.349°°	−19.229°°
		(2.343)	(2.379)
Urban population of 20,000 or more, not adjacent to a metro area		−14.627°°	−18.211°°
		(3.244)	(3.284)
Urban population of 2,500 to 19,999, adjacent to a metro area		−5.203°°	−7.296°°
		(2.015)	(2.067)
Urban population of 2,500 to 19,999, not adjacent to a metro area		−0.763	−4.119
		(2.187)	(2.277)
Completely rural or less than 2,500 urban population, adjacent to a metro area		9.922°°	7.500°°
		(2.779)	(2.803)
Completely rural or less than 2,500 urban population, not adjacent to a metro area		19.537°°	15.529°°
		(2.587)	(2.680)
West			10.213°°
			(1.874)
Midwest			8.937°°
			(1.245)
Northeast			6.034°°
			(2.083)
Area of county (log)			0.382
			(0.663)
Constant	−124.380°°	−153.355°°	−142.215°°
	(5.161)	(7.485)	(8.233)

NOTE: Standard errors in parentheses. The sample includes all counties in the Hunger in America survey minus counties with implausible estimates of coverage. These implausible estimates occur when the number of locations per person exceeds 0.002 and where the number of days open per location exceeds 0.4. $N = 2,910$.
°$p < .05$. °°$p < .01$.

most rural types of counties have more food-providing locations, the other counties have fewer locations, all else equal, than counties in metro areas with populations of 1 million or more.[10] The South has fewer locations, all else equal, than the other three regions. The size of the county has no statistically significant influence on the number of food-providing locations.

In Table 6, we turn to the number of days that a provider is open as our metric of food bank coverage. With respect to sign and statistical significance, the results are similar to those found in Table 5. The only exception is that the Northeast, all else equal, does not have more days open than the South.

Table 7 considers the impacts of the same set of factors on the number of pounds of food distributed. Results are similar to those found with the other metrics of distribution. The exceptions are that the number of food insecure persons is positive and statistically significant across all three columns; the association of counties with urban populations of 2,500 to 19,999, adjacent to a metro area; and urban population of 2,500 to 19,999, not adjacent to a metro area with number of pounds is both statistically insignificantly different from counties in metro areas with a population of 1 million or more. The Northeast distributes fewer pounds, all else equal, than the South.

A unifying theme of this volume is the blurring of boundaries between urban and rural areas. In the context of our article, this issue may be framed with respect to the distribution of food. We do so in Table 8, where we examine whether a county being adjacent to a metro area, controlling for other factors, influences the provision of food. This is enabled by the structure of the Rural-Urban Continuum Codes, whereby the groupings 4 and 5, 6 and 7, and 8 and 9 all have the same population cutoffs but differ by whether they are adjacent to a metro area. For example, categories 6 and 7 both include counties with an urban population of between 2,500 to 19,999, while the former is adjacent to a metro area and the latter is not. In Table 8 the regressions are the same as found in Tables 5 through 7; only now we consider, with a sample comprising categories 4 through 9, whether the county is adjacent to a metro area.[11] In contrast to the previous multivariate results, where we did see differences by the rural-urban divide, the coefficient on whether a county is adjacent to a metro area is statistically insignificant and small. There are three other departures from the previous tables, perhaps due to the dropping of categories 1 through 3—the region of the country is generally statistically insignificant, the size of the county is positively associated with the distribution of food, and the number of food insecure persons is now statistically insignificant in two of the three models.

Conclusion

Food insecurity is not evenly distributed geographically across the United States. Instead, we see distinct differences by the rural-urban divide, especially once we break things down by region. In aggregate terms, we do see that areas with greater need are receiving more food from food banks. When we use the number of food providers as our metric, there is twice as much coverage in remote rural counties compared to the largest metropolitan counties. While not as stark, we

TABLE 6
Determinants of Number of Days Open for Feeding America Food Providing Locations

	(1)	(2)	(3)
Total population (log)	2.526°°	2.534°°	1.469°°
	(0.485)	(0.500)	(0.562)
Number of food insecure persons (log)	0.402	1.176°	2.228°°
	(0.475)	(0.471)	(0.528)
Counties in metro areas of 250,000 to 1 million population		−1.399°°	−1.487°°
		(0.512)	(0.517)
Counties in metro areas of fewer than 250,000 population		−2.576°°	−2.920°°
		(0.544)	(0.550)
Urban population of 20,000 or more, adjacent to a metro area		−4.110°°	−4.544°°
		(0.618)	(0.629)
Urban population of 20,000 or more, not adjacent to a metro area		−3.237°°	−3.904°°
		(0.855)	(0.869)
Urban population of 2,500 to 19,999, adjacent to a metro area		−1.364°	−1.613°°
		(0.531)	(0.547)
Urban population of 2,500 to 19,999, not adjacent to a metro area		−0.337	−0.875
		(0.577)	(0.602)
Completely rural or less than 2,500 urban population, adjacent to a metro area		2.070°°	1.765°
		(0.733)	(0.742)
Completely rural or less than 2,500 urban population, not adjacent to a metro area		4.137°°	3.523°°
		(0.682)	(0.709)
West			2.907°°
			(0.496)
Midwest			1.672°°
			(0.329)
Northeast			0.416
			(0.551)
Area of county (log)			−0.083
			(0.175)
Constant	−26.746°°	−32.822°°	−30.739°°
	(1.346)	(1.974)	(2.178)

NOTE: Number of days open is divided by 1,000. Standard errors in parentheses. The sample includes all counties in the Hunger in America survey minus counties with implausible estimates of coverage. These implausible estimates occur when the number of locations per person exceeds 0.002 and where the number of days open per location exceeds 0.4. $N = 2,910$.
°$p < .05$. °°$p < .01$.

TABLE 7
Determinants of Number of Pounds Distributed for Feeding America Food Providing
Locations

	(1)	(2)	(3)
Total population (log)	0.950°°	1.053°°	0.744°°
	(0.229)	(0.236)	(0.265)
Number of food insecure persons (log)	0.494°	0.791°°	1.117°°
	(0.225)	(0.222)	(0.247)
Counties in metro areas of 250,000 to 1 million population		−0.986°°	−1.056°°
		(0.236)	(0.237)
Counties in metro areas of fewer than 250,000 population		−1.235°°	−1.418°°
		(0.252)	(0.254)
Urban population of 20,000 or more, adjacent to a metro area		−1.749°°	−1.931°°
		(0.284)	(0.288)
Urban population of 20,000 or more, not adjacent to a metro area		−1.520°°	−1.915°°
		(0.394)	(0.399)
Urban population of 2,500 to 19,999, adjacent to a metro area		−0.366	−0.479
		(0.248)	(0.253)
Urban population of 2,500 to 19,999, not adjacent to a metro area		0.117	−0.167
		(0.270)	(0.280)
Completely rural or less than 2,500 urban population, adjacent to a metro area		1.246°°	1.137°°
		(0.347)	(0.349)
Completely rural or less than 2,500 urban population, not adjacent to a metro area		2.078°°	1.772°°
		(0.324)	(0.334)
West			1.528°°
			(0.239)
Midwest			0.653°°
			(0.153)
Northeast			−0.505°
			(0.253)
Area of county (log)			0.014
			(0.084)
Constant	−12.875°°	−16.272°°	−16.096°°
	(0.648)	(0.943)	(1.047)

NOTE: Number of pounds is divided by 1,000,000. Standard errors in parentheses. The sample includes all counties in the Hunger in America survey minus counties with implausible estimates of coverage. These implausible estimates occur when the number of pounds per person exceeds 90. N = 2,758.
°$p < .05$. °°$p < .01$.

TABLE 8
Determinants of Distribution for Feeding America Food Providing Locations for Rural-
Urban Continuum Codes 4 through 9

	Number of Locations	Number of Days Open	Number of Pounds Distributed
Total population (log)	2.194°°	0.488°°	0.140°°
	(0.465)	(0.097)	(0.036)
Number of food insecure persons (log)	0.768	−0.034	0.096°°
	(0.434)	(0.090)	(0.033)
Adjacent to a metro area	−0.084	−0.076	−0.010
	(0.226)	(0.047)	(0.017)
West	−0.094	0.171°	−0.017
	(0.414)	(0.086)	(0.032)
Midwest	0.973°°	0.140°	0.005
	(0.269)	(0.056)	(0.020)
Northeast	7.281°°	1.055°°	−0.010
	(0.531)	(0.110)	(0.039)
Area of county (log)	0.550°°	0.071°	0.025°
	(0.154)	(0.032)	(0.012)
Constant	−26.603°°	−4.364°°	−1.978°°
	(1.640)	(0.341)	(0.132)
n	1,814	1,814	1,667

NOTE: The sample includes all counties in the Hunger in America survey minus counties with implausible estimates of coverage as noted in Tables 5 through 7.
°$p < .05.$ °°$p < .01.$

also see much better coverage in remote rural areas when we use our two other measures—the number of days open per person and the number of pounds of food distributed per person.

This high degree of coverage in rural areas is directly related to the member food bank programs provided by Feeding America. The most common program model in operation, including in rural areas, is a traditional food pantry—a physical location where grocery products are distributed for off-site use, usually for preparation in the recipient's residence. A variation of this model that can be particularly appropriate in rural areas is a mobile food pantry, a program in which a food bank makes a same-day distribution without involving a receiving agency; this model can often involve distribution from a Feeding America truck directly to clients in need.

While the presence of charitable food assistance in rural areas is an important component of efforts to reduce food insecurity in these communities, no comprehensive plan to reduce food insecurity can overlook the importance of SNAP. As is the case with the distribution of charitable food, the proportion of the population receiving SNAP in rural areas is higher than in either metropolitan or micropolitan areas (14.6 percent versus 10.9 percent and 13.8 percent, respectively)

(Bailey 2014). These higher rates may reflect food banks' efforts to promote SNAP participation and provide application assistance in rural communities. Considering the successes of Feeding America food banks and the USDA in promoting food assistance in rural areas, perhaps other nongovernment and government groups that are charged with directing resources toward geographic areas that are underserved should emulate these programs.

Appendix

Map the Meal Gap

The county-level estimates of food insecurity in Map the Meal Gap are established as follows. First, we begin by establishing the extent of food insecurity for each state for each year from 2001 to 2014. Our state-level measures of food insecurity are defined at the person-level where persons are defined as food insecure if they live in a food insecure household. This is consistent with how the measures of food insecurity at the person-level are delineated in the official USDA report (see, e.g., Coleman-Jensen et al. 2015, Table 1A). With these state-level food insecurity rates, we estimate the following model of food insecurity:

$$
\begin{aligned}
FI_{st} = \alpha + \beta_{UN}UN_{st} + \beta_{POV}POV_{st} + \beta_{MI}MI_{st} + \beta_{HISP}HISP_{st}, \\
+ \beta_{BLACK}BLACK_{st} + \beta_{OWN}OWN_{st} + \mu_t + \upsilon_s + \varepsilon_{st}
\end{aligned}
\tag{1}
$$

where s is a state, t is year, UN is the unemployment rate, POV is the poverty rate, MI is median income, HISP is the percent Hispanic, BLACK is the percent African American, OWN is the percent of persons living in owned (rather than rented) housing units, μ_t is a year fixed effect, υ_s is a state fixed effect, and ε_{st} is an error term. (The coefficient estimates for the most recent MMG are in Table A1.) Our choice of variables was first guided by the literature on the determinants of food insecurity; we included variables that have been found to influence the probability of someone being food insecure.[12] However, we are constrained with our methods to include only those that are available both in the CPS and American Community Survey (ACS).

In our second step, we use the coefficient estimates from step 1 plus data for the same variables defined at the county level to generate estimated food insecurity rates for individuals in every county. We use 2010–2014 ACS five-year estimates for all variables at the county level except for unemployment rates, which reflect one-year (2014) annual averages from the Bureau of Labor Statistics (BLS).

This can be expressed in the following equation:

$$
\begin{aligned}
FI^{*}_{csT} = \hat{\alpha} + \hat{\beta}_{UN}UN_{csT} + \hat{\beta}_{POV}POV_{csT} + \hat{\beta}_{MI}MI_{csT} + \hat{\beta}_{HISP}HISP_{csT} +, \\
\hat{\beta}_{BLACK}BLACK_{csT} + \hat{\beta}_{OWN}OWN_{CST} + \mu_T + \nu_s
\end{aligned}
\tag{2}
$$

where c denotes a county and T denotes the year from which the county-level variables are defined.[13]

TABLE A1
Estimates of the Impact of Various Factors on Food Insecurity at the
State Level, 2001–2014

	Coefficient (SE)
Poverty rate	.169°°
	(.054)
Unemployment rate	.529°°
	(.102)
Median income	−.003
	(.002)
Percent Hispanic	−.153°
	(.064)
Percent African American	.121
	(.065)
Percent homeownership	−.107°°
	(.039)
2002 (year fixed effect)	.000
	(.003)
2003 (year fixed effect)	.004
	(.004)
2004 (year fixed effect)	.014°°
	(.004)
2005 (year fixed effect)	.009°
	(.004)
2006 (year fixed effect)	.014°°
	(.003)
2007 (year fixed effect)	.019°°
	(.004)
2008 (year fixed effect)	.042°°
	(.004)
2009 (year fixed effect)	.027°°
	(.006)
2010 (year fixed effect)	.022°°
	(.006)
2011 (year fixed effect)	.023°°
	(.005)
2012 (year fixed effect)	.025°°
	(.005)
2013 (year fixed effect)	.028°°
	(.005)
2014 (year fixed effect)	.030°°
	(.006)
Constant	.150°°
	(.032)

NOTE: The omitted year for the year fixed effects is 2001. The data used are taken from the December supplements of the 2001–2014 Current Population Survey.
°$p < .05$. °°$p < .01$.

Notes

1. Rural-Urban Continuum Codes are defined by the Office of Management and Budget (OMB). They classify metropolitan counties by the population of their metro areas and nonmetropolitan counties by urbanization and adjacency to a metro area. There are three metro and six nonmetro categories. For more details about these definitions, see https://www.ers.usda.gov/data-products/rural-urban-continuum-codes/ documentation/; and for a listing of the codes by year, see https://www.ers.usda.gov/data-products/rural-urban-continuum-codes.

2. The South comprises Delaware, Washington DC, Florida, Georgia, Maryland, North Carolina, South Carolina, Virginia, West Virginia, Alabama, Kentucky, Mississippi, Tennessee, Arkansas, Louisiana, Oklahoma, and Texas; the West comprises Arizona, Colorado, Idaho, Montana, Nevada, New Mexico, Utah, Wyoming, Alaska, California, Hawaii, Oregon, and Washington; the Midwest comprises Illinois, Indiana, Michigan, Ohio, Wisconsin, Iowa, Kansas, Minnesota, Missouri, Nebraska, North Dakota, and South Dakota; and the Northeast comprises Connecticut, Maine, Massachusetts, New Hampshire, Rhode Island, Vermont, New Jersey, New York, and Pennsylvania.

3. An "affirmative response" is sometimes based on a "yes/no" categorization. In other cases, respondents are asked about whether an outcome happened "often," "sometimes," or "never." A response of "often" or "sometimes" is considered an "affirmative response."

4. The Feeding America network comprises one national office and 200 food banks that together serve nearly every county in the United States. Each food bank partners with a network of local agencies (including some that are faith-based and others that are not) that operate grocery and meal programs to provide food to people in need.

5. Based on the categories in HIA, the following programs are defined as locations that provide food-based HIA: afterschool snacks, BackPack Programs, Child Congregate Feeding Programs (non–Kids Cafe), Commodity Supplemental Food Program (CSFP), community gardens, community kitchens, day dare, food-bank operated meal programs, food-bank operated pantry programs, food pantries, group homes, home-delivered grocery programs, home-delivered meals, Kids Cafe Programs, mobile pantries, other pantry programs, school pantry programs, senior brown bag and food box distributions, rehabilitation programs, residential programs, senior congregate meals, senior grocery programs, senior mobile, shelter, transitional housing, just-in-time delivery, soup kitchens, and Summer Food Service Program (SFSP). The following other programs are programs operated by Feeding America agencies but they do not provide food as their main role: clothing/furniture assistance, tax preparation, GED programs, general information and referrals, health clinics, housing assistance, job training, legal assistance, Medicaid/CHIP, National School Breakfast Program, National School Lunch Program, nutrition education, other nonfood, transportation assistance, utility assistance, and WIC outreach.

6. The categories are as follows: "one day per week," 52 days; "certain days each week," 156 days; "seven days per week," 365 days; "once per month," 12 days; "certain days each month," 36 days; "certain months of the year," 4 days; "once a year," 1 day; and "irregular or ad hoc schedule," 6 days.

7. While pounds of food is not often used as a metric in other contexts, it is still extensively used within food banks.

8. All comparisons are statistically significant with at least a 95 percent confidence level unless otherwise noted. With respect to weights, we treat all counties identically, irrespective of size.

9. In the first column the coefficient is positive but statistically insignificant.

10. The exception is counties with urban populations of 2,500 to 19,999, not adjacent to a metro area where the effect is also negative but statistically insignificant.

11. The other variables included are the same as the third column of Tables 5 through 7.

12. For a recent review for food insecurity in households with children, see Gundersen and Ziliak (2014); and for an earlier broader review, see Gundersen, Kreider, and Pepper (2011).

13. For a broader discussion of MMG, see Gundersen, Engelhard, and Waxman (2014).

References

Aday Lu Ann, Beth Quill, and Cielito Reyes-Gibby. 2001. Equity in rural health and health care. In *Handbook of rural health*, eds. S. Loue and B. Quill, 44–72. New York. NY: Springer.

Auchincloss, Amy, and Wilbur Hadden. 2002. The health effects of rural-urban residence and concentrated poverty. *Journal of Rural Health* 18:319–36.

Bailey, Jon. 2014. *Supplemental Nutrition Assistance Program and rural households*. Lyons, NE: Center for Rural Affairs.

Bartfeld, Judith, Craig Gundersen, Timothy Smeeding, and James P. Ziliak, eds. 2015. *SNAP matters: How food stamps affect health and well being*. Stanford, CA: Stanford University Press.

Burton, Linda, Daniel Lichter, R. Baker, and John Eason. 2013. Inequality, family processes, and health in the "new" rural America. *American Behavioral Scientist* 57 (8): 1128–51.

Coleman-Jensen, Alisha, Matthew Rabbitt, Christian Gregory, and Anita Singh. 2015. *Household food security in the United States in 2014*. Economic Research Report No. 194. Washington, DC: Department of Agriculture, Economic Research Service.

Fields, Bronwyn, Jeri Bigbee, and Janice Bell. 2016. Associations of provider-to-population ratios and population health by county-level rurality. *Journal of Rural Health* 32:235–44.

Gundersen, Craig, Emily Engelhard, and Elaine Waxman. 2014. Map the Meal Gap: Exploring food insecurity at the local level. *Applied Economics Policy and Perspectives* 36 (3): 373–86.

Gundersen, Craig, Brent Kreider, and John V. Pepper. 2011. The economics of food insecurity in the United States. *Applied Economic Perspectives and Policy* 33 (3): 281–303.

Gundersen, Craig, and James P. Ziliak. Fall 2014. Childhood food insecurity in the U.S.: Trends, causes, and policy options. *The Future of Children* 24 (2): 1–19.

Gundersen, Craig, and James P. Ziliak. 2015. Food insecurity and health outcomes. *Health Affairs* 34 (11): 1830–39.

Kaufman, Brystana, Sharita Thomas, Randy Randolph, Julie Perry, Kristie Thompson, George Holmes, and George Pink. 2016. The rising rate of rural hospital closures. *Journal of Rural Health* 32:35–43.

Kreider, Brent, John V. Pepper, Craig Gundersen, and Dean Jolliffe. 2012. Identifying the effects of SNAP (food stamps) on child health outcomes when participation is endogenous and misreported. *Journal of the American Statistical Association* 107 (499): 958–75.

Lichter, Daniel, Domenico Parisi, Michael Taquino, and Brian Beaulieu. 2008. Race and the micro-scale spatial concentration of poverty. *Cambridge Journal of Regions, Economy, and Society* 1:74–91.

Peters, David. 2012. Income inequality across micro and meso geographic scales in the midwestern United States, 1979–2009. *Rural Sociology* 77:171–202.

Simmons, Leigh, Bonnie Braun, Richard Charnigo, Jennifer Havens, and David Wright. 2008. Depression and poverty among rural women: A relationship of social causation or social selection? *Journal of Rural Health* 24:292–98.

Tarasuk, Valerie, Joyce Cheng, Claire Oliveira, Naomi Dachner, Craig Gundersen, and Paul Kurdyak. 2015. Health care costs associated with household food insecurity in Ontario. *Canadian Medical Association Journal* 187 (14): E429–E436.

Tolbert, Charles, F. Carson Mencken, T. Lynn Riggs, and Jing Li. 2014. Restructuring of the financial industry: The disappearance of locally owned traditional financial services in rural America. *Rural Sociology* 79:355–79.

Vargas, Clamencia, Cynthia Ronzio, and Kathy Hayes. 2003. Oral health status of children and adolescents by rural residence, United States. *Journal of Rural Health* 19:260–68.

Neighborhood Problems across the Rural-Urban Continuum: Geographic Trends and Racial and Ethnic Disparities

By
ERIN YORK CORNWELL
and
MATTHEW HALL

Neighborhood problems such as abandoned buildings, broken windows, and crime are often seen as urban problems. However, the recent housing crisis, shifting demographics, and deepening inequality may have increased neighborhood problems outside of cities. This article describes trends in neighborhood quality across the rural-urban continuum and considers how these trends differ by race/ethnicity. We use data from the 1985 to 2013 American Housing Survey to examine neighborhood problems surrounding a sample of 125,049 housing units in central cities, suburbs, exurbs, and rural areas. We find that rates of neighborhood problems are consistently highest in cities, but they have been steadily increasing in nonmetropolitan areas. We also find that disparities in exposure to neighborhood problems among racial and ethnic groups are not limited to cities: blacks and Latinos living outside of metropolitan areas are increasingly and disproportionately exposed to neighborhood problems. Further research should examine both the causes and consequences of neighborhood problems across the rural-urban continuum.

Keywords: neighborhood quality; disorder; racial/ethnic inequality; urban; suburban; rural

Housing and neighborhood conditions are critical foci in social science research in part because they are both a product and a mechanism of social stratification. Classic

Erin York Cornwell is an assistant professor in the Department of Sociology at Cornell University. She is an affiliate of the Center for the Study of Inequality and the Cornell Population Center. Her research examines how housing and neighborhood contexts contribute to inequalities in access to resources, social connectedness, and individual outcomes such as health.

Matthew Hall is an associate professor in the Department of Policy Analysis and Management at Cornell University. He serves as a training director for the Cornell Population Center and is an affiliate of the Center for the Study of Inequality. Both a sociologist and a demographer, his research focuses on racial/ethnic inequality, immigration, and neighborhood change.

Correspondence: eyc46@cornell.edu

DOI: 10.1177/0002716217713171

formulations of spatial attainment theory suggest that as families achieve higher earnings and accumulate greater wealth, they will move to higher-quality housing and neighborhoods (Massey and Denton 1985). These areas are likely to provide access to more resources, better schools, and more employment opportunities, in turn enhancing educational attainment, earnings, and wealth (see Sampson 2012). Higher-quality residential contexts are also characterized by fewer neighborhood problems, such as broken windows, abandoned buildings, junk or litter, and crime. These residential conditions threaten residents' health by increasing stress (Hill, Ross, and Angel 2005) and fear (Ross and Jang 2000), and by heightening risks of depression (Latkin and Curry 2003), respiratory illnesses (Rosenbaum 2008), and disability (Steptoe and Feldman 2001). And together, conditions of neighborhood physical and social disorder can lead to social withdrawal, distrust, and isolation (Ross, Mirowsky, and Pribesh 2001; Steenbeek and Hipp 2011; York Cornwell and Behler 2015).

While important and insightful, prior research examining individual exposure to neighborhood problems has largely focused on the distribution of problems within urban contexts and their consequences for urban residents (Burke, O'Campo, and Peak 2006; York Cornwell and Cagney 2014). In fact, neighborhood problems are commonly conceptualized as urban problems, stemming from patterns of urban growth as well as urban economic and social processes (e.g., Massey and Denton 1998; Wilson 1987; Sampson, Raudenbush, and Earls 1997). Consequently, relatively little is known about the prevalence, distribution, or consequences of neighborhood problems outside of the city. This is despite the fact that approximately 46.2 million Americans live in nonmetropolitan counties (U.S. Department of Agriculture 2016), and demographic change over the last several decades has been dominated by population growth outside of central cities (Guest and Brown 2005). The geographic spread of population growth outside of cities has been driven by the suburbanization of blacks and new immigrants (Timberlake, Howell, and Staight 2010) and by rural Hispanic growth in new destinations (Lichter 2012). Concurrently, the loss of rural jobs to urban areas, and the selective out-migration of young, educated whites have reshaped conditions in rural settings (Carr and Kefalas 2009). However, prior work has not examined in depth the extent of racial/ethnic disparities in residential quality within both metropolitan and nonmetropolitan areas.

In this article, we use data from the 1985 to 2013 American Housing Survey (AHS) to examine trends in residential conditions within a nationally representative sample of 125,049 housing units located across central cities, suburbs, exurbs, and nonmetropolitan areas. First, we examine the prevalence of neighborhood problems—including abandoned buildings, buildings with bars on windows, and perceived crime—across the rural-urban continuum over the past 30

NOTE: We are grateful for comments and feedback on early versions of this work from Steven Alvarado, Kendra Bischoff, Benjamin Cornwell, Anna Haskins, Peter Rich, and Laura Tach. We also thank Dan Lichter, Jim Ziliak, and participants in the New Rural-Urban Interface conference at the University of Pennsylvania.

years. We then examine trends in racial/ethnic disparities in residential quality. That is, we explore to what extent racial/ethnic minorities are increasingly or decreasingly likely to be exposed to neighborhood problems inside and outside of the city.

We find that neighborhood problems are most common in central cities, and they have increased since 2007. However, we also observe gradual, long-term growth in neighborhood problems outside of the central city. With respect to racial and ethnic disparities in residential quality, we find that disparities in exposure to neighborhood problems have been relatively stable, or declining, in central cities and suburban areas. However, blacks and Latinos living in exurbs and rural areas are increasingly disadvantaged compared to their white counterparts. Some, but not all, of these widening disparities are seemingly the result of the Great Recession and its economic aftermath. Our findings call into question the assumption that neighborhood problems are strictly urban problems and suggest the emergence, or strengthening, of structural barriers that limit minorities' access to high quality neighborhoods outside of urban areas.

Residential Quality across the Rural-Urban Continuum

Research on residential mobility typically assumes that migration from central cities to suburbs provides households with access to higher-quality housing and neighborhoods (Alba and Logan 1992; Logan et al. 1996). This assumption stems, in part, from patterns of migration, urban growth, and economic development, which have driven investment and disinvestment in central cities and suburbs over the past 60 years. Metropolitan development following World War II was characterized by massive investment in, and household migration to, the suburbs. New housing stock and increased tax bases contributed to higher quality residential contexts in suburbs (Jackson 1985).

Urban deindustrialization, beginning in the 1970s, widened economic and racial inequalities between central cities and suburbs. Economic shifts away from manufacturing led to massive job losses in central cities, particularly in cities that once had a strong manufacturing base, such as those in the Rust Belt (Massey and Denton 1998; Wilson 1987). Subsequent economic decline, reduced tax revenues, and unmaintained infrastructure have contributed to the emergence of neighborhood problems such as dilapidated or abandoned buildings in central cities (Skogan 1990). However, since the 1990s, gentrification—or increases in the socioeconomic status of previously poor, inner-city neighborhoods (see Brown-Saracino 2010)—has brought middle- and upper-class residents back to some central cities. At the same time, the demolition of public housing and rising rents in central cities have pushed the poor and African Americans out to the suburbs (Allard and Roth 2010; Goetz 2011; Hyra 2012).

One of the central issues that we address in this article is the intriguing possibility—indeed the likelihood—that neighborhood problems have also diffused beyond the nation's central cities. Indeed, several scholars have argued recently that suburban housing stock is deteriorating, particularly in older inner-ring sub-urbs, and this may increase the presence of neighborhood problems (Allard and Roth 2010; Holliday and Dwyer 2009; Kneebone and Berube 2013; Murphy 2010). Recent work also suggests that suburbs are becoming more diverse due to a growing proportion of minority residents (Frey 2001), as well as an influx of immigrants who bypass central cities to settle directly in suburbs (Singer 2009).

These trends are tightly intertwined with the suburbanization and ruralization of poverty. Over the past two decades, the rate of growth of poverty in suburban areas has vastly exceeded that within central cities (Howell and Timberlake 2013). And, similar to the effects of urban deindustrialization noted above, underdevelopment within rural communities has led to higher rates of unem-ployment and extreme economic immobility for residents (Eason 2017). Rural residents with more education and greater resources have migrated to metropoli-tan labor markets (Carr and Kefalas 2009). But the long-term economic depres-sion and the concentration of poverty in rural regions (Lichter and Schafft 2016) may have eroded neighborhood quality there.

It is important to note that the housing crisis and economic recession of the mid-2000s also worsened neighborhood conditions for many Americans, not just those in central cities. Unemployment rates in metropolitan and nonmetropoli-tan areas followed similar upward trajectories during the recession, but recovery has been slower in nonmetropolitan areas (Hertz et al. 2014). Foreclosures were more frequent in suburban than urban areas (Hall, Crowder, and Spring 2015), and clusters of foreclosures often result in abandoned or unkempt properties and weakened local tax bases, which may hamper efforts to maintain services and infrastructure (Chernick, Langley, and Reschovsky 2011; Lucy 2010). Consistent with this, Allen (2013) finds that abandoned buildings increased faster in the suburbs than in central cities from 2005 to 2009.

In this article, we question the commonplace assumption that neighborhood problems are largely urban problems and that suburban and rural areas provide safe havens from crime and social disorganization. Our goal is to examine trends in the presence of neighborhood problems across central cities, suburbs, and nonmetropolitan areas. We examine long-term trajectories, over the past three decades, as well as more recent upticks in neighborhood problems that may stem from the recent economic recession.

Race/Ethnicity and Spatial Attainment in Metropolitan and Nonmetropolitan Areas

An ancillary goal is to document trends in racial and ethnic disparities in neigh-borhood quality within central cities, as well as suburban, exurban, and rural areas. Theories of locational attainment typically posit that greater income and wealth provide the economic freedom to leave declining or impoverished urban neighborhoods for higher-quality housing in middle-class or affluent suburbs (Logan et al. 1996; Massey and Denton 1985). This process has led to a spatial

fragmentation of urban life and the growing concentration of poverty and affluence across the urban hierarchy. Recent work highlights substantial neighborhood income segregation within metropolitan areas (Firebaugh and Farrell 2016;
Reardon and Bischoff 2011), suburbs (Kneebone 2012), and small towns and
nonmetropolitan counties (Lichter, Parisi, and Taquino 2012). Spatial clustering
of economic disadvantage can lead to a decline in the quality of the surrounding
built environment, which in turn reduces land and property values, diminishes
the local tax base and the provision of services, and results in economic disinvestment (Skogan 1990).

But socioeconomic resources are not the only factor that alternatively presents
barriers or drives access to high-quality neighborhoods. According to the place
stratification model, structural constraints and discrimination in the housing market limit housing opportunities for racial/ethnic minorities, including African
American and Latino households (Alba and Logan 1992; Freeman 2008). African
Americans are especially unlikely to convert upward socioeconomic mobility into
higher-quality neighborhoods and housing. African Americans in central cities
tend to live in lower-quality neighborhoods and housing compared to whites,
even if they share similar levels of education and income (Logan et al. 1996;
Friedman and Rosenbaum 2007; Rosenbaum 1996; Woldoff and Ovadia 2008).
Hispanics and Asians are more spatially integrated with whites (Rugh and Massey
2014), although some studies find that they reside in lower-quality neighborhoods (Allen 2013; Rosenbaum 1996).

Previous research has focused on disparities in residential quality inside the
central city, but areas outside the city are also highly differentiated by income and
race. For example, African Americans in the suburbs live in poorer and lower-
quality neighborhoods than whites, even when they possess the same socioeconomic resources as whites (Logan 2014; Friedman and Rosenbaum 2007).
Latinos and Asians in the suburbs tend to live in neighborhoods that are equal to
or just slightly lower quality than those of whites, although recent immigration
has intensified disadvantages for Latinos (Logan et al. 1996; Friedman and
Rosenbaum 2007). This suggests that the place stratification model carries over
into the suburbs, sorting blacks, in particular, into lower-quality suburban
neighborhoods.

During the past two decades, residential segregation and clustered economic
disadvantage have been increasing in small towns and rural areas, particularly in
new immigrant destinations (Lichter, Parisi, and Taquino 2016; Hall 2013;
Kneebone 2012). These trends have led to rural ghettos and ethnic enclaves, in
which rural poor minorities are trapped, stigmatized, and spatially isolated from
middle-class and affluent areas (Eason 2012, 2017). At the same time, increasing
diversity may drive perceptions of social disorder. The growth of new Hispanic
boomtowns and the influx of poor African Americans in suburbs have raised concerns about increasing density, social disorganization, and crime (see Crowley
and Lichter 2009; Murphy 2012). This may portend increasing disparities in
exposure to (or perceptions of) neighborhood problems at the rural-urban fringe
and in remote rural areas, a possibility that we explore in this article.

Data and Methods

To assess trends in neighborhood quality across metropolitan and nonmetropolitan areas, we rely on nearly three decades of data from the AHS. The AHS is a longitudinal survey of a nationally representative sample of housing units in the United States between 1985 and 2013. The original 1985 sample includes 53,558 housing units, each followed and reevaluated every two years (or until the unit is demolished or removed from the housing stock). To maintain national representation, the AHS regularly replenishes the sample with new housing units. In total, the full panel tracks housing outcomes for 125,049 units. We exclude observations when a unit is unoccupied, because key neighborhood, housing, and demographic information is generally lacking for these units.

Our outcomes of interest capture various aspects of the neighborhood surrounding each housing unit, based on information provided by housing occupants. Specifically, we characterize neighborhood problems along three dimensions: (1) the presence of *abandoned or vandalized buildings* within 300 feet of the housing unit, (2) the presence of *buildings with bars on windows* within 300 feet of the housing unit, and (3) whether the respondent perceives the *presence of crime* in the surrounding neighborhood. These measures represent useful proxies of social disorder associated with economic dislocations, crime, and population decline and out-migration.

Our analysis of trends in these outcomes focuses on their variation across the rural-urban continuum and across racial/ethnic groups. We use detailed geographic information provided by AHS to determine the spatial location of each housing unit. Specifically, we classify units into one of four types of areas based on metropolitan and urban statuses: (1) central cities within metropolitan areas, (2) urban metropolitan areas outside of the central city (hereafter called "suburbs"), (3) rural areas within metropolitan areas (hereafter called "exurbs"), and (4) all nonmetropolitan areas (hereafter called "rural areas").[1]

The race/ethnicity of housing unit occupants is determined via the reference person's (household head's) self-reported race and Hispanic origin. Our full sample includes members of all racial/ethnic groups, but we focus on results for three major groups: non-Hispanic whites, non-Hispanic blacks, and Hispanics of any race. We are not able to consider nativity status because the AHS did not begin collecting this information until 2001.

Our analyses of trends in these measures are adjusted for several household characteristics. These include socioeconomic status (educational attainment and total [logged] household income), family structure (presence of children, marital status, and gender of the household head), and housing status (whether the home is owner-occupied and whether the current occupants are new to the housing unit). We additionally include indicators distinguishing between the four census regions and a dummy variable for the format of the survey, which accounts for the AHS's shift to an electronic form in 1997.

We use logistic regression to fit measures of neighborhood problems to a year polynomial. Our basic model can be expressed in the following form:

FIGURE 1
Predicted Probabilities of Nearby Abandoned Buildings, by Geographic Location

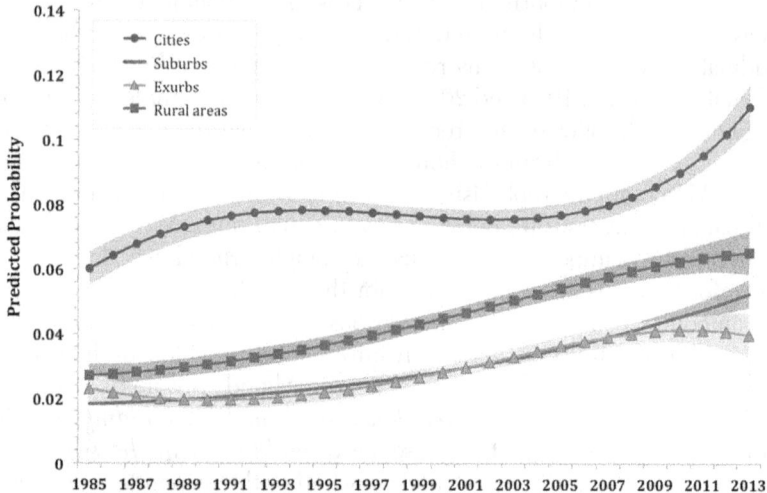

SOURCE: American Housing Survey, 1985–2013.
NOTE: $N = 438,196$ observations. All models control for householder education, marital status, tenure, gender, age, income, length of residence, and regional location. Shaded areas around trend lines depict the 95 percent confidence intervals.

$$\text{logit}\left(\pi_{jut}\right) = \beta_0 + \beta_1\mathbf{T} + \beta_2 Geo_u + \beta_3 Race_{ut} + \beta_4\left(Geo_u \,{}^\circ\, \mathbf{T}\right) + \beta_5\left(Race_{ut} \,{}^\circ\, \mathbf{T}\right) + \beta_6(Geo_u,$$
$${}^\circ\, Race_{ut}) + \beta_7\left(Geo_u \,{}^\circ\, Race_{ut} \,{}^\circ\, \mathbf{T}\right) + \beta_8\mathbf{W}_{ut} + \varepsilon_u$$

where (π_{jut}) is binary neighborhood outcome j for unit u in year t; $\mathbf{T}$ is a cubic expression of years since 1985; Geo_u is a set of indicators for geographic location of the unit; $Race_{ut}$ is a set of indicators for the race/ethnicity of the householder at time t; and $\mathbf{W}_{ut}$ is a vector of demographic characteristics of the occupants. The time polynomial is allowed to vary by geography, race, and their interaction to assess differential trends in neighborhood problems over the 1985 to 2013 period. Standard errors are clustered at the housing unit level. We report the results of these models in graphical form as predicted probabilities with 95 percent confidence intervals.

Results

We begin by describing trends in residential quality, from 1985 to 2013, within metropolitan and nonmetropolitan areas. Figures 1, 2, and 3 show predicted probabilities of neighborhood problems, adjusted for householder characteristics, census region,

FIGURE 2

Predicted Probabilities of Nearby Buildings with Bars on Windows, by Geographic Location

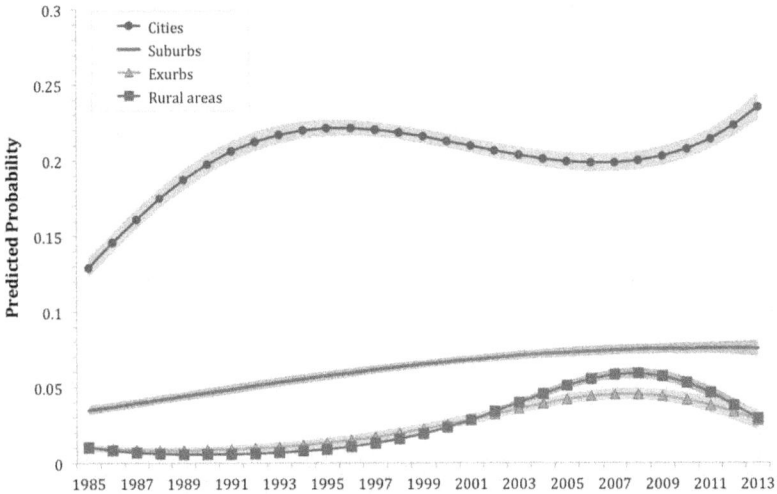

SOURCE: American Housing Survey, 1985–2013.

NOTE: N = 438,196 observations. All models control for householder education, marital status, tenure, gender, age, income, length of residence, and regional location. Shaded areas around trend lines depict the 95 percent confidence intervals.

and survey format. Probabilities of exposure to abandoned or vandalized buildings (Figure 1) and bars on windows (Figure 2) are highest for residents of central cities, and they have increased since 2007. By 2013, for residents of central cities, the predicted probability of living within 300 feet of an abandoned or vandalized building is .11, and the probability of living near a building with bars on the windows is .23.

Outside of the central city, the probability of living near abandoned or vandalized buildings is lower, but it has been steadily increasing since 1985. The steepest increase in exposure to abandoned buildings is observed in rural areas, where the probability of living near abandoned or vandalized buildings has more than doubled, from about .03 to .07. Probabilities of exposure to bars on windows were very low outside of the central city in 1985, but they have modestly increased in suburbs, exurbs, and rural areas.

Figure 3 shows the trends for householders' perception of the presence of crime in the neighborhood. Crime is most commonly reported around housing units in central cities. In 1985, the probability of perceiving crime in the surrounding neighborhood was about .25 for residents of central cities. The probability increased through the mid-1990s, then decreased to the mid-2000s, and then increased after 2007. This pattern generally follows that of the probability of nearby buildings with bars on windows, which may be indicative of residents' concerns about crime. And it is roughly consistent with the national decrease in

FIGURE 3
Predicted Probabilities of Perceived Neighborhood Crime, by Geographic Location

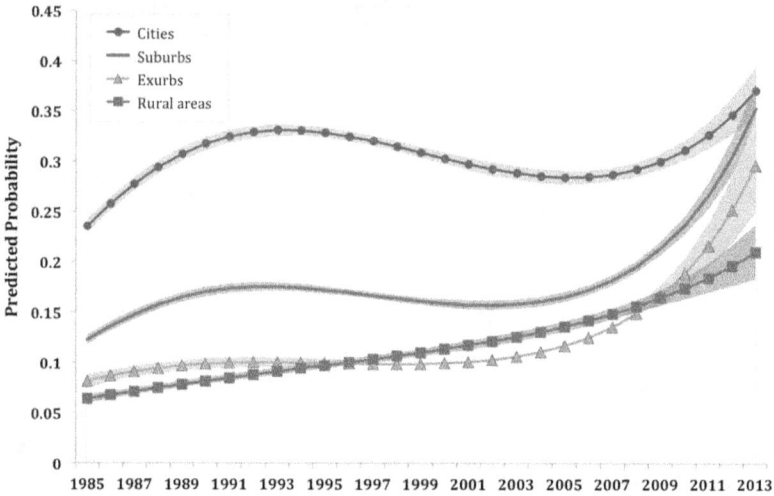

SOURCE: American Housing Survey, 1985–2013.
NOTE: N = 531,265 observations. All models control for householder education, marital status, tenure, gender, age, income, length of residence, and regional location. Shaded areas around trend lines depict the 95 percent confidence intervals.

rates of violent and property crime during the 1990s and early 2000s (U.S. Department of Justice 2010).

Outside of the central city, the probabilities of perceiving crime within one's neighborhood are highest in suburban areas. The likelihood of perceiving neighborhood crime sharply increased in the suburbs and exurbs after 2007, a pattern that may reflect exaggerated fears caused by an increase in the population, immigrants, and the poor (Crowley and Lichter 2009). In fact, in 2013, the probabilities of perceiving neighborhood crime among suburban residents (.35) and exurban residents (.30) approached that of central city dwellers (.37). Residents of rural areas have had a more than threefold increase in the probability of perceiving neighborhood crime across this time period (from .06 to .21). But the increase has been gradual, with no evidence of a post-2007 uptick.

Racial disparities in residential quality

Since 1985, all four of the geographic areas that we examine have become more racially and ethnically diverse. As shown in Figure 4, the proportion of Hispanic householders has doubled in central cities, and it has nearly tripled in suburbs, exurbs, and rural areas. These increases likely include recent immigrants living in new immigrant destinations outside of the central city (Lichter, Parisi, and Taquino 2016), but we are unable to differentiate householders by

FIGURE 4

Race/Ethnicity of AHS Householders within Cities, Suburbs, Exurbs,
and Rural Areas, 1985 and 2013

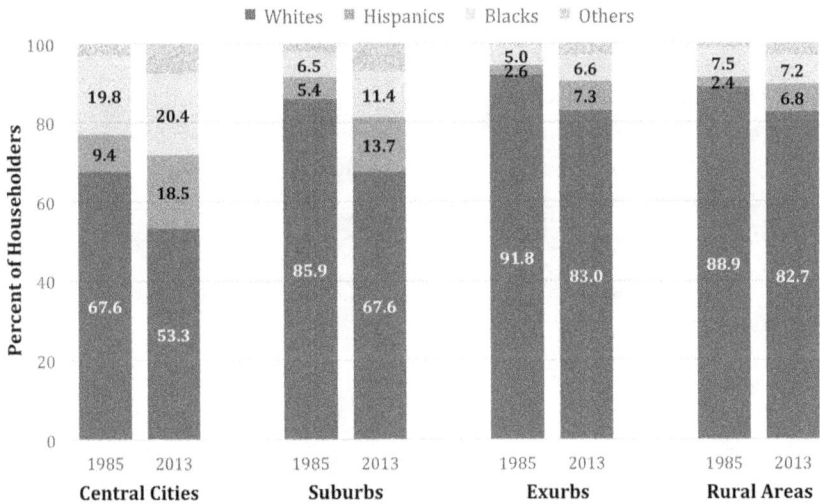

SOURCE: American Housing Survey, 1985–2013.

nativity status. The proportion of African American householders in central cities
has been relatively stable from 1985 to 2013, around 20 percent. However, the
proportion of African Americans in suburbs has nearly doubled—from 6.5 percent in 1985 to 11.4 percent in 2013. The proportion of African Americans in
exurban areas has also increased slightly over the time period, but it has remained
low in rural areas.

Next we examine whether African Americans and Hispanics inside and outside
of the central city are disproportionately likely to be exposed to neighborhood
problems. To describe general trends, we present figures showing predicted
probabilities of exposure to each of the neighborhood problems across racial/
ethnic groups within central cities, suburbs, exurbs, and rural areas.

We begin by considering abandoned or vandalized buildings. As shown in
Figure 5, in central cities, the predicted probability of exposure to abandoned or
vandalized buildings has slightly increased for both blacks and whites, but the gap
between black and white households has not notably changed from 1985 to 2013.
Hispanics' exposure to abandoned buildings in central cities has declined since
1985, making them less disadvantaged compared to whites in 2013. We observe
a similar pattern in the suburbs and in rural areas. Exposure to abandoned buildings has modestly increased for all groups, but blacks' disadvantage compared to
whites has remained relatively consistent over the past 30 years.

In exurban areas, exposure to abandoned or vandalized buildings was equally
unlikely for black, Hispanic, and white households in 1985, but new gaps have
emerged. In 2013, black householders' predicted probability of living near

FIGURE 5
Predicted Probabilities of Living near Abandoned Buildings, by Race/Ethnicity

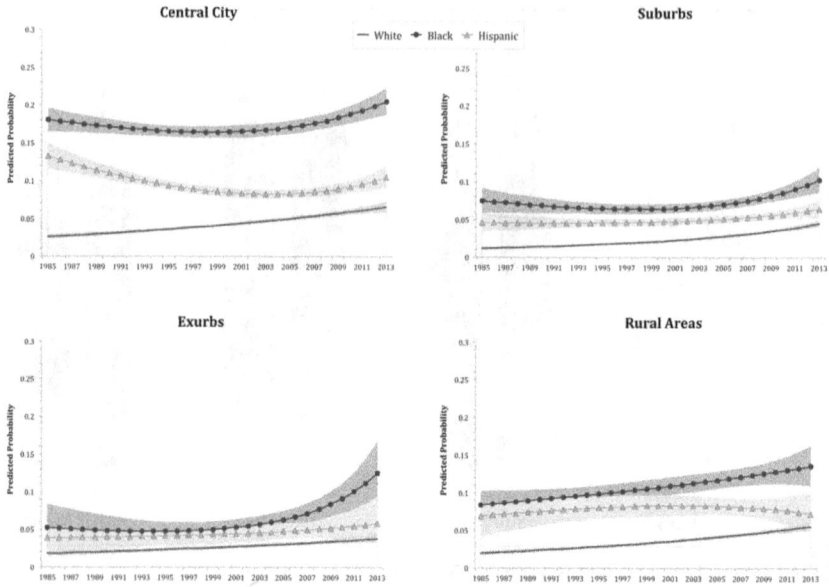

SOURCE: American Housing Survey, 1985–2013.
NOTE: Models control for householder education, marital status, tenure, gender, age, income, length of residence, and regional location. Shaded areas surrounding the trend lines indicate 95 percent confidence intervals.

abandoned buildings (.13) is more than twice that of Hispanics (.06) and three times that of whites (.04). Much of the disproportionate increase in blacks' risk of exposure to abandoned buildings in exurban areas occurred after 2007. These trends reflect a stable and modest gap in exposure to abandoned or vandalized buildings among whites and Hispanics in exurban areas, but a recently growing disadvantage for blacks.

Figure 6 shows trends in racial/ethnic disparities in exposure to bars on windows. Blacks and Hispanics in central cities are substantially more likely than whites to live near buildings with bars on the windows. In 1985, the probability of reporting bars on windows among black and Hispanic householders was more than three times as great as that among whites (.32 for Hispanics, .31 for blacks, and .09 for whites), and the magnitude of these disparities has been quite stable over the past 30 years. In suburban areas, we also observe a relatively stable gap between black and white householders' probability of exposure to buildings with bars on windows. However, a slight decrease in Hispanics' exposure to buildings with bars on windows since the early 2000s has led to the convergence of black and Hispanic probabilities.

In exurban areas, disparities in exposure to buildings with bars on windows have widened. In 1985, the likelihood of exposure to buildings with

FIGURE 6
Predicted Probabilities of Nearby Buildings with Bars on Windows, by Race/Ethnicity

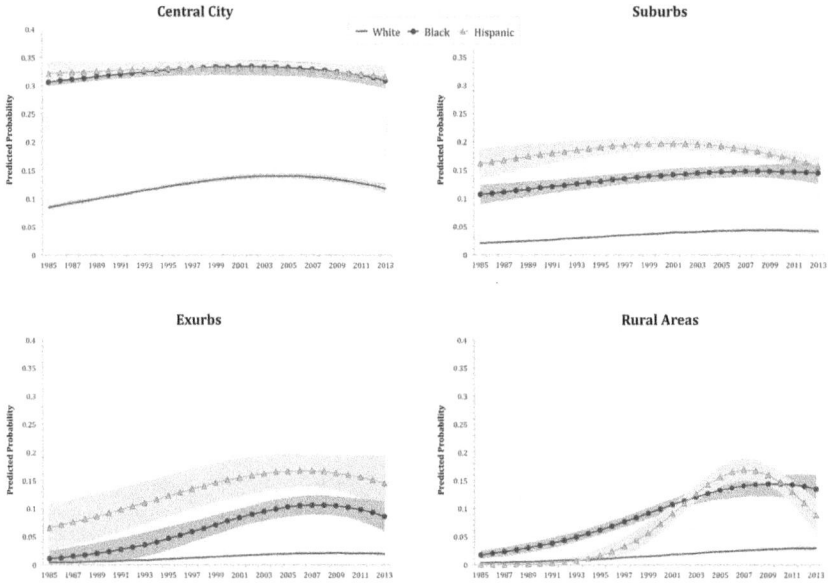

SOURCE: American Housing Survey, 1985–2013.
NOTE: Models control for householder education, marital status, tenure, gender, age, income, length of residence, and regional location. Shaded areas surrounding the trend lines indicate 95 percent confidence intervals.

bars on windows was quite low for white and black householders (.00 and .01, respectively), and slightly higher for Hispanics (.07). Exurban whites' probability of exposure to buildings with bars on windows has changed very little, but the probability increased markedly for Hispanics and blacks in the exurbs, leading to predicted probabilities in 2013 of .14 for Hispanics and .10 for blacks (compared to .02 for whites).

We also observe growing disparities in exposure to bars on windows in rural areas. In 1985, the probability of living near buildings with bars on windows was near zero for all three groups. However, blacks' predicted probabilities increased over this time period, so that by 2013 they were four times more likely than white residents to live near buildings with bars on windows (.14 and .03, respectively). Hispanic householders' exposure to buildings with bars on windows grew rapidly from the mid-1990s to the mid-2000s, followed by a decline. Nevertheless, Hispanic householders in rural areas are now three times more likely than whites to live near buildings with bars on the windows (.09 compared to .03 for whites).

Finally, in Figure 7, we consider disparities in the perception of crime. In 1985, black householders in central cities had a predicted probability of .30 of perceiving crime in their neighborhoods, compared to .22 and .23 among Hispanics and whites, respectively. The likelihood of perceiving crime in one's neighborhood increased for all three groups through the early 2000s, and then

FIGURE 7
Predicted Probabilities of Perceived Crime in the Surrounding Area, by Race/Ethnicity

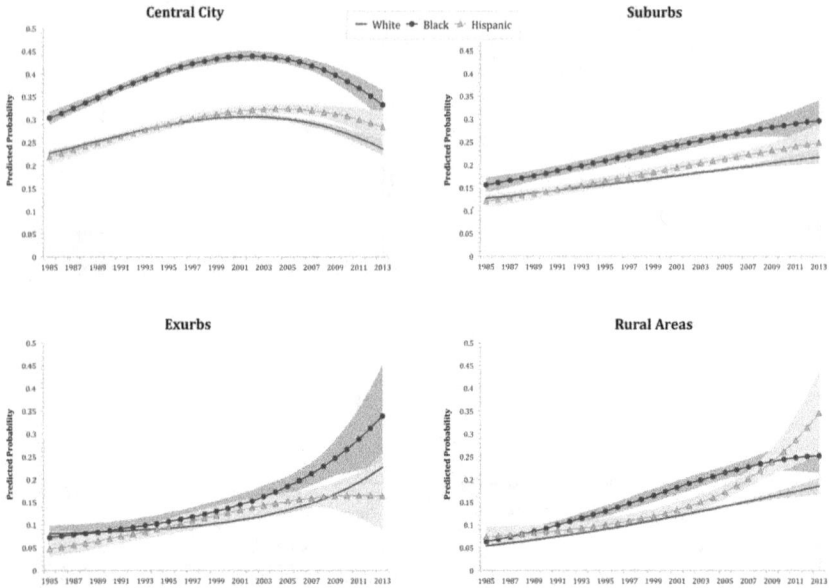

SOURCE: American Housing Survey, 1985–2013.
NOTE: Models control for householder education, marital status, tenure, gender, age, income, length of residence, and regional location. Shaded areas surrounding the trend lines indicate 95 percent confidence intervals.

declined, particularly among blacks. Overall, the racial/ethnic gaps in perceived crime have remained relatively stable, with blacks and Hispanics more likely than whites to report crime in their area in 2013 (probabilities of .33, .28, and .24, respectively).

Gaps between suburban blacks, Hispanics, and whites have slightly widened over this time period, with suburban blacks' disadvantage increasing the most. In 2013, the probability of perceiving crime in the neighborhood among black suburban residents was .30, compared to .25 and .22 among Hispanic and white residents, respectively.

Disparities in perceived crime have increased most markedly in exurban and rural areas. In exurbs, the probability of perceiving crime in one's neighborhood was very low for all groups in 1985. The likelihood of perceiving crime increased for all groups through 2007, after which we observe an uptick in the probability of exposure to nearby crime among blacks. The sharp increase among exurban blacks brings their probability of perceiving crime (.33, compared to .23 for whites and .16 for Hispanics) in line with that observed among blacks in central cities (.33) in 2013.

In rural areas, the probability of perceived crime was very low for all three groups in 1985, but perceived crime has increased and disparities have emerged.

The gap between black and white residents of rural areas has increased since 1985, and a sharp uptick in Hispanics' probability of exposure to crime since 2005 leads to the emergence of a gap between Hispanic and white householders. In 2013, rural Hispanic householders had a .34 probability of perceiving crime in their neighborhood, compared to .25 among black households and .19 among whites. These probabilities put rural Hispanics on par with probabilities of exposure to crime observed among black residents in central cities (.33), suburban areas (.30), and exurban areas (.33). However, probabilities of perceived crime in 2013 are lower for rural whites (.18) than for whites in other areas. As a result, the gap between blacks, Hispanics, and whites in perceived crime is larger today in rural areas than in central cities.

Conclusion

Prior research has largely considered neighborhood problems as characteristic of disadvantaged inner-city neighborhoods, stemming from patterns of urban growth and reflecting urban economic and social processes (e.g., Massey and Denton 1998; Wilson 1987; Sampson, Raudenbush, and Earls 1997). Building from this, scholarship on locational attainment typically assumes that moving out of the city allows individuals to escape neighborhood problems (Logan et al. 1996). However, recent population growth and rising poverty in the suburbs, as well as in small towns and rural areas, raises questions as to whether neighborhood problems are limited to central cities. At the same time, increasing diversity in suburban and rural areas (Hall and Lee 2010; Kneebone 2012; Lichter, Parisi, and Taquino 2012) suggests that residential conditions in these areas may be increasingly internally differentiated, leading to racial and ethnic disparities in exposure to neighborhood problems.

In this article, we used panel data following a national sample of housing units over nearly three decades to describe trends in the distribution of neighborhood problems across and within urban, suburban, exurban, and rural locations. Several key findings have emerged. First, abandoned and vandalized buildings, buildings with bars on the windows, and perceptions of crime are most common in central cities, but the risk of exposure to these problems has been increasing over the past 30 years for residents of all areas, including those in suburban, exurban, and rural areas. These results affirm that neighborhood problems are not just big city or urban problems.

Differences in the timing of increases in neighborhood problems across urban and rural areas suggest variation in their causes. For example, we observe a post-2007 uptick in abandoned or vandalized buildings and bars on windows in central cities, but not in exurbs or rural areas. This may reflect the negative consequences of fore-closures and the economic recession for metropolitan neighborhoods and tax bases (Allen 2013; Chernick, Langley, and Reschovsky 2011; Lucy 2010).

We also observe sharp increases since 2007 in perceived crime within all four geographic areas. These results suggest similarities in the way that the economic recession has shaped crime patterns or the perception of crime across the urban-rural divide. It is unclear, however, whether changing perceptions of crime reflect objective conditions or the politics of fear. For example, perceptions of crime in small towns and rural areas may stem from different crimes or different symbols of crime than those in central cities (Eason 2017), as well as from changing demographics and increasing immigrant concentration (Crowley and Lichter 2009). And features of the built environment such as land use and the presence of retail shops may condition the relationship between reported crime and perceived crime (Foster et al. 2013). Further research should explore the underpinnings of the growing perception of crime across the rural-urban continuum and its consequences for individuals and the communities where they reside.

In exurban and rural areas, risks of exposure to abandoned buildings, bars on windows, and crime have steadily increased over the past three decades, reflecting a gradual change in residential conditions that likely stems from longer-term processes. These may include declining built environments and the aging of the housing stock outside of metropolitan areas, as well as persistent or increasing poverty. Another possibility, drawing from social disorganization theory, is that increasing poverty, instability, and diversity in nonmetropolitan areas has eroded localized social cohesion and collective efficacy. As a result, residents may increasingly lack the ability to work together to address neighborhood problems (Sampson 2012; Sampson and Morenoff 2006). But because most of this research has focused on urban contexts, it is unclear whether residents of sparsely populated areas conceptualize their surrounding area as a neighborhood with the potential for social organization (DeMarco and DeMarco 2010). A critical direction for further research, then, is to explore the social and economic conditions that give rise to neighborhood problems outside of the city.

Our most important finding is that racial and ethnic disparities in neighborhood conditions are not limited to the central city. Consistent with prior work, we observe substantial racial and ethnic disparities in exposure to neighborhood problems in the central city (Friedman and Rosenbaum 2007; Allen 2013), as well as in the suburbs (Logan 2014; Logan et al. 1996; Friedman and Rosenbaum 2007). However, disparities in central cities and suburbs have been relatively stable—or even declining—over the past 30 years.

Yet racial and ethnic disparities in perceived neighborhood problems appear to be *increasing* in exurban and rural areas. Specifically, we observe widening disparities in exposure to abandoned buildings in exurban and rural areas, as well as in exposure to crime in exurban areas, so that blacks are more likely than their Latino and white counterparts to be exposed to these conditions. We also find a growing gap separating blacks and Latinos from their white counterparts in the risk of exposure to bars on windows in exurban and rural areas and exposure to crime in rural areas. Many of these changes have been gradual, but there is some evidence that the economic recession of the late 2000s contributed to racial/ethnic disparities in exposure to abandoned buildings and crime.

Based on our findings, we cannot assume that residing outside of the central city provides access to higher-quality neighborhoods and a safe haven from social disorder. This appears to be true only for whites. We find that whites who reside outside of the city have lower probabilities of exposure to neighborhood problems than those who live in the central city. Regardless of where they live, minorities are more likely than whites to be exposed to neighborhood problems, and these disparities are increasing. Strikingly, minorities in suburban, exurban, and rural areas as of this writing are no less likely than those in central cities to perceive that crime is a problem in their area. Thus, even when minorities are not stuck in declining or disadvantaged inner-city neighborhoods (Sharkey 2013), they are not getting the same advantages—in terms of residential quality—as are their white counterparts.

Growing neighborhood problems in exurbs and rural areas, and racial and ethnic disparities in exposure to neighborhood problems, are of critical concern. Expanding racial disparities may reflect that the diversification of nonmetropolitan areas has also led to the emergence, or strengthening, of structural barriers that limit minorities' access to high-quality neighborhoods in suburban, exurban, and rural areas. Differential exposure to neighborhood problems could contribute to growing gaps in economic attainment, health, and well-being among minorities who reside outside of the city. Further research should consider the causes of perceived neighborhood problems and their consequences within a wider range of urban and nonurban geographies. Research should also direct greater attention to patterns of rural-urban migration, as well as residential segregation, white flight, and inequality across the rural-urban continuum. Much policy-related work has been devoted to improving living conditions and reducing neighborhood inequalities within the central city. Urgent attention is needed to address the possibility of growing disadvantages in residential contexts of minorities who reside outside of urban areas.

Note

1. The AHS contains more precise information on nonmetropolitan areas, distinguishing between "urban nonmetropolitan" and "rural nonmetropolitan," but the number of housing units occupied by black and Hispanic occupants in these areas is very small. Moreover, supplemental analysis of overall trends in neighborhood and housing quality suggested that these two types of areas have substantively and statistically similar trajectories of change.

References

Alba, Richard D., and John R. Logan. 1992. Analyzing locational attainments. *Sociological Research and Methods* 20:367–97.

Allard, Scott W., and Benjamin Roth. 2010. *Strained suburbs: The social service challenges of rising suburban poverty.* Washington, DC: Brookings Institution Metropolitan Policy Program.

Allen, Ryan. 2013. The distribution and evolution of physical neighborhood problems during the great recession. *City & Community* 12:260–79.

Brown-Saracino, Japonica, ed. 2010. *The gentrification debates.* New York, NY: Routledge.

Burke, Jessica Griffin, Patricia O'Campo, and Geri L. Peak. 2006. Neighborhood influences and intimate partner violence: Does geographic setting matter? *Journal of Urban Health* 83:182–94.

Carr, Patrick J., and Maria J. Kefalas. 2009. *Hollowing out the middle: The rural brain drain and what it means for America*. Boston, MA: Beacon Press.

Chernick, Howard, Adam Langley, and Andrew Reschovsky. 2011. The impact of the Great Recession and the housing crisis on the financing of America's largest cities. *Regional Science and Urban Economics* 41:372–81.

Crowley, Martha, and Daniel T. Lichter. 2009. Social disorganization in new Latino destinations? *Rural Sociology* 74:573–604.

DeMarco, Allison, and Molly DeMarco. 2010. Conceptualization and measurement of the neighborhood in rural settings: A systematic review of the literature. *Journal of Community Psychology* 38:99–114.

Eason, John M. 2012. Extending the hyperghetto: Toward a theory of punishment, race, and rural disadvantage. *Journal of Poverty* 16:274–95.

Eason, John M. 2017. *Big house on the prairie: Rise of the rural ghetto and prison proliferation*. Chicago, IL: The University of Chicago Press.

Firebaugh, Glenn, and Chad Farrell. 2016. Still large, but narrowing: The sizable decline in racial neighborhood inequality in metropolitan America. *Demography* 53:139–64.

Foster, Sarah, Matthew Knuiman, Lisa Wood, and Billie Giles-Corti. 2013. Suburban neighborhood design: Associations with fear of crime versus perceived crime risk. *Journal of Environmental Psychology* 36:112–17.

Freeman, Lance. 2008. Is class becoming a more important determinant of neighborhood attainment for African-Americans? *Urban Affairs Review* 44:3–26.

Frey, William. 2001. *Melting pot suburbs: A Census 2000 study of suburban diversity*. Washington, DC: Brookings Institution.

Friedman, Samantha, and Emily Rosenbaum. 2007. Does suburban residence mean better neighborhood conditions for all households? Assessing the influence of nativity status and race/ethnicity. *Social Science Research* 36:1–27.

Goetz, Edward. 2011. Gentrification in black and white: The racial impact of public housing demolition in American cities. *Urban Studies* 48:1581–1604.

Guest, Avery M., and Susan K. Brown. 2005. Population distribution and suburbanization. In *Handbook of population*, eds. Dudley L. Poston and Michael Micklin, 59–86. New York, NY: Springer.

Hall, Matthew. 2013. Residential integration on the new frontier: Immigrant segregation in established and new destinations. *Demography* 50:1873–96.

Hall, Matthew, Kyle Crowder, and Amy Spring. 2015. Variations in housing foreclosures by race and place, 2005–2012. *The ANNALS of the American Academy of Political and Social Science* 660:217–37.

Hall, Matthew, and Barrett Lee. 2010. How diverse are U.S. suburbs? *Urban Studies* 47:3–28.

Hertz, Tom, Lorin Kusmin, Alex Marré, and Tim Parker. 2014. *Rural employment trends in recession and recovery*. August. Washington, DC: U.S. Department of Agriculture, Economic Research Service. Available from https://www.ers.usda.gov/webdocs/publications/err172/48731_err172.pdf.

Hill, Terrence D., Catherine E. Ross, and Ronald J. Angel. 2005. Neighborhood disorder, psychophysiological distress, and health. *Journal of Health and Social Behavior* 46:170–86.

Holliday, Amy L., and Rachel E. Dwyer. 2009. Suburban neighborhood poverty in U.S. metropolitan areas in 2000. *City & Community* 8:155–76.

Howell, Aaron J., and Jeffrey M. Timberlake. 2013. Racial and ethnic trends in the suburbanization of poverty in U.S. metropolitan areas, 1980–2010. *Journal of Urban Affairs* 36:79–98.

Hyra, Derek. 2012. Conceptualizing the new urban renewal: Comparing the past to the present. *Urban Affairs Review* 48:498–527.

Jackson, Kenneth. 1985. *Crabgrass frontier: The suburbanization of the United States*. New York, NY: Oxford University Press.

Kneebone, Elizabeth. 2012. *The growth and spread of concentrated poverty, 2000 to 2008–2012*. Washington DC: The Brookings Institution Metropolitan Policy Program.

Kneebone, Elizabeth, and Alan Berube. 2013. *Confronting suburban poverty in America*. Washington, DC: Brookings Institution Press.

Latkin, Carl A., and Aaron D. Curry. 2003. Stressful neighborhoods and depression: A prospective study of the impact of neighborhood disorder. *Journal of Health and Social Behavior* 44:34–44.

Lichter, Daniel T. 2012. Immigration and the new racial diversity in rural America. *Rural Sociology* 77:3–35.

Lichter, Daniel T., Domenico Parisi, and Michael C. Taquino. 2012. The geography of exclusion: Race, segregation, and concentrated poverty. *Social Problems* 59:364–88.

Lichter, Daniel T., Domenico Parisi, and Michael C. Taquino. 2016. Emerging patterns of Hispanic residential segregation: Lessons from rural and small-town America. *Rural Sociology* 81:483–518.

Lichter, Daniel T., and Kai A. Schafft. 2016. People and places left behind: Rural poverty in the new century. In *The Oxford handbook of the social science of poverty*, eds. David Brady and Linda Burton, 318–40. New York, NY: Oxford University Press.

Logan, John R. 2014. *Separate and unequal in suburbia. Census Brief prepared for Project US2010*. Available from http://www.s4.brown.edu/us2010.

Logan, John R., Richard D. Alba, Tom McNulty, and Brian Fisher. 1996. Making a place in the metropolis: Locational attainment in cities and suburbs. *Demography* 33:443–53.

Lucy, William H. 2010. *Foreclosing the dream: How America's housing crisis is reshaping our cities and suburbs*. Washington, DC: APA Planners Press.

Massey, Douglas S., and Nancy A. Denton. 1985. Spatial assimilation as a socioeconomic outcome. *American Sociological Review* 50:94–106.

Massey, Douglas S., and Nancy A. Denton. 1998. *American apartheid: Segregation and the making of the underclass*. Cambridge, MA: Harvard University Press.

Murphy, Alexandra K. 2010. The symbolic dilemmas of suburban poverty: Challenges and opportunities posed by variations in the contours of suburban poverty. *Sociological Forum* 25:541–69.

Murphy, Alexandra K. 2012. "Litterers": How objects of physical disorder are used to construct subjects of social disorder in a suburb. *The ANNALS of the American Academy of Political and Social Science* 642:210–27.

Reardon, Sean F., and Kendra Bischoff. 2011. Income inequality and income segregation. *American Journal of Sociology* 116:1092–1153.

Rosenbaum, Emily. 1996. Racial/ethnic differences in home ownership and housing quality, 1991. *Social Problems* 43:403–26.

Rosenbaum, Emily. 2008. Racial/ethnic differences in asthma prevalence: The role of housing and neighborhood environments. *Journal of Health and Social Behavior* 49:131–45.

Ross, Catherine E., and Sung Joon Jang. 2000. Neighborhood disorder, fear, and mistrust: The buffering role of social ties with neighbors. *American Journal of Community Psychology* 28:401–20.

Ross, Catherine E., John Mirowsky, and Shana Pribesh. 2001. Powerlessness and the amplification of threat: Neighborhood disadvantage, disorder, and mistrust. *American Sociological Review* 66:568–91.

Rugh, Jacob S., and Douglas S. Massey. 2014. Segregation in post-civil rights America. *Du Bois Review: Social Science Research on Race* 11:205–32.

Sampson, Robert J. 2012. *Great American city: Chicago and the enduring neighborhood effect*. Chicago, IL: The University of Chicago Press.

Sampson, Robert J., and Jeffrey D. Morenoff. 2006. Durable inequality: Spatial dynamics, social processes, and the persistence of poverty in Chicago neighborhoods. In *Poverty traps*, eds. Samuel Bowles, Steven N. Durlauf, and Karla Hoff, 176–203. Princeton, NJ: Princeton University Press.

Sampson, Robert J., Stephen Raudenbush, and Felton Earls. 1997. Neighborhoods and violent crime: A multilevel study of collective efficacy. *Science* 227:918–23.

Sharkey, Patrick. 2013. *Stuck in place: Urban neighborhoods and the end of progress toward racial equality*. Chicago, IL: The University of Chicago Press.

Singer, Audrey. 2009. *The new geography of United States immigration*. Washington, DC: Brookings Institution.

Skogan, Wesley G. 1990. *Disorder and decline: Crime and spiral of decay in American neighborhoods*. Berkeley, CA: University of California Press.

Steenbeek, Wouter, and John R. Hipp. 2011. A longitudinal test of social disorganization theory: Feedback effects among cohesion, social control, and disorder. *Criminology* 49:833–71.

Steptoe, Andrew, and Pamela J. Feldman. 2001. Neighborhood problems as sources of chronic stress: Development of a measure of neighborhood problems, and associations with socioeconomic status and sealth. *Annals of Behavioral Medicine* 23:177–85.

Timberlake, Jeffrey M., Aaron J. Howell, and Amanda J. Staight. 2010. Trends in the suburbanization of racial/ethnic groups in US metropolitan areas, 1970 to 2000. *Urban Affairs Review* 47:218–55.

U.S. Department of Agriculture (USDA). 2016. *Rural American at a glance*. Economic Information Bulletin 162, Economic Research Service. November. Washington, DC: USDA. Available from https://www.ers.usda.gov/webdocs/publications/eib162/eib-162.pdf.

U.S. Department of Justice. 2010. Uniform crime reporting statistics. Washington, DC: FBI, U.S. Department of Justice. Available from http://ucrdatatool.gov.

Wilson, William J. 1987. *The truly disadvantaged: The inner city, the underclass, and public policy*. Chicago, IL: The University of Chicago Press.

Woldoff, Rachel A., and Seth Ovadia. 2008. Not getting their money's worth: African-American disadvantages in converting income, wealth, and education into residential quality. *Urban Affairs Review* 45:66–91.

York Cornwell, Erin, and Rachel A. Behler. 2015. Urbanism, neighborhood context, and social networks. *City & Community* 14:311–35.

York Cornwell, Erin, and Kathleen A. Cagney. 2014. Assessment of neighborhood context in a nationally representative study. *Journals of Gerontology* 69B (S2): S51–S63.

The Cardiovascular Health of Young Adults: Disparities along the Urban-Rural Continuum

By
ELIZABETH LAWRENCE,
ROBERT A. HUMMER,
and
KATHLEEN MULLAN
HARRIS

U.S. young adults coming of age in the early twenty-first century are the first cohort to grow up during the obesity epidemic; justifiably, there is much concern about their cardiovascular health. To date, however, no research has examined the extent to which there are disparities in young adult cardiovascular health across the urban-rural continuum. We examine this topic using data from the National Longitudinal Study of Adolescent to Adult Health (Add Health). We find that young adults who live in metropolitan core areas exhibit more favorable cardiovascular health than individuals who live in smaller communities and that population density largely accounts for this association. Further, individuals living in more densely populated areas in young adulthood relative to during adolescence have better cardiovascular health than those who live in areas similar or less dense than their adolescent residence. Our results strongly suggest that the physical and social features of communities represent important contexts for young adult cardiovascular health.

Keywords: rural; urban; population density; cardiovascular health; young adulthood; Add Health

The U.S. obesity epidemic began among adolescents in the mid- to late 1990s (Lee et al. 2011). By the late 2000s, 37 percent of young adults were obese and another 33 percent were overweight (Hussey et al. 2015; Harris 2010). The

Elizabeth Lawrence is a postdoctoral fellow in the Carolina Population Center at the University of North Carolina at Chapel Hill. Her research examines social inequality and health, with a focus on how individuals' educational and health trajectories develop together over the life course.

Robert A. Hummer is the Howard W. Odum Distinguished Professor of Sociology and a fellow of the Carolina Population Center at the University of North Carolina at Chapel Hill. His research focuses on health and mortality disparities across the life course, with particular attention given to the emergence of disparities in early and mid-life.

Correspondence: lizlaw@unc.edu

DOI: 10.1177/0002716217711426

early onset and rapid rise in obesity among young adults will threaten their cardiovascular health and future work lives for decades to come. Rising inequality and the slow pace of economic recovery after the Great Recession have furthermore forced many young adults to return home to live with their parents while they finish advanced degrees or find employment (Fry 2013), redistributing many of these young adults to rural areas or in the micropolitan and commuting areas of cities. In our highly stratified society, however, educational and work opportunities remain increasingly concentrated in large cities (Burton et al. 2013). Given these dramatic shifts in the health, social, and economic contexts in which young people live, it is critically important to understand young adult cardiovascular health in the United States and, in particular, how young adult cardiovascular health differs across residential contexts.

We use data from the National Longitudinal Study of Adolescent to Adult Health (Add Health) to take important steps toward better understanding disparities in young adult cardiovascular health in the United States across the urban-rural continuum. We use a measure of "ideal cardiovascular health" developed by the American Heart Association (Lloyd-Jones et al. 2010) that considers body weight, blood pressure, and other indicators of cardiac and vascular health. First, we document patterns of ideal cardiovascular health among young adults across the urban-rural continuum, as well as according to patterns of residential change from adolescence to young adulthood. Second, we specify multivariate models of ideal cardiovascular health to better understand why there are differences in young adult cardiovascular health across the urban-rural continuum. We focus on the population density of the census tract within which individuals live as one potentially important explanation for differences in young adult cardiovascular health across the urban-rural continuum. We also focus on early life and adolescent factors that are predictors of both young adult geography of residence and cardiovascular health, as well as on young adult socioeconomic, social, and

Kathleen Mullan Harris is the James E. Haar Distinguished Professor of Sociology, a fellow of the Carolina Population Center, and the director of the Add Health Study at the University of North Carolina at Chapel Hill. Her research focuses on social, behavioral, and biological linkages in health across the life course.

NOTE: This research was supported by the National Institutes of Health under Ruth L. Kirschstein National Research Service Award (F32 HD 085599) from the Eunice Kennedy Shriver National Institute of Child Health and Human Development. We are grateful to the Carolina Population Center and its NIH center grant (P2C HD050924) for general support. We thank conference attendees, two anonymous reviewers, and the editors Dan Lichter and Jim Ziliak for their helpful comments. A prior version of this article was presented at The New Rural-Urban Interface Conference in September 2016. This research uses data from Add Health, a program project directed by Kathleen Mullan Harris and designed by J. Richard Udry, Peter S. Bearman, and Kathleen Mullan Harris at the University of North Carolina at Chapel Hill, and funded by grant P01-HD31921 from the Eunice Kennedy Shriver National Institute of Child Health and Human Development, with cooperative funding from twenty-three other federal agencies and foundations. Special acknowledgment is due Ronald R. Rindfuss and Barbara Entwisle for assistance in the original design. Information on how to obtain the Add Health data files is available on the Add Health website (http://www.cpc.unc.edu/addhealth). No direct support was received from grant P01-HD31921 for this analysis.

family structure factors that may account for cardiovascular health differences across the urban-rural continuum.

We contribute to the understanding of cardiovascular health disparities in several ways. First, research on geographic-based health disparities has tended to focus on morbidity, disability, and mortality patterns among the middle-aged and elderly populations (Glasgow, Morton, and Johnson 2004), with relatively little attention given to young adults. This is an important oversight because today's young adults face a far different social, economic, and epidemiologic context than young adults in the past. Second, we provide greater detail on the geographic context of young adults' residence through the use of both rural-urban commuting area (RUCA) codes and a measure of neighborhood population density based on census tracts. The RUCA codes and population density are correlated but distinct measures, and population density may be an important explanatory factor for health disparities across the rural-urban continuum. Third, we use high-quality, longitudinal, individual-level data to consider geographic context of young adult residence, changes in residential context between adolescence and young adulthood, and cardiovascular health. A longitudinal analysis is particularly important because of the permeability of rural-urban boundaries and selection processes that shape individuals' decisions to move to or stay in different locations as they make the transition to adulthood. Fourth, we identify and assess the extent to which several different sets of explanatory variables account for differences in young adult cardiovascular health across the urban-rural continuum in the United States.

Geography and adult health in the United States

Generally, adults who live in rural communities have poorer health than those living in more urban areas (Anderson et al. 2015; Monnat and Pickett 2011). Whereas mortality rates in the mid-twentieth century were higher in cities than in rural areas, this pattern has since reversed (Cossman et al. 2010). Mortality is now higher in rural areas, in large part due to higher rates of heart disease (Cossman et al. 2010; Eberhardt and Pamuk 2004; Fontanella et al. 2015; Morton 2004; Singh and Siahpush 2014). Health behaviors are also generally worse in rural areas; importantly, obesity and tobacco use are more common in these areas compared to in cities (Agunwamba et al. 2016; Befort, Nazir, and Perri 2012; Rhew, Hawkins, and Oesterle 2011; Roberts et al. 2016).

Much of the research focusing on rural health emphasizes less access to health care among adults living in rural areas. Perhaps the most well-documented disparity is that health care providers are fewer and farther away in rural areas, compared with urban areas, and rural residents tend to use fewer health care services compared with their urban counterparts (Agency for Healthcare Research and Quality 2014; Caldwell et al. 2016; Hummer et al. 2004; Purnell et al. 2016). Yet health care access is at best only a partial explanation of geographic health disparities (Hartley 2004). Indeed, the economic circumstances of rural residents appears to be an important source of their poor health relative to people living in urban areas (Probst et al. 2011). Shifts in the U.S. economy have moved jobs out of production facilities in rural areas, with cities now offering more and more service, financial, and technology-based employment opportunities. These changes have resulted in fewer employment opportunities for those in rural areas (Burton et al. 2013). The lower economic well-being of people in rural areas may lead to unhealthy stress-related behaviors, such as smoking, illegal drug use (e.g., opiates), alcohol abuse, unhealthy diet, and inactivity, all of which have detrimental consequences for cardiovascular health, even in early adulthood (Pampel, Krueger, and Denney 2010; Thoits 2010).

While the documentation of urban-rural health disparities is a fundamental first step, it is important that researchers move beyond an urban-rural dichotomy to better understand more detailed and nuanced measures of geography of residence. Most research examining geographic differences in health uses a simplified operationalization of rural versus urban residential context, which does not acknowledge the connections and blurring between rural and urban spaces (Lichter and Brown 2011). Research taking a more nuanced approach generally demonstrates that health disparities are not based on a simple urban-rural dichotomy. W. L. James (2014), for example, reports heterogeneity in mortality rates across nonurban areas of the United States; he finds that areas adjacent to small towns with populations ranging from 2,500 to 19,999 have the highest mortality rates in the United States. Cossman and colleagues (2010) also show that classifying areas as simply urban or rural obscures important heterogeneity in health patterns across U.S. geographic areas. Thus, our analysis incorporates a rural-urban continuum of residence (i.e., RUCA codes) to more comprehensively operationalize the geography of young adult residence.

Differences in cardiovascular health across the urban-rural continuum may in part be explained by the environmental features of communities. In particular, the population density of the local area in which individuals live differs across the urban-rural continuum and may help to shape cardiovascular health. More densely populated areas may have greater street connectivity and walkability and may offer more or better options for increasing physical activity and improving nutrition; access to retail outlets, health care sites, and social services may also be enhanced in densely populated areas (Galea and Vlahov 2005; Saelens, Sallis, and Frank 2003). Higher population density may also help to facilitate social connections between individuals, which has been shown to exhibit a strong association with cardiovascular health in the United States (Y. C. Yang et al. 2016). Densely populated areas may also attract young adults who are highly educated and affluent because educational and high-paid employment opportunities are more plentiful in these areas compared with less densely populated areas (Burton et al. 2013).

Another potential explanation for differences in young adult cardiovascular health across the urban-rural continuum highlights differences among individuals that may lead them to both live outside of metropolitan cores and/or less densely populated areas and have worse cardiovascular health. Rather than the rural or small city contexts reflecting fewer economic opportunities, the low socioeconomic status (SES) of rural and small city residents may be the result of more educated individuals (or those seeking more education) leaving such areas, also known as the "brain drain" (Burton et al. 2013). Similarly, the unhealthy behaviors observed in rural and smaller urban areas may result from individuals who engage in these behaviors also preferring to live in smaller and/or less dense areas. However, little research explores the extent to which geographic health differences may be due to the *composition* of people living in different communities in the United States, and to our knowledge, no research examines cardiovascular health disparities across the urban-rural continuum among young adults.

To summarize, our research questions are as follows:

1) First, does the cardiovascular health of U.S. young adults differ according to the type of urban or rural area within which they live?
2) Second, to what extent does the population density of the area within which individuals live explain young adult differences in cardiovascular health across the urban-rural continuum?
3) Third, to what extent do demographic, socioeconomic, and behavioral compositional factors—measured both during adolescence and young adulthood—explain differences in young adult cardiovascular health across the urban-rural continuum?
4) Finally, do young adults who live in different geographic contexts compared to adolescence (either in terms of the urban-rural continuum or in terms of population density) exhibit better or worse cardiovascular health in young adulthood relative to those who live in similar contexts across the transition to adulthood?

Methods

Data

We use data from Add Health. These data are nationally representative, following a cohort of adolescents into young adulthood. The first wave of data (wave I) surveyed adolescents ages 12 to 19 in 1994–1995, with follow-ups 1 year later (wave II; 1995–1996), 7 years later (wave III; 2001–2002), and 14 years later (wave IV; 2008–2009). Each wave of data provides a wealth of information on health, SES, and other social circumstances. We focus on cardiovascular health and residential location in wave IV, when respondents are aged 24 to 34, but also consider a number of variables from wave I to identify factors that are associated with both residential location and young adult cardiovascular health. Our sample includes the 12,252 respondents who participated in wave IV, have a valid sampling weight, do not report being pregnant or probably pregnant at the time of the survey, and are not missing on the outcome variable.

Measures

Our outcome measure is a binary indicator of ideal (versus not ideal) cardiovascular health, a concept defined by the American Heart Association (AHA). The AHA introduced ideal cardiovascular health as a tool to monitor and spur efforts to improve cardiovascular health and reduce deaths from cardiovascular diseases and stroke (Lloyd-Jones et al. 2010). It is based on seven indicators that tap into key dimensions of health behavior and health, including body weight, physical activity, smoking, diet, cholesterol, blood pressure, and blood glucose. Subsequent to the initial report identifying the concept of ideal cardiovascular health, a number of studies have demonstrated its strong association with mortality and morbidity (e.g. Dong et al. 2012; Ford, Greenlund, and Hong 2012; Q. Yang et al. 2012). We operationalize *ideal cardiovascular health* using AHA guidelines defining ideal health behaviors and health factors (Lloyd-Jones et al. 2010). Based on available data in Add Health, we measure ideal cardiovascular health based on individuals exhibiting six or more of the following: (1) did not smoke in the last 30 days; (2) have a body mass index (BMI) less than 25; (3) had five or more physical activity sessions per week; (4) consume less than four sugar-sweetened beverages per week;[1] (5) have a total cholesterol in the bottom seven deciles and no reports of lifetime hyperlipidemia diagnosis or recent use of an antihyperlipidemic medication in the previous four weeks; (6) have systolic blood pressure less than 120, diastolic blood pressure less than 80, and no reports of lifetime hypertension diagnosis or recent use of antihypertensive medications; and (7) have no report of lifetime diabetic diagnosis or recent use of antidiabetic medication, and no indication of diabetic or prediabetic levels of glucose (fasting glucose less than 100 milligrams per deciliter [mg/dl], nonfasting glucose levels less than 200 mg/dl, and HbA1c less than 5.7).[2] Smoking, physical activity, sugar sweetened beverage consumption, and diagnoses were self-reported by respondents. Interviewers measured height and weight, which were used to calculate BMI and blood pressure. Dried blood spots were assayed to determine cholesterol and glucose levels (for details on these protocols and measures, see Entzel et al. 2009; Whitsel et al. 2012, 2013).

Our main independent variable is the RUCAs (U.S. Department of Agriculture [USDA] 2016), which are linked to the individual records of Add Health. For both waves I and IV, the census tract in which the respondent resides is linked to the RUCA code. Wave IV tracts are identified using census boundaries in the year 2000, and wave I tracts are based on 1990 U.S. Census boundaries. RUCA codes are taken from these same census files. RUCA categories include: metropolitan area core, metropolitan area high commuting, metropolitan area low commuting, micropolitan area core, micropolitan area high commuting, micropolitan low commuting, small town core, small town high commuting, small town low commuting, and rural areas (Morrill, Cromartie, and Hart 1999). Appendix Table A1 displays the characteristics of the ten categories. Because some of the categories have a small number of respondents, we combine high and low commuting zones for metropolitan, micropolitan, and small town areas. Thus, we end up with seven different RUCA categories. Further information on RUCA codes can be obtained from the USDA (2016). We measure residential change through comparing movement in or out of metropolitan core areas from adolescence (wave I) to young adulthood (wave IV), categorizing individuals as having lived in metropolitan core areas at both time points, at neither time point, in adolescence but not young adulthood, or in young adulthood but not adolescence. Because small percentages of individuals live in other types of locations at either wave I or wave IV, we are unable to examine patterns other than metropolitan core location (versus nonmetropolitan core location).

We also consider population density at the neighborhood or census tract level, measured as the number of people per square kilometer living in each respondent's residential tract. For wave IV, population density is identified with American Community Survey five-year estimates (2005–2009); and for wave I, 1990 U.S. Census data provide values for population density. Because the distribution of this variable is skewed, we take the natural log of the value at each wave.[3] We show quartiles of the original population density measure in the descriptive statistics. We also create a measure of change in population density from adolescence to young adulthood. We compare census tract population density in waves I and IV and identify those people who lived in a less dense context over time, those who lived in a more densely populated area over time, and those who remained in a similarly dense area over time. Similarity in density (or stability) is defined as living in an area that was within 223 people per square kilometer of the individual's adolescent population density, as this value represents the mean population density increase among those who were at the same location at waves I and IV. We do not distinguish whether the change in population density is due to residential mobility or changes in the environment. Population density is associated with RUCA; those living in core areas have higher average density than those in commuting or rural areas, but the range of population density for each of the RUCA codes is large. Importantly, the variation in population density is sufficient to allow for simultaneous analysis of both RUCA codes and population density.

We also examine a number of factors that may be associated with both residential location and cardiovascular health in young adulthood. Sociodemographic factors include interview age, sex, race/ethnicity, and nativity status. Interview age is years of age at time of interview, and sex is a dichotomous variable indicating if the respondent is female.[4] Race/ethnicity is a mutually exclusive categorical variable that identifies individuals as non-Hispanic white, non-Hispanic black, Hispanic, and other. Other race/ethnicity includes Asian/Pacific Islander, American Indian/Alaska Native, and those selecting "other" for race. Nativity status is a variable that includes three categories: respondents and their parents were born in the United States, respondents were born in the United States and their parents were foreign-born, and respondents were foreign-born.

Other compositional factors that may explain young adult differences in cardiovascular health along the urban-rural continuum include adolescent SES, health and health behaviors, and residential location. Socioeconomic background is operationalized through parent educational attainment and household income-to-needs collected in wave I. Parent educational attainment is a continuous measure of years of education representing the average years for the mother and father, or the single measure for those with information only for the mother or father. Income-to-needs is the ratio of the reported household income to the U.S. Census–defined poverty threshold for that year and household size.

Adolescent health includes BMI, depressive symptoms, smoking status, self-rated health, number of physical activity sessions, and alcohol consumption, all measured in wave I. BMI is measured the same as young adult BMI, but height and weight are self-reported in adolescence.[5] Depressive symptoms is a continuous, standardized measure combining responses to nineteen questions from the Center for Epidemiological Studies-Depression (CES-D) battery. Smoking status is a dichotomous indicator representing whether the respondent reported any smoking in the last 30 days. Self-rated health in adolescence is a 5-point scale ranging from *poor* to *excellent*. Number of physical activity sessions combines how often the respondent reports participating in activities in the last seven days. Three questions capture a range of activities, such as participation in sports and working out at the gym. Alcohol consumption is a categorical indicator representing alcohol consumption in the previous 12 months. Those reporting no alcohol consumption are compared to those who report usually consuming one drink, two drinks, or more than two drinks during the times they had an alcoholic drink.

A number of indicators measure achieved SES and the social environment in young adulthood, which also represent potential explanations for cardiovascular health differences across the urban-rural continuum. Educational attainment, household income-to-needs, and employment status represent young adult SES. Educational attainment includes categories for less than high school, high school diploma, some college, and college degree or more (referent). Income-to-needs is a continuous measure that is the ratio of the household's total income to the poverty threshold defined by the U.S. Census for each year and household size. Employment status is represented with three categories: full-time employment (30+ hours per week), part-time employment (10–29 hours per week), and unemployed (less than 10 hours per week). We define individuals as having high social integration if they report two or more of the following: being married, having six or more close friends, attending church twelve or more times in the past year, and volunteering in the past year. Those meeting this criterion are coded 1 for high social integration, and all others are coded 0. We create a dichotomous measure for young adults who live with children using the wave IV household roster.

Analytic approach

We first examine descriptive statistics of ideal cardiovascular health across young adult RUCA codes, young adult population density, movement into or out of metropolitan core areas from adolescence into young adulthood, and changes in population density. Because there are no studies examining the health correlates of a nationally representative sample of U.S. young adults by residential location, we devote considerable space to describing these patterns. Our logistic regression analysis begins by baseline differences in young adult cardiovascular health across the urban-rural continuum. Subsequently, we add in substantive groups of characteristics (population density, sociodemographic factors, adolescent characteristics, and young adult characteristics) to the models to assess the extent to which they help to explain associations between the RUCA measures and ideal cardiovascular health. We do not directly compare results from different logistic regression models, but base our conclusions on general patterns. Variance inflation factor tests produced no evidence of multicollinearity.

All analyses adjust for the complex sampling design to ensure representativeness. We use multiple imputation for those who are missing values on some independent variables to retain the full sample. All independent and dependent variables are used to inform the imputation model. We do not impute values for our outcome variable, ideal cardiovascular health, and we have complete information for young adult RUCA codes, young adult population density, adolescent RUCA codes, age, sex, and young adult educational attainment. We impute less than 1 percent of values for race/ethnicity, nativity status, adolescent depressive symptoms, adolescent self-rated health, adolescent physical activity, young adult marital status, living with children, young adult employment, and adolescent population density. We impute 2.2 percent of values for parent education, 23.5 percent for adolescent income-to-needs, 2.5 percent for adolescent BMI, 17.9 percent for adolescent smoking, 1.7 percent for adolescent alcohol consumption, and 6.6 percent for young adult income-to-needs.

Results

Descriptive results

Table 1 displays descriptive statistics. Just 7 percent of young adults aged 24 to 34 have ideal cardiovascular health. The average number of ideal indicators for individuals is 3.32, or just under one-half of the maximum of 7. These figures clearly indicate that this young adult cohort has far from ideal cardiovascular health. The percentages of young adults with healthy physical activity (54 percent), who are nonsmokers (60 percent), who have ideal blood sugar (62 percent), and who have ideal cholesterol (65 percent), while far from 100 percent, are much higher than the percentages with healthy BMI (33 percent), who consume few or no sugar-sweetened beverages (29 percent), and who have ideal blood pressure (29 percent), for which only one-third or less exhibit healthy levels.[6]

Nearly three-quarters (71 percent) of young adults live in a metropolitan core, with an additional 10 percent in high- or low-commuting areas around these cities. A smaller number of individuals live in tracts described as micropolitan, small town, or rural. We divide young adult population density into quartiles in Table 1, so each represents roughly one-quarter of young adults. Table 1 also shows changes in residential context from adolescence to young adulthood. The majority of young adults (63 percent) lived in a metropolitan core in both adolescence and young adulthood. Smaller proportions lived in a metropolitan core in adolescence and a smaller community in adulthood (12 percent), lived in a smaller community in adolescence and in a metropolitan core during young adulthood (8 percent), or did not live in a metropolitan core in either adolescence or young adulthood (17 percent). The largest proportion of individuals (38 percent) experienced an increase in population density from adolescence to adulthood, though nearly the same number lived in a place with similar density (36 percent).

TABLE 1

Weighted Means of Young Adult Ideal Cardiovascular Health across Residential Location Measures

	Population	Ideal CVH (6–7 Indicators)	# Ideal CVH Indicators	Ideal CVH indicators						
				BMI <25	5+ Physical Activity Sessions	<3 SSB in Last Week	Not Current Smoker	Ideal Blood Sugar	Ideal Blood Pressure	Ideal Cholesterol
Population		0.07	3.32	0.33	0.54	0.29	0.60	0.62	0.29	0.65
Young adult RUCA										
Metropolitan core	0.71	0.07	3.39	0.34	0.55	0.31	0.62	0.63	0.30	0.64
Metropolitan high/low commuting	0.10	0.06	3.25	0.30	0.52	0.27	0.56	0.64	0.30	0.65
Micropolitan core	0.07	0.06	3.17	0.28	0.50	0.26	0.61	0.59	0.25	0.69
Micropolitan high/low commuting	0.03	0.04	2.99	0.30	0.50	0.16	0.55	0.57	0.28	0.63
Small town core	0.03	0.03	3.15	0.28	0.49	0.25	0.53	0.60	0.32	0.68
Small town high/low commuting	0.02	0.06	3.01	0.31	0.51	0.20	0.52	0.61	0.23	0.64
Rural	0.04	0.04	3.18	0.31	0.54	0.25	0.54	0.62	0.26	0.67
Young adult population density										
< 186.06 people/km²	0.28	0.05	3.16	0.29	0.52	0.25	0.56	0.61	0.28	0.66
186.08–955.90 people/km²	0.26	0.07	3.36	0.33	0.52	0.31	0.62	0.64	0.30	0.63
956.00–2,352.27 people/km²	0.27	0.07	3.34	0.35	0.54	0.30	0.59	0.63	0.29	0.64
2,353+ people/km²	0.19	0.08	3.49	0.35	0.58	0.31	0.66	0.61	0.32	0.66

(continued)

TABLE 1 (CONTINUED)

	Population	Ideal CVH (6–7 Indicators)	# Ideal CVH Indicators	BMI <25	5+ Physical Activity Sessions	$\leq$3 SSB in Last Week	Not Current Smoker	Ideal Blood Sugar	Ideal Blood Pressure	Ideal Cholesterol
Adolescent to young adult RUCA										
Metro core to metro core	0.63	0.07	3.37	0.34	0.55	0.30	0.61	0.63	0.30	0.64
Metro core to other	0.12	0.06	3.26	0.30	0.53	0.28	0.56	0.65	0.28	0.65
Other to metro core	0.08	0.09	3.50	0.36	0.55	0.32	0.66	0.64	0.32	0.65
Other to other	0.17	0.05	3.10	0.29	0.50	0.22	0.57	0.58	0.27	0.67
Adolescent to young adult change in density										
Decreasing	0.25	0.06	3.27	0.30	0.54	0.28	0.61	0.60	0.29	0.65
Stable	0.36	0.05	3.19	0.31	0.52	0.26	0.57	0.62	0.28	0.64
Increasing	0.38	0.09	3.48	0.37	0.56	0.32	0.63	0.64	0.31	0.65

SOURCE: Add Health.
NOTE: Analysis adjusts for complex sampling design. $N = 12,252$.

Although levels of ideal cardiovascular health are very low among young adults living in all types of places, there are clear differences across geographic locations. Individuals living in metropolitan cores and denser areas demonstrate the highest proportion with ideal cardiovascular health, as well as the highest average number of ideal cardiovascular health indicators. Rural areas lag well behind, though small town core areas have the lowest percentage of individuals with ideal cardiovascular health. The results indicate that RUCA codes do not demonstrate a linear relationship with ideal cardiovascular health, in line with previous research showing that mortality rates are not graded across rural-urban continuum codes (James 2014). People living in higher density areas in young adulthood also exhibit higher proportions of ideal cardiovascular health. Focusing on changes in the geography of residence across the transition to adulthood, the cohort that lived in a metropolitan core in young adulthood and in a smaller community in adolescence has the highest proportion of individuals with ideal cardiovascular health, followed by those who lived in metropolitan core areas in both adolescence and young adulthood. The longitudinal approach to population density indicates that ideal cardiovascular health is most common among those who experience increases in density during the transition to adulthood. Young adults in rural and less densely settled areas in young adulthood suffer a significant cardiovascular health disparity that will likely be revealed in higher rates of mortality in older age and in lower overall life expectancy.

Additional descriptive statistics (see the appendix, Tables A2 and A3) demonstrate that there are systematic individual differences in many social, economic, behavioral, and health characteristics by both RUCA code of residence and population density. Notably, those living in denser areas have higher adolescent and young adult SES and generally better adolescent health and health behaviors.

Multivariate models of young adult cardiovascular health by geography of residence

Table 2 presents odds ratios and significance levels from logistic regression models predicting ideal cardiovascular health. Model 1 shows that, compared with those residing in metropolitan core areas, young adults living in metropolitan commuting, micropolitan commuting, small town core, and rural areas are significantly less likely to have ideal cardiovascular health. Those living in micropolitan core and small town commuting areas exhibit no difference in ideal cardiovascular health relative to individuals in metropolitan core areas.

When population density is added in model 2, only small town core residents have significantly decreased odds of ideal cardiovascular health. With the addition of demographic controls in model 3, there are no differences in ideal cardiovascular health across the RUCA codes. Population density is a particularly important explanation for young adult differences in cardiovascular health across the urban-rural continuum. Moreover, individuals who live in more densely populated areas are more likely to have ideal cardiovascular health compared to people who live in less densely populated areas. These results remain in subsequent models, with population density attenuating somewhat with the inclusion

TABLE 2
Odds Ratios for Logistic Regression Models Predicting Young
Adult Ideal Cardiovascular Health

	Model 1	Model 2	Model 3	Model 4	Model 5
Young adult RUCA (metro core)					
Metropolitan high/low commuting	0.73**	0.99	1.12	1.12	1.11
Micropolitan core	0.80	0.94	1.15	1.14	1.28
Micropolitan high/low commuting	0.52*	0.76	0.88	0.90	0.95
Small town core	0.35***	0.46**	0.55	0.60	0.69
Small town high/low commuting	0.75	1.14	1.62	1.95	2.13*
Rural	0.50**	0.77	0.95	0.90	0.87
Young adult logged population density		1.10**	1.17****	1.12***	1.08**
Age at wave IV			0.95	1.06*	1.05
Female			4.22****	4.34****	3.92****
Race/ethnicity (white)					
Black			0.25****	0.32****	0.39****
Hispanic			0.51****	0.86	0.97
Other			0.93	0.88	0.87
Nativity (U.S. born)					
Parents foreign born			0.86	0.88	0.80
Foreign born			1.84***	1.81**	1.67**
Background SES (wave I)					
Income-to-needs				1.02	1.01
Parent education				1.16****	1.08***
Adolescent health (wave I)					
BMI				0.84****	0.84****
Depressive symptoms				0.94	1.00
Smoker				0.68**	0.81
Self-rated health				1.14**	1.08
Physical activity sessions				1.01	1.00
Alcohol consumption (none)					
Usually 1 drink				1.03	0.96
Usually 2 drinks				0.95	0.85
Usually > 2 drinks				1.09	1.01
Adolescent residence (wave I)					
Logged population density				1.00	1.01
RUCA code (metro core)					
Metro/micro high/low commuting				1.20	1.11
Micro core				1.22	1.13
Small town core				0.78	0.67
Small town high commuting				0.91	0.86
Rural area				1.60**	1.50**

(continued)

TABLE 2 (CONTINUED)

	Model 1	Model 2	Model 3	Model 4	Model 5
Young adult factors (wave IV)					
Educational attainment (BA+)					
< High school					0.37°°°
High school					0.35°°°°
Some college					0.53°°°°
Income-to-needs					1.04°°°
Employed (full time)					
Not employed					1.14
Part time					1.12
High social integration					1.28°°
Living with kids					0.91
Constant	0.08°°°°	0.04°°°°	0.05°°°	0.01°°°°	0.07°°°

SOURCE: Add Health.

NOTE: Analysis adjusts for complex sampling design. Referent is in the parentheses. $N =$ 12,252.

$°p < .10.$ $°°p < .05.$ $°°°p < .01.$ $°°°°p < .001.$

of additional covariates. For example, the inclusion of young adult educational attainment, income-to-needs, employment status, social integration, and living with children in model 5 results in a 33 percent reduction in the association between population density and ideal cardiovascular health (compared to model 4); the associations between education, income, and ideal cardiovascular health are particularly strong. This suggests that the higher SES of individuals who live in more densely populated areas is in part responsible for their more favorable young adult cardiovascular health. Nonetheless, young adults who live in higher-density areas continue to exhibit significantly higher odds of ideal cardiovascular health, net of background and young adult factors. Figure 1 displays the predicted probabilities of ideal cardiovascular health for individuals living in the densest, least dense, and average density areas (and otherwise have characteristics equivalent to the referent group or population mean). Although the overall levels of ideal cardiovascular health are low, the relative differences in predicted probabilities are large, with individuals living in the highest density areas in young adulthood exhibiting more than twice the probability of being in ideal cardiovascular health compared with those who live in low density areas.[7]

Table 3 presents models examining the same outcome, ideal cardiovascular health, but now considers residential location patterns of stability and change from adolescence to young adulthood. Compared to individuals who lived in metropolitan core areas in both adolescence and young adulthood, those who did not live in metropolitan core areas in either life stage have 38 percent reduced odds of ideal cardiovascular health in young adulthood. Further, those who lived in metropolitan core areas as adolescents but who live in smaller communities in young adulthood have 25 percent lower odds of ideal cardiovascular health in

FIGURE 1
Predicted Probabilities of Ideal Cardiovascular Health across Young
Adult Population Density

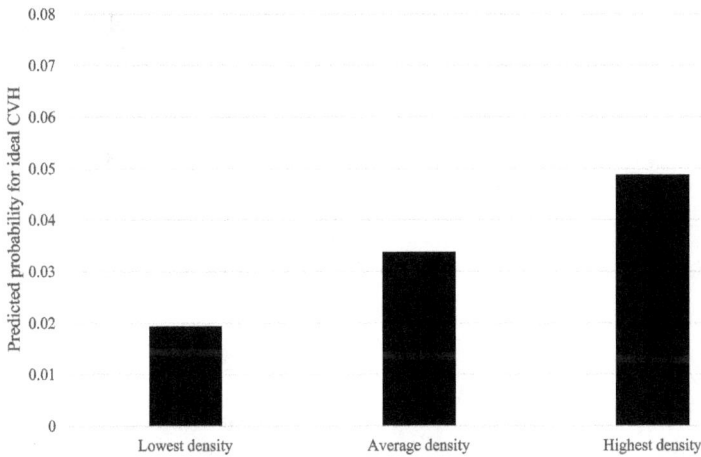

SOURCE: Add Health.
NOTE: Predicted probabilies computed from Table 2, model 5. Other than population density measures, calculations assume characteristics equivalent to the referent group (for categorical variables) or sample mean (for continuous variables). Analysis adjusts for complex sampling design. N = 12, 252.

young adulthood compared with those who consistently lived in a metropolitan core. These differences do not persist once other variables are considered, and, like the previous set of results, population density and demographic characteristics account for the observed differences across the rural-urban continuum categories. Model 2 demonstrates that individuals who live in a more densely populated area in young adulthood compared with their residential context in adolescence have higher odds of ideal cardiovascular health relative to those who remained in a similarly dense area during the transition to adulthood. Adolescent and young adult factors appear to attenuate the association, but those who live in increasingly dense residential areas are 32 percent more likely to have ideal cardiovascular health, net of all covariates (model 5).[8]

Discussion

This study seeks to identify the extent to which U.S. young adult cardiovascular health differs across the rural-urban continuum and what may account for these differences. Our results show that young adults who live in metropolitan core areas (71 percent of young adults) exhibit better cardiovascular health than young adults who live outside of these core areas. Even more striking, young adults who live in low-density areas have worse cardiovascular health than young adults who live in more densely populated areas. Further, the strong association between the

TABLE 3
Odds Ratios from Logistic Regression Models Predicting Young Adult Ideal
Cardiovascular Health

	Model 1	Model 2	Model 3	Model 4	Model 5
Adolescent to young adult RUCA (metro core to metro core)					
Metro core to other	0.75*	0.89	0.84	0.90	0.98
Other to metro core	1.27	1.16	1.16	1.06	0.96
Other to other	0.62***	0.71**	0.81	1.00	1.06
Change in population density (stable)					
Decreasing		0.96	1.14	1.13	1.06
Increasing		1.48***	1.65****	1.43***	1.32**
Age at wave IV			0.96	1.06*	1.05
Female			4.18****	4.33***	3.93****
Race/ethnicity (white)					
Black			0.27****	0.34***	0.41****
Hispanic			0.56***	0.91	1.02
Other			0.96	0.92	0.91
Nativity (U.S. born)					
Parents foreign born			0.92	0.90	0.81
Foreign born			1.99***	1.85***	1.71**
Background SES (wave I)					
Income-to-needs				1.02*	1.01
Parent education				1.16****	1.08***
Adolescent health (wave I)					
BMI				0.84****	0.84***
Depressive symptoms				0.94	1.00
Smoker				0.67***	0.81
Self-rated health				1.13*	1.08
Physical activity sessions				1.01	1.00
Alcohol consumption (none)					
Usually 1 drink				1.04	0.97
Usually 2 drinks				0.95	0.85
Usually > 2 drinks				1.09	1.01
Young adult factors (wave IV)					
Educational attainment (BA+)					
< High school					0.38***
High school					0.35****
Some college					0.53****
Income-to-needs					1.05***
Employed (full time)					
Not employed					1.14
Part time					1.13
High social integration					1.27**
Living with kids					0.89
Constant	0.08****	0.06****	0.09***	0.01****	0.10**

SOURCE: Add Health.
NOTE: Analysis adjusts for complex sampling design. Referent is in the parentheses. N = 12,252.
*p < .10. **p < .05. ***p < .01. ****p < .001.

population density of individuals' census tract and their odds of ideal cardiovascular health explains the association between rural-urban residence and cardiovascular health in our statistical models. The strength of the association between density and cardiovascular health is further bolstered by our examination of residential changes across the transition to adulthood, which shows that individuals who lived in more densely populated areas as they transitioned to adulthood have higher odds of ideal cardiovascular health compared with individuals who lived in similarly dense or less dense areas over time. This finding supports results from other studies that demonstrated greater physical activity and reduced BMI among residents of dense or compact areas (e.g., Ewing et al. 2014; Frank et al. 2005; James et al. 2013).

The mechanisms behind the strong association between young adult residence in a densely populated context and cardiovascular health could be compositional in that there are other unobserved factors that we have not accounted for that may explain the association. We have controlled for adolescent health behaviors and health factors to help mitigate selection effects, but it could be that there are other factors shaping the migration of healthy young adults to denser areas. This intranational process could be similar to that in the international migration and health literature, which has shown that immigrants have better health than their U.S.-born counterparts (Hummer, Melvin, and He 2015). Alternatively, mechanisms underlying the association may be contextual in that it is the physical and social environment in dense areas that promotes health (Sparks 2012), and cardiovascular health in particular. Perhaps most likely, the environments and people within dense areas coexist in a reciprocal relationship that reinforces certain patterns and behaviors (Cummins et al. 2007). Individuals have preferences and constraints for where they live, including opinions on walkability and proximity to recreation (Berry et al. 2010). Built and social environments may sort these preferences into different lifestyles. Families seek large homes, nice cars, and attractive lawns as a sign of financial well-being and comfort and as a source of differentiation from those of lower status, such as families living in inner-city public housing. Low-density neighborhoods make large homes and cars affordable and convenient. These relatively large homes and cars make it easy to obtain, transport, and store large amounts of nonperishable foods and, in turn, are more comfortable for bigger bodies. Government institutions also support low-density neighborhoods with large homes and cars, providing wide roads and free parking, among other comforts (Jackson 2009). In contrast, other individuals may seek out dense areas for their activity, diversity, and vibrancy. These dense areas are marked by public spaces that can be difficult for bigger bodies to navigate (Brewis et al. 2016). Expenses associated with owning a car, driving, and parking in dense areas may incentivize walking, cycling, and use of public transportation, and smaller residences may prevent the acquisition of a large amount of food. Across these different communities, the environments and social and cultural norms can propagate a way of life, with important health consequences.

Prior research has often used a rural-urban distinction to measure lifestyle and health differences across residential areas, but this simple dichotomy obscures the complexity of location in today's increasingly blurred society (Lichter and Brown

2011). The enhanced rural-urban RUCA continuum is a much more refined catego-rization of residential space, but these rigid categorizations cannot accommodate the blurring, crossing, and shifting of boundaries. Yet environmental features still distin-guish communities and the residents that reside in them from one another. And based on our findings, the population density within which individuals live appears to be a dimension of residential life that is especially important for a set of important health outcomes in early adulthood and, thus, a dimension that cannot be ignored in future work on the topic. Moreover, density is not only a feature of large metropolitan cities but also of smaller cities, small towns, and rural areas, which may make it an important consideration for population health in all types of residential spaces.

As individuals select into different communities and these environments accom-modate and encourage different lifestyles, health disparities across contexts may grow. We focus on ideal cardiovascular health here to foreshadow future cardiovas-cular conditions that today's young adults have yet to experience. For today's young adults whose future health and longevity are threatened by the obesity epidemic, these spatial differences may only become more important in the future. Fairly strong differences across population density may widen as young adults settle into their current locations, raise families, and perpetuate their lifestyles. At the same time, rural-urban interdependence may obscure spatial disparities. Research on health and place will need to consider how boundaries are blurred and traversed to identify salient features of social and physical environments.

Appendix

TABLE A1
RUCA Codes with Descriptors

Classification	Description
Metropolitan area core	30% of the population is in an urbanized area (urban-ized area has population of 50,000 or more)
Metropolitan area high commuting	Primary flow 30% to urbanized area
Metropolitan area low commuting	Primary flow 10%–30% to urbanized area
Micropolitan area core	30% of the population is in a large urban cluster (large urban cluster has population of 10,000 to 49,999)
Micropolitan area high commuting	Primary flow 30% or more to a large urban cluster
Micropolitan area low commuting	Primary flow 10%–30% to a large urban cluster
Small town core	30% of the population is in a small urban cluster (small urban cluster has population of 2,500 to 9,999)
Small town high commuting	Primary flow 30% or more to a small urban cluster
Small town low commuting	Primary flow 10%–30% to a small urban cluster
Rural areas	Primary flow is to a tract that is not an urbanized area or an urban cluster

SOURCE: U.S. Department of Agriculture (2016).

TABLE A2
Weighted Means of Covariates across Residential Location Categories in Young Adulthood (Wave IV)

| | | Young Adult RUCA | | | | | | | Young Adult Population Density in People / km² | | | |
| | | Metropolitan | | Micropolitan | | Small Town | | | | | | |
	Population	Core	High/Low Commuting	Core	High/Low Commuting	Core	High/Low Commuting	Rural	<186.06	186.08–955.90	956.00–2,352.27	2,353+
Population		0.71	0.10	0.07	0.03	0.03	0.02	0.04	0.28	0.26	0.27	0.19
Sociodemographics												
Age at wave IV	28.38	28.38	28.48	28.33	28.25	28.35	28.37	28.43	28.41	28.34	28.34	28.46
Female	0.49	0.49	0.47	0.47	0.52	0.48	0.43	0.49	0.49	0.49	0.49	0.47
Race/ethnicity												
White	0.69	0.64	0.85	0.67	0.81	0.73	0.79	0.85	0.80	0.74	0.65	0.48
Black	0.15	0.15	0.09	0.25	0.13	0.24	0.19	0.12	0.13	0.15	0.16	0.18
Hispanic	0.12	0.16	0.05	0.04	0.04	0.01	0.01	0.01	0.04	0.09	0.15	0.25
Other	0.04	0.05	0.01	0.04	0.03	0.02	0.01	0.01	0.03	0.03	0.04	0.09
Nativity status												
U.S. born and parents U.S. born	0.87	0.84	0.94	0.95	0.95	0.97	0.99	0.98	0.95	0.90	0.87	0.72
Parents foreign-born	0.07	0.09	0.03	0.03	0.05	0.02	0.00	0.01	0.03	0.06	0.08	0.16
Foreign-born	0.05	0.07	0.03	0.02	0.01	0.01	0.00	0.01	0.02	0.04	0.05	0.12
Background SES (wave I)												
Parent education	13.06	13.18	12.86	13.18	12.74	12.38	12.40	12.19	12.76	13.24	13.16	13.07
Income-to-needs	2.90	3.04	2.77	2.52	2.59	2.90	3.00	2.35	2.64	2.93	2.99	3.13
Adolescent health (wave I)												
BMI	22.56	22.41	22.83	22.67	22.53	23.05	23.69	23.34	22.88	22.34	22.45	22.55
Depressive symptoms	-0.05	-0.05	-0.08	-0.08	0.00	-0.02	-0.15	-0.06	-0.04	-0.08	-0.05	-0.03
Smoker	0.34	0.32	0.39	0.31	0.44	0.38	0.40	0.43	0.40	0.34	0.34	0.26
Self-rated health	3.86	3.88	3.83	3.84	3.87	3.71	3.83	3.77	3.83	3.89	3.86	3.89
Physical activity sessions	5.46	5.53	5.31	5.49	5.14	5.45	5.52	4.83	5.25	5.49	5.44	5.76

(continued)

| | | Young Adult RUCA | | | | | | | | Young Adult Population Density / People / km² | | |
| | | Metropolitan | | Micropolitan | | Small Town | | | | | | |
	Population	Core	High/Low Commuting	Core	High/Low Commuting	Core	High/Low Commuting	Rural	<186.06	186.08–955.90	956.00–2,352.27	2,353+
Alcohol consumption												
None	0.52	0.52	0.49	0.57	0.50	0.55	0.49	0.50	0.50	0.53	0.52	0.54
Usually 1 drink	0.10	0.10	0.09	0.10	0.11	0.08	0.09	0.10	0.09	0.10	0.10	0.11
Usually 2 drinks	0.08	0.08	0.07	0.10	0.09	0.09	0.06	0.07	0.08	0.08	0.08	0.07
Usually > 2 drinks	0.30	0.30	0.35	0.23	0.30	0.28	0.36	0.33	0.32	0.30	0.30	0.27
Young adult factors												
Educational attainment												
Less than high school	0.09	0.08	0.10	0.08	0.10	0.12	0.09	0.15	0.10	0.09	0.09	0.07
High school diploma	0.27	0.25	0.32	0.30	0.35	0.39	0.45	0.38	0.35	0.25	0.25	0.24
Some college	0.34	0.34	0.36	0.38	0.37	0.32	0.31	0.28	0.35	0.35	0.35	0.30
College degree or more	0.30	0.33	0.22	0.24	0.17	0.17	0.15	0.20	0.20	0.31	0.31	0.38
Household income-to-needs	3.74	3.97	3.73	3.12	3.03	2.41	2.77	2.73	3.23	3.89	3.78	4.20
Employment												
Unemployed	0.71	0.72	0.73	0.69	0.70	0.61	0.72	0.63	0.68	0.72	0.71	0.72
Part time	0.09	0.09	0.08	0.08	0.11	0.07	0.09	0.07	0.08	0.09	0.10	0.08
Full time	0.20	0.19	0.19	0.23	0.19	0.32	0.19	0.31	0.23	0.19	0.19	0.20
High social integration	0.52	0.50	0.54	0.57	0.65	0.57	0.54	0.59	0.56	0.54	0.51	0.45
Living with children	0.46	0.42	0.56	0.54	0.62	0.64	0.56	0.57	0.58	0.47	0.43	0.32

SOURCE: Add Health.
NOTE: Analysis adjust for complex sampling design. $N = 12,252$.

TABLE A3
Weighted Means of Covariates, across Transition to Adulthood Residential Location Categories

	Population	Adolescent to Young Adult				Adolescent to Young Adult Change in Population Density		
		Metro Core to Metro Core	Metro Core to Other	Other to Metro Core	Other to Other	Decreasing	Stable	Increasing
Population		0.63	0.12	0.08	0.16	0.25	0.36	0.38
Sociodemographics								
Age at wave IV	28.38	28.40	28.42	28.19	28.37	28.51	28.38	28.30
Female	0.49	0.49	0.46	0.52	0.49	0.48	0.50	0.48
Race/ethnicity								
White	0.69	0.64	0.87	0.69	0.73	0.57	0.77	0.68
Black	0.15	0.14	0.05	0.24	0.24	0.19	0.13	0.14
Hispanic	0.12	0.17	0.06	0.03	0.01	0.18	0.07	0.13
Other	0.04	0.05	0.02	0.05	0.02	0.06	0.03	0.05
Nativity status								
U.S. born and parents U.S. born	0.87	0.83	0.93	0.93	0.97	0.81	0.92	0.86
Parents foreign-born	0.07	0.10	0.03	0.03	0.02	0.10	0.05	0.08
Foreign-born	0.05	0.07	0.03	0.03	0.01	0.08	0.03	0.06
Background SES (wave I)								
Parent education	13.06	13.10	12.96	13.82	12.59	12.71	12.86	13.47
Income-to-needs	2.90	3.04	3.01	3.00	2.27	2.62	2.73	3.26
Adolescent health (wave I)								
BMI	22.55	22.47	22.62	21.95	23.12	22.72	22.73	22.29
Depressive symptoms	-0.05	-0.04	-0.11	-0.10	-0.04	-0.03	-0.03	-0.09
Smoker	0.34	0.33	0.40	0.28	0.37	0.33	0.39	0.30
Self-rated health	3.86	3.87	3.87	3.94	3.78	3.83	3.82	3.93
Physical activity sessions	5.46	5.53	5.50	5.53	5.13	5.27	5.40	5.65

(continued)

TABLE A3 (CONTINUED)

	Population	Adolescent to Young Adult				Adolescent to Young Adult Change in Population Density		
		Metro Core to Metro Core	Metro Core to Other	Other to Metro Core	Other to Other	Decreasing	Stable	Increasing
Alcohol consumption								
None	0.52	0.52	0.48	0.56	0.55	0.51	0.51	0.54
Usually 1 drink	0.10	0.10	0.10	0.10	0.09	0.10	0.09	0.11
Usually 2 drinks	0.08	0.08	0.08	0.07	0.09	0.08	0.08	0.07
Usually > 2 drinks	0.30	0.30	0.35	0.28	0.27	0.31	0.31	0.28
Young adult factors (wave IV)								
Educational attainment								
Less than high school	0.09	0.09	0.10	0.04	0.11	0.11	0.11	0.06
High school diploma	0.27	0.26	0.31	0.17	0.37	0.28	0.33	0.22
Some college	0.34	0.34	0.37	0.34	0.33	0.35	0.33	0.34
College degree or more	0.30	0.32	0.22	0.45	0.20	0.26	0.23	0.38
Household income-to-needs	3.74	3.94	3.61	4.22	2.85	3.68	3.38	4.11
Employment								
Unemployed	0.71	0.71	0.71	0.77	0.67	0.70	0.69	0.73
Part time	0.09	0.09	0.08	0.07	0.08	0.10	0.09	0.08
Full time	0.20	0.20	0.20	0.16	0.25	0.20	0.23	0.18
High social integration	0.52	0.49	0.54	0.57	0.59	0.50	0.53	0.52
Living with children	0.46	0.42	0.55	0.40	0.58	0.50	0.53	0.38

SOURCE: Add Health.

NOTE: Analysis adjust for complex sampling design. $N = 12,252$.

Notes

1. The AHA healthy diet components include levels of fruit and vegetable, fish, whole grain, sodium, and sugar-sweetened beverage consumption (Lloyd-Jones et al. 2010). We set the sugar-sweetened beverage threshold based on their definition of no more than thirty-six ounces per week, assuming that one serving is twelve ounces.

2. Measures for total cholesterol, blood pressure, and glucose are designed to be as close to AHA guidelines as possible given our available information. For example, Add Health does not provide absolute concentrations for cholesterol given the assay method (Whitsel et al. 2013).

3. We tested for threshold values and squared terms to determine nonlinear relationships between population density and ideal cardiovascular health, but the logged term produced the best fitting models.

4. We tested for interactions between residential location and gender, but none was significant.

5. BMI based on self-reported height and weight is correlated with measured BMI (in adolescence at wave II) at over .99.

6. Our rates for BMI and blood sugar are similar to overall percentages of U.S. adults reported by Lloyd-Jones and colleagues (2010). Our measures of physical activity and total cholesterol reflect greater (or healthier) percentages, likely due to variable construction. The percentage of individuals consuming a healthy amount of sugar-sweetened beverages is much higher than the 0.5 percent of U.S. adults who meet the AHA healthy diet criterion. Rates of nonsmoking and healthy blood pressure are lower for our sample compared to U.S. adults, which may reflect the unique environment and behaviors of the young adult cohort.

7. The association between the population density of the tract within which individuals live and cardiovascular health appears to be largely driven by those within metropolitan core areas. The association between population density and cardiovascular health is nearly identical in a full model that includes all covariates but constrains the sample to those in metropolitan core areas, but the effect of population density is smaller and nonsignificant for the same model among those not living in metropolitan core areas.

8. Using number of ideal cardiovascular health indicators instead of a yes/no distinction produced no substantive differences in the results.

References

Agency for Healthcare Research and Quality, U.S. Department of Health and Human Services. 2014. *National healthcare disparities report*. Available from http://www.ahrq.gov/research/findings (accessed 8 September 2016).

Agunwamba, Amenah A., Ichiro Kawachi, David R. Williams, Lila J. Finney Rutten, Patrick M. Wilson, and Kasisomayajula Viswanath. 2016. Mental health, racial discrimination, and tobacco use differences across rural-urban California. *Journal of Rural Health*, Online First.

Anderson, Timothy J., Daniel M. Saman, Martin S. Lipsky, and M. Nawal Lutfiyya. 2015. A cross-sectional study on health differences between rural and non-rural US counties using the County Health Rankings. *BMC Health Services Research* 15:441–49.

Befort, Christie A., Niaman Nazir, and Michael G. Perri. 2012. Prevalence of obesity among adults from rural and urban areas of the United States: Findings from NHANES (2005–2008). *Journal of Rural Health* 28 (4): 392–97.

Berry, Tanya R., John C. Spence, Chris M. Blanchard, Nicoleta Cutumisu, Joy Edwards, and Genevieve Selfridge. 2010. A longitudinal and cross-sectional examination of the relationship between reasons for choosing a neighbourhood, physical activity and body mass index. *International Journal of Behavioral Nutrition and Physical Activity* 7 (1): 57–68.

Brewis, Alexandra, Sarah Trainer, SeungYong Han, and Amber Wutich. 2016. Publically misfitting: Extreme weight and the everyday production and reinforcement of felt stigma. *Medical Anthropology Quarterly*, Online First.

Burton, Linda M., Daniel T. Lichter, Regina S. Baker, and John M. Eason. 2013. Inequality, family processes, and health in the "new" rural America. *American Behavioral Scientist* 57 (8): 1128–51.

Caldwell, Julia T., Chandra L. Ford, Steven P. Wallace, May C. Wang, and Lois M. Takahashi. 2016. Intersection of living in a rural versus urban area and race/ethnicity in explaining access to health care in the United States. *American Journal of Public Health* 106 (8): 1463–69.

Cossman, Jeralynn S., Wesley L. James, Arthur G. Cosby, and Ronald E. Cossman. 2010. Underlying causes of the emerging nonmetropolitan mortality penalty. *American Journal of Public Health* 100 (8): 1417–19.

Cummins, Steven, Sarah Curtis, Ana V. Diez-Roux, and Sally Macintyre. 2007. Understanding and representing "place" in health research: A relational approach. *Social Science & Medicine* 65 (9): 1825–38.

Dong, Chuanhui, Tatjana Rundek, Clinton B. Wright, Zane Anwar, Mitchell S.V. Elkind, and Ralph L. Sacco. 2012. Ideal cardiovascular health predicts lower risks of myocardial infarction, stroke, and vascular death across whites, blacks and Hispanics: The Northern Manhattan Study. *Circulation* 125 (24): 2975–84.

Eberhardt, Mark S., and Elsie R. Pamuk. 2004. The importance of place of residence: examining health in rural and nonrural areas. *American Journal of Public Health* 94 (10): 1682–86.

Entzel, Pamela, Eric A. Whitsel, Andrea Richardson, Joyce Tabor, Suzanne Hallquist, Jon Husey, Carolyn T. Halpern, and Kathleen Mullan Harris. 2009. *Add Health Wave IV documentation: Cardiovascular and anthropometric measures.* Available from http://www.cpc.unc.edu/projects/addhealth/documentation (accessed 21 November 2016).

Ewing, Reid, Gail Meakins, Shima Hamidi, and Arthur C. Nelson. 2014. Relationship between urban sprawl and physical activity, obesity, and morbidity—Update and refinement. *Health & Place* 26:118–26.

Fontanella, Cynthia A., Danielle L. Hiance-Steelesmith, Gary S. Phillips, Jeffrey A. Bridge, Natalie Lester, Helen Anne Sweeney, and John V. Campo. 2015. Widening rural-urban disparities in youth suicides, United States, 1996–2010. *JAMA Pediatrics* 169 (5): 466–73.

Ford, Earl S., Kurt J. Greenlund, and Yuling Hong. 2012. Ideal cardiovascular health and mortality from all causes and diseases of the circulatory system among adults in the United States. *Circulation* 125 (8): 987–95.

Frank, Lawrence D., Thomas L. Schmid, James F. Sallis, James Chapman, and Brian E. Saelens. 2005. Linking objectively measured physical activity with objectively measured urban form: Findings from SMARTRAQ. *American Journal of Preventive Medicine* 28 (2): 117–25.

Fry, Richard. 2013. *A rising share of young adults live in their parents' home.* Washington, DC: Pew Research Centers Social and Demographic Trends. Available from www.pewsocialtrends.org (accessed 21 November 2016).

Galea, Sandro, and David Vlahov. 2005. Urban health: Evidence, challenges, and directions. *Annual Review of Public Health* 26:341–65.

Glasgow, Nina, Lois Wright Morton, and Nan E. Johnson, eds. 2004. *Critical issues in rural health.* Ames, IA: Blackwell Publishing.

Harris, Kathleen Mullan. 2010. An integrative approach to health. *Demography* 47 (1): 1–22.

Hartley, David. 2004. Rural health disparities, population health, and rural culture. *American Journal of Public Health* 94 (10): 1675–78.

Hummer, Robert A., Jennifer E. Melvin, and Monica He. 2015. Immigration, health, and mortality. In *International encyclopedia of social and behavioral sciences*, vol. 11, 2nd ed., ed. James D. Wright, 654–61. Oxford: Elsevier Press.

Hummer, Robert A., Jan Pacewicz, Shu-Chuan Wang, and Chiquita Collins. 2004. Health insurance coverage in nonmetropolitan America. In *Critical issues in rural health*, eds. Nina Glasgow, Lois Wright Morton, and Nan E. Johnson, 197–210. Ames, IA: Blackwell Publishing.

Hussey, Jon M., Quynh C. Nguyen, Eric A. Whitsel, Liana J. Richardson, Carolyn Tucker Halpern, Penny Gordon-Larsen, Joyce W. Tabor, Pamela P. Entzel, and Kathleen Mullan Harris. 2015. Characteristics and reliability of in-home anthropometry: The National Longitudinal Study of Adolescent to Adult Health, wave IV. *Demographic Research* 32 (39): 1081–98.

Jackson, Kenneth T. 2009. A nation of cities: The federal government and the shape of the American metropolis. *The ANNALS of the American Academy of Political and Social Science* 626 (1): 11–20.

James, Peter, Philip J. Troped, Jaime E. Hart, Corinne E. Joshu, Graham A. Colditz, Ross C. Brownson, Reid Ewing, and Francine Laden. 2013. Urban sprawl, physical activity, and body mass index: Nurses' Health Study and Nurses' Health Study II. *American Journal of Public Health* 103 (2): 369–75.

James, Wesley L. 2014. All rural places are not created equal: Revisiting the rural mortality penalty in the United States. *American Journal of Public Health* 104 (11): 2122–29.

Lee, Hedwig, Dohoon Lee, Guang Guo, and Kathleen Mullan Harris. 2011. Trends in body mass index in adolescence and young adulthood in the United States: 1959–2002. *Journal of Adolescent Health* 49 (6): 601–8.

Lichter, Daniel T., and David L. Brown. 2011. Rural America in an urban society: Changing spatial and social boundaries. *Annual Review of Sociology* 37:565–92.

Lloyd-Jones, Donald M., Yuling Hong, Darwin Labarthe, Dariush Mozaffarian, Lawrence J. Appel, Linda Van Horn, Kurt Greenlund, Stephen Daniels, Graham Nichol, and Gordon F. Tomaselli, et al. 2010. Defining and setting national goals for cardiovascular health promotion and disease reduction: The American Heart Association's strategic impact goal through 2020 and beyond. *Circulation* 121 (4): 586–613.

Monnat, Shannon M., and Camille Beeler Pickett. 2011. Rural/urban differences in self-rated health: Examining the roles of county size and metropolitan adjacency. *Health & Place* 17 (1): 311–19.

Morrill, Richard, John Cromartie, and Gary Hart. 1999. Metropolitan, urban, and rural commuting areas: Toward a better depiction of the United States settlement system. *Urban Geography* 20 (8): 727–48.

Morton, Lois Wright. 2004. Spatial patterns of rural mortality. In *Critical issues in rural health*, eds. Nina Glasgow, Lois Wright Morton, and Nan E. Johnson, 37–45. Ames, IA: Blackwell Publishing.

Pampel, Fred C., Patrick M. Krueger, and Justin T. Denney. 2010. Socioeconomic disparities in health behaviors. *Annual Review of Sociology* 36:349–70.

Probst, Janice C., Jessica D. Bellinger, Katrina M. Walsemann, James Hardin, and Saundra H. Glover. 2011. Higher risk of death in rural blacks and whites than urbanites is related to lower incomes, education, and health coverage. *Health Affairs* 30 (10): 1872–79.

Purnell, Tanjala S., Elizabeth A. Calhoun, Sherita H. Golden, Jacqueline R. Halladay, Jessica L. Krok-Schoen, Bradley M. Appelhans, and Lisa A. Cooper. 2016. Achieving health equity: Closing the gaps in health care disparities, interventions, and research. *Health Affairs* 35 (8): 1410–15.

Rhew, Isaac C., J. David Hawkins, and Sabrina Oesterle. 2011. Drug use and risk among youth in different rural contexts. *Health & Place* 17 (3): 775–83.

Roberts, Megan E., Nathan J. Doogan, Allison N. Kurti, Ryan Redner, Diann E. Gaalema, Cassandra A. Stanton, Thomas J. White, and Stephen T. Higgins. 2016. Rural tobacco use across the United States: How rural and urban areas differ, broken down by census regions and divisions. *Health & Place* 39:153–59.

Saelens, Brian E., James F. Sallis, and Lawrence D. Frank. 2003. Environmental correlates of walking and cycling: Findings from the transportation, urban design, and planning literatures. *Annals of Behavioral Medicine* 25 (2): 80–91.

Singh, Gopal K., and Mohammad Siahpush. 2014. Widening rural-urban disparities in all-cause mortality and mortality from major causes of death in the USA, 1969–2009. *Journal of Urban Health* 91 (2): 272–92.

Sparks, P. Johnelle. 2012. Rural health disparities. In *International handbook of rural demography*, eds. László J. Kulcsár and Katherine J. Curtis, 255–71. Dordrecht, the Netherlands: Springer.

Thoits, Peggy A. 2010. Stress and health major findings and policy implications. *Journal of Health and Social Behavior* 51 (1 Supplement): S41–S53.

U.S. Department of Agriculture (USDA) Economic Research Service. 2016. Rural-urban commuting area codes. Available from http://www.ers.usda.gov/data-products (accessed 7 September 2016).

Whitsel, Eric A., Carmen C. Cuthbertson, Joyce W. Tabor, Alan J. Potter, Mark H. Wener, Patric A. Clapshaw, Ley A. Killeya-Jones, Carolyn T. Halpern, and Kathleen Mullan Harris. 2013. Add Health Wave IV documentation: Lipids. Available from http://www.cpc.unc.edu/projects/addhealth/documen tation (accessed 21 November 2016).

Whitsel, Eric, Joyce W. Tabor, Quynh C. Nguyen, Carmen C. Cuthbertson, Mark H. Wener, Alan J. Potter, Ley A. Killeya-Jones, and Kathleen Mullan Harris. 2012. Add Health Wave IV documentation: Measures of glucose homeostasis. Available from http://www.cpc.unc.edu/projects/addhealth/docu mentation (accessed 21 November 2016).

Yang, Quanhe, Mary E. Cogswell, W. Dana Flanders, Yuling Hong, Zefeng Zhang, Fleetwood Loustalot, Cathleen Gillespie, Robert Merritt, and Frank B. Hu. 2012. Trends in cardiovascular health metrics and associations with all-cause and CVD mortality among US adults. *Journal of the American Medical Association* 307 (12): 1273–83.

Yang, Yang Claire, Courtney Boen, Karen Gerken, Ting Li, Kristen Schorpp, and Kathleen Mullan Harris. 2016. Social relationships and physiological determinants of longevity across the human life span. *Proceedings of the National Academy of Sciences* 113 (3): 578–83.

Reconsidering Territorial Governance to Account for Enhanced Rural-Urban Interdependence in America

By
DAVID L. BROWN
and
MARK SHUCKSMITH

The urban-rural interface is structured by intense social, economic, and environmental interdependencies among urban and rural places. Accordingly, we argue that the rural-urban interface should be governed in a new, hybrid manner—one that accounts for both place-based and relational exigencies. The United States lacks a coherent, coordinated approach to multijurisdictional planning and governance, but multijurisdictional governance can and often does succeed through cooperation at the state and local levels. To illustrate this point, and to ground the theoretical discussion, we present three examples of multijurisdictional planning that are effective at the local level, and one example that has failed to accomplish such goals. Governance of the zone of rural-urban interactions will be more effective and accountable if policies and programs involve not only the constituent municipalities located in this space, but also the social, economic, and environmental relationships in which these communities are embedded.

Keywords: urban-rural interface; territorial; relational; multijurisdictional governance; mobilities turn; soft spaces; spaces of engagement

In U.S. politics, "taking back control" has become a populist theme. But how do local communities and their governments engage with forces of change that transcend their boundaries?

David L. Brown is international professor of development sociology at Cornell University. He is past president of the Rural Sociological Society and past chair of the American Sociological Association's Section on Development Sociology. He is the author or editor of ten books, most recently the Routledge International Handbook of Rural Studies (2016).

Mark Shucksmith is a professor and director of Newcastle University Institute for Social Renewal, UK. He is the author or editor of twelve books, most recently the Routledge International Handbook of Rural Studies (2016). He was awarded the OBE by Queen Elizabeth in 2009 for services to rural development and to crofting.

Correspondence: dlb17@cornell.edu

DOI: 10.1177/0002716217706495

Rural and urban communities all face the challenge of territorial governance in an ever more interdependent world, where many people feel increasingly powerless in the face of forces beyond their democratic control.

America's new rural-urban interface is a case in point, structured by ever more intense social, economic, and environmental interdependencies among urban and rural places and an inability individually to address the broader forces of change. Without cooperation, or coordination at a higher level, local governance is unable to respond effectivity to the challenges of an increasingly interdependent world. One-size-fits-all policies such as the Personal Responsibility and Work Opportunity Reconciliation Act of 1996 (e.g., "welfare reform"), for example, instituted work and training requirements that, while realistic for urban persons, were unattainable for the rural poor in the absence of explicit mechanisms that link rural persons to urban training, child care, and transportation services (Jensen and Chitose 1997). In addition, focusing on one community at a time deflects attention from the collective needs and opportunities that exist in the broader field of multijurisdictional relationships. The result is waste and inefficiency, redundant programs, and missed opportunities for more strategic, effective, and accountable governance. Moreover, competition and conflict between neighboring places reduces the possibilities for cooperative solutions to challenges in the rural-urban interface (OECD 2013). This is especially true in areas such as emergency medical service, fire suppression, and education. In education, for example, go-it-alone strategies often result in a loss of services in smaller rural schools, and even school closures, while intercommunity cooperation in such areas as administrative services, procurement, and the teaching of specialized advanced placement courses could contribute to the viability of local rural schools while guaranteeing access to high-quality education regardless of a student's place of residence.

This article develops a conceptual framework for examining the dynamic organization of communities located in the rural-urban interface, a conceptualization that provides guidance for more effective governance of interaction and interdependence. Castells wrote in 1997 of the "annihilation of space" brought about by advances in information technology, modern transportation, and other societal and global transformations facilitated by deregulation, devolution of authority, ever more mobile capital and labor, and heightened corporate penetration throughout national and global space. Interestingly, much the same language was used in 1852 by Frederick Douglass to describe how the railway, steamship, and telegraph incubated and intensified new patterns of spatial interaction. Here, we examine what such a networked and interdependent world, and associated developments in social science theory, namely, a "relational turn" (Massey 2004)

NOTE: The authors would like to acknowledge the advice and suggestions of two anonymous reviewers. Mark Tewdwr-Jones, Mike Woods, Andy Pike, Dan Lichter, and those attending the TARRN Network meeting in Belfast in May 2016 also made helpful suggestions. As usual, any errors remain the authors' responsibility. This work was supported by USDA NIFA multistate research grant # 1597800 as administered by the Cornell University Agricultural Experiment Station.

and a "mobilities turn" (Urry 2007), implies for the ways we understand the interface between rural and urban space and its governance. More generally, we explore the challenges and opportunities of governing at the urban-rural interface, which, we argue, now requires a more cooperative logic rather than the traditional logic of nested hierarchical, spatial governance (Gualini 2006).

Our goal is to illustrate how current definitions and thinking about political geography represent a conceptual roadblock to spatial integration and governance at the rural-urban interface. We begin by explaining the "rural-urban interface." We then examine emerging patterns of social and economic organization in the rural-urban interface, along with a hybrid conceptualization that acknowledges growing interdependence among bounded places located hierarchically along the rural-urban continuum. We consider the current status of multijurisdictional governance at the regional and local levels, and illustrate how our hybrid approach contributes to more effective and accountable solutions to problems facing people and communities in the rural-urban interface. Our theoretical discussion is grounded in four examples of multijurisdictional governance, which effectively highlight a new perspective on spatial planning shaped by a relational understanding of space and place (Graham and Healey 1999; Healey 2007). This new perspective challenges our current understanding of autonomous bounded territorial entities, and proposes instead that spatial and social boundaries are increasingly porous—hence the term *soft spaces*, introduced later in this article (Paasi and Zimmerbauer 2016, 76). We conclude with some observations about the challenges and opportunities of using a hybrid territorial/relational lens to conceptualize and implement rural-urban governance.

The New Rural-Urban Interface

Social scientists, policy-makers, and social commentators have long observed that a growing amount of social, economic, demographic, political, and environmental activity occurs in the rural-urban interface.[1] Until recently, this urban-rural space (e.g., peri-urban, urban fringe, or rurban) has been thought of as almost entirely under urban control—political and economic influences that radiate outward from the urban core or city. Early regional economic theory, and much contemporary thinking, conceptualized metropolitan regions as an asymmetric set of social and economic relationships whereby the center dominates the hinterland, and places in the hinterland possess little or no collective agency. Shucksmith (2008, 63) has characterized this mode of thought as "cities as the locomotives of economic development, and rural areas as carriages being pulled along in the wake of the great modern metropolis." Ward (2006, 52) has argued that such thinking "reproduces a rural development problem. It establishes and reinforces out-of-date notions of geographic centrality and hierarchies, and it actively marginalises places, consigning them to the periphery, dividing and polarising." This city-centric thinking is the legacy of central place theory (Christaller 1933/1966; Losch 1940/1954), as synthesized, enhanced, and imported into American research on regional economy and society by Bogue (1950), Berry (1967), and many other scholars. Previous research has documented the growing demographic and economic dominance of the nation's large cities (Fischer and Hout 2008). Moreover, central place theory continues to form the fundamental basis of the American system of statistical geography, especially the core-based concepts of metropolitan statistical areas, micropolitan statistical areas, and noncore areas (U.S. Census Bureau 2013).

Recently, however, scholars have reconsidered the hierarchical nature of spatial relationships constituting U.S. metropolitan regions. The urban-rural interface is conceptualized as a space of social and economic interdependence and interpenetration rather than a social or symbolic boundary separating urban from rural life (Lichter and Brown 2011; OECD 2013). The demographic and economic hegemony of the nation's large cities is unmistakable, along with the asymmetrical nature of the power relationship between central cities and hinterland communities. Yet recent scholarship has observed an acceleration in the volume of urban-rural transactions but has begun to question the extent of asymmetry and the relative lack of autonomy possessed by peripheral places, at least in certain types of transactions, such as food security, waste management, recreation and leisure, and environmental services (Lichter and Brown 2014). Similarly, Scott (2011, 857) has argued that the interstitial spaces lying between metropolitan areas are undergoing significant transformation "as they become increasingly articulated with the rhythms and cultures of the modern metropolis," and scholars such as Harrison and Heley (2014, 1118) and Cloke (2006, 19) suggest that this "urbanization of the rural" is accompanied by "ruralization of the urban" as processes of deconcentration, decentralization, and gentrification lead the urban form to adopt very strong rural characteristics.

In this article we employ a relational[2] perspective to examine the spatial organization of the rural-urban interface. We see the interface as a space that is produced and reproduced by social, economic, environmental, and other types of transactions that occur on a regular basis and are part and parcel of a metropolitan region's essential organization and structure. We see these rural-urban relationships whether they involve commuting and labor market mobility, land use changes, direct marketing of urban services or agricultural produce, or the hauling of urban trash to rural landfills as providing possibilities for collaboration on one hand and conflict on the other. These relationships are infused with power, the deployment of which is often opaque and obscured. The rural-urban interface is not neatly bounded by governmental or politico-administrative borders. It is a multilevel, polycentric space where governance flows across units and jurisdictions (Homsy and Warner 2013), a "space of flows" as Castells (1989) terms it.[3] In this article, we critique approaches that unduly privilege governmental units and fail to engage with the social, economic, political, and environmental relationships in which places are embedded.

In principle, an approach that addresses both relational and territorial aspects of the settlement system could be achieved, as noted above, either by hierarchical coordination from a higher level of government or by horizontal cooperation. The next section explains why we believe that the coordinated approach is decreasingly possible in contemporary America. We then set out an alternative, cooperative conceptual framework to help policy-makers consider how to design and implement effective and accountable governance structures in support of people and communities in the rural-urban interface. Our framework is derived from the new spatial planning literature, as articulated by scholars such as Allmendinger and Haughton (2009), Gualini (2006), and Paasi (2013). While it embraces relational thinking, it also acts within legally sanctioned spaces (Allmendinger, Chilla, and Sielker 2014; Shucksmith, Brown, and Vergunst 2012; Cox 1993). Hence, our framework features a hybrid of territorial and relational thought, addressing both bounded political and administrative territories and the social, economic, and environmental relationships in which these communities are enmeshed and embedded.

A Lack of Coordination: The Rise and Fall of National-Level Regional Planning in the United States

The U.S. federal government does not have an overarching regional development policy (OECD 2010). A 2009 World Development Report background paper contended that regional policy in the United States comprises "a complex web of (often poorly) integrated programs … that operate at different and often overlapping scales" (Hewings, Feser, and Poole 2009, 2). The report goes on to observe that the "degree of coordination across spatial governance regimes is often ad hoc at best." Moreover, Drabenstott (2006) has shown that only a small fraction of U.S. development-oriented programs actually focus on either place-specific development, for example Housing and Urban Development's (HUD's) Community Development Block Grant Program; or broader area and regional development, for example, the Commerce Department's network of multicounty economic development districts (EDD). Instead, the majority of development-related funding and program effort is focused on physical infrastructure, education, and housing programs that occur in specific, bounded places. These observations are consistent with Storper et al.'s (2015) recent study of San Francisco's and Los Angeles' differing fortunes since 1970. They concluded that "it is not realistic to propose that regions devise formal strategies for regional economic development in the U.S. There would be no agency to implement them even if they were well designed. … In addition, existing interests in fragmentation and overlap are entrenched and supported by a widely shared ideology of community economic development and local control" (Storper et al. 2015, 227).

The United States did not always suffer from a relative lack of national-level programs promoting and supporting multijurisdictional planning and development. In fact, as late as the early 1980s, the United States had a robust system of substate regionalism. At that time, a wide variety of regional councils and agencies was supported by federal grant programs. These councils operated in both metropolitan and nonmetropolitan areas. Nonmetropolitan regional councils tended to place emphasis on general management, planning, and policy advice to local governments, while metropolitan councils devoted attention to planning in such specific areas as environmental quality and transportation (Stam and Reid 1980). Most of the programs assisted regional organizations that performed specific functions, such as transportation, land use planning, or economic development. Some of the federal programs, however, such as those focusing on health care planning, only assisted substate regional organizations devoted to particular functions.[4] Most, but not all, of these federal programs were available nationwide.

Substate regionalism began after World War II in the United States, and accelerated greatly during the early 1970s. For about a decade, the federal government had a significant impact on the growth of substate regionalism. According to research by the Advisory Commission on Intergovernmental Relations (ACIR; 1977), only five federal planning grant programs for community development used an area-wide approach in 1964. By 1972, there were twenty-four such programs, and thirty-two by 1976 (ACIR 1979). Beginning in the late sixties, the federal government coordinated general purpose regional development programs through a network of A-95 regional clearinghouses. In addition, regional planning and service delivery for single functions such as health care, transportation, mental health, and environmental quality management were also developed during this time. Federally mandated planning in general, and substate regionalism in particular, dwindled by the late 1970s. Neither the Carter nor the Reagan administration nor Congress was willing to sustain it (Bowman and Franke 2008). The Reagan administration was especially hostile to the idea of federal planning. With its supply side view of the market, the culture of planning was seen to limit the reach of market mechanisms, and to substitute professional for consumer judgment (Melhado 2006). Accordingly, nationally managed substate regionalism virtually disappeared in the United States after 1980.[5]

Toward Cooperation: A Territorial Framework for Examining Governance of the Rural-Urban Interface

Without regional or subregional governance, atomized local government is likely to lose its capacity to perform effectively in an increasingly interdependent, networked, and neoliberal world (Lewis et al. 2013). This will take place in the face of market and other forces, which transcend spatial or place boundaries. Jobs are offshored, services centralized or withdrawn, and decisions made far away in boardrooms and offices without knowledge of or commitment to the places concerned.

Some scholars have characterized these transformations in terms of the differential mobility of people in places, arguing that this difference is becoming an increasingly potent stratifying factor of life chances in our late modern or postmodern times, because the differential mobility of people in places constrain some while enabling others, whether in urban or rural settings (Urry 2007).

These ideas have become widely adopted in sociology to the extent that they are referred to as a "mobilities turn." Complementary to this is the "relational turn," which is being explored by geographers and planners, both in Europe and America. They focus on the social and networked nature of space and scale (Friedmann 1993; Amin 2004; Massey 2004, 2005; Thrift 2004), and the increasingly "porous" nature of boundaries and borders (Amin 2002, 391). These writers dispute "the idea that space can be understood as a 'container' and scales as nested hierarchies of bounded and partitioned spaces" (Allmendinger, Chilla, and Sielker 2014, 2703). Nevertheless, there is a recognition that portraying relational and territorial spaces as unduly dichotomous may be unhelpful, and that both may be significant.

This raises many questions for both rural and urban studies. Most fundamentally, recognition of the networked nature of space and scale, and the porous nature of boundaries and borders might call into question the notion of "place" itself, place-based development, the rural-urban binary implicit in rural or urban studies, and, important for this article, the liminal space of the rural-urban interface. However, we argue that, while the extent and nature of mobility have increased in contemporary society and new forms of mobility are restructuring people's social and economic lives, people still solve the challenges of everyday life in places that are meaningful for them (Shucksmith, Brown, and Vergunst 2012; Beynon and Hudson 1993). Accordingly, we reject a simple territorial versus relational dichotomy, and see the rural-urban interface as a synthesis of place-based relationships and broader relational processes, both of which must be addressed. In other words, local governance might draw upon and employ a range of relational networks that stretch beyond the local jurisdiction, but these are still simultaneously lodged within their territories (Allen and Cochrane 2010).

To this end, "Local and regional actors construct 'spaces of engagement' (or networks of association) that link them to regional, national, or supranational institutions in order to secure their local 'spaces of dependence'—areas in which their prosperity, power, or legitimacy relies on the reproduction of certain social relations" (Mackinnon 2010, 5). Other attempts to overcome the territorial/relational dualism have drawn on a range of theories, or revived the concept of localities in terms of absolute, relative, and relational space (Jones and Woods 2014; Anderson and McFarlane 2011). Jones and Woods (2014) make the important point that to have analytical value any locality must have both material coherence and imagined coherence. In other words, there must both be institutional structures that hold a locality together and provide vehicles for collective action, and there must also be a shared sense of identity that makes that place meaningful as a space of collective action.

So while increasing mobilities and global flows are restructuring the nature of rural-urban and global-local relationships, places still matter. Many institutions such as councils are still place-based and places still have meaning for those who live there. The challenge for governance in the rural-urban interface is to simultaneously acknowledge the legitimacy of place-based interests while also engaging with transcendent inter-place relationships through constructing spaces of engagement.

This combination of relational and territorial insights has implications for multilevel governance in many spheres, and not only with respect to the rural-urban interface. First, this calls into question how we conceive of place-based policies, whether characterized as "bottom-up" (endogenous) or "top-down" (exogenous) in rural studies, "place-shaping" in urban studies and planning (Forester 1999), and "asset-based community development" or "community capitals" approaches (Flora and Flora 2008).

Our perspective on governance in the rural-urban interface is shaped by the notion of networked development (Shucksmith 2012; Lowe, Murdoch, and Ward 1995; Ray 2006). This notion proposes that social and economic development processes combine bottom-up, internal (endogenous) forces and top-down, external (exogenous) forces. The local necessarily interacts with the extra-local in contemporary networked society, with importance attached to both vertical (hierarchical) and horizontal networks (Schucksmith 2010). Critical to the socioeconomic development process are those institutions, actors, and networks that have the capacity to link businesses, communities, and institutions involved in governance at a variety of scales. Networked development therefore involves not only deliberative governance and territorial place shaping, but also institutional capacity building and sharing of responsibilities with an enabling state and other external actors (Shucksmith 2012). Places need to be integrated within wider networks and structures so that external resources can be readily appropriated when they are absent or damaged in the local setting, and to secure their wider spaces of association in a networked world.

Challenges to fundamental spatial concepts such as territory, border, and place have also been central to recent developments in planning theory, notably the emergence of a new "spatial planning" founded upon a relational understanding of space and place (Graham and Healey 1999; Healey 2007). While planners "have traditionally thought and practiced with and through clearly bounded scales (national, regional, local), in this century the new spatial planning is imposing relationally inscribed concepts ... into the lexicon of spatial planners" (Heley 2013, 1325). "Relational thinking has challenged the understanding of the world as a simple continuum of bounded territorial entities and suggests that regions are social constructs and results of power struggles, and that their borders are increasingly porous" (Paasi and Zimmerbauer 2016, 76). Nevertheless, consistent with our contention that governance should reflect a combination of relational and territorial thinking, the legitimacy and accountability of planners is still seen to reside in bounded territories, with their electorates, laws, and regulatory codes. For this reason, Cochrane and Ward (2012, 7) argue that "policy-making has to be understood as both relational and territorial, as both in motion and simultaneously fixed, or embedded in place. Rather than seeing this as an inherently contradictory process, however, what matters is to be able to explore the ways in which the working through of this tension serves to produce policies and places, policies in place."

In the absence of hierarchical coordination at the regional or subregional level, cooperation between local jurisdictions offers, in principle, an alternative approach to engaging with the relational forces of change that transcend political and administrative boundaries. But can they succeed in practice in enabling policymaking that is both territorial and relational?

Practical attempts to govern the rural-urban interface more effectively through a hybrid of relational and territorial thinking at the state and local level have indeed emerged in the United States. We have seen in the previous section that the decline of national-level coordination of regional planning in the United States frustrates the need to address both territorial and relational aspects of governance, and this section has advanced an alternative conceptual approach that makes a case for cooperation. We turn now, in the next section, to concrete examples of relational governance in action at the state and local levels, suggesting that such cooperation may be more feasible and appropriate to the American context than hierarchical coordination. These examples ground the theoretical discussion, and show how the relational and territorial perspectives help U.S. planners and policy-makers to reassert the promise of multiscalar governance and planning in the rural-urban interface.

Multijurisdictional Governance and Planning in the United States: Cooperative Approaches

While we have seen that the United States lacks a coherent national approach to multijurisdictional governance, many states, and some metropolitan areas, have developed thoughtful and innovative approaches to assist in regional planning and development. These schemes can be comprehensive and multifunctional in nature, or focused on a particular function such as waste management, fire protection, or water supply. We provide three examples of effective state-level comprehensive planning and development schemes to show that multijurisdictional planning and governance exists and succeeds in the United States and to describe their similarities and differences of focus and organization. These examples are all consistent with the hybridized territorial and relational approach to rural-urban interface governance proposed above. We also include one example of a lack of cooperation frustrating effective governance.

Walworth County's comprehensive plan

In 1999, the Wisconsin Legislature enacted the "smart growth" law that provided a new framework for the development, adoption, and implementation of comprehensive plans by counties, cities, villages, and towns (Southeastern Wisconsin Regional Planning Commission 2009). A good example of this was developed by Walworth County. Walworth, located in the southeast corner of the state, comprises the Whitewater-Elkhorn micropolitan statistical area. Its 102,000 persons are spread across fifteen towns that include five small cities, ten villages, and open country. In addition, it is contiguous to both the Milwaukee and Racine metropolitan statistical areas. Accordingly, Walworth County is squarely in the rural-urban interface. In response to the state's requirements, Walworth County, in cooperation with thirteen of its fifteen towns, prepared a multijurisdictional comprehensive plan that includes issues and opportunities; housing; transportation; utilities and community facilities; agricultural, natural, and cultural resources; economic development; intergovernmental cooperation; land use; and implementation (Walworth County Wisconsin 2010). The plan was developed, and is governed, by a smart growth technical advisory committee that includes one elected representative from each participating town and five Walworth County board representatives at large. The technical advisory committee, the county board, and the participating towns designed a public participation plan at the onset. This essential part of the process seeks to obtain a high level of public input throughout the course of the planning. Hence, the Walworth plan exemplifies the territorial and relational thinking that we propose in this article.

The comprehensive land use plan through the year 2035 is among the most important impacts of Walworth County's multijurisdictional approach. The county-wide land use plan was developed to achieve basic consistency among the fifteen individual town land use plans while at the same time promoting long-standing county planning objectives of protecting important natural and agricultural resources and preserving the unique characteristics of the county, while accommodating expected growth and development (Walworth County Wisconsin 2009).

Flagstaff, Arizona's fire suppression initiative

Flagstaff, Arizona, is located in the middle of the world's largest contiguous ponderosa pine forest. According to forest ecologists at the University of Northern Arizona, decades of putting fires out has caused the forest to get too dense, making it more susceptible to big, hot, devastating fires. Without action, unnaturally large and severe wildfire exacerbated by climate change will destroy the forests and put communities at risk. Faced with this probable fate, the Four Forest Restoration Initiative (FFRI) was established to conduct landscape-scale restoration planning and implementation to protect critical wildlife habitat, safeguard communities, and create jobs. The goal is to restore a vast set of forests, grasslands, and springs in Arizona's high country.

After decades of devastating wildfires and a year of discussions, the U.S. Forest Service, other natural resource agencies, community leaders, environmentalists, scientists, and private industry leaders established the FFRI to restore forest ecosystems on four national forests in Arizona. The initiative includes a multiparty monitoring effort to share diverse perspectives between multiple interests and stakeholders, to foster understanding, and to incorporate the latest scientific evidence concerning environmental and forest management. The FFRI is a collaborative effort involving more than thirty individual public and private entities. This diverse group includes the city of Flagstaff and other municipalities, the county, the state, the timber industry, the National Park Service, and the U.S. Forest Service. These stakeholders meet monthly, do research, and work with the Forest Service to create small controlled fires and remove brush and weeds that can lead to large uncontrolled fires that endanger communities, housing, and wildlife. This is a collaborative process. FFRI differs

from many past forest management schemes in that it pays attention to both territorial entities such as local government, and to the relationships that link them
together in a sociobiological ecosystem. In other words, the initiative's organizational model is consistent with the hybrid territorial/relational model put forth in
this article, and the urban-rural interface that envelops Flagstaff and its environs
is part of the ecosystem being managed by FFRI.

New York City's watershed

Watershed management is a clear example of successful multiscalar governance of natural resources (Bloomquist and Schlager 2005). Watersheds are often
located, at least in part, in the rural-urban interface. Hence, this is a good example through which to examine how the (cooperative and competitive) relationships joining urban and rural communities can be mobilized to structure and
regulate the use of water located in the hinterland of large cities. Since decisions
about the control of water are made by individuals and groups, developing unified authorities involving multiple jurisdictions is especially challenging. We
examine this process through the lens of the New York City (NYC) watershed.

NYC obtains its water from a system of reservoirs located in the Catskill Mountains
and the Hudson River Valley (see Figure 1). The water is of exceptionally high quality, and requires less treatment and filtration than other urban water systems. Hence,
social and economic activities occurring in the vicinity of NYC's water sources
increase the risks of contamination and the need for expensive filtration and other
kinds of treatment. Not surprisingly, NYC seeks to control land use in the vicinity of
its reservoirs by purchasing conservation easements and by restricting economic
activities such as dairy farming. In the early 1990s, NYC proposed regulatory actions
that aroused fears that agriculture and other economic activities in the watershed
would be significantly curtailed. Specifically, NYC's proposed regulations would have
produced buffer zones around water sources, restricted construction of new sewer
connections, and led to significant land purchases by the city around reservoirs and
water courses. These potential outcomes generated contentious negotiations between
NYC and forty-one communities located in the watershed.

The forty-one localities each had a strong individual interest but lacked a collective "regional identity." NYC's proposed regulatory actions awakened a long-
held and widespread view of NYC as an "oppressor" of rural towns that dated
back to the early part of the twentieth century when the city constructed the
West of Hudson Water System (Pfeffer and Wagenet 2003). This oppositional
view helped to spur a community development process among the forty-one
towns in the NYC watershed that resulted in the establishment of the Coalition
of Watershed Towns. This coalition negotiated a mutually advantageous memo-
randum of agreement (MOA) with NYC in 1997. The MOA permitted NYC to
purchase land or conservation easements if NYC agreed not to exercise eminent
domain to acquire land for watershed protection. In addition, the Watershed
Protection and Partnership Program, involving NYC and the forty-one watershed
towns, was established as a mechanism to protect the watershed's ecology, while
at the same time protecting the social and economic vitality of the watershed

FIGURE 1
The New York City Watershed

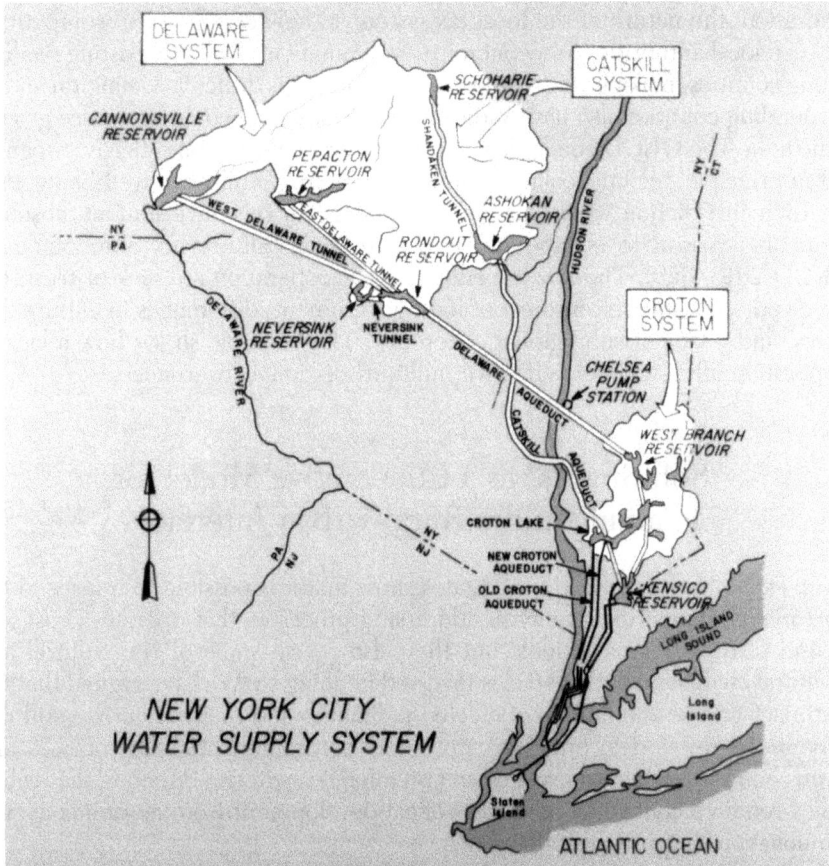

communities. Hence, this multiscalar governance process "encompasses the interests of both water quality protection for downstream consumers, and the social and economic well-being for upstream residents" (Pfeffer and Wagenet 2003, 114). This integrated, regional watershed management system provides a mechanism for accountability that sets performance standards and responds to diverse community interests (Bloomquist and Schlager 2005). As a result, NYC has avoided costly infrastructure and operating expenditures while upstate communities have been able to seek development initiatives consistent with the MOA.

Lexington, Kentucky

A recent OECD report (2013) on rural-urban partnerships shows that, despite the potential advantages of a cooperative approach to multijurisdictional governance, substantial obstacles to cooperation remain, particularly in their case study, Lexington, Kentucky. The report showed that trust is lacking between the individual county governments composing Lexington's metropolitan region, and, in addition, the nature of the local tax system stimulates aggressive competition between local authorities for economic development and adds to existing rivalries among counties, making cooperation and partnerships difficult. Lexington and its surrounding counties also have radically different perspectives on future growth in the area. The OECD concludes that "while virtually all local officials recognize that in principle, regional collaboration could improve collective well-being, they fear their jurisdiction would lose in the process. In this environment, absent a compelling reason to collaborate, it is safer politically to act autonomously" (OECD 2013, 329). The key impediments to cooperation are lack of trust, the perceived economic self-interest of local government, differences in culture and values, and a lack of subregional coherence. This example shows how a lack of cooperation often hampers effective multijurisdictional governance.

"Soft Spaces" as a Cooperative Model for Planning in the Rural-Urban Interface

These examples from the United States show that it is possible to transcend the territorial/relational dichotomy in addressing processes that operate across and beyond territorial jurisdictions, but they also reveal some of the cultural and structural challenges and obstacles involved in doing so. We have argued that the legitimacy and accountability of elected politicians and their executives still rest in bounded territories, but they must now confront relational processes and porous boundaries that transcend but also inhabit territories. Meeting these challenges requires conceptual and theoretical development from academia as well as innovations in practices of governance.

In this final section, we raise the question of whether the concept of "soft space," inspired by developments in European and UK planning and economic development practice, might offer potential in both these respects for America. Indeed, Allmendinger and Haughton (2009) introduced the concept of soft space to show how relational thinking can influence not just research and spatial analysis but also spatial policy and practice. They noticed that spatial planning, while still tied legally to set boundaries for formal plans, was in practice also operating informally beyond its jurisdiction. Planners had found ways of extending their reach over "soft spaces," beyond the borders of their jurisdiction, to address processes that stretched further afield, such as housing demand, commuting, and water supplies. This was achieved by working with a broad range of public, private, and civil society actors who were able to transcend individual jurisdictions and thereby engage with complex, multilayered, fluid, and, sometimes, fuzzy scales of policy and governance arrangements.

In short, planners have already been found to be at work in subregions that do not conform to politico-administrative boundaries, often in city-regions[6] or in other urban-rural interfaces, such as around London. This responds to a policy impetus to break away from the shackles of preexisting patterns of governance that are viewed as slow, bureaucratic, or not reflecting the real geographies of problems and opportunities (Allmendinger and Haughton 2009, 619). Allmendinger, Chilla, and Sielker (2014, 2705) therefore conceptualize soft spaces as new spaces for governance that can be relatively enduring or ephemeral, formal or informal, centrally sanctioned or locally driven. They argue that these spaces provide an opportunity to address mismatches between administrative and functional areas by creating bespoke spaces for dealing with specific issues such as regeneration, integrating different sectors such as transport, infrastructure, and education, in processes operating at various scales.

The bottom line—and why we think these concepts are critical to American thinking about governance and policy development in the rural-urban interface—is that soft spaces are hybrids of territorial and relational space. They are so both conceptually and in practical application, enabling (bounded) municipalities or communities and their executives to engage with relational flows and processes that transcend boundaries. For this reason, the developing literature on soft space and fuzzy boundaries may be an avenue worth exploring for U.S. practitioners and U.S. political and social scientists.

To that end, a brief introduction to that literature is sketched here. The soft space approach has some practical advantages that enable cooperation to proceed even where there are significant obstacles to formal collaboration. Perhaps its most attractive feature is its informality and the scope afforded for creativity and experimentation (alongside political deniability). Indeed, it is this experimental and political dimension to multijurisdictional schemes that allows them to be used politically, testing strategies and approaches to an issue without ceding ultimate authority (Allmendinger, Chilla, and Sielker 2014, 2706). This, of course, is double-edged and has its dangers alongside the advantages.

Thus, a potentially serious criticism of such informal approaches, and a challenge both for practice and academia, is what we characterize as the dark side of multijurisdictional governance: that is, the potential of such practices to obscure power arrangements and be nondemocratic. Soft spaces may allow experiments and initiatives to escape democratic scrutiny to the benefit of powerful actors, while obscuring where power actually resides. For example, Allmendinger and Haughton (2009) argue that the development of (so-called) sustainable communities in the Thames Gateway in the spaces between formal agencies and plans and strategies has been used to overcome resistance to new housing development. Olsen and Richardson (2011, 361) see such use of multijurisdictional governance as a way of camouflaging contested spatial politics, while Paasi and Zimmerbauer (2016, 88) emphasize that power in such processes derives not from one electorate or its officers but is embedded in a complex assemblage of actors, interactions, interests, negotiations, struggles, and events that occur through networks, perhaps facilitating capture of democratic processes by social elites. This raises the question of how to enjoy the advantages of working in this informal, creative way while also ensuring transparency and accountability.

From an analytical perspective, we offer two further criticisms of the concept of soft space, neither of which may impede its practical governance application to rural-urban interaction. First, the soft spaces may only loosely be said to create hybrids of territorial and relational space, since they only seem to apply to contiguous territories and relations that overspill administrative boundaries, rather than in circumstances where it is harder to map relational space on to territorial space. In this sense, soft spaces may be more akin to Jones and Woods's (2014) lens of *relative space* than *relational space*. This may matter less when focusing on subregional or regional rural-urban interdependencies than if we were concerned with the noncontiguous urban-rural interdependencies of the global agrifood complex, for example. Second, because soft space derives from planning theory, it still privileges governments (local, regional, and national) as social and political actors, despite the diminished role of local governments under neoliberalism in an interconnected world.

These emerging approaches to transcending the territorial/relational dichotomy have advantages and dangers, therefore, some of which may be inherent but others may be avoidable. The concepts of soft space and fuzzy boundaries emanate from a substantial international literature from which American academics and practitioners can draw in developing appropriate approaches to conceptualizing and addressing pressing issues in the rural-urban interface.

Conclusion: The Promise of Relational Governance at the Rural-Urban Interface

In this article we have framed the rural-urban interface as a social and economic space that is produced and reproduced by social, economic, political, and other kinds of relationships between urban and rural communities. Rather than being a boundary that divides rural from urban space, the interface is a zone of intense interaction that links rural and urban people and communities. We drew on ideas from European planning and geography to develop a conceptual framework for examining the dynamic structures and processes that construct the interface, and as a basis for multiscalar governance of rural-urban space where diverse processes are structuring and restructuring everyday life. The dynamic model we propose is a hybrid of territorial and relational spaces that enables (bounded) electorates and their executives to engage with relational flows and processes that transcend political and municipal boundaries.

This hybrid of territorial and relational thinking identifies the real geographies of problems and opportunities, thereby minimizing the mismatch between administrative and functional areas. Places, with their institutions, governments, histories, and legacies, matter in present-day America, but these entities are embedded in complex multiscalar networks where much social, economic, and political life is transacted. Hence, governance in the rural-urban interface can be more effective, responsive, and accountable where both territorial and relational aspects of rural and urban space are considered and accounted for in policy development and program administration.

We have argued that the soft space approach is flexible and dynamic, but that it carries a risk of obscuring power relationships and undermining democratic governance. Instead we propose a hybrid, cooperative approach that, while still flexible and experimental, can help to minimize the antidemocratic tendencies of soft space because concrete communities have histories, legacies, and identities, or what Jones and Woods (2014) have called material and imagined coherence. We used diverse examples to ground our discussion of the hybrid governance model, and to demonstrate that these theoretical concepts can be translated into real-world practice, so long as we also learn from experiences and studies in the UK and Europe as well as those in the United States. Our perspective includes not only the network society of enhanced connectivity and interdependencies, but also the changed role of government and administrative borders and place-based actors.

Consistent with our contention that a hybrid approach can be effective and accountable, Storper and his colleagues (2015) showed that San Francisco's superior performance in terms of gross value added (GVA) per capita compared with that of Los Angeles is at least partly related to its adoption of multijurisdictional governance. They observe that while neither San Francisco nor Los Angeles has a single regional development agency with powers to coordinate regional development policies, "nevertheless, many regionally important projects are carried out by either the biggest cities in the region or by special-purpose agencies created by political coalitions among the cities and counties," including, for example, water supplies and transport infrastructure (Storper et al. 2015, 145). However, the study concludes that San Francisco has learned about the benefits of multiscalar cooperation and has built effective institutions for cooperation since the 1950s, with the councils in the Bay Area learning how to collaborate effectively, while "Los Angeles county inspires competition and rejection by its neighbor counties" (Storper et al. 2015, 168).

These authors draw attention to the relational processes that cut across administrative territories: "metropolitan regions rarely have agencies whose role is to promote regional economic development but instead rely on a patchwork of cities and counties and their many departments and agencies ... this is a problem because economies operate at regional scales, with causes and effects that do not respect the borders of cities and counties or the different powers of their dizzying array of agencies and policies" (Storper et al. 2015, 226). Indeed, while many factors are involved, Storper and colleagues find that networks and relational landscapes are far more significant to the divergence of these regional economies (Storper et al. 2015, 169–70, 201–8) than the usual factors used to explain urban growth. Entrepreneurs in San Francisco were able to draw on boundary-spanning economic and social networks, which enabled them to combine knowledge from different fields as well as to facilitate the emergence of an innovative organizational ecology and an open source culture.

We believe that governance of the rural-urban interface will be more effective and accountable if policies and programs involve not only the constituent municipalities located in this interface but also the social, economic, and environmental relationships in which these communities are embedded. This hybrid approach can produce effective governance at the urban-rural interface, in potentially contentious areas as waste management; infrastructure development; changing land use patterns, including but not limited to the location of housing; economic activities; municipal facilities such as transportation and waste water treatment plants; environmental protection and natural resources management; and local food systems.

Notes

1. While this article focuses on the United States, the general framework that we develop is relevant to highly developed, capitalist economies in general. The framework that we propose is largely influenced by the European, the UK in particular, planning and social geographic literatures.

2. A "relational perspective" means that we focus on the relationships between people that may stretch across space. These include, for example, market relations, power relations, gender relations.

3. Flows of people, workers, capital, information, waste, and so on.

4. For example, Area Agencies on Aging (AAAs) were established under the Older Americans Act (OAA) in 1973 to respond to the needs of those 60 and older in every local community. There are currently more than 670 AAAs around the country.

5. Two exceptions to the demise of multijurisdictional planning and development programs in the United States should be mentioned: (a) The Appalachian Regional Commission (ARC) and (b) The U.S. Department of Commerce's Economic Development Administration (EDA). The ARC's purpose is to ameliorate regional underdevelopment through "the coordinated effort of a regional development organization working with state and local development units" (Hewings, Feser, and Poole 2009, 7; Isserman and Rephann 1995). The EDA is one of the only U.S. programs explicitly tasked with promoting substate regional planning and development. EDA's top three priorities include: (a) supporting long-term coordinated economic development, (b) supporting innovation and competitiveness, and (c) encouraging entrepreneurship (U.S. EDA 2007).

6. A city-region is the functional region around a city, consisting of several areas of local government.

References

Advisory Commission on Intergovernmental Relations (ACIR). 1977. *A catalogue of federal grant-In-aid programs to state and local governments: Grants funded FY 1975.* A- 52a. Washington, DC: U.S. Government Printing Office.

Advisory Commission on Intergovernmental Relations (ACIR). 1979. *A catalogue of federal grant-in-aid programs to state and local governments: grants funded FY 1978.* A-72. Washington, DC: U.S. Government Printing Office.

Allen, John, and Allan D. Cochrane. 2010. Assemblages of state power: Topological shifts in the organization of government and politics. *Antipode* 42 (5): 1071–89.

Allmendinger, Phil, Tobias Chilla, and Franziska Sielker. 2014. Europeanizing territoriality: Towards soft spaces? *Environment and Planning A* 46 (11): 2703–27.

Allmendinger, Phil, and Graham Haughton. 2009. Soft spaces, fuzzy boundaries, and metagovernance: The new spatial planning in the Thames gateway. *Environment and Planning A* 41(3): 617–33.

Amin, Ash. 2002. Spatialities of globalisation. *Environment and Planning A* 34 (3): 385–99.

Amin, Ash. 2004. Regions unbound: Towards a new politics of place. *Geografiska Annaler B* 86 (1): 33–44.

Anderson, Ben, and Colin McFarlane. 2011. Assemblage in geography. *Area* 43 (2): 124–27.

Berry, Brian J .L. 1967. *Geography of market centers and retail distribution.* Englewood Cliffs, NJ: Prentice Hall.

Beynon, Huw, and Ray Hudson. 1993. Place and space in contemporary Europe: Some lessons and reflections. *Antipode* 25 (3): 177–90.

Bloomquist, William, and Edella Schlager. 2005. Political pitfalls of integrated watershed management. *Society and Natural Resources* 18 (2): 101–17.

Bogue, Donald. 1950. *The structure of the metropolitan community: A study of dominance and subdominance*. Ann Arbor, MI: University of Michigan Press.

Bowman, Ann, and James Franke. 2008. The decline of substate regionalism. *Journal of Urban Affairs* 6 (4): 51–63.

Castells, Manuel. 1989. *The informational city: Information technology, economic restructuring, and the urban regional process*. Cambridge, MA: Blackwell Publishers.

Castells, Manuel. 1997. *The rise of the network society*. London: Blackwell Publishers.

Christaller, Walter. 1933/1966. *Die zentralen orte in suddeutschland* [*Central places in southern Germany*]. Trans. by C. W. Baskin. Englewood Cliffs: Prentice Hall.

Cloke, Paul. 2006. Conceptualising rurality. In *The handbook of rural studies*, eds. Paul Cloke, Terry Marsden, and Patrick Mooney, 18–28. London: Sage Publications.

Cochrane, Allen, and Kevin Ward. 2012. Researching the possibilities of policy mobility: Confronting the methodological challenges. Guest editorial. *Environment and Planning A* 44 (1): 5–12.

Cox, Kevin R. 1993. The local and the global in the new urban politics: A critical view. *Environment and Planning D: Society and Space* 11 (4): 433–48.

Douglass, Fredrick. 1852. What, to the Slave, Is the 4th of July? Speech in Rochester, New York. Available from http://www.blackpast.org/1852-frederick-douglass-what-slave-fourth-july.

Drabenstott, Mark. 2006. Rethinking federal policy for regional development. *Economic Review* 91 (1): 115–42.

Fischer, Claude, and Michael Hout. 2008. *Century of difference: How America changed over the last 100 years*. New York, NY: Russell Sage Foundation.

Flora, Cornelia, and Jan Flora, eds. 2008. *Rural communities: Legacy and change*. 3rd ed. Boulder, CO: Westview Press.

Forester, John. 1999. *The deliberative practitioner: Encouraging participatory planning processes*. Boston, MA: MIT Press.

Friedmann, John. 1993. Towards a non-Euclidian mode of planning. *Journal of the American Planning Association* 59 (4): 482–84.

Graham, Stephen, and Patsy Healey. 1999. Relational concepts of space and place: Issues for planning theory and practice. *European Planning Studies* 7 (5): 623–46.

Gualini, Enrico. 2006. The rescaling of governance in Europe: New spatial and institutional rationales. *European Planning Studies* 14 (7): 881–904.

Harrison, John, and Jesse Heley. 2014. Governing beyond the metropolis: Placing the rural in city-region development. *Urban Studies* 52 (6): 1113–33.

Healey, Patsy. 2007. *Urban complexity and spatial strategies: Towards a relational planning for our times*. London: Routledge.

Heley, Jesse. 2013. Soft spaces, fuzzy boundaries and spatial governance in post-devolution Wales. *International Journal of Urban and Regional Research* 37 (4): 1325–48.

Hewings, Geoffrey, Edward Feser, and Ken Poole. 2009. *Spatial/territorial development policies in the United States*. Background paper. World Development Report: Reshaping Economic Geography. Washington, DC: World Bank. Available from http://siteresources.worldbank.org/INTWDRS/Resources/477365- 1327525347307/8392086-1327527757537/Hewings.pdf.

Homsy, George, and Mildred Warner. 2013. Climate change and the co-production of knowledge and policy in rural USA communities. *Sociologia Ruralis* 53 (3): 291–310.

Jensen, Leif, and Yoshimi Chitose. 1997. Will workfare work? Job availability for welfare recipients in rural and urban America. *Population Research and Policy Review* 16 (4): 383–95.

Isserman, Andrew, and Terance Rephann. 1995. The economic effects of the Appalachian regional commission. *Journal of the American Planning Association* 61 (3): 345–65.

Jones, Martin, and Michael Woods. 2014. New localities. *Regional Studies* 47 (1): 29–42.

Lewis, Nick, Richard Le Heron, Hugh Campbell, Matthew Henry, Erena Le Heron, Eric Pawson, Harvey Perkins, Michael Roche, and Christopher Rosin. 2013. Assembling biological economics: Region-shaping initiatives in making and retaining value. *New Zealand Geographer* 69 (3):180–96.

Lichter, Daniel, and David L. Brown. 2011. Rural America in an urban society: Changing spatial and social boundaries. *Annual Review of Sociology* 37:565–92.

Lichter, Daniel, and David L. Brown. 2014. The new rural-urban interface: Lessons for higher education. *Choices* 29 (1): 1–6.

Losch, August. 1940/1954. Die raumliche ordnung der wirtschaft [*The economics of location*]. Trans. by Walter Woglom and Wolfgang Stolper. New Haven, CT: Yale University Press.

Lowe, Philip, John Murdoch, and Neil Ward. 1995. Networks in rural development: Beyond endogenous and exogenous models. In *Beyond modernisation: The impact of endogenous rural development*, eds. Jan D. van der Ploeg and Gert van Dijk, 87–105. Assen, the Netherlands: Van Gorcum.

Mackinnon, Danny. 2010. Reconstructing scale: Towards a new scalar politics. *Progress in Human Geography* 35 (1): 21–36.

Massey, Doreen. 2004. The political challenge of relational space: Introduction to the Vega Symposium. *Geografiska Annaler B* 86 (1): 3.

Massey, Doreen. 2005. *For space*. London: Sage Publications.

Melhado, Evan. 2006. Health planning in the United States and the decline of public-interest policymaking. *Milbank Quarterly* 84 (2): 359–440.

OECD. 2010. *Regional development policies in OECD countries*. Paris: OECD. Available from http://www.oecd.org/gov/regional- policy/regionaldevelopmentpoliciesinoecdcountries.htm .

OECD. 2013. *Rural-urban partnerships: An integrated approach to economic development*. Paris: OECD.

Olsen, Kristian, and Tim Richardson. 2011. The spatial politics of spatial representation: Relationality as a medium for depoliticization? *International Planning Studies* 16 (4): 355–75.

Paasi, Anssi. 2013. Regional planning and the mobilisation of regional identity: From bounded spaces to relational complexity. *Regional Studies* 47 (8): 1206–19.

Paasi, Anssi, and Kaj Zimmerbauer. 2016. Penumbral borders and planning paradoxes: Relational thinking and the question of borders in spatial planning. *Environment and Planning A* 48 (1): 75–93.

Pfeffer, Max, and Linda Wagenet. 2003. Communities of interest and the negotiation of watershed management. In *Pathways for getting to better water quality: The citizen effect*, eds. Lois Wright Morton and Susan Brown, 109–19. New York, NY: Springer.

Ray, Chris. 2006. Neo-endogenous rural development in the EU. In *The handbook of rural studies*, eds. Paul Cloke, Terry Marsden, and Patrick Mooney, 278–91. London: Sage Publications.

Scott, Allen J. 2011. A world in emergence: Notes towards a resynthesis of urban economic geography for the 21st century. *Urban Geography* 32 (6): 845–970.

Shucksmith, Mark. 2008. New Labour's countryside in international perspective. In *New Labour's countryside: Rural policy in Britain since 1997*, ed. Michael Woods, 59–78. Bristol, UK: Polity Press.

Shucksmith, Mark. 2010. Disintegrated rural development? Neo-endogenous rural development, planning and place shaping in diffused power contexts. *Sociologia Ruralis* 50 (1): 1–14.

Shucksmith, Mark. 2012. *Future directions in rural development*. Dunfermline, UK: Carnegie UK Trust. Available from http://www.carnegieuktrust.org.uk/publications/future- directions-in-rural-development-full-report/.

Shucksmith, Mark, David L. Brown, and Jo Vergunst. 2012. Constructing the rural-urban interface: Place still matters in a highly mobile society. In *Rural transformations and rural policies in the US and UK*, eds. Mark Shucksmith, David L. Brown, Sally Shortall, Jo Vergunst, and Mildred Warner, 287–306. New York, NY: Routledge.

Southeastern Wisconsin Regional Planning Commission. 2009. Community assistance. Available from http://www.sewrpc.org/SEWRPC/communityassistance/AdvisoryServices.htm.

Stam, Jerome, and Norman Reid. 1980. *Federal programs supporting multicounty substate regional activities: An overview*. Rural Development Research Report No. 23. Washington, DC: USDA-ERS.

Storper, Michael, Thomas Kemeny, Naji Makarem, and Taner Osman. 2015. *The rise and fall of urban economies: Lessons from San Francisco and Los Angeles*. Palo Alto, CA: Stanford University Press.

Thrift, Nigel. 2004. Transurbanism. *Urban Geography* 25 (8): 724–34.

Urry, John. 2007. *Mobilities*. Cambridge: Polity Press.

U.S. Census Bureau. 2013. *Metropolitan and micropolitan areas*. Available from http://www.census.gov/population/metro/.

U.S. Economic Development Administration (EDA). 2007. *What you need to know about your economic development administration*. Washington, DC: U.S. EDA.

Walworth County Wisconsin. 2009. Multijurisdictional comprehensive plan. Fact Sheet No. 5. Available from http://www.sewrpc.org/SEWRPCFiles/CommunityAssistance/Smartgrowth/Walworth/fact_sheet_walworth_5.pdf.

Walworth County Wisconsin. 2010. *A multi-jurisdictional comprehensive plan for Walworth County: 2035.* Community Assistance Planning Report No. 288. Available from http://www.sewrpc.org/SEWRPCFiles/Publications/CAPR/capr-288-comprehensive- plan-for-walworth-co-2035.pdf.

Ward, Neil. 2006. Rural development and the economies of rural areas. In *A new rural agenda*, ed. Jane Midgley, 46–67. Newcastle upon Tyne: Ipprnorth.

⑤SAGE track

Authors!
Submit your article online with SAGE Track

SAGE Track is a web-based peer review and submission system powered by ScholarOne® Manuscripts

The entire process, from article submission to acceptance for publication is now handled online by the SAGE Track web site. 300 of our journals are now on SAGE Track, which has a graphical interface that will guide you through a simple and speedy submission with step-by-step prompts.

SAGE Track makes it easy to:

- Submit your articles online

- Submit revisions and resubmissions through automatic linking

- Track the progress of your article online

- Publish your research faster

⑤SAGE

⑤SAGE research**methods**

The essential online tool for researchers from the world's leading methods publisher

From basic explanations to advanced discussion, **SAGE Research Methods** will lead you to the content you need

More content and new features added this year!

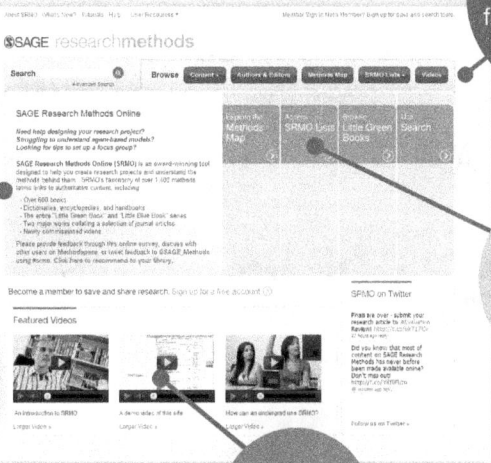

"I have never really seen anything like this product before, and I think it is really valuable."

John Creswell, University of Nebraska–Lincoln

Discover **Methods Lists** – methods readings suggested by other users

Watch video interviews with leading methodologists

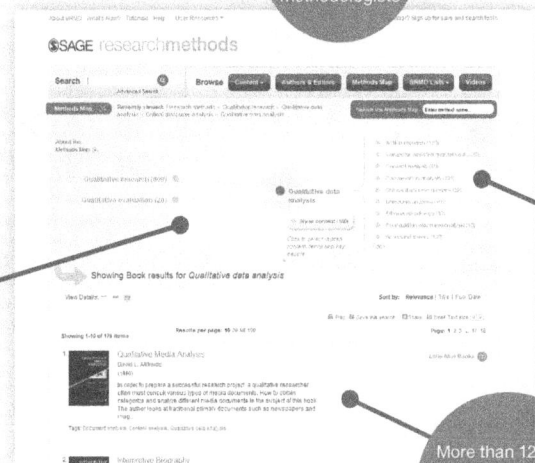

Explore the **Methods Map** to discover links between methods

Based on a custom-designed taxonomy with over 1,400 qualitative, quantitative, and mixed methods terms

More than 120,000 pages of book, journal, and reference content to support your learning

find out more at
www.sageresearchmethods.com

THE IMPACT OF THE SOCIAL SCIENCES: How Academics and their Research Make a Difference

Simon Bastow, Patrick Dunleavy, and Jane Tinkler, *all from London School of Economics*

Foreword by Kenneth Prewitt, *Columbia University*

In the modern globalized world, some estimates suggest that around 40 million people now work in jobs that 'translate' or mediate advances in social science research for use in business, government and public agencies, health care systems, and civil society organizations. Many large corporations and organizations across these sectors in the United States are increasingly prioritizing access to social science knowledge. Yet, the impact of university social science continues to be fiercely disputed. This key study demonstrates the essential role of university social science in the 'human-dominated' and 'human-influenced' systems now central to our civilization. It focuses empirically on Britain, the second most influential country for social science research after the US. Using in-depth research, the authors show how the growth of a services economy, and the success of previous scientific interventions, mean that key areas of advance for corporations, public policy-makers, and citizens alike now depend on our ability to understand our complex societies and economies. This is a landmark study in the evidence-based analysis of social science impact.

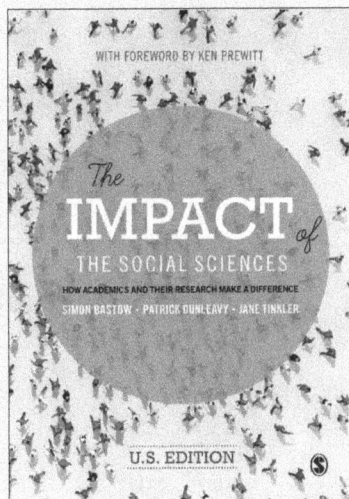

PAPERBACK ISBN: 978-1-4462-8262-5 • FEBRUARY 2014 • 326 PAGES

LEARN MORE AT SAGEPUB.COM!

www.ingramcontent.com/pod-product-compliance
Lightning Source LLC
Chambersburg PA
CBHW060312030426
42336CB00011B/1003